# *Psychological Healing*

# Psychological Healing

Historical and Philosophical Foundations of
Professional Psychology

## Paul C. Larson

RESOURCE *Publications* · Eugene, Oregon

PSYCHOLOGICAL HEALING
Historical and Philosophical Foundations of Professional Psychology

Resource Publications
An Imprint of Wipf and Stock Publishers
199 W. 8th Ave., Suite 3
Eugene, OR 97401

www.wipfandstock.com

PAPERBACK ISBN: 978-1-5326-0059-3
HARDCOVER ISBN: 978-1-5326-0061-6
EBOOK ISBN: 978-1-5326-0060-9

Manufactured in the U.S.A.                                    MAY 16, 2017

To MY PARENTS, JAY and Patricia Larson whose love of reading books on history got me started on this path. To Dr. Sterling M. McMurrin who was my inspiration and model of a scholar and academician. To Rev. John Wade, Ammon Hennacy, and Bruce (Utah) Phillips who were my mentors in social justice. To Dr. Ted Packard who chaired my doctoral dissertation and was a mentor in professional psychology. Above all to my students for whom I've labored long to present this vision of our common heritage and the legacy of those who have gone before us in this noble profession of healing by psychological means.

# Contents

# Preface

THE PURPOSE OF THIS book is to serve as a text for the course often known as history and systems in a graduate curriculum for training health service psychologists (HSP). That is the current designation for practitioners of psychology licensed to provide health care, encompassing the fields of clinical and counseling psychology. Programs in both those specialties lead to eligibility for a license to practice as a health care provider. The profession of psychology is much like the profession of medicine in that both are based on scientific foundations with traditions of empirical and experimental research as well as traditions of clinical judgment. The field of professional psychology is both a science and a skilled professional service. Many psychologists serve in academic roles only, doing research and teaching. Areas of applied psychology include specialties working in schools and other settings. School psychologists provide many services similar to clinical and counseling but in the context of primary or secondary schools. They are usually regulated by a different agency than the one that licenses other occupations. Forensic psychologists are often licensed as health care providers and provide services to correctional facilities, court evaluations, and consultation to attorneys. Industrial-organizational, consulting, or business psychologists are also a long-standing area of professional applied psychology, though that field is generally not licensed by states or provinces. Thus, some doctoral level psychologists teach and conduct research, others provide a variety of applications of psychology, and some provide health care services. This book seeks to at least touch upon most of those areas of applied psychology, though the focus clearly is on those that offer health care services. Healing implies the clinical context and that is the main focus of the historical and philosophical narrative.

I chose as the title of the book, *Psychological healing*, in order to focus on the role of the professional psychologist as health care provider. The analysis of the role of healer or helper requires reference to the history of other healing or helping professions. Many specific occupations fill the social role of healing. Part of our origins as psychologists is shared with the other healing professions. Across history and cultures the broader social role of healing takes many forms, some of which can be readily recognized as antecedents of our current definition of the role in contemporary American and Western societies, though others seem exotic and unfamiliar. All, however, serve that common purpose of helping people to become more whole, more healthy and more effective. The promise of psychology is that its knowledge and skills can lead one to that better condition, the practitioner is the guide.

A course in history and systems of psychology or similar titles exists in most undergraduate and graduate programs in psychology. It has been a required element in the curriculum in clinical and counseling psychology training programs which are accredited by the American Psychological Association (APA). This requirement coverage of both the philosophical and historical bases of present thought and practice are important areas for psychologists in training.

## Competencies for practice

American psychology has begun to shift its emphasis in training health service psychologists toward a competency-based model (Rubin, Bebeau, Leigh, Lichtenberg, Nelson, Portnoy, Smith & Kaslow, 2007; Rudolfa, Bent, Eisman, Nelson, Rehm & Ritchie, 2008). Currently 12 basic competencies have been identified and grouped into two broad domains. The foundational competencies include: Reflective practice-self assessment, scientific knowledge-methods, relationships, ethical-legal standards-policy, individual-cultural diversity, and interdisciplinary systems. Functional competencies include: assessment-diagnosis-case conceptualization, intervention, consultation, research-evaluation, supervision-teaching, and management-administration.

An important one is the competency in individual and cultural diversity, sometimes simply called diversity or multiculturalism. This focus has grown from an understanding that contemporary society is comprised many groups of peoples based on such factors as race, gender, ethnicity, language, sexuality, age, socio-economic status and religion. The goal of this competency is to engage in practice with persons of diverse backgrounds with greater sensitivity to these differences. A core part of the American ethos is the fact that we are a nation of immigrants from all over the world. This has led to a changing demographic. In the twenty first century, we will become a nation of minorities where no group based on race or ethnicity will be in a majority. It is likely that practitioners will serve people who are different from themselves and therefore require a deeper knowledge of their background as well as a more open attitude to understanding their values and hopes. A significant rationale for the study of history is that it can increase awareness of how the diversity of our modern world came about. The history of peoples and their migrations is essential to understand the complexity of our society and to relate with sensitivity to the range of people who seek professional aid and comfort.

Professional psychologists are trained to examine the individual life history and it is in this context that a lack of knowledge in the historical and cultural factors can impede effective service. Thus, teaching students in this profession needs covering not only of the profession itself but of the historical context which makes up the current moment in time as an expression of that diversity of histories. It is all the more important that those who provide health care services are responsive to a much wider range of human differences than in previous decades. The major focus of this book is to supply a perspective of the current diverse populations we serve. That will help clinicians in training to be culturally competent providers through an understanding of how the diversity of our world came to characterize the diversity of our population.

Multicultural and diversity training begins with a comprehensive understanding of world history. Gergen (1973) elsewhere argued that history is a foundational discipline for social psychology. He bases his claim from the human science perspective that the explanation of particularity is a common activity for historians and social psychologists. In order to appreciate the global scope of the diversity found in modern industrialized countries with complex populations of multiple races, ethnicities, languages, religions and cultures, a global focus in the telling of history is mandatory. Our modern world increasingly brings practitioners into contact with people who may differ from their own backgrounds and require some attitudinal sensitivity toward and knowledge of various flavors of human diversity. This book deals more extensively with world history than most similar text books and the rationale is the importance of understanding the origins of the present world for dealing with patients from diverse backgrounds.

It is a truism to say we live in a global world. Everyone's life is affected by forces and events in far distant lands; what effects appear locally create ripples in the social body that touch each of us, even if faintly. Therefore attention given here is from a global perspective, despite the daunting scope of the task. The sections on earlier historical periods in the helping role as well as Asian alternative approaches is part of this thrust for a broader coverage. Greater attention is also paid to the early spiritual world views since this gave birth to all the other major world religions. While many therapists are secular in their world view, many of their clients have a personally significant spiritual or religious tradition. This adds yet another reason to teach a broader perspective, as psychology seeks to train its practitioners to deal not only with people from different parts of the world, but ideas and practices whose origin lies abroad. One current example is mindfulness; it arose from a meditative practice particular to but not exclusively from Buddhism and is now a widely taught element of evidence-based practice.

Psychology has come to recognize the importance of spirituality and religion as a factor in human diversity requiring inclusion in the broad mandate for cultural competence. Greater attention to Eastern ideas and practices is critical to understanding recent developments in therapeutic psychology of basic mindfulness as a tool in treating a wide range of human problems. To understand the context of psychological healing requires a broader understanding of the overall structure of world history, since it defines the very cultural diversities we deal with in the modern world. Greater attention to the various forms of Western spiritual ideas and practices are immediately relevant for study as well.

## An imbalance in the historiography of psychology

The goal of this book is to articulate a broad vision of the historical and theoretical foundations of modern *professional* psychology. This is a different task from most previous authors of texts in the history of psychology. I have elsewhere argued (Larson, 2002) that most previous text books relate the history of the *science* of psychology as their primary focus, and only touch upon the development of the profession in the latter chapters dealing with more recent developments. Even then it is given only brief coverage along with other developments in psychology, such as the cognitive revolution. This is understandable since the greatest market for textbooks on the history of psychology is in broad university based programs which include both undergraduate and graduate students. The course generally aims at attracting both undergraduate majors as well as graduate trainees. Thus, it is forced into a framework that emphasizes the totality of psychology as it relates to an academic discipline focused on research and teaching. Besides, most previous text book authors have been academic psychologists by training.

In contrast to a long line of histories of scientific psychology, Reisman (1991) sets out a major history of clinical psychology. Yet Reisman only begins his narrative with the beginning of organized psychology as a science in the 1870s onward, not touching on any earlier developments. The early branches of professional psychology, clinical, counseling, school and organizational/industrial, have been treated in more specific works (e.g. Whitely, 1980) including the histories of their particular division within APA represented by various special foci (Dewsbury, 1996, 1997, 1998, 1999, 2000, 2002, 2004).

Texts in the history of psychiatry have paved the way in attempting a longer historical scope across time and covering a wider geographical coverage, though still frequently Euro-centric (Ackerknecht, 1959; Alexander & Selesnick, 1966; Bromberg, 1937; Ehrenwald, 1976; Zilboorg, 1941). Howells (1975) is a notable exception in his global focus of the history of psychiatry. Histories of psychology generally limit coverage of ancient and medieval contributions to early chapters in the book, generally viewing pre-scientific psychology as less relevant to the current status of psychology. Indeed, the tone is often triumphalist. Previous eras were mired with superstition and only recently has scientific approaches moved the field forward.

The field of the history of mental health as a broad human concern has emerged with its own literature, though usually slanted in favor of the medical model and its contributions (Bell, 1980; Howells & Osborn, 1984; Roccataglia, 1986; Rosen 1968; Scull 1981). The broad survey texts have given way to more focused monographs taking up in detail particular regions, time periods, or therapeutic approaches.

What is needed is a text with a primary focus on the *profession* of psychology that begins at the very roots of healing by psychological means, even before our modern profession emerged. What this means is that the social role of the helper is taken as the key element. Professional psychology, after all, is a service occupation. Taking such a focus allows the exploration of many approaches to healing, including medical and spiritual forms of healing, since the modern differentiation of specific healing modalities as both professional and scientific disciplines is a few centuries old at best.

This book takes up the challenge to tell the story of a profession, psychology, and to ground it in a history of the profession of healing, very broadly conceived. It is grounded in an analysis of the role of professional psychologist as it stands at the early twenty-first century in primarily the United States as primarily a health care profession, but also consultative and educational as well, though the role of the clinician and counselor take a primary spot. Clinical and counseling psychology in the United States are the two forms of professional practice that are licensed by governmental authorities along with other occupations affecting public health.

## The plan of the book

The first chapter lays out the conceptual framework for understanding the nature of helping and healing as well as some key issues and metaphors in the historical narrative. The second chapter covers the broad topic of spiritual healing. Of all the social roles, certainly among the oldest is that of a spiritual leader. Anthropologists first popularized the term *shaman* for the earliest type of healer and spiritual leader. Later as settled communities developed, formal priesthoods emerged. These two roles are still present today as types of practitioners of the healing arts and are part of psychology's heritage. In the third chapter the history of the classical Western approaches to healing. Chapter four covers the approaches that evolved in the classical periods of Eastern civilizations of the Indian subcontinent and east Asia, especially China.

Chapter five takes European history from the end of the ancient world through the Middle Ages, the Renaissance, and the early modern period. Chapter six covers further developments leading the rise of modernity. The seventh chapter, talks about the rise of the sciences both the natural and human sciences. Most students have just heard of a singular science, the natural science approach, and the idea of two different philosophies of science is largely unheard of. Particular attention therefore is given to the origins of the human sciences and its signature methdological tool, qualitative research. Chapter eight tells the story of the development of psychology as an experimental science as well as the early ventures into practice. Chapter nine goes into more detail on the emergence of psychometric testing and quantification. The following four chapters, 10, 11, 12, and 13, trace the development of four important theoretical orientations of therapy. In the clinical psychology program of the Chicago School of Professional Psychology's (TCSPP) Chicago campus, the founding clinical psychology program for the institution, these four different streams of therapeutic theory are taught. Beginning with Psychoanalysis in chapter 10, then behaviorism in chapter 11, including cognitive-behavioral approaches, humanistic-existential psychology is covered in chapter 12, and social systems theory in chapter 13. Finally, in chapter 14 the history of professional psychology is covered beginning with World War II and bringing the narrative up to the current time.

This book uses the convention of the Common Era (CE) and Before the Common Era (BCE) to denote the most widely accepted way of speaking of historical dates. The common era is based on the Christian calendar and reflects the dominance of European ways of thinking over the last several centuries. Other calendrical systems are used by other religions. The author wishes to avoid the clearly sectarian reference of AD which comes from the Latin for year of our Lord, or BC standing for before Christ. Dates are noted as either before the Common Era (BCE) or during it (CE). As we get into chapters where there is exclusive reference to events in the Common Era, even the CE will be dropped.

# 1

# Conceptual Framework for a History of Psychological Healing

## Suffering and healing: The fiduciary relationship

THE FOCUS OF THIS book is the evolution of psychological healing. It was a deliberate choice to emphasizes this broader focus on the role of the healing more generally. The health service psychologist is one of many health care providers. In the field of occupational definitions, helping and healing are broad occupational categories with many specific occupations under that umbrella. They all share a common task of bringing improvement to the lives of those who seek help. Any understanding of the role of helping or healing must be grounded in an understanding of the nature of human suffering and the particular features of the helping relationship. The primary feature is the fiduciary nature of the relationship; it is built on trust. The second feature is the degree of preparation for assuming the role of healer. Let us tackle this issue first

### Professional occupations

There are several features that define an occupation as a profession. One of the most important is the nature of the balance of power within the relationship. It is unequal. The client has a more urgent need for the professional's skill and good will to meliorate the problems the client brings to the encounter. It is this very asymmetrical nature of the helping relationship which provides the legal justification for regulation. The sufferer needs help; the professional can offer it. Recognizing this power imbalance is the basis for ethical constraints on the nature of the therapeutic relationship.

At its heart, the professional relationship is based on trust; that is, it is a fiduciary one. The client has an urgency of need that makes them vulnerable. The professional has both skill and expertise that the client needs. The client trusts the professional in several important ways. First, the client trusts the professional to perform certain functions in a competent and ethical manner. Second, the client trusts the professional to act to support the client's interests, not their own. Whatever guidance is given in the course of a professional relationship should benefit the client. Self-serving actions are seen as violating that ethical principle. The fee should be the only benefit the professional receives. The implication of this is that the concept of interests is central to understanding the fiduciary obligation of the professional. While this is a complex issue, one easy way of determining interests is to ask the question who has a stake in the outcome of the professional relationship, and what are the gains or losses that could result? There needs to be a clear understanding of the interests of the parties and an adherence to ethical standards of practice to insure that the vulnerability of the client is not an opportunity for exploitation or advantage to the professional.

We are not the only profession which is based in a fiduciary relationship. Indeed, one could generalize it to many specific occupational roles. Clearly all health care services are fiduciary. Lawyers, accountants and others have as one of their components the fact that clients must disclose deeply personal information in order for the skills of the professional to be effectively brought to bear on the matter at hand. The client, therefore, is vulnerable. One can make a case that even hair care professionals have a sort of fiduciary relationship, given the importance that appearance plays as a social signal. We trust that we will be able to project the type of image of our self we intend. But the trust we place in other occupations is less critical in many ways than health care and law.     Two other aspects distinguish professional occupations from others; a longer education requirement and the necessity to use independent judgment in the application of the skill. The length of education is generally the main feature that we use to distinguish professions from other sorts of skilled service occupations which may also involve some degree of trust on the part of the client. Most occupations termed professions require post-graduate degrees (a masters or doctoral degree). All persons living in modern societies depend on the basic competence of people to do their jobs, be they operators of railroad engines or plumbers and electricians, but the health care professions are among the most demanding in terms of the time for preparation because the knowledge and skills are so complex. The current market place also contains a wide range of non-licensed care givers with few or no regulation of formal training or preparation. Life coaches, psychic readers and advisors and other lay healers are sought out and readily found in most communities. Spirituality rather science is often the major epistemological basis for their claim of a power to heal.

The second aspect of professionalism is the independent exercise of judgment in a complex fiduciary relationship. This is the basis for the license to practice independently without supervision provided as an employee in an organization. The successful use of good judgment is rewarded by clients referring other clients; its failure can result in loss of license, lawsuit for negligence, and other sanctions including mandatory supervision and further training. The various codes of ethics supplement state regulations as hedges around the exercise of judgment.

Medicine has traditionally allowed only doctoral level practitioners as independent licensed practitioners, though nurses with masters degrees and physicians assistants with bachelors or masters degree often exercise wide-ranging independence, especially in rural areas where direct contact with a physician may be difficult. In the psycho-social arena of healing, masters level practitioners also have been granted independence of practice. The front line of mental health services is now carried out largely by masters level practitioners. Indeed, one of the challenges of the modern professional psychologist will be to identify and offer those additional services that the doctoral degree can offer such as supervision, administration, program development and evaluation.

## Suffering.

Let's face it, no one wants to see a psychologist. People come to see a therapist only when their own resources for self-help have been insufficient. A person generally comes to encounter a professional helper during a period of distress, though the complaining party may sometimes be the people who have to live with the person. Clients usually have been suffering for some time, trying self help or other means, until they are forced to acknowledge things aren't working well.

The clinical context touches upon the deepest aspects of our vulnerabilities as humans, our distress at loss, change and, often, just ordinary existence. Faced with the existential reality of knowledge of our own ultimate death, we nonetheless move forward and create or find meaning in the various activities and relationships of our world. At times we cannot quite seem to fill that existential void and feel a sense of meaninglessness or perhaps a more free floating sense of being uprooted and drifting. Whether the crisis that brings someone into see a psychologist is an acute trauma or loss or a subtle shift in an on-going malaise that now can be no longer tolerated, people come to seek our care when they feel weak and incapable.

The chief reason for this reluctance is the stigma of mental illness. While people with physical ailments receive sympathetic attention, people with non-visible illnesses often do not. People with emotional or behavioral problems tend to be seen as either weak willed, or even morally culpable for their own suffering, hence are subject to negative evaluation by others. Blaming the victim for their own problems is much more common with psychological problems than with clear cut medical ones. However, there are medical conditions where stigma is present. Things dealing with sexuality, for example, are tinged with the moral framework we place on intimate relationships. Our knowledge of the role of smoking and lung cancer likewise result in self blame by those who smoke and have contracted the illness. So that attribution of personal responsibility for the origin and maintenance of a condition lead to stigmatization of the victim regardless of how psychological or physical the nature of the symptoms are. Overall, however, the mind-body duality has resulted in psychological difficulties being treated very differently from physical ones. The problem of identifying clear cut physical markers of a condition or its causes has made the origins of these problems more difficult to discern than abnormal blood chemistry or images of broken bones. The causes of emotional or mental suffering are complex and involve factors that are subjective as well as objective. This makes the field of psychotherapy and counseling more complicated. Detailed discussion of etiological matters is outside the scope of this work, but reductionist approaches that seek only biological bases or dismiss them altogether should be avoided.

While medicine has made more inroads in the public consciousness for preventative activities or regular opportunities for a physical examination to detect early signs of disease, psychology has not been as successful in promoting preventive care. The positive psychology movement has appealed to people not in distress, but who wish to use psychological techniques and knowledge for personal growth and self-improvement. Wellness programs in corporate and other contexts offer psychological services through psycho-educational groups as training and education rather than therapy. So if you present psychological knowledge or skills as tools for well-being, a wide range of teaching and consulting options are possible to provide services.

There are other applications of psychology that avoid the stigma of mental illness. In the business context, the consulting psychologist is often called in when the organization is experiencing dysfunction, though there is some greater use of psychologists as agents of routine and hygienic or preventative activity rather than restorative. In the educational contexts, students who are not doing as well as expected are singled out for referral for services, but the context as a whole is grounded more in change as normal development. In forensic psychology not only may they may not want to see a psychologist, but they are forced to do so in the context of coercive social institutions such as jails and prisons. So across contexts the role of the professional helper can be seen very differently by the subjects of professional attention. In the clinical context, there is a clearer focus on urgent human needs as a fundamental element in health and well-being.

## Healing.

When I once broached the title of this book to my students and asked for feedback they tended to shy away from the word healing. It sounded too dichotomous, implying cure, and few of them had the confidence that what they would be undertaking would usually result in that sort of dramatic outcome. They expected to help their clients improve and saw movement along a continuum from worse to better as an achievable goal for their professional endeavors. It is true that they were first years students and had not yet had the experience of seeing someone make the type of transformative change which might justifiably be called a cure. Those experiences are rare enough for most clinicians anyway. So their caution is understandable.

Yet another concern of the students was the close identification of healing with medicine as a profession. Healing was something particular to medicine and not psychology. Some of them started with pre-med courses only to find they lacked either interest or skill in the pre-requisite science courses. Others come from the humanities and many come from other majors in the social and behavioral sciences. Regardless of how they came to psychology, the student, once in a doctoral program, needs to develop an identity as a psychologist distinct from though related to medicine. As will be seen, psychology has had to struggle to become an independent profession and separate itself from medicine and other healing arts and sciences.

Healing also is problematic when the prognosis is guarded or terminal. How can one expect to heal another when they are in the final phase of life? How can one speak of healing when they have a chronic condition that will never completely remit? The answer to the question comes from the root meaning of healing, to make whole. Even in the case where life is ebbing or where a long period of disability is ahead, the prospect of living out one's time with a greater sense of meaning and integration justifies the use of the term healing.

Meaning is the currency of psychological healing. If circumstances present an individual with certain losses of traditional sources of meaning, then the healing occurs through both accepting and transforming meanings. People can endure, even thrive, after having been beaten down, after experiencing major limits in functional capacities; they can be remarkably resilient. They can find new sources of meaning and purpose in their lives. Indeed, any successful adaptation to disability requires a re-assessment of one's place in life. We are able to go on after loss and suffering. The literature on near death experiences reports how many people come out of such a catastrophe with changed perspectives and values. How well we can facilitate such change as rehabilitation psychologists varies; as in all therapy the outcome is only partly within our or even our client's control.

A consequence of the very nature of our profession, its exposure to human suffering, is the potential for burn out (Freudenberger, 1975). Mental health professionals are known to be at greater risk for this sort of disillusionment and impaired professional performance. It is not easy taking on the pain of others, and successful therapists soon learn how to create psychological distance from their clients' problems when they go home at night. Learning how to re-create oneself through leisure activities or other means is a vital skill to acquire in one's graduate training.

So the very nature of the profession of psychology involves dealing intimately and frequently, with others in distress. This fact sets the key ethical fact in defining professionalism; the establishment and maintenance of a relationship of trust. In legal terms, this is a fiduciary relationship. The relatively unequal situation of the participants with regard to need sets this relationship apart. The client needs some combination of comfort as well as guidance for alleviating the suffering. The therapist is, hopefully, not nearly so needy emotionally or personally. The therapist expects some compensation for services rendered, and offers skill of service. The aim of the services provided are to serve the benefit of the other. This means the therapist must curb self-interest. Other obligations of care as well as all the other specific principles contained in statutes, case law or professional code of ethics flow from the basic fact that people trust us with their lives, health and well-being. Most professional relationships are between strangers. As we shall see, the earliest layers of history of psychological healing show a closer connection when societies were organized around tribal or village life where most people were known to some closer degree than now customary. In the fiduciary or professional relationship we use psychological means to meliorate their suffering as completely as feasible under their circumstances. The exposure to the suffering of others creates an occupational risk of suffering ourselves as well as giving poor service because of burn out. But those are simply the conditions of our vocation. Persevering in it across a career usually requires more than occupational choice, it requires a sense of calling or vocation to take on this sort of job. It is not pleasant or easy to wade into the depths of misery to bring our clients out onto dry land again, but that is what we do.

## Psychological means

We have now discussed the ethical basis for the professional relationship in the fiduciary quality of an imbalance of power in therapeutic relationships between a person in need for care and a health service provider. The aim of all professional healing, no matter what manner is the relief of suffering through skillful means by the healer. What then distinguishes psychological means from other means of healing? How does psychology stake out its domain? If it shares the contexts of human suffering with all other health care professions or even the importance of forming a fiduciary relationship with the client, how does psychology differ in its methods? What marks out our discipline?

An easy answer comes from the method of subtraction. Unlike medicine, we cannot perform surgery, and, with a few but perhaps growing exceptions, we cannot prescribe medications. Likewise, psychologists are not licensed for therapeutic touch, healing by the laying on of hands. The practice of manual or manipulative medicine by osteopaths, chiropractor, or the use of therapeutic touch, as in nursing, physical and occupational therapy or massage therapy is beyond our scope unless we get separate and additional training.

All we have as psychologists is verbal social interaction as our medium. We talk, that's just about all we can do, so we had better do it very well. This means that a foundational and core skill will be gaining expertise in modes of effective communication and good interpersonal relationships. We share the medium of therapeutic conversation with other psycho-social helping professions. Psychologists differ from social workers, counselors, and other practitioners not so much in what we do but in areas of emphasis, since there is that basic commonality of verbal interaction as the medium. Furthermore the basic skills are the formation of a therapeutic relationship through active listening and creating an empathetic understanding of the client's needs; the story of the evolution of that skill set comes later. Beyond that core set of relationship skills, there are real differences based on theory for how the therapeutic conversation should be structured. Psychologists distinguish themselves on the basis of the doctorate as the major entry level credential. Presumably, the additional years of training give psychologists an advantage of depth of understanding, and more finely developed skills than practitioners with a masters degree. Our early and continued specialization in formal structured testing as an assessment tool is one of the few areas of specialization that have not been as widely used by other masters level practitioners.

The interview as a form of dyadic interpersonal interaction is shared by all of the healing arts as well as several other occupations. We share the clinical interview with the psycho-social or mental health healing professions as well as medicine and the other bio-medical health professions. Here a distinction must be made between the bio-physical therapies, where the interpersonal dynamics are a part of rapport building, but where the content focus is on physical or medical conditions, and the psycho-social therapies where the interpersonal dynamics are crucial, and where the content focus is more the personal psychological and social problems. As noted above, the stigma that still exists around mental illness is an active factor in the reluctance of people to use psychological services. But with the broad field of clinical health and rehabilitation psychology, psychological means are applied to primarily physical or medical conditions.

We also share the interview with law, which is also a licensed profession because of its fiduciary nature, and likewise the focus is on the broader psycho-social arena of personal functioning. Journalism and many qualitative social science researchers, likewise have interviewing as a core professional skill and activity. Given the large range and scope of occupations which rely on verbal interviews and interactions with others, what marks the type of communication engaged in by counselors, psychotherapists and psychologists?

We know that human communication takes place through a variety of media. Both verbal utterances as well as the non-verbal visual and auditory actions are part of the message. At even closer levels of distance between sender and receiver, smell communicates, and at even closer levels we communicate by touch and taste. All of the expressive bodily and behavioral channels are the para-linguistic means by which we affirm, modify, or deny the verbal linguistic message. The juxtaposition between linguistic and para-linguistic channels is the source of amazing variety in meanings ranging from humorous, ironic, deceitful, and many other nuances of meaning. There are differences between verbal or visual textual language and the pictorial, gestural, or vocal intonational features of language, and the whole field of pragmatics in linguistics is based on an understanding that language is embedded in this larger communicative context in broader aspects of social life. We do things with words as well as communicate specific meanings, and of course, meanings are extremely context dependent.

Jerome Frank and his wife (Frank & Frank, 1991) authored the seminal work, *Persuasion and healing.* Its title made it clear that what it spoke to was the common mechanism by which all healing fundamentally takes place, the skill of verbal persuasion. He described the major structural similarity between the varieties of counseling, therapy on the one hand and other forms of creating social or opinion change, including thought reform and spiritual healing. He had a whole chapter on the placebo effect in therapy. The common thread running through all ways of bringing about change was persuasion as a social skill enacted in some professional role. Counseling and psychotherapy are but a specific range of types of verbal persuasion, as Frank noted. The key elements are a credible ritual and a positive response set. There has to be a shared understanding of the means by which change will occur. In Western psychotherapy the credible ritual is a specific type of dialog or therapeutic conversation. In pre-literate societies and in modern spiritual healing today, there is a different ritual form, but the participants both enact a series of interchanges they believe will work. Through these enactments the initial induction of hope is nurtured and promoted. If there has to be an initial investment on the part of the client that change is possible, the process of therapy has to put that to work and create some favorable results.

Yalom & Leszcz (2005) echoed the importance of the instillation of hope in therapy. It is one of the curative factors in group therapy, and by extension all forms of therapy. One part of the healing process in medicine is likewise instillation of hope. But hopefully, the therapist can provide more specific forms of help, ones that efficiently move the process along toward specific results. So in each case, the particulars of counseling and therapy are shaped to the particulars of the client's situation in some manner. There is also hope in both the healer and the client that the means employed have worked with this sort of problem before and are effective. All therapists have to at least achieve this minimal level of change in the client.

Hopefully, we add more than just hope and belief in a better future in some way. This is the domain of specific treatments for specific conditions, where hope is applied to particular sets of circumstances. This is where the various schools and styles of therapy differ. The concepts that are used to frame the common understanding of how to proceed and the specific techniques or sequences of techniques for inducing change all take place within the general framework of a life face to face social interaction in the form of a conversation, a dialogue. Each session is time limited and the number of sessions constitutes a course of treatment. These same circumstances hold regardless of the nature of the conceptual framework, Frank taught us that both spiritual and scientific modes of healing work for these basic reasons.

Health care in general is moving toward a more integrative model of service delivery, so HSPs are going to be interacting with people of other helping or healing professions. This is why APA has established the need for a basic competency in interdisciplinary systems and consultation as a functional competency. This is consistent with the emergence of a holistic, bio-psycho-social model us needed (Engel, 1977; Pryzwansky & Wendt, 1987). Given the nature of world views as elaborated below, we should also acknowledge spiritual elements in the holistic perspective. Psychologists may differ as to their philosophical positions on the mind-body problem; encompassing both materialistic reductionists and full secularists, through a variety of spiritual positions. Indeed, a bio-psycho-social-spiritual integrative framework is both possible and an important asset. Most psychologists don't spend much time concerned with this philosophical issue, but a more pragmatic understanding of the inter-penetration of biological, psychological and social factors in explaining the complexity of observed human behavior as well as phenomenological variety of experience.

## Health service psychology: A naturalistic description

The nature of the profession as an occupation can be described in terms of two sets of ideas. One set broadly describes what psychologists do; that is, the roles, activities and contexts of the practitioner, the other set looks at the competencies needed for skilled practice; the knowledge, skills, and attitudes (KSA) used by the practitioner. The original formulation from industrial/organizational psychology and personnel management is knowledge, skills and aptitudes. But NCSPP has reformulated this slightly to emphasize the complex interpersonal and cultural attitudes that are critical in forming fiduciary relationships. The first model, roles, activities, and contexts, looks at the big picture and defines the nature of what the professional does in light of where, to whom, and for what purpose the service is provided. The second model, focuses on the elements underlying the successful performance of activities within a role and in a certain context. Job descriptions and evaluation measures are often organized around a set of KSAs for each position. The competencies involve complex sets of knowledge, skills and attitudes and is evaluated by benchmarks taking into consider level of training issues identifying the characteristics of the minimally competent practitioner.

## Roles.

The concept of role is one of the core concepts in all of social theory. The dramaturgical metaphor, a phrased used by the sociologist Goffman (1959), was expressed eloquently by Shakespeare's allusion to the world being a stage upon which we play our own individual roles, coming into and leaving the drama in the course of time and events. Roles are a set of social expectations which frame the nature of social interactions, giving them structure, providing them with scripts. Playing roles pervades every part of the fabric of daily human experience. Roles and scripts form the structure of social interactions. They are the framework around which people improvise in carrying on daily life. Rodseth & Novak (2000) used the anthropological distinction between the plaza and the hearth to describe the locus where roles are enacted. Familial roles are played out primarily in the privacy of home; public roles are played out in a variety of contexts. Occupational roles are ideally spelled out explicitly in job descriptions so that supervision and reward for successfully performance or consequences of unsuccessful performance can be applied.

## Activities.

The activities are more concrete than the roles. These are the things that fill billable hours and are summarized as an individual session of professional service. In traditional mental health contexts, this usually means the 50 minute hour, though as psychologists integrate into primary care, the length of a session may be quite brief (e.g. billable in 15 minute increments). In the educational context this can be a class session; in the organizational psychology context this is a consultation session. For most of professional psychology this is some form of verbal live, face to face interaction, what is termed direct client contact. But it is not so much the length of time for a session that is important here but what activity or activities are conducted during that period of time.

Counseling or psychotherapy is the activity with greatest frequency. Assessment, including formal psychological testing is another common activity. Consultation with other practitioners is becoming an increasingly important activity as part of interdisciplinary care. Supervision of students and other professionals is also common. Indeed, the 12 competencies mentioned in the preface are activities of health service psychologists (HSP).

These are complex skills, and they require a high degree of self-awareness and reflection to maintain the therapeutic relationship. Two competencies involve awareness of self and the impact of self on others, relationship and reflective practice. They overlap somewhat with the concept of attitude in the KSA analysis as they deal with a particular approach to the nature of relationship. The performance of counseling and psychotherapy is also inherently improvisatory. No matter how much you study the theories and read clinical manuals, in the end, you engage in dialog with a client and face unforeseen disclosures during the session. While that practitioner may have little time to reflect on a session while it is on-going, the process of professional growth and development requires some time to review and incorporate new insights (Schön, 1983, 1987).

Labov and Fanshel (1977) hold that the root activity in psychotherapy is therapeutic conversation. We engage in a certain type of dialog. Being a specialized discourse, it is different from ordinary social conversation. The concept of discourse communities comes from the disciplines of socio-linguistics and anthropology. A group of people who are in conversation with each other form a discourse community. They have their own frames of reference and usually a set of specialized terms and knowledge that is particular to the needs of the group. The therapist is part of the discourse community of mental health specialists. Together the therapist and client jointly create as shared discourse reflecting an intersection of ideas and notions from both worlds, the world of the patient and the world of the professional. The skill in doing therapy is making the best match possible between the interpersonal and cultural worlds of both parties so more harmonious working become possible. Use of technical jargon is one of the problems in communication with patients. One of the obligations of psychologists and others is to use plain language in communications.

## Contexts.

The performance of the professional role and its related activities takes place in certain contexts. The contexts are both physical and social. Each session takes place in specific physical locations, and those rooms and buildings are structured by people to facilitate certain social relations rather than others. The contexts form an ecology of helping. Roger Barker (1903-1990) pioneered the concept of behavior setting as the basis for an ecological view of human life (Barker 1968; Barker & assoc, 1978). Barker initially thought the environment accounted for the largest amount of behavior, though later adapted his views to be more reflective of other factors (Sabar, 2014).

One example of challenges arising from this is the situation of many clinical health psychologists. The typical psychotherapists office has some chairs and perhaps an end table and lamp and conveys a more relaxed conversational atmosphere. The examination room of medical facilities is built around the exam table and associated gear. When a psychologist steps into such a room to evaluate or treat a patient they are faced with very different furniture and physical structure than the typical psychologist's office. Also group therapy space is very different from the typical conference room in offices. They are built around large tables, whereas psychologists prefer conducting group sessions in an open space with a circle of chairs so that everybody can face each other without the barrier of the table. These examples illustrate the impact of the physical context on the social context of therapy.

Beyond the physical differences in the structuring of the space is another aspect of context; the social and organizational. There are significant differences in the structures of hospitals, prisons, schools or businesses, both in terms of the physical structures and the social contexts. There are also significant differences in the social contexts based on whether the organizations are governmental or private, and if private, if they are for-profit or not-for-profit corporations. In nearly all organizations there is a hierarchical structure, a chain of command. This means that the activities and roles of professional psychologists are part of a network of supervision and management of clinical service. There are differences in the social context between the office of a solo practitioner in private practice, and that of the employee of an organization. Team treatment as a model for delivery of services require the psychologist to understand and be sensitive to other sorts of practitioners and other staff whose roles may differ quite extensively.

In addition, the mode of reimbursement for services varies and dictates substantial differences in the expectation of privacy. Cash payment insures the highest degree of privacy; forensic matters have no expectation of privacy because of the need of the legal system to have its proceedings public. All forms of third party payment require the patient to sign a release of information so that use of services can be monitored for necessity and accuracy of contractual arrangements.

Part of the context is also conceptual; that is, governed by different sets of metaphors or ideas. There are distinct assumption found in educational, health care, correctional/forensic, or business contexts. In two contexts, the clinical and the forensic, there is an assumption of the abnormality of the situation of the client. In education and business, there are generally assumptions that the client is normal. In education there is a focus on the age-appropriate development of children that distinguishes the context from most adult contexts. The positive psychology movement aims to provide the benefits of psychological principles and techniques to a normal population rather than a population that is suffering from some form of malady or illness. Wellness is a key concept and moves beyond the assumption of pathology and the need for diagnosis. It also moves beyond the concept of medical necessity which is the basis of third party reimbursement of services under health care insurance plans.

Finally the very size of the organization sets many of the contextual features by which the helping roles and activities are performed. Bureaucracy increases as a function of size and complexity. The degree of personal service is maximized in individual private practice, and minimized in large scale institutions. Part of the management goals are often to keep a high degree of personal service even within the need for regimentation and standardization inherent in large organizations.

## Competencies for practice

As noted in the preface (Rubin et al 2007; Rudolfa et al 2009), The America Psychological Association has adopted a competency based model of training for Health Service Psychologists (HSP). The National Council of Schools and Programs in Professional Psychology (NCSPP), which represents the Psy.D. programs, systematically developed a competency based model of the skills to be taught during training and are the basic set of tools which the end product, an entry level professional psychologist should possess (Peterson, McHolland, Bent, Davis-Russell, Edwall, Polite, & Stricker, 1991; Peterson, Peterson, Abrams & Stricker, 1997). These early versions of competencies from NCSPP established much of the framework for the current model adopted by APA.

A competency is the skilled performance of a craft or a profession. Twelve basic competencies have been identified and grouped into two broad domains. The foundational competencies include: Reflective practice-self assessment, scientific knowledge-methods, relationships, ethical-legal standards-policy, individual-cultural diversity, and interdisciplinary systems. Functional competencies include: assessment-diagnosis-case conceptualization, intervention, consultation, research-evaluation, supervision-teaching, and management-administration. A competency is measured by acts of performance; at first closely supervised, then ultimately upon demonstration of competency, the practitioner is licensed for independent practice.

A competency is comprised of a particular set of knowledge, skills, and attitudes (KSA). The acronym is familiar to those in industrial/organizational psychology and personnel management. The A in the acronym was originally abilities, but the nature of helping and healing requires a set of attitudes about oneself and one's relationship to the persons one serves. In addition to satisfactory academic performance, clinicians in training must demonstrate competence in certain skilled activities, particularly communication.

## Knowledge.

The knowledge component of competency includes the whole realm of psychology augmented by significant input from both biological and sociological poles of the bio-psycho-social sciences. In their accreditation standards for curricula in clinical our counseling psychology, APA spells out a variety of core subjects that have to be covered and are considered the foundations of psychological science and practice. The various courses on biological, cognitive-affective and social bases of behavior as well as developmental psychology and the history and philosophy of psychology are among the core scientific basis of practice. Scientific methods and applications of basic psychological research and knowledge of developmental stages are important aspects of training as well.

The functional competencies relate to activities described earlier in the scope of practice. These comprise the broad definitions of the activities performed with and for the client. Assessment and intervention are very broad domains that are comprised of other specific activities like testing, counseling, and so on. The higher level competencies deal with the contexts of practice; supervision, consultation, interdisciplinary systems awareness.

## Skills.

The foundational and core skill set is human communication skills. The author has argued (Larson, 2006) that rhetoric describes very closely that skill. As will be discussed later, one key archetype of healing comes from rhetors, early practitioners of the art of persuasive speech. The core skill is basically human communication. Practicing psychology is a type of skilled performance, a craft as noted by British social psychologist,

Michael Billig (1996). He coined the term *witcraft* to encompass the use of rhetoric as persuasion to make a living, particularly as applied to psychology as a social discipline. This was a serendipitous term, coupling the ancient concept of craft as skill to intellectual or ideational activities. Witcraft is a social skill, a communicative skill, a facility in artfully structuring human relationships through interaction. As so considered, it is a foundationally important skill for professional practice in psychology. Indeed, we live by our wits, our ability to put together cogent series of exchanges in the therapeutic conversation and relationship. We don't vend products, we provide a service. We only provide material objects incidentally to the service, as an educational aide. In the end, the client needs to come away feeling some benefit; that imposes the obligation of attention to outcome.

### Attitudes.

What are the attitudes that go along with the knowledge of human experience and behavior and the skilled practice of persuasive communication? The competencies of reflective practice and individual/cultural diversity require a degree of openness to examination of one's own attitudes and acceptance of difference that can be both hard to describe in behavioral terms, and essential for maintaining the quality of relationship that leads to healing. Keep in mind the fiduciary obligation to act in the best interests of the other imply certain attitudes.

One key ethical assumption is non-violence. For words to work, fists have to be restrained. We generally don't focus much attention on this basic working assumption unless one happens to work with a population that is prone to aggression and possibly even violence. A significant number of human problems arise out of our inability to manage anger both at the interpersonal level and the broader social level. Counseling and psychotherapy work primarily at that more local and small scale of individuals in the immediate social relationships, but as social psychologist Kurt Lewin would show, psychologists can bring their professional knowledge and skills to bear on problems of social conflict. Assaults on psychologists are fortunately rare, but anyone who has worked in hospital settings has had to at some point confront how best to defuse an assaultive client situation. Psychologists become have increasingly involved in court-ordered anger management programs for domestic battery offenders and others. This means that we have to take seriously the task of creating an atmosphere that promotes the use of dialog in lieu of force.

Rogers (1951) identified 3 conditions that the therapist must provide for successful therapy to occur. We will deal with him later in the text. For now we note that empathetic understanding of the client, unconditional positive regard and genuineness are those conditions. In the context of the KSA analysis, they are key attitudes. More broadly speaking, unconditional positive regard is simply being non-judgmental with regard to who the client is or what they have done or said, at least to the best of one's abilities. The opportunity for an open discussion of difficult matters without interruption or argumentation is a key for establishing a working basis of interpersonal trust. Empathic understanding is also one of the key aspects of the therapeutic relationship that was associated with positive outcome. So successful was his early program of research on counseling and psychotherapy that the basic skill set in communicating and listening is largely derived from his work. Increasingly, additional research on the common factors of therapy found through meta-analysis and other reviews of research point to the importance of the therapeutic relationship in favorable outcome. The relationship competency in the current APA formulation inculcates these important attitudinal and skilled behavioral approaches of active listening and a client-centered value structure. Generating an empathetic understanding of the other was a key to Rogers' work. I now introduce limenality, a concept broader than empathy which integrates diversity awareness.

## Limenality as a core skill and attitude.

A limen is a threshold that marks a boundary between one space and another. We literally cross through a limen when we pass through a door dividing interior space. The term limen, as a threshold, was first used in perceptual psychology or psychophysics to denote the boundary between an imperceptible and a perceptible stimulus. The concept of limen as a physical or perceptual boundary leads to some broader reflections on interpersonal and social boundaries. Boundaries can be spatial, separating from one room from another, or temporal boundaries between past and present, or even social boundaries arising from being or not being a member of a particular group. Most boundaries can be crossed by bridges linking the lands, concepts, or groups of people which are separated. In each case there is a psychological threshold through or across which a passage can be found.

The anthropologists Arnold Van Gennep (1909/1960) and Victor Turner (1969/1995) used the term limenality as part of their theory of rites of passage. This class of activities is a broad and important anthropological and social psychological concept. The rite of passage moves a person from one social role to another. Many rites are age related, the passage beginning biological fertility onset at adolescence, marriage, and finally burial of the dead mark times when one's role shifts. Limenality is the term for that ambiguous period when participants in rites of passage are in between social roles. For a period of time one is no longer a boy or girl, but is not yet a man or woman. It is a time and space for transition and transformation. Work is done to prepare the candidate for the next stage of life and the roles of that phase. For the spiritual healer, limenality is also the ability to cross between the world of the mundane and the space of spiritual communion. As we shall see in a subsequent chapter, spiritual healing originated with techniques for moving between worlds, the mundane and the spiritual. Trance was the medium, the bridge if you will, that allowed the healer to connect the two worlds briefly in the rite of healing.

Limenality is here focused more as a description for a set of skills key for two competencies of psychological practice; relationship and individual cultural diversity. Both competencies share the common task of being able to enter into the perspective of the other, to walk between the two worlds of self and other and establish a bridge of communication, trust, and empathetic understanding. Counselors and therapists are taught the skills of empathic listening and communicating. But the need for culturally competent practice also requires understanding the nature of group differences and how they impact the dyadic therapeutic relationship, or even how the intervention strategy should be targeted at a couple, family, group, or community level as well. The individual must be seen in cultural context, because part of their perspective or frame of reference is the various things each person shares with some other groups of people.

This leads to another important distinction, the difference between the insider's and the outsider's perspectives. The emic, or the insider's perspective, and the etic, or outsider's perspective were first formulated by Pike (1954) for understanding aspects of linguistics. The sort of knowledge of a language that the native speaker has is distinguished from the outsider's frame of reference, or the experience of an outsider learning to speak the language. Comparative linguistics is possible only from an etic perspective. The emic/etic dichotomy has been extended to mean more generally the insider and outsider perspective and is applied to all manner of cross-cultural phenomena (Headland, Pike & Harris, 1990). So the goal of limenality is to maximize the ability to take on the insider's point of view with regard to individuals and social groups as closely as possible. The greater the skills the better the understanding of the differences in perspectives, and hence the possibility of finding bridges of communication. The goal of didactic and experiential work in multicultural and diversity training is to help the participant move from a completely etic perspective with regard to another social group or set of groups to one closer to and more sensitive toward the emic perspective held by members of that group.

Time also marks boundaries. Our understanding of time is strongly linear with the present marking the boundary between past and future. At the change of a year, the Romans honored the god Janus, for whom January is named. Janus was literally a two-faced deity. One face was turned to the future, one to the past. Cognitive psychology has demonstrated how important memory is to our sense of self, and how important imagination is to planning the future. With temporal boundaries we are always balanced in the present moment with glimpses of our past and visions of our future. Janus' fulcrum point at the threshold of the present can reminds us of the dialectical balance between poles of life remembered and plans, hopes and dreams for the future.

Limenality is all about boundaries and the ability to cross them fluidly. But boundaries are inherent in all life. Each life is based on cells and each cell has a boundary. If it were not permeable then input needed for metabolism would not pass, nor waste products from that metabolism, so permeability and stability of boundaries are both necessary for life. We all have experiences of crossing some boundaries and finding others impermeable. We will see later how psychologist Kurt Lewin expands on this with the concept of life space.

The theory articulated here is based on the foundational concept of perspective, or point of view. Perspective is a dialectical concept; meaning that each perspective only makes sense in terms of its relation to the context of the broader community of discourse of other perspectives. It is a relational concept in that it mediates between self and other, whether as individual (empathy) or as a member of a group (emic/etic). Each individual perceives the world from an ever shifting physical location that gives a particular perceptual perspective. But perspectives can also be the expressed opinions of the individual as well as express or inferred perspectives of groups of people. Perspectives exist in discourse communities and represents a foundational emphasis on the concrete social matrix of human culture. The elements of the message are meant to convey the individual's perspective with regard to any particular topic of dialog. Every individual and every group has perspectives, and human culture is the sum total of messages about perspectives which have been passed across the boundaries of individual, group and cultural differences and across time. Each individual person has many perspectives, depending on the object of the link between that person and another person, live, imagined or implied. This network of persons in relationship constitutes the social environment. If a social matrix is composed of individual elements which are linked in the matrix by specific bonds or associations, then perspectives are the real or potential links between the various nodes conceived in the abstract as a system.

The practice of the profession of psychology requires a tripartite set of skills, a high degree of awareness of self, of the other person as individual and of the nature of the relationship between self and other, what we often term process awareness as it implies awareness of the impact of self on other and other on self. Reflective self awareness is critical in understanding potential barriers in the relationship or communicative process. It is also important in the self care of the practitioner as a human being and as a professional. Some degree of mutuality of feelings is required to be able to see the other, so there is a zone of engagement with the other. This mutuality of engagement in the process of therapy has long been viewed under the rubric of transference/counter-transference. A high degree of reflexive thought is needed to track both the shifting meanings of the client's narrative, and our own reactions as therapists. This ability to track simultaneously both the other and the self in interaction is termed limenality. It facilitates creating bridges between people.

Limenality requires an ability to shift between perspectives, between our own as individuals providing input, and that of the client or recipient of our services. We are bridge builders; we establish relationships with others who express need. We build a relationship of trust based on our initial contacts and circumstances and hope to engage the client in an on-going stream of interactions with the goal of helping them, healing them in some way or degree.

The therapeutic conversation is a dialectic because it is an exchange of perspectives within a discourse community. But it also develops over time with a back and forth flow of interactions. It does so in sequence, each communication involving some degree of potential reference to material laid down. Each utterance is conditional, in part, on what was said before. All conversations and friendships have that sort of dialectic, but therapeutic ones have a heightened sense of need and require a different sort of skill than ordinary conversation. This is a critically important point, because it makes the nature of psychotherapy a stochastic, or probabilistic process rather than one that is entirely deterministic.

Knowing self is a necessary condition for knowing the other. Indeed the self is often known only in terms of its relationship to others, what is termed the looking glass self. The person of the therapist is the tool of therapy. A therapist lacking self awareness is a poor tool because they haven't practiced the same set of skills we teach others. The Delphic admonition know thyself means that the practitioner must practice the tool of awareness and reflection if they expect to be able to teach it to others. The awareness of self in relationship to other reflects the dialectical, back and forth, quality of crossing borders and bridging chasms. This necessity to live our values to a certain degree and to be able to present our self as tool to the other in need dovetails perfectly with our roots in rhetoric as the master discipline of persuasion by verbal means.

## Epistemology and metaphors

A metaphor is a way of extending thought beyond the literal, it suggests new possibilities. It links one thing with another, though they are dissimilar in many ways; the metaphor is the bridging cognitive link between dialectical opposites as well as other seemingly unrelated things. It creates the spark of transmission across the boundary, and marks the passage of the old into new. The metaphor is a primary embodiment of a creative act, opening up new possibilities.

Stephen Pepper (1891-1972), a Stanford philosopher, saw the importance of metaphor in the development of Western ideas about epistemology, or the area of philosophy dealing with how we justify our claims of knowledge of the world. There are a number of macro level sets of beliefs, what he called world hypotheses that describe major epistemological positions over the history of Western philosophy. Each has a root metaphor as part of the glue that holds the related set of ideas about the world and our knowledge of it. His most well known work is *World hypotheses: A study in evidence* (1942). He used the more tentative term, hypothesis, to emphasis the provisional character of all knowledge, and the process of testing of belief against reality, which has become the hallmark of empirical philosophy and science. We can use the more contemporary phrase, world view, without missing the basic point he was making. A world view is a collection of beliefs, assumptions, whether firm or tentative that shape our individual cognitive structures and the collective structure of knowledge as set forth in publicly available media and preserved across generations. We all hold world views as individuals; our modern understanding of individual personal cognitive structures, have implicit beliefs or folk philosophy as part of the landscape of the mind.

Pepper saw six basic world views, which he labeled, animism, mysticism, formism, mechanism, organicism, and contextualism. Each of these world views is organized around a root metaphor that expresses the basic ideas in an pithy and easily communicated manner. The person is a root metaphor for animism; for mysticism he seems to suggest revelation via the mystical experience; for formism, structure and classification is the root metaphor; for mechanism, the machine; for organicism, the living organism; and for contextualism, the text or historical event is the root metaphor.

The first two of the six world hypotheses he rejected because the basis of their warrants or justifications ultimately lie in the personal spiritual experience of the individual, or faith in the prophetic voice of another. Therefore, they are not suitable for rational justification and critique. The four remaining world hypotheses, or world views, he deemed as basically acceptable. Each of us as critical thinkers tends to prefer one, though we may hold views from each. The preference of one over another world view was based on the assumptions one was willing to make about the world, and thus were in some sense a primitive axiom-like sort of preference, with foundational impact. This embraces a pluralistic views of epistemologies, which is keeping with his general embrace of the pragmatic tradition in American philosophy, started by one of psychology's founding fathers, William James. Many views can be seen as acceptable, varying in their strengths, weaknesses, the things they help explain well, and the things they seem to stumble on.

Within psychology several authors have presented his ideas in the context of their own theoretical work and used him to highlight their particular perspective. Sarbin (1986) sees his narrative psychology as embodying the contextualist world view. Schwartz (1984) claimed the organicist world view as literally embodying a unifying mind-body holism expressed in systems theory. Lyddon (1995) seeks to advance a constructivist position in psychology by invoking the contextualist world view of Pepper. Altman and Rogoff (1987) used Pepper's schema of classification of world views to advance an transaction, interactionist perspective in terms of person environment relationships. Recently, Steven Hayes (Hayes, Hayes, Reese & Sarbin, 1993) has viewed his contemporary brand of behavioral therapy, acceptance and commitment therapy (ACT) as stemming from a constructivist world view. Each of them recasts aspects of Pepper's original formula to address a slightly different area of concern.

As we probe the development of the theoretical and scientific bases of professional psychology we can see that various theories emphasize or draw strongly from one or more of these world views. For example, trait theory seems to come out of a structural or formistic thrust in psychology. The traits are part of the taxonomy or classificatory structure of types. Behaviorism clearly emphasized mechanism, or determinate relationships between stimulus and response or alternatively, operant behavior and environmental reinforcement pattern. Humanistic psychology clearly emphasizes organicism in its holistic and molar focus. To the extent that all psychologies rely on the communicative nature of humans, all forms of psychology share in the contextualist point of view as well. Narrative and discourse are primary in psychology and the dialectic of text and context is a fundamental process. Thus, Pepper's system allow some degree of comparisons across theories or areas of interest in psychology as well as summarizing epistemic warrants or justifications.

## History as the archaeology of mind

Now we examine a final metaphor that is about the nature of history itself, the metaphor of depth and layering. The metaphor and graphic symbol of the arrow of time point to a linearity about time. We spoke earlier about the limenal perspective of the present, caught between past and future in the fleeting now. Time moves from the past into the future and so an ever extending line becomes the structure of our memories, recollections and projected into the future as hopes and plans. We rely on stories told to us by others as well as stories read about or viewed in other media to give us a knowledge of our own past as well as the past of others. Our imagination carries us into the future.

One way of ordering this line of time is actually literally true with regard to both geological and human history. Time is underfoot; in a very literal sense the deepest layer is the oldest layer. This principle of stratigraphy is the foundation of geology, paleontology and archaeology as scientific disciplines. As an example of the metaphor of depth as literally true; in the Grand Canyon of the Colorado River in the American West we can descend through layers of geological time as we go deeper into the canyon, we finally come to the bedrock schist upon which all other layers are deposited. Thus the study of the layering of deposits, stratigraphy is a profoundly important metaphor for understanding human history.

Psychodynamic theory has likewise been based in the metaphor of depth psychology. The surface dimension was consciousness and the deeper layer is the unconscious. The primal dichotomy is conscious versus unconscious is important. Each individual has her or his own developmental history, so the layering of the unconscious has some parallel with physical strata, the oldest is the deepest. The most primitive psychic material, the bedrock of our personal planet, are the habits and modes of being that we often term temperament; experience deposits material encoded in some manner in memory, even unconscious memories. These are often termed habits.

The stream of thinking emphasizing unconscious processes works like an archaeologist, excavating a site, exposing artifacts, and interpreting them in context. The therapist or analyst works backward from the present layers into as many of the past as needed to address the problem at hand. Memory is the ground upon which the layers of the person are deposited. But the compaction of memories means that some decay and become as dust, like friable products covered by collapsed walls or drifting sands. Others become rock hard and endure in their shape across time. Forgetting or not learning in the first place, is a basic and ordinary cognitive process. So personal memory, like history itself, is an evolving project. The metaphor of depth, of layers not only speak to the physical organization of things as in archaeological dig sites, but the ways in which individual persons form themselves and respond to the experiences they have across their life-time. That is the subject matter of professional psychology. We function as agents of uncovering and interpreting in context, at least to the extent that we adopt or make use of the psychodynamic frame of clinical theory. The purpose of clinical theory is to set out modes of excavation of symbolic material as well as to set out the canons of interpretation in light of psychological stratigraphy. The process of excavation is conducted at each therapeutic interview, it's like digging a trench through a landscape, exposing covered material.

## Streams of transmission and professional training

Streams of transmission is another metaphor for the nature of history. The physical basis for the metaphor is the network of creeks which become streams, which flow into rivers, larger rivers still, and eventually emptying into a sea or ocean. As water flows down from heights to the lowlands, so time flows onward like a river. Moments merge into moments and soon our lives are structured into events, stages and phases, in a hopefully long sequence from beginning to end. Both the physical basis of the metaphor as well as the experience of time share the act of flow or flux.

A stream of transmission in the domain of education can be seen in the passing on of knowledge, skills, and professional attitudes. It is a metaphor that fits quite well as a description of the nature of professional training. The teacher of clinical practice must articulate both the scientific and conceptual bases of clinical judgement as well as mentor the development of skills involved in becoming a competent practitioner. The role of the teacher is to transmit the collective wisdom of the profession to the next generation of practitioners, knowledge, skills, and attitudes of professionalism. All of this unfolds over time in a program of study as knowledge and skills form competencies.

A graphic representation of the metaphor of streams of transmission is a branching tree structure. Many small creeks flow downward coalescing into rivers and so on. At the beginning in the heights are many, but in the end there is one great ocean into which all of the multiplicities resolve into unity. This is also physically embodied in the pedigree charts of genealogy, but in a reverse direction. The start is the individual person and the branching tree structure fans out across successive earlier generations of parents, grandparents, and so on. A descendant chart can also fan out from a common ancestor and show successive generations of children, grand children, and so on.

Many branching tree structures of a historical nature have a common origin or an end point and fan out forward or backward in time.

Asynchronous branching tree structures also are useful, such as the outline structure for writing or the indexing of material into sections and topics shows how ubiquitous this cognitive tool is. It is the basis of the organization of the display of files and folders on digital storage media. Networks of all sorts can be modeled using same node-link-node which is the graphic basis of the branching tree structure, though networks don't have to have a single origin point, but may be self contained. Organization charts are another example of graphic type.

The branching tree structure is the graphically similar to genealogical charts because it literally embodies time and generations. All life comes from life and the history of life is written in our genes. Ultimately we have a common genetic ancestor way back in time and share our genes with all other living beings on the planet to a greater or lesser extent. The phrase most recent common ancestor (MRCA) is found in evolutionary biology and is the point at which species differ, and from which different lines of succession begin. We have billions of distant cousins. At some point sexual reproduction and dimorphism emerged and has become the means of reproduction of complex animals. Most human creation myths start with a primal couple, and all the human races come from them. So we all share some place as a descendant in the branching tree structure of the human species and evolutionary biology traces the history of speciation across the variety of living and extinct life forms. When we look at our genealogical chart as an individual we see our particularity as the point of origin and the web of ancestors retreating into the mists of distant time.

The biologist Steven Gould (1986) has noted that in geology, paleontology and evolutionary science, history matters. It is the homology of various fossil finds across time that give meaning and order to the lineages of speciation and descent. Indeed he calls those, along with astronomy, the historical sciences because the possibilities for experimental control and manipulation are negligible. Psychology, also, is a historical science, though most psychologists might not agree. As Gergen (1973) noted, particularly in social psychology we are faced with the prospect that earlier findings may differ because of what is called cohort effects, the particular aspects of culture which change over time. The scientist is tasked with explaining how the series of events come to pass that bring about the present. So real and particular events, including people and their motives are part of the things to be explained by history, and many types of science including psychology.

Professional psychology is a human activity deeply grounded in particularity or individuality. In a later chapter this point will be emphasized as a distinction between a natural science and a human science approach to psychology. In the clinical context we refer to the particularity of each individual's life history. Each person is unique in some regards. The goal of the clinician is not to formulate general knowledge about all possible cases, but to deal with the particular case present. The clinician as scientist may also seek to find regular patterns that emerge across individuals and across time, but that is work in a different context. While randomized controlled trials (RCT) have the advantage of rigorous controls over the variable that exhibit causative influences on outcome, real clinical practice has to deal with the client who walks in off the street with their particular set of issues and life history. The clinical interview aims at eliciting the needed background information particular to the client in order to see their situation from as close to their perspective as possible which maintaining one's professional stance. Even now, as we treat individuals, couples, families, groups and even organizations and communities, we deal with particular ones. Each social group has its unique history, just as each individual organism does. The primary tool of the clinician is the individual case history.

The importance of the transmission of both knowledge and skill in practice has examples in the context of two spiritual systems and one secular system. In Tibetan Buddhism the transmission of authority to use a set of spiritual practices is conveyed through an empowerment where both the doctrines and the techniques are conveyed. Unlike Western faiths which are more focused on creeds, the focus in that form of Buddhism is on practice of meditation technique in a disciplined manner over time. The knowledge of the theology or world view is embedded in the very nature of the practices, or sadhannas. The sense of continuity of practitioners in a stream of teachers and students is an important part of the flavor of Tibetan spirituality. High lamas are lineage holders, that is, they literally hold the keys to certain knowledge and techniques which are essential and which must be passed on. East monk, lama, or lay person receives empowerments, ritual transmissions of knowledge with a vow to practice it for the benefit of all sentient beings. Tracing one's lineage from teacher to teacher and knowing that one is part of a chain of practitioners going back to the Buddha is part of the social context of practice. It is the transmission of not only what to do, but how to do it skillfully, with grace and compassion.

The other example comes from the West. In Roman Catholic, Eastern Orthodox, Anglican and some other Protestant traditions the concept of a stream of transmission is Apostolic succession. All priests in a valid line were ordained by others holding valid ordination traceable ultimately to St. Peter or one of the other disciples of Jesus. There is a direct line of authority that provides a continuity of authority to perform the sacraments and pass on the teachings.

The secular example is psychoanalysis where there is a similar, very literal stream of transmission in terms of the link created through the experience of personal analysis. All analysands can trace their lineage of transmission back to Freud by knowing who psychoanalyzed their analyst, and so on back to the founder. Most other schools of therapy do not quite as formally have the sort of stream of transmission as is seen in psychoanalysis. Psychoanalysis requires an experiential process, just like training in meditation. The other schools of psychotherapy do not formally require any personal experience as a receiver of therapy in order to practice it. There are some exceptions.

Hypnosis, for example, would be almost impossible to teach without directly experiencing it as well. Humanistic psychology, as a broad stream is highly experiential, and participation in workshops at a personal level is seen as very important, though formal credentialing and training is not always highly structured. Generally, most other forms of counseling and therapy are passed on without such personal experiential processes.

A stream of transmission represents the passing on of knowledge and skills from one generation to another succeeding one through training and mentoring. While formal academic course work can expose the students to the theory of assessment and intervention, and even initial role plays may help get a beginning feeling of competence in the actual doing of it, it is the subsequent apprenticeship in practicums or other pre-doctoral training programs where the hands-on portion of clinical education really occurs. Experiential learning is an aspect of training that in nearly all instances requires the sort of supervised exposure and guidance implied in the metaphor of a steam of transmission. Apprenticeship in healing is a technical and a personal process as well. It is a process of training by not just formal instruction, but by observation of example, and supervised practice. Ideally, it should also involve opportunity for self reflection and examination to shape the attitudes necessary for limenality as the bridge to the other.

One of my favorite myths which illustrates the stream of transmission comes from ancient Greece. Apollo was the Olympian deity with special power of healing. He had a son, Asklepios (often spelled in the Latin form, Asclepius). The centaurs were a rowdy bunch of creatures, half horse and half human. In mythology they were quite animalistic in their lusts and aggression, but the noblest of the Centaurs was Chiron. Apollo entrusted his son Asklepios to Chiron to raise and transmitted the gift of healing to Chiron. Chiron then instructed Asklepios in the healing arts and he later became the chief deity of healing and medicine. Chiron stands in the middle of a stream of transmission from Apollo to Asklepios. Chiron is also seen as a model for the wounded healer. He and Hercules (Gk. Heracles) were battling some other centaurs when Chiron was struck by an arrow. Though he survived the wound the pain never ceased and he asked Zeus as a gift to allow him to die so his pain would end. The wish was granted, but he became immortalized in the constellation of Sagittarius. Chiron, the wounded healer, transmits the gift of healing which he gives to Asklepios who then trains others in the arts of healing, but as the wounded healer, there are burdens that only death can release him from. This stands as a powerful metaphor for would be healers. There are limits to what can be accomplished, but the calling requires one to pass on the craft to others; and they continue the tradition in a lineage of healing.

## Larson's role archetype theory

My first experience teaching the history of professional psychology to clinical psychology students came with the charter class of Wright State University's School of

Professional Psychology, and I repeated it until I left in 1987 to come to Chicago. Over the course of that time I came to see the way in which certain basic role descriptions characterized the developments which led to the emergence of professional psychology. I found particular resonance with Jung's concept of archetype. If one focuses on the social role of healing, the possibilities of connection between current manifestations and ancient roots are made easier to understand through this concept. An archetype is a cluster of psychological processes and content embodied in myth and symbols. In this sense, the roles are enactments of the various metaphors by which human healing have been understood and practiced across time and cultural space. They constitute the collective set of meanings for the sorts of interactions that go into helping and healing and are part of our unconscious psychological framework of understanding.

Professional psychology is an amalgam of four archetypal roles; first, of the shaman and priest or priestess, second the physician, third the teacher, and fourth the scientist. The first three are old enough to be truly archetypal in their cross-cultural validation and duration. The scientist is a more recent social role and the archetypal network of meanings is less well differentiated. The role of the scientist has become a staple of popular culture (e.g. the mad scientist). Science as a belief system seems to have come to dominate the world's intelligentsia. The very promise of science in technology, medical cures, and its authority to pronounce what is reality has made it a major epistemological font. The central role that science has come to play in modern life certainly underscores its importance as a reference point in the warrants or justifications of the authority of professional psychology.

The shaman represents the primordial spiritual healer, arising out of animism as a world view. The priest or priestess were more socialized roles that emerged in what Taylor (1977) termed the era of hydraulic civilizations (roughly from Neolithic (7,000-2,500 BCE) through Bronze Age (2,500-800 BCE). The foundation of both social roles for healing was almost exclusively spiritual in nature. With the emergence of urban centers, structures such as temples, and social organization and occupational specialization, the archetype of the physician begins. Although still largely mixed with various spiritual world views and practices, this is probably the first archetype to emerge with the possibility of secular healing by means of skilled technique or special knowledge of the material plane. Physicians as technicians rather than priests were found in ancient Egypt and Greece. Particularly in the Greek cultural sphere, a well organized tradition of healing through technology rather than charm or prayer evolved and was passed on to the Roman empire.

In Classical Greece, the first professional teachers emerged to teach effective use of speech. From that came rhetoric and philosophy. In the classical Greco-Roman civilization around the Mediterranean, the Stoic and Epicurean teachers of philosophy held that studying and practicing a philosophy could transform one's life and make for greater well-being. So teaching at its earliest point of professional development was about not just the logic of rigorous and clear thinking, but about understanding the emotions and motivations and being able to live a balanced life in which all of those components contribute to harmony.

The role of scientist became the epitome of empirical philosophy as it inspired European technological advances which fostered European cultural domination through colonization. By the nineteenth century the modern sciences emerged as specific disciplines in the academic tradition. The twentieth century saw the emergence of development of the profession and science of psychology into its modern forms and the full maturation of the various archetypes whose streams led into the large and flowing river of our profession today.

These four archetypal roles are with us today. As psychologists we deal with matters of ultimate concern for people, and provide comfort at times of grief, pain, and loss. Whether one's world view is spiritual or secular, when we deal with matters of ultimate concern we are in an area first explored by those working in a spiritual world view. In that sense we still have a foot in the world of spirituality. We are embodied beings and thus we suffer from ailments of the body. This requires us to understand and be comfortable with the world of physiology and medicine, and things of the body in general. Many of our techniques are grounded in an education mode, teaching people to think, feel, and behave in new and different ways. The archetype of the teacher resonates in sympathetic vibration across the millennia. Finally, as we observe, measure and seek to understand what we do and find ways to enhance and refine it, the archetype of the scientist guides us forward. Science informs practice, practice informs science and new skills are passed along in a continuing stream of transmission of the modes of psychological healing. These four archetypal roles now come together in the role of the professional psychologist. Here is how the story unfolds.

# 2

# Spiritual Healing

We begin our history of healing through psychological means by considering spiritual healing. It is the first archetypal role for healing which emerged in human culture. It is first embodied in the role of the shaman then later the role of priest or priestess. This role arises from a spiritual world view rather than the secular one now associated with science. Some sort of spirituality has been the most common world view throughout the greatest period of human history and across the greatest spread of geography. Indeed, it is only relatively recently, the last three hundred years or so, that a completely secular world view has emerged as an alternative to the spiritual view.

In recent decades some scholars have distinguished between spirituality and religion. Spirituality refers to the personal, even private experience of encounter with the Divine, whereas religion represents the public and social affiliation with a community of people who share a set of myths and rituals to honor their understanding of the Divine. Some still see religion and spirituality as too similar to really distinguish between them. But one thing that has prompted the division is the emergence of many people who are dominantly secular in their world view, do not feel particularly drawn to participating in traditional religions, but also feel a tug or pull toward something beyond the individual. In America one of the fastest growing groups are those who in surveys of religious orientation would check a box titled *none* or something similar. This is an example of the possibility of a secular spirituality, if that isn't an oxymoron.

Most forms of spiritual thought are theistic in nature, that is, they personify the Divine in form of a person. Non-theistic forms of spirituality view the Divine or sacred as an impersonal force, law, principle of creation, ground of being, etc. These forms become sources of ultimate meaning and therefore foundations of spirituality. Evidence for the existence of a spiritual world view comes from the earliest artifacts of human history; objects of art which seem to express some vision of another world. So the tug of spiritual world views is pulling on a long rope of connection.

## Knowledge and mystery

There are a number of great and profound mysteries. The first is existence itself. Why is it that anything exists? The second is life itself. Why do some things live? The third is consciousness. Why am I aware that I exist and am alive? The fourth is suffering and death. Why do we all die and in the meantime also experience suffering? The fifth is significance. What is the point and purpose of my existence and that of all living beings and all nature?

First philosophy then science are the human attempts to address these mysteries. Philosophy is based on human reason, science is based on reason plus observation. Science seeks to find explanation for things in lawful principles of nature. Let's see how much we can explain without supernatural forces. One of the most interesting things about the history of science is that as far as we have pushed natural law explanations, at the very boundary of what we know is still mystery, the unknown. Science acts as if everything is knowable and pushes us to find ways of knowing through the processes of nature. It has come very far and will continue to deepen our understanding of the world, but I doubt that it will ever explain everything. Mystery remains a hard fact of existence.

What is our response to mystery? The heart of spiritual experience is that we experience those fundamental mysteries as somehow tied up with something we respond to as sacred, as worthy of the most profound and ultimate reverence. Religion then takes those spiritual experiences and finds ways of sharing them with others and making some rational sense of it in light of what else we know. We have come to a common understanding that spirituality is that personal and private experience of encounter with the mystery as divine or sacred, and religion is that corporate, social, and public expression of those sentiments.

Are spiritual/religion and science in conflict? My answer is no, they are separate ways of knowing. Like the allegory of the blind men and the elephant, each grasps a different aspect of ultimate truth. Taken together, we have a more complete picture of the world as knowledge and mystery.

Empedocles said that the two most fundamental forces in the cosmos are attraction and replusion, movement toward or away from some thing. This is consistent with a secular physics of elecro-magnetism. It is also consistent with basic psychology. We as humans are either drawn toward or away from various other people, various activities, and various beliefs.

How do we come to know anything, or perhaps more precisely, how do we justify our beliefs? Reason was the first answer. This is the answer of philosophy. Science couples reason with observation. Both seek to minimize the influences of other human characteristics, particularly emotion. Emotion is viewed by both as irrational. I prefer to use the term non-rational; there's less of a pejorative tone to it.

Love is the most prevalent example of a non-rational motive in human life. Falling in love is not something that one reasons about, it just happens. Complicated as it is, with the possibility of it not being returned by one's beloved, we nonetheless view it as one of the most important aspects of human existence. So the lesson is clear, a fully human life must be lived with both reason and emotion. While we often need to guide our actions to balance reason and emotion and express them both in ways that are congenial to others, we do need both the rational and the non-rational for a complete existence. That's convenient because we can't help having both, so we might as well come to a harmonious relationship between them.

Finally, as noted in the previous chapter we come to the problem of human suffering. Spiritual healing was the first means by which we as humans sought to give comfort and presence to each other in the face of suffering. Some have been called to do this as a vocation. In spiritual terms, this is the pastoral function, to minister to people in times of suffering, and also, to celebrate with them in times of joy. Either way, it is how we care for each other in some of the most important ways. That is our story.

## Cultural context: Human beginnings

If we take the current story of cosmic development from physics, the universe originated in a Big Bang some 13.7 billion years ago and by about 4.5 billion years ago the galaxies, star systems, and planets formed, including our own planet Earth orbiting our Sun. So our local history is about that old. Nearly all elements which make up living beings on Earth came from nuclear fusion within stars, so we literally are star children. After numerous geologic eons, periods and epochs we arrive at a time when mammals begin to dominate the life forms of the planet after several catastrophic mass extinctions of other life forms, most recently the dinosaurs. There is a growing consensus among scientists that we may be entering a period called the Anthropocene, where human activities shape the planetary ecology in profound ways. The beginning of global warming is a sign that this period is already showing signs of our significant effects on climate. Satellite pictures of the earth at night clearly show the visible signs of population centers through the wealth of artificial lighting in urban areas.

By about 60 million years ago primates emerge and by about 4 million years ago we find fossils of the genus *Australopithecus*, the oldest in the lines of primates which could be ancestors or a collateral line feeding into the genus *Homo,* of which humans are the current representative species. By about 2.5 to 1.5 million years ago we find fossils of *homo habilis* or handy man known for the growing variety of stone tools. Our direct line of *homo sapiens* emerges about 200,000 years ago. Fossil evidence is found in Africa, the Eurasian land mass, Australia and the Americas showing the humans had populated the globe completely between 40,000 and 10,000 years ago. Antarctica only being populated by sparse groups of scientists in the last several decades. With regard to the Americas, the current debate concerns how far back to push the arrival of humans. The previous data suggested a date around 11,000 (BCE) for the arrival of people in the Americas, associated with a tool style known as the Clovis point, but new sites have unearthed evidence of slightly older artifacts verified by radiocarbon dating. However much details may change, the central conclusion remains most of the earth's land mass and many of its islands were inhabited by humans migrating out of Africa.

Moving from geological time scales and paleontology to human archaeology, we can classify the development of our species from several standpoints, but the most common one for the oldest eras is a system based on the dominant tools found. Stone tools were used in the Paleolithic, or old stone age (1 million to 10,000 years before present, B.P.), and the Neolithic eras, or new stone age (10,000 BCE to 3,000 BCE). With discovery of metallurgy we call the succeeding ages the Chalcolithic (copper using) era, the Bronze Age (3,000 to 1,000 BCE) and the Iron Age (1,000 BCE to the end of classical antiquity, approx, 700 CE). The pace was slow until fairly recently, when technological developments began to compound and create a momentum of change. More recent technologies mark the arrival of the Industrial Revolution and now the Digital age.

For the greatest part of time humans pre-history we got our sustenance from hunting animals and foraging for plant food and therefore were nomadic, moving around seasonal resources. Social organization rarely developed beyond bands of related families. The native peoples of the Great Plains in the United States, were in many ways living lives that had existed unchanged for millennia prior to the advent of European explorers and later settlers. The degree to which the bands were nomadic depended on the relative abundance of the climate in the lands they occupied and the density of population. Tropical climates afforded abundant amounts of food, temperate climates offered seasonal fluctuations of abundance and want, and arctic climates were harshest and yet people adapted and sustained themselves across time.

A crucial development was language. Many thousands of years before writing, oral language existed and it provided the tool from which human culture developed. Communication provided our species with an advantage over other species as bands of humans could coordinate hunting activities. Large mammals such as mammoths could provide protein for our brains to grow more complex. Language also allowed shared knowledge about the cycles of ripening plants also gathering food from vegetation also was enhanced.

One of the earliest signs of the emergence of a spiritual world view is burial of the dead which we find evidence of in the Paleolithic era. In addition, early art strongly suggests a sense of awe and reverence toward life and its mysteries. Two such early art works are the Venus of Willendorf, from around 25,000 years ago and the cave painting known as the Shaman of Trois-Frères from 13,000 years ago. The first is a figurine with exaggerated female characteristics which suggest a veneration of the fertility of women and the mystery of childbirth. The latter suggests a mastery over animals for the purpose of successful hunt and a spiritual connection between human and animals. A most dramatic example of cave art is the recently discovered art in the Chauvet cave in France. The documentary film, *Cave of forgotten dreams* (2010) shows the esthetic beauty and sublime feelings found in early human art. It is likely that some social role emerged, a specialist in spiritual matters, to whom the people would look for healing as well. This figure we will term the *shaman* as a generic label for the oldest layer of healing by psychological means.

The Neolithic era saw significant changes that resulted in dramatic transformations of the human situation. This era sees the domestication of plants and animals and the beginnings of village life as nomadic peoples settled in communities. This made agricultural and herding economies possible. The surplus of food that came about resulted in population increases. Villages eventually grew to become cities. Taylor (1977) uses the term hydraulic civilizations to characterize the late Neolithic cultural centers that emerged in fertile river valleys about the fourth to second millennium BCE. They were called hydraulic because of their use of irrigation to expand agriculture. With more food then larger populations flourished allowing cities, social stratification to emerge. These societies developed metallurgy, first with copper. Then they discovered that mixing it with tin produced bronze, a harder metal that could hold an edge for weaponry.

In Africa, the Nile fed the growth of Egyptian civilization. In the Near East, the land between the two rivers, the Tigris and Euphrates, known as Mesopotamia, flourished in what is now Iraq. In the Indian sub-continent the Indus river was the home of the earliest civilization in that area. In east Asia, Chinese civilization emerged based around the Huang-ho and Yangtze rivers. Soon other high civilizations emerged in the Mekong, the Ganges and Bramaputra river basins as well. In the Americas, however, the high civilizations emerged in coastal or mountainous regions. What made the river based civilizations so productive was the invention of irrigation, which expanded the areas that could be put under cultivation. That made the early communities, cities, villages, tempting targets for nomadic warriors. Especially in Eurasia, the grassy steppe land where the horse was domesticated created a recurring conflict between settled villagers and horseback riding archers. China built walls to keep out predation by mounted warriors. Indo-European peoples came into Europe in waves and populated the Anatolian peninsula, Iran and the Indian subcontinent. Much later Turkic tribes came and settled.

Urban life allowed these river based to emerge as civilizations. Oral language became embodied in writing, marking the transition from pre-history to history. Social differentiation and hierarchical structures developed as population grew. This brings the possibility of kingdoms and empires and not just chiefdoms which characterized smaller societies. The division of labor and the emergence of craft specialists either in soldiering or pottery making, or healing became common. Most civilizations began creating large monumental buildings of stone. These were nearly all designed as sacred sites or temples. By this time we have evidence of priesthoods who serviced the temples.

So the shaman of nomadic band cultures evolved into the priests and priestesses of the variety of deities and families of deities, or pantheons, found in emerging civilizations. Healing became a technical specialty of the priestly groups. While we will see in the next chapter how the physician becomes separated out as a special occupation and becomes increasingly based in empirical findings. Across time, though religious and spiritual leaders took on other functions, they retained a primary role in healing. This continues to today as part of healing, as noted above, includes finding meaning and purpose even in the midst of serious illness, disability or loss. Ultimately the existential issues of life, embodiment, death, choice and limitation are dealt with by both spiritual, bio-medical and psycho-social practitioners.

For many years I have taught the sort of world view and healing practices that go with the earliest layers of spiritual healing in a three-fold fashion. Animism is the theory; magic is the technology, and the shaman, priest or priestess is the practitioner.

## Animism: Theory for spiritual healing practices

The word animism was first used to describe a spiritual or religious philosophy by the British anthropologist Edward Burnett Tylor (1832-1917). In this world view, all things are alive. They are or have spirits; some spirits have bodies, others do not. Things we now would recognize as inanimate were seen as living beings such as the Sun, Moon, the earth itself, the sky, seas, mountains and so on. The earth itself was a living being, known in ancient Greece as Gaia. Pepper (1942) identifies the person as the root metaphor of animism. The individual person who has consciousness projects that consciousness out onto the world and views them as other persons. The concept of soul, spirit or psyche is the extension of the experiencing and acting individual. We now recognize that the world divided into inanimate objects as well as living or animate beings, but in the earliest stages of human culture all things were imbued with a vital essence. This belief persists in the form of an impersonal life force energy that permeates all things; we'll come back to that idea later.

Personification can be done deliberately as well as instinctively. When we anthropomorphize our animal companions, we likewise engage in personification. With animals, particularly mammals, the extension of the experience of personhood to the other begins to make a bit more sense. We know that some animals form strong bonds with humans and, of course, vice versa. In contemporary America many people relate to their companion animals as family, referring to themselves as the father or mother and their dog or cat as their child. We now know that the higher up the phylogenetic scale of biological evolution one goes, the more the animals share behavioral characteristics with humans and have their own cognitive processes consistent with their neural organization, so ascribing to them consciousness and some of the qualities of personhood seems more fitting.

One can see some form of primitive sensory or cognitive processing far down on the phylogenetic scale of animals. Plants and bacteria or viruses, though we concede them to be living beings, we typically do not treat them as having some form or manner of consciousness. An important and oft cited paper on the philosophy of mind raised the question of what it is like to be a bat (Nagel, 1974). In that piece he notes that the nature of mind is to have a sense of what it is like to be that thing, having a subjectivity. He doesn't explore how far down the ladder of being one can go with the ascription of mind, but he does describe at least some of the characteristics we would expect of those things which are enminded as well as embodied. Animism would challenge the assumption that there is a limit to some degree or quality of consciousness. It is clearly harder to perceive the sun, moon, earth, wind, sea and sky as living beings, let alone persons. Nonetheless animism has its current defenders (Harvey, 2006).

The world is divided into at least two realms, the sacred and the profane, or mundane (Eliade, 1961). This is the basis for the philosophical distinction between the natural world and the supernatural world. Religious explanations of events in the natural world often invoking the action of the deity or several deities. Storms were cause by Zeus or Odin or others. As secular thought challenged these ascriptions naturalistic explanations based on laws became the hallmark of science. Most spiritual philosophies still hold to a distinction between these two realms of reality. The goal of the religious professional, the shaman, was to pass from one world to another and back again to gain knowledge of the cause of illness and the path to health.

What is the theory of health and illness in an animistic world view? Basically, health is harmony on both the mundane and spiritual planes of existence; illness is the result of imbalance, disharmony in some way or other. Clements (1932) outlined the major categories of specific factors that account for the imbalance. Among them are violation of taboo (performance of a forbidden act), it opposite, failure to perform an obligatory act, soul loss, spirit possession, and active malevolence by another being (bewitching, hexing). When spiritual philosophies evolve into the more recognizable modern world religions, we see the addition of illness as a punishment from God for transgression of divine commandments.

Even in modern spiritual philosophies arising from later developments, there is still a major conceptual continuity in terms of the concept of balance. Most of the Asian healing arts we will consider in a succeeding chapter involve some impersonal spiritual life force (e.g. in Chinese, *chi*, *qi*, in Japanese, *ki*) and define health or illness in terms of the balance of yin/yang or other psycho-spiritual forces and fluids. Balance and moderation is also at the heart of many of the clinical philosophies found in Hellenistic Greece and Rome which arose in the waning days of the pagan ancient world. Thus a variety of conceptions of illness use the principle of balance to define health and imbalance as a cause of illness. Only the type of things which are in or out of balance have changed as our intellectual tools have become more sophisticated and cross-pollinated from the ideas of other cultures.

Animism was the earliest expression of the primitive concept of soul, spirit, or even impersonal spiritual force pervades all modern forms of spiritual philosophy. Though the diversity of spiritual and religious practice changed significantly with the advent of organized religion. One of the salient threads of continuity across time is the belief in something other than the ego, the self, or the individual; that something other is the realm of spirit. As we shall see later, transpersonal psychology is accepting of something transcendent to the individual ego, however that may be defined.

## Magic: The technology

The animistic world view leads naturally to magic as a technology. Magic is the means of making things happen in accordance with the individual will. While the typical assumption is that the action is supernatural in nature, it has always been recognized that some degree of instrumental action on the mundane or ordinary plane of existence can be effective in addition to action on a spiritual plane. Indeed the link between the mundane and the spiritual world is how magic works according to the dictum, "As above, so below." That saying from the Hermetic corpus, a body of magical writings from late antiquity is a central principle; what action is taken in one realm has an effect in the other. In the end, even the most consummate magician must recognize the limitation of her or his skill when coming up against forces and spiritual powers greater than oneself. These most powerful spirits are accorded the status of deities, gods and goddesses. Monotheism comes along much later, but even in those religions magicians were recognized as figures in European cultures into the early modern era. From the modern period onward magic has evolved into a spiritual practice promoting communion with the Divine (Gray, 1975).

Sir James Frazer (1854-1941), in his classic tome on comparative mythology, *The Golden Bough* (1950/1922), made the link between the mundane and spiritual realms central as a law of sympathy. All magic, according to Frazer relies on this law of sympathy for its effect. Whatever sorts of things and processes we might find in the mundane world of ordinary experience (below) have a sympathetic connection to similar things and processes at the spiritual level (above). The literal etymology of sympathy is *feeling with* so whether we use it in the more familiar context of interpersonal relations or this specialized meaning, the common thread is the perceptible link between two entities or realms. This link between the sacred and the mundane acts as a conduit for transmission of action between the realms, from one to another and back again. Later, this sympathetic connection would be described in terms of vibrations and resonant harmonies.

Sympathetic magic has two major aspects, homeopathic magic and contagious magic. In homeopathic magic, like brings about like; mimesis is the operative principle. If one wishes a successful bison hunt, one enacts a hunt with a kill and sacrifice. If one wants to inflict pain or wound another, one creates a doll in the target person's image and does to it what one wants to happen to the live target. Contagious magic is based on the concept of spiritual essence, power or fluid. Each part of our body contains a portion of our spiritual self and if it can be obtained by another it can be used for good or ill toward that person. In the first examples, one would don the skin and horns of the bison as one became the bison for ritual purposes, for they contain the vital essence of the bison. In the second example of a malevolent hex on another human, not only should one use homeopathic magic and construct a poppet doll, or likeness of the other, but one should obtain some part of the target person, some spittle, a clipping of hair, or a finger nail paring. That morsel would then charge the doll with the spiritual force of the intended victim, thus sealing the action not only through homeopathic but through contagious magic as well.

That personal power can be transmitted from one person to another in the course of healing. This is the spiritual basis of therapeutic touch. In the Christian New Testament, there is the story of Jesus passing through a crowed market and feeling the power drain out of him when a woman touched his garment in passing (Luke 8:44-46). This palpable spiritual power was found throughout human history. In medieval through early modern Europe, the therapeutic touch was often found in royalty, though lay healers also are chronicled. Finally, prior to the birth of modern psychodynamic therapies, Mesmerism used the magnetic pass. The hands would pass across the patient's body from head to feet, transmitting the magnetic fluid to the sufferer and in reverse to remove the trance which accompanied the fluid.

There is a long history of continuity in the use of spirits in magic. Conjuring up spirits has been a basic activity of those who practice these spiritual arts. There are some differences in the ways spirits are used, however. One could invoke them into one's own person, a very dangerous procedure because it could lead to spirit possession, or one could more safely evoke them into a protective circle separated from the magician. This was the favored practice of many Renaissance or Elizabethan magicians, like John Dee. One could also travel outside one's body. This is technically termed ecstasy. We now think of it as an extreme state of joy, but its earlier meaning is staying outside one's body as a conscious soul or spirit for a period of time.

These techniques lead us into a discussion of the techniques at the very heart of shamanism, the trance. The principle use of the altered state of consciousness is to travel from the mundane world to the spirit world. There the shaman sees what factor, force, or spirit is causing the current illness in the patient and brings back the key to the therapeutic procedures. Much magical work involves attaining an altered state of awareness through which one communicates with the spiritual realm. All sorts of specific uses and activities follow depending on the purpose for which magic is used. While psychoactive chemicals were known and used, so also were a variety of non-chemical means such as rhythmic drumming, chanting, dancing or still and quiet contemplation.

## The Shaman as Practitioner

The term *shaman* comes from the Siberian Chuckchee people, but it has now become a generic term for the individual practitioner of spiritual healing in all sorts of societies. We will use it in that generic sense. It covers folk healers within a wide range of ancient and contemporary cultures who operate out of a largely spiritual framework, possibly animistic in the world view, and are not trained in modern scientific medicine. It is most closely associated historically with pre-literate hunter-gatherers, but is found in village societies and even in modern urban areas of developed countries. There is a long history of continuity as well as a geographic spread in terms when and who might be called shamanic practitioners (Walter & Fridman, 2004).

Shamanic healers exist today not only in the few bands of nomadic or semi-nomadic peoples like the Sami who follow herds of reindeer or other large mammals across the northern reaches of Eurasia, but also in Siberia where the indigenous language gave us this now generic term. They also continue to exist in settled communities as either the most available healer in rural areas, or as an alternative healer in a modern metropolis where more mainstream medical professionals are available. Crook (1997) describes how there is an overlay of religions as societies develop. In Ladakh, where he studied the relationship between Buddhism and shamanic practices, he found that the people went to the monastery and the lamas for one set of concerns, while still using shamanic healers and diviners for other purposes. They co-existed with a later and more formalized organized religion overlaying the earlier animistic base. Shamanic practitioners are found often in recent immigrant communities where they provide some continuity between cultures of origin and new host cultures. Hmong shamans followed the rest of the migrants from Vietnam to America following our war there in the nineteen sixties and seventies. Native American healers, likewise exist not only on reservations but in urban settings too. Finally, the anthropologist Michael Harner has studied under shaman in several cultures and now packages workshops and retreats to teach what he calls core shamanism to Westerners who seek a different and older form of spiritual practice (Harner, 1990).

How does one become a shaman? The path for becoming a shaman is quite different from what most students of professional psychology recount as the path for their occupational choice. For them it is often not a choice, but a solution to a personal crisis. The path usually wound through a dark valley involving a personal crisis that brought one to sense a calling or vocation as a shaman. The anthropological literature highlights the many ways in which the ones chosen for this vocation often have some sort of marginalizing condition or status. They may not fit gender or sexual orientation roles, they may suffer from seizure disorders or other maladies, they may have symptoms of mental illness or in some other way stand out as different from their own communities (Silverman, 1967). The personal crisis, whatever its nature is often resolved by becoming a healer. They often seek out an existing shaman to help resolve the crisis and find out that they can only resolve it by becoming one. The penalty for refusal is usually madness or death, so it is part of a spiritual ordeal.

Thus begins the tradition of the wounded healer, as in our story of Chiron. Even today a common joke about psychotherapists is that they go into the field to fix their own problems. The kernel of truth is that it takes some interest in and willingness for self exploration to become a successful psychotherapist. Many of us are drawn to the field by a variety of personal histories which push us toward self exploration and reflection as well as altruistic motives for helping others. For some of us the choice stems from multiple reasons, but often that same sense of a calling for a vocation is among them. Hopefully the process of training for both shamans and professional psychologists weeds out those who are too damaged by their own personal histories to be helpful to others. Also, hopefully professional training helps develop the student's capacity for self awareness and reflection as part of honing the self as tool for the practice of healing.

The term vocation has been used in modern Western spiritual traditions to refer to the sense of personal calling that motivates someone to take up the ministry or to take up the religious life in a monastic order in those traditions that have such groups. There a sense of the working of a higher power or purpose, a force beyond one's own personal wishes and plans. One does not choose a profession of spiritual work and healing, one is called. Not all who become professional healers do so by a spiritual calling, a vocation. Some of the secular minded still sense that there is a particular goodness of fit between their values and choice of career and can participate in their own way in the experience of vocation.

Once the person accepts the call, they then must apprentice as a novice to a master shaman for not only further healing but training in the arts of healing. Castaneda (1968) tells the story of his apprenticeship to a Yacqui medicine man Don Juan. The data of the book came from his doctoral dissertation in anthropology at University of California, Berkeley, though its authenticity has been challenged. Regardless of whether we view this as an ethnographic report or a novel, it is very instructive chronicle about spiritual development in an animistic world view. The process of apprenticeship gives the novice the tools to manipulate spiritual realities and their mundane manifestations.

How does the shaman heal? The common thread through the many historical and cultural differences, is that the healer works on the spiritual plane to bring about the healing. The trance is used as a vehicle for the shaman to enter the spirit world, find the basis for the problem and the path that must be followed for healing to occur. Diagnosis and therapy are the twin phases or aspects of the professional relationship. One assess the problem presented, formulates a theory of the case and then prescribes the treatment, involving the client in the process of healing. In spiritual healing the diagnostic process is termed divination. Trance is usually central to the process of divination, though a variety of other means are used as well.

There are two ways one can enter into a trance according to Fischer (1971). These are the path of stillness and the path of activity; the former is termed trophotropic and the latter is termed ergotropic. He uses terms coined in the study of autonomic nervous system, first by Hess, then more recently by Gellhorn & Kiely (1972). The trophotropic states are entered into through eyes-closed, inward-focused, physically still types of mind training. These are common known as meditative techniques. The erogotropic states are entered into through eyes-open, outwardly-focused, physical activity. This is your traditional shamanic drumming, chanting, moving, dancing. It is also the runner's high in aerobic activity. Both paths lead to altered awareness and if deliberately cultivated can be used in a variety of ways. Western rational culture, however, tends to be skeptical of all forms of altered consciousness as sources of knowledge, though recently meditative practices have become more acceptable in psychology, particular in the context of stress management.

Divination is the use of spiritual practices to answer personal questions or guide choices. It has been understood psychologically by Jung through his principle of synchronicity. The most common form of divination is sortilege, or casting lots. There is something about a random event like picking a card or reading tea leaves that according to the practitioners allows a portal to open so the spiritual realm, and through the principle of sympathy, can direct the signs to reveal the future. This is the mantic function, so particular types of divination are named by their medium. Among the earliest types of divination was reading the cracks in bones tossed into the fire (scapulomancy); the spots of the liver of a sacrificed animal (hepatomancy), and later, the turn of a card (cartomancy). Jung's preface to Wilhelm's translation of the classic Chinese divinatory text, the *I Ching* laid out how randomness events occurring together at the same time, though they may not reflect causal influence, may nonetheless be seen as a reflection, a mirror or speculum of the forces that are intertwined at that moment and related to the client's inquiry.

Obviously, any augury or divination involves matching symbol systems. The client and their concerns create one set of symbol systems. The device or medium of divination comprise another set of possible symbol systems. The divination is the art of creating the match between one and the other symbol systems, and linking it to some specific action the client may take to further their purposes. In this conceptualization, a Rorschach test is no different in principle from a Tarot card reading. Both are means of having the client project their own symbol systems and personal needs, hopes and fears into a set of stimuli, producing a response that is partly random and partly personal. The resultant discussion of the projection of the client becomes the divination of the path ahead. There are some similarities in purpose and process between psychological assessment and divination (Larson 2016).

Once a way out of the present problem is found by consultation with the spirit world or with spiritual forces, then the shaman must lay out a longer and more thorough path by which the suffering of the client may be relieved. In classical shamanism this involves a multi-model ritual series of actions. There is often a preparatory phase in which the person engages in sacrifices, fasts, and other forms of denial of ordinary gratifications as a way of showing their sincerity to the spiritual forces controlling the outcome. The use of drumming, props, incense, costumes, movement, and so on engages all the senses. The healing in traditional shamanic practice is not usually done on a solitary person. It certainly involves the family of the suffering person. It may even involve the whole village or community. Healing is a social event. The universe is composed not only of spiritual beings and forces, but our fellow humans. Illness is sometimes seen as the result of violation of taboo (spiritual prohibitions) or failure to meet ritual obligations, including breaches of social relationships. One person's actions reverberate through the network. To heal a disturbed social network, the involvement of all nodes in the network may be needed. So the shaman must be a social creature and involve all the various spiritual forces and persons but the mundane persons who constitute the social proximal environment of the sufferer. As above so below; as with one, so with all.

As noted above, the rituals of the shaman are multi-modal processes. That is, they involved not just talk but chant, song, dance, drumming, masks and other props. In our modern frame of reference, they were full scale artistic productions. All these elements which are now part of our modern expressive therapies (e.g. art, music, dance/movement, drama therapies). The origins of these modern uses of the arts in healing come from shamanic practice. Likewise, the full artistry of a Catholic, Orthodox or Anglican High Mass begins with the simpler forms that were used by early shamans. The value of all the tools of pageantry is their ability to heighten the emotional engagement and involvement of the sufferer, family and community in the healing process. The underlying principle behind those tools is to muster the social support of those who care about the sufferer to aid in the healing activity. The shaman binds up the social wounds that may have caused the ruptures in community which were expressed as illness; the shaman makes right that which has been disjointed at both a spiritual, an individual psychological and a social level.

In summary, animism is a spiritual philosophy which uses personification to create or discover a world spirits, a spiritual world. The direct experience of contact with the divine is the basis of authority, and it localizes in the person. Magic is a technology involving manipulation of spiritual forces to produce results in the mundane world. The shaman is the quintessential individual practitioner of psychological healing, working through the limenal capacity to travel between the spiritual and mundane world through trance as source of healing power.

## Priesthoods, temples and civilizations

The shaman was transformed into the priest or priestess with the arrival of village life, and especially, when villages became cities. The earliest city-states arose in the fertile river valleys and mark Taylor's (1977) hydraulic civilizations mentioned earlier. From the development of urban centers, spirituality became focused around large temple complexes built in honor of the local deity. In Egypt, the cities of Memphis and Thebes were important. In Mesopotamia, modern Iraq, the cities of Uruk, Lagash, Ur were among the earliest cities in the Sumerian culture, the first to have writing and pass on to us a written legacy. In the Indus valley the cities now known as Mohenjo-Daro and Harrapa flourished. Urban life and temples seem to emerge together along with palaces as signs of kingship. The fabric of social life became more differentiated and diverse. Social stratification and social classes developed.

The key difference between the role of the shaman and that of the priest or priestess was the transmission of authority. In less populated and less differentiated societies, the power to heal was something that was personal to the healer. The ability of the shaman to contact the divine forces and to harness them for curing the sick was based on their personal capacity to use trance for contact with the spirit world and to engender hope and belief in healing. With the advent of formal religion organized around temples and other building complexes, authority became transferred through ordination. The social conferral of authority to conduct healing in the context of the temple marked a taming of the free lance practitioner.

Temples were not only edifices, but they were communities. Because of their central role in the ideological basis of community, they were also places of literacy. In most societies the first scribes were priests as well. Soon temples took in grain or other agricultural surpluses from the lands controlled by the city-state. They became distribution points of that surplus when lean times came. Thus the temples acquired an economic role as well as a spiritual role. They acquired a political role in consort with the king who was the chief warrior and ruled by power of arms. Spirituality, or at least organized religion, and politics have been linked from the earliest of times. The temple as well as the palace of the ruler were the major cultural centers of early civilizations. Writing as well as many of the decorative and performing arts developed as much in the temples as in the palaces of these early city-states. The term cult is used in a neutral anthropological sense in this book. It refers simply to the social structure of a religion; the network of priests, the physical structures of temples, the mythic structures told to the people, the relationship of the people to their deities. The modern usage of cult often implies coercion, control or manipulation, but that sense is not used here.

The era of formal organized religions ushers in a sort of layering of spiritual views. Most of the beliefs of animism pass unchanged into the polytheistic religions of classical antiquity. But cults to one deity are replaced later as another rises in popularity. Religions encounter each other through war, trade or migration and as they do the possibility of religious syncretism arises, that is, blending aspects of the foreign into the native. The technology of magic changes little. As writing takes hold, formal theologies emerge and attempts to provide more sophisticated accounts, not only in terms of extended narrative stories, but with early attempts to provide a rational system of beliefs.

Across most cultures, the divine manifested in both male and female form. The divine family, like the human family, contained male and female deities. Religious professionals mirrored this spiritual and sexual dichotomy. The servants of the divine were both male and female, taking on the role of priest or priestess. Mostly, but not always, the temple servants of a female deity were female and likewise for male deities. Apulius, a Roman novelist writes about the male priests of the goddess Cybele, the galli as they were called. But there also existed in many animistic societies some representation of the both/and genders, the divine androgyne, Hermes-Aphrodite (Hermaphrodite). The one beyond the duality of gender. Other societies were decidedly patriarchal and emphasized the primacy of the male deity, even if they acknowledged a multiplicity of male and female deities. Johan Jacob Bachofen (1815-1887) was an early proponent of the idea that the early societies were matriarchal, and were later supplanted by cultures dominated by aggressive male warrior gods (1967/1861). Gimbutis (2007/1974) has brought together her own extensive research as well as others in an updated understanding of the gender issue as well as practices around the deities of ancient Europe.

The Indo-European peoples came into India, supplanting the earlier Harrapan civilization with the modern set of male dominated pantheon of deities familiar to Hindus. In Greece, the more female focused Minoan civilization was replaced by the Olympic pantheon of deities as the Dorians came down the Greek peninsula from their steppe homeland. So a good deal of evidence confirms the arrival of peoples with pantheons of deities led by a male figure, but since the earlier civilizations they supplanted were generally prior to writing, our inferences about their social organization is always be more tentative. The extent to which those societies were matriarchal or a simply more gender balanced sharing of spiritual power or civic power cannot be firmly established.

Despite the dominance of the pantheons of the classical era by male deities, there was still representation of the divine in both male and female forms. It was later that the monotheistic religions of Judaism, Christianity and Islam came to dominate the area around the Mediterranean. These religions had a single deity, quite clearly represented as a male. Thus a problem for Western culture is the recovery of the divine feminine. Dan Brown's novel (2003) *The DaVinci Code* tackles that issue, highlighting the current debate about the role of women in spiritual leadership, or even as embodiment of the divine. The Tantric tradition in India, to be discussed later, emphasized the complementary nature of male and female energies in the divine dance of phenomena, as well as its sexual expression. Many cultures centered around the Mediterranean also kept a balance between male and female deities. They are paired as divine mothers and fathers, or sometimes mothers and sons (e.g Zeus and Hera, Astarte and Adonis, Attis and Cybelle, and so on).

Pepper's other unacceptable world view was mysticism. He is less clear about the root metaphor for this, but he seems to focus on the nature of the mystical experience, especially in revealed religions. These are the Abrahamic monotheisms, Judaism, Christianity, and Islam. One of the features of modern monotheisms is their emphasis on the divine revelation to prophets of commandments for the guidance of human affairs. In mysticism he seems to have in mind the development of more sophisticated forms of spirituality that came as civilizations developed from the earlier level of nomadic bands of hunter-gatherers. But mysticism is a very broad category of spiritual practices and philosophies that cuts across all forms and eras of religion (Underhill, 1961/1911).

The story of the evolution of civilizations and their healing theories and practices will now unfold over the primal layer of animism as the earliest spiritual theory, magic as the earliest healing technology and the shaman and priest or priestess as the person charged with the role of healing. Just as layers of spiritual philosophy overlay one another, so too our modern understanding of psychological healing as a scientific enterprise overlays the bedrock of spiritual healing. Whether we personally have a spiritual world view or not, many of our clients do. They may have a mixture of earlier and later versions of spirituality. Our task is to honor the roots we share in common while providing those elements of the past which are transferrable and work as well today and in eras long gone.

## Summary

In this chapter spiritual healing was described as the tool of the first archetype of psychological healing, the shaman, priest, or priestess. Based in a view of the world that includes some form or aspect of a spiritual side of being, the practitioner mobilizes the hope of the patient and the support of the social environment to bring about the healing. From the earliest days of human culture through the rise of hydraulic civilizations, the practitioner changed from a more individualistic shaman to socially organized priesthoods in temples. While there are significant cultural differences between societies in various parts of the world throughout pre-history and history, the common thread was the clear link to an ultimate source of meaning and purpose called spirit. This mode of healing continues into the present, though what we will see next is secular modes of healing arising in several cultures in ancient times and setting the stages for secular frameworks which constitute the modern practice of healing by psychological means.

# 3

# Foundations of Western Thought and Practice

## The West as a cultural phenomenon

WHAT IS THE WEST? In broad and conventional terms, it is the set of cultures that evolved in Western Europe. From there it spread by exploration and colonization to the rest of the world. It is also a set of ideas and technologies and perspectives which originated locally in Europe and expanded globally. Western ideas now penetrate all societies. The basis of the presence is both material and ideological. The goods and ideas pioneered by the West have become foundational in the global society. The current era is now dealing with the consequences of that hegemony and seeking to arrive at a more globally balanced civilization. Contact between European and other cultures were significantly changed by the West's technological advance in navigation and firearms from the 15th through 19th centuries. Over the course of the era economic control and political colonization followed. In its wake came the spread of languages, religion, laws and customs. But where and how did Western Europe come to be a dominant force?

The ideological foundation of Western culture comes from two sources. One is the monotheistic religion of Judaism, especially as it was retained as a cultural influence later through its offshoot, Christianity. This results in the moral and spiritual foundations of European countries and their colonial descendants to one degree or another. The second foundation was the philosophy, technology and arts of Greece, and later its Roman successor. This gives us the artistic, philosophical, and technical-scientific, basis of European cultures. While in the early period, the Judaic influence remained localized to the Near East, Greek influence, particularly after Alexander of Macedon became wide spread both into Asia and eastward and southward into the other parts of the Mediterranean world and north Africa.

The West, of course, cannot be known completely except by its dialectical relationship to the East; the Occident and the Orient. These were the quintessential polarities that defined Western thought as it positioned itself in contrast to its neighbors. Indeed, at the present geo-political moment, the Islamic world is seen as engaged in a major struggle against the West. But the beginnings of that story comes in a subsequent chapter not this. This story deals with the foundations upon which the West was built. On a spirituality derived foundation drawn from the Judaeo-Christian religions, history added the gift of Greek philosophy and medical skill. The West was born.

## Judaic roots: Monotheism and ethics

One main stream in the Western transmission is the particular religious and ethical tradition that begins among the Semitic peoples and features a belief in one God who reveals his plan for humans through prophets. The monotheistic religions are Judaism, Christianity and Islam, in that order of development. As noted previously, all three of these monotheistic religions are termed Abrahamic as they all claim a spiritual lineage through the patriarch Abraham, who is revered in all of these faith traditions.

The story of God's revelation to humans is contained in the Hebrew Bible, or Tanach, which Christians call the Old Testament of their Bible. Tanach is an acronym for Torah (the Law), Nevi'im (the Prophets) and Chutuvim (the Writings). Indeed, the Jews are also known as the people of the Book, for their reverence for the Bible. Muslims accept the broad narrative of the Bible, but have a different telling of the story in their sacred book, the Q'uran. The Biblical story begins with creation, the first people, Adam and Eve, and their short stay in the Garden of Eden. Human suffering enters the world with their disobedience to the commandment to not eat the fruit of the tree of knowledge of good and evil. Many generations pass, wickedness prevails, and God causes a universal flood wiping out all but Noah and his kin. From that point the narrative continues to the story of Abraham, also known as Abram or Ibrahim. He lived in the ancient Mesopotamian city of Ur of the Chaldees, in modern Iraq, where US troops have recently been at war. Many early cultures allowed human sacrifice under certain conditions. As Abraham was about to sacrifice his son, it was revealed that this practice should not continue and a Covenant or pact between God and Abraham and his descendants ensued. The agreement holds that if he and his descendants would acknowledge only him and obey his commandments as revealed through the prophets, they would multiply and inherit the land of Canaan, the promised land. The religions of their neighbors, various pantheons of polytheism deities, both male and female, was rejected in favor of one God, monotheism.

The notion of a prophet who communicates directly with God is a hallmark of the Western religious tradition. Moses was among the most significant prophets for all three monotheistic religions. He was the main figure in the mythic axis point in the Judaic tradition; the Exodus of the Jews from slavery in Egypt into freedom. Most of the world's religions have a charismatic founding figure, a great teacher, guru, prophet or savior; each tradition casts that leader in the role of supreme teacher or exemplar quite differently. Although other prophets preceded Moses and followed after him, he is among the most important ones for Judaism and is generally seen as that sort of founding teacher.

The Biblical story continues with an account of bondage in Egypt and their subsequent liberation. This still resonates through the Western world as a framework for the calls to social justice. The civil rights movement of the 1950s, 60s and onward were driven by the rhetoric of the promised land, the call to righteousness, the call of a people in bondage charging them with strength for their coming journey into freedom. Of all of the founding narratives of great religions, this one alone has the liberation from slavery as its major theme. It took the rest of the world several millennia to adopt this ethical stance. Slavery was accepted as a fact of life throughout the rest of the ancient world and even in modern societies until the nineteenth century. Even today, the story of the Exodus sounds a clarion call for an ethic of autonomous self-determination by peoples and individuals.

The major gift of the Judaic tradition is a focus on law and ethics. Laws did not originate in the Judaic tradition; after all, Hammurabi, the Babylonian king promulgated a code of laws some centuries before the Mosaic story. But the claim common to the Western monotheisms is that the laws are revealed by God through the prophets. After the Exodus from Egypt, the Israelites wandered in the desert and from Mt. Sinai, God revealed to Moses what Jews call the Torah, or law. This set of laws is collectively known as the Ten Commandments. It forms the backbone of the Jewish religion.

The Israelites entered Canaan and took over the land after battles with the existing people. They ultimately formed a united Kingdom, which saw its zenith. Many scholars question the dating and origin of belief in an afterlife and a divine judgment with reward for the faithful and punishment for the evildoer, but those ideas have become fundamental to understanding the modern versions of Judaism, Christianity and Islam. The Hebrew narrative of lawgiving and the imperative to live in accordance with those laws has been a historically successful version of the idea of divine justice.

The kingdom of Israel eventually emerged after battles with the existing Canaanite inhabitants. Its high point occurred under Kings Solomon and David. The religion of the Jews centered around sacrificial rites in the Temple in Jerusalem conducted by a priestly class, the Cohenim. Dietary and other codes sought to distinguish the Jews from their polytheistic neighbors. Many subsequent prophets railed against the Israelites for abandoning one or another commandment.

Israel is located between the two powerful civilizations of Egypt and those arising in Mesopotamia, the lands between the Euphrates and Tigris rivers in modern Iraq. The united kingdom of Israel split into two kingdoms, Israel in the north and Judah in the south. The northern kingdom, Israel, was conquered by the Assyrians and deported to some unknown destination, sparking the legend of the lost tribes of Israel. The southern kingdom soon fell to the Neo-Babylonian empire, and were deported to Babylon.

It was here that Judaism was radically transformed by its exposure to another stream in the Western tradition, but from a non-Semitic people, the Persians. The Babylonian captivity ended when Cyrus, the king of the Achaemenid Persian dynasty conquered Babylon. As a result, the Jews came in contact with the Persians who followed a dualistic religion founded by their prophet Zoroaster, or Zarathustra (ca 650 - 550). This religion holds the cosmos is in a struggle between the god of light, Ahura Mazda, and the god of darkness, Ahriman, or Angra Mainu. Many scholars accept that the notion of a heaven and hell, a final judgment and salvation of the soul were first taught in Persia, and brought back to Israel after release from Babylon. Whatever tendencies toward dichotomous thinking in terms of good versus evil, sacred versus profane got heightened through contact with a thorough going dualistic philosophy. Israel was a province, or satrapy, of the Persian empire until it was conquered by Alexander the Great and his Macedonian and Greek armies.

Alexander passed through and installed pagan temples and the worship of Greek gods. Israel became a province of the Seleucid kingdom which succeeded Alexander. The Jews revolted under the leadership of the Maccabees, which the holiday of Hanukkah recounts. Finally as Rome rose to prominence, it incorporated Israel as a province. The Jews revolted in the first century CE, but were brutally crushed and dispersed throughout the Roman empire, beginning the modern diaspora of the Jews. It was not until the nineteenth century that modern Zionism emerged as a movement for return and settlement in their ancestral lands. Out of these experiences the modern form of Rabbinic Judaism emerged, along with Christianity in the centuries beginning the common era (CE). Islam was the third Abrahamic spiritual tradition which began with the revelation of God to Mohammed (570-632 CE) in the seventh century of the modern era.

## Madness and healing in ancient Israel

We touched on theories of illness both physical and mental as part of the narrative about spiritual healing. The most severe forms of mental illness have historically been termed madness, though we prefer the more modern term psychosis. Extreme forms of suffering reverberate throughout literature and practice in Western cultures, epitomizing the dark fear of psychological disintegration. We sometimes harbor that primal fear that we, too, could become mad and loose our sanity.

In the Bible, there is the poignant narrative concerning King Saul and David (I Samuel, 16:1-et seq.). Saul probably had some type of bipolar disorder, because he fluctuated between periods of deep depression and periods of clarity and reason. It is conceptualized by the writer of I Samuel as evil spirits seizing him and changing his behavior. During one of these troubled periods, Saul asks his advisors to bring a young shepherd, David, who was known to be skilled with the harp. He comes forth and is able to soothe Saul's madness by his skillfully playing of beautiful music; the first recorded instance of healing through music. There was also later a falling out between David and Saul, partly related to the overly close relationship between David and Jonathan. David's love for Jonathan, " . . . deeper than the love of women . . .." (2 Samuel 1:26) has, since at least the Renaissance, served as a Biblical support for same sex relationships.

One cause of madness is punishment for disobeying God's commands (Deuteronomy 28:23). This teaching has led many to feel their illness is punishment from some transgression and is still serves to support the stigmatization of mental illness. This tendency to blame the victim for their illness is not confined to the West, but this scriptural passage gives rise to such blame. We will see in the next chapter how the doctrine of reincarnation is used to likewise attribute moral and spiritual significance to illness and misfortune, though within a very different framework.

## The Greek world

The second major founding influence on Western culture is ancient Greece, and it successor, Rome. The cultural sphere of ancient Greece ringed the Eastern Mediterranean. Greece comes at the southern tip of the Balkan peninsula; it narrows near Athens, at the isthmus of Corinth which connects the Peloponese, or lower part of Greece to the mainland, or peninsula Greece. There are a large number of islands in the Aegean Sea between Greece and Asia Minor. The largest island is Crete, home of the Minoan civilization, the dominant force in the second millennium BCE and the one with the oldest of the Greek cultures. On the mainland, the Achaeans had great cities at Mycenae, Argos and other parts of peninsular Greece. On the mainland of Anatolia there were a number of Greek cities; forming the region was known as Ionia. Close to the narrow passage to the Black Sea was Troy, whose struggles against the Achaean Greeks was the basis of the founding mythic cycle of Greece, as told by Homer in the *Iliad* and the *Odyssey*. On the western side of the Balkans, Greeks also settled in Sicily and along the boot of Italy, a land known as Magna Graecia.

The period of events recounted by Homer took place in the Bronze age. Then across the Mediterranean around 1100-800 BCE there was a general collapse of civilizations, known as a Dark age. The classical period when the great works of philosophy, drama, poetry, science, politics and history is known as the Hellenic period (ca 800 bce – 330 BCE). The cultural dominance of Athens (lead *polis* or city in the region known as Attica) in the Greek world was both intellectual, artistic, economic, and sometimes political. It was part of a vital community of independent city-states which grew up in the mountainous mainland. The geographic isolation of cities in a mountainous region was similar to the isolation of islands in the Aegean Sea, so both maritime and peninsular Greece was shaped by these relatively independent governments and societies. This geographically enforced local autonomy made for an often fractious group of states. Athens and Sparta vied for regional hegemony, and the Peloponnesian wars in the fifth century BCE saw both Athens and Sparta and their allies locked in conflict. Actual governments were not always democracies, as we now understand that political system. Athens and other states did lead the way with experimentation with republics and legislative bodies as collective forms of leadership, but autocracies, kingdoms and military dictatorships were also present. As noted before, however, slavery was accepted as a fact of life and so what shoots of democracy sprang up did so on the soil of an economy based in part on slaves.

Greek concerns focused eastward with the rise of the Achaemenid dynasty of Persia. Most of Ionia on the mainland of Asia came under Persian control in the fifth century BCE. The Persians invaded Greece successfully early several times in the fifth century, but were ultimately defeated and pushed out of Europe following the land battle of Marathon, the sea battle of Salamis (480 BCE) and the a final land battle at Plataea (479 BCE). The Greeks had only been able to unite and think about the conquest of Persia by Philip I of Macedon. Under his son Alexander the Great (330 BCE) the Greeks took back Ionia, defeated one after another Persian force sent to meet them. Alexander conquered the area known as the Levant, now Syria and Lebanon, took Palestine and Egypt, then Babylon, and finally taking the Persian capitol of Persepolis. He then pushed eastward taking the lands known as Bactria and Sogdiana, now parts of central Asia and Afghanistan. Even further eastward he pushed moving down the Indus river. But his troops were tired and wanted to return home to enjoy the rest of their lives in peace. Reluctantly he agreed and returned to Babylon where he died in 323 BCE. The period of Alexander and his empire mark the beginning of the Hellenistic era in Greek history. Greece came under Roman rule in 146 BCE, but the broad cultural themes which emerged in Hellenistic times persisted throughout much of the rest of Roman antiquity, ending with the onset of what is called the European dark ages (ca. fifth century through ninth century CE).

## The archetype of the physician

We now undertake the first discussion of the archetype of the physician as a component of the professional role for psychologists. In current usage, healing is seen as primarily a medical activity. Yet as we have seen already, healing's older roots are spiritual. Spiritual healing uses tools which are primarily verbal, the magical incantation or spell. The history of Greek medicine also shows a prominent role for spiritual approaches. The Asklepian tradition was focused in temples, but over time the influence of the Hippocratic tradition made the physician a more secular occupation.

The domain of medicine in the modern world of diverse health care professionals emphasizes the physical means of healing. As noted above, prescribing medications, surgery and other invasive procedures, and the use of hands for manipulation of the body (manual medicine), have been the defining techniques of medicine. The physician's sole right to prescribe medication has begun to erode, as dentists, optometrists, many nurse practitioners and now even several U.S. states have granted limited prescription privileges to psychologists. Many disciplines such as massage therapy and body work have taken up the therapeutic touch of the body independent of medicine. Many diagnostic and uncomplicated treatment procedures in primary care facilities are now done by non-physicians such as nurse practitioners, physician assistants and emergency medical technicians (EMT).

The earliest evidence of the physician comes from ancient Egypt. Imhotep (fl. 2650-2600 BCE) is credited as a polymath, someone with multiple talents. He was a physician, an architect and the vizier of the pharaoh Djoser. He later became deified as a healing god, and his temple sites frequently were sites of pilgrimage for healing. Supplicants would often make offerings in the form of ceramic models of the body part which was ailing them. We find this practice of ceramic offering migrating to Greece their healing temples, and continuing into Roman times.

Asklepios, was the Greek god of medicine. Let me briefly recap the myth, though previously mentioned. It says Asklepios was a half-son of Apollo by the mortal Koronis, a Thracian princess. He was raised by Chiron, the most civilized of the generally animalistic centaurs. Chiron received the healing arts directly from Apollo and transmitted them to Asklepios, thus establishing the divine stream of transmission of the healing arts in Greek culture. The cult of Asklepios as a healing fraternity which embodied the older shamanic traditions, yet it facilitated the emergence of a *techne*, or skill, of quite secular nature. In its later years in Roman civilization, it returned to its more spiritual roots (Kerényi, 1959).

According to legend, Asklepios was married to Epione, and had several children. His daughter Panacea is symbolic of the universal medicine, the one cure-all. Hygieia is the goddess of health and prevention; hence the origin of our term hygiene for healthy practices. His sons Machaon and Podaleirios divided the world of medicine into surgery and internal medicine, and his son Telesphoros was associated with the process of recovery. That basic divide of specializations between internal medicine and surgery persists in modern medicine.

The physicians who became priests of Asklepios were collectively known as the sons of Asklepios. It was sometimes a tradition passed on in families, but open to new recruits. The symbol of Asklepios is a staff with a snake entwined around it. The Asklepian staff has a single snake and is drawn as a naturalistic tree branch. It is often confused with the staff of Hermes, the caduceus, which has two snakes twined around a more polished rod, with wings on the top. Hermes was both the messenger or herald of the gods, hence winged heels; he was also the patron of commerce, thieves, and the symbol of both mystery and gnosis.

The practitioners were centered around a temple. This meant that sufferers had to be well enough to travel to where one was located. Indeed, part of the healing process were the sacrifices that had to be made in order to complete this journey or pilgrimage. The main temples of Asklepios were in Epidauros and the island of Kos. In Roman times there was a great temple of Asklepios in Rome itself, on an island in the Tiber River. In the temples, there was usually a central room where the image of the deity was kept and where offerings and other ceremonies sought to connect with the divine. The temples were the centers of learning and of healing.

The major feature of Asklepian healing was dream incubation. That is, supplicants were led into the temple at night for sleep with the understanding that Asklepios would come to them in a dream which was then interpreted by the priests the next morning. The temples had a particularly interesting architectural characteristic which related to this healing practices. The *tholos*, was often built on a spiral pattern, going from outer to an inner chamber by a circular or spiral path. In some sites it would even go below ground. The reason for this was the association of healing power with *chthonic* forces (those powers emanating from the underworld, the world of the dead). The snake which twines around Asklepios' staff, of course, lives on or under the ground and so represents those forces beneath us. In Jungian terms, these chthonic forces are our unconscious processes. The central chamber was large enough to accommodate a crowd. One psychologist, Dr. Edward Tick (2001), has revived the process as a healing workshop, working particularly with Vietnam veterans with post-traumatic stress disorder (PTSD).

Hippocrates is usually thought to be the founder of the Greek medical tradition, though his contributions were predated by the Asklepian tradition. While the Asklepian tradition bridges the spiritual and the secular phases of medical specialization, Hippocrates reflects the roots of the current medical tradition based in secular technical skill. Hippocrates' school came over a period of time when the possibility of a secular world view emerges within the culture. Modern scholarship doubts that the body of writings now attributed to Hippocrates came from one author. The body of writings under his name are known as the Hippocratic Corpus. It is probable that even in ancient times his name became a touchstone of credibility, and anyone who wanted their writings to have credibility had to put forth the manuscript as written by Hippocrates. The approach of the Hippocratic approach to health is quite secular, and his aphorisms start with a very eloquent statement of the human condition. The challenge for the healer is "first, do no harm" (Hippocrates, ca 5th cent BCE/2003).

He and his followers emphasized the physical aspects of causation of illness, though not quite in a modern way. He wrote on such important aspects of our physical environment as the purity of air and water. But the Hippocratic Corpus is most closely associated with humoral theory. This theory holds that the key physical elements of the body are four vital fluids; blood, phlegm, yellow bile (Gk. *choler*) and black bile (Gk. *melancholer*). Of those four, three actually exist, the fourth, black bile does not. Health came from a balance (Gk. *eucrasia*) of these fluids, and illness signaled an imbalance (Gk. *dyscrasia*). To this theory was added the philosophy of physics taught by Empedocles (fl. 450 BCE). He held that the four fundamental elements of the world were earth, air, fire and water. To the four elements and the four humors were added the four qualities, hot, cold, dry and moist. So blood was warm and wet, phelgm was cold and wet, choler was hot and dry and melancholer was cold and dry.

This led to the system of personality as temperaments, or biological dispositions. People could be described as sanguine, phlegmatic, choleric or melanchoic. The sanguine personality was sunny and optimistic, cheerful and outgoing. The phlegmatic temperament was slow to react, calm, and methodical. The choleric temperament was easily provoked to anger, highly excitable and often difficult to be with. The melancholic was prone to periods of depression and brooding and pessimistic. The Hippocratic theory of medicine, including the temperaments, had its best systematic statement in the works of the Roman physician Galen (131-201 CE), who passed on the best of Greco-Roman medicine of his era. His works were cited by both European and Arab physicians well into the modern era.

The physician would diagnose which of these was in excess or deficiency and pre-scribe accordingly. As these ideas continued to evolve in the ancient world, practices began to focus more and more on blood, since it was easy to drain off. Bloodletting became standard practice in medicine. The striped pole we now associate with barbers symbol-izes the bloody towels of the surgeon-barbers of Medieval and Renaissance times. In the years when most were illiterate that colorful sign showed people where they could go for treatment. The theory of bad blood evolved, and even as late as the 1790s, American physician and founder of American psychiatry, Benjamin Rush used leeches to drain of impure blood to restore the health of his patients. His leech jar is on display at the Smith-sonian Institution. In this sense, the four-humor theory is probably the longest lasting theory of medicine, in existence in one form or another from the mid first millennium BCE up to the advent of modern biomedical theory based on microbiology.

## Healing by word

Healing by use of words or discourse begins with the archetype of the shaman/ priest(ess), continues through the archetype of the physician, but reaches a new un-derstanding with the archetype of the teacher. The Spanish physician and scholar, Pedro Lain Entralgo (1970) wrote a major treatise on the history of psychiatry titled, *Therapy of the word in classical antiquity*. In this, he sets out the thesis that healing by word shifted over the course of time and the development of new understandings of the power of language. There are three modes that explain the data according to Entralgo, the use of language as magic spell or charm, the *epóde*, the use as prayer, or *euche*, and the use of speech as cheerful or persuasive speech, *terpnos logos*. Clearly, forms of psychological healing based in a spiritual world view relied on the potency of spell or prayer. The cheerful or persuasive speech is the basis of the modern practice of counseling and psychotherapy and have a more secular or humanistic basis of efficacy.

The two spiritual modes of verbal healing can be distinguished as follows. In the case of incantation, spell, or charm, the language of command is used. Even references to magic, sorcery and so on in the Bible acknowledges the importance of the name of the spirit. By knowing the name, one controlled the spirit. Hence, most classical, me-dieval and renaissance books of magic are compendiums of names of various spirits which could be conjured to do the bidding of the magician, at least if he or she were themselves powerful enough to control the spirit rather than being controlled and going mad. The European fairy tale of Rumpelstiltskin is a remnant of the belief in the power of control by uttering a person's name.

In Greek magic, according to Entralgo, the approach was less of command and one of cajoling or persuading. Spirits had to be seduced, won over, charmed into co-operating. The speaker used language to entice through promises, flattery, threats, etc. This was a transitional phase which was important because it begins to herald the recognition of the social basis of even spiritual activity. In either case, the spell or incantation has largely disappeared from conventional spiritual practices, though it survives in folk religions and modern pagan revival practices

In prayer, or *euche*, this persuasive use has been further refined and expressed, now with humbleness in the form of supplication. While spirits might be controlled by command or persuasion, deities must be approached with humility and entreaty. This type of healing is still preserved in the various genres of spiritual healing techniques; hymns, liturgies, offertories, litanies and laments directed toward God.

This leaves the last type, the fully persuasive use of language, which is *terpnos logos* in Greek. This leads naturally into a discussion of the first practitioners of this art and skill, to the rhetors of ancient Greece. In terms of healing, this represents the emergence of a fully secular and technological use of language for healing purposes, without recourse to spiritual means.

## Early Greek philosophy

The tradition of healing by teaching begins during Greek and Roman times, though a secular tradition of healing by words alone in a secular manner did not survive antiquity. Philosophy is not often thought of as healing, but having true knowledge of the world has always been held to be an important asset in managing human life and decision making. Philosophy in classical antiquity was actually seen as therapeutic and as a guide to living the good life, or eudaemonia, as it was called which we will discuss in detail below.

The history of Western philosophy takes Socrates as its main founder. But he wasn't the first to engage in speculation about the nature of reality. Many of those earlier philosophers, known as the Pre-Socratics hailed from Ionia, that part of the classical Greek world now part of Turkey facing the Aegean Sea. Though they spoke and wrote on many topics, the pre-Socratics are best known for seeking to establish what the fundamental elements of the world are. They sought the *phusis* or the basic nature of the physical world. Our term physics and metaphysics come from that linguistic root. Metaphysics is the branch of philosophy dealing with basic categories of existence and substance that characterize the universe. Various pre-Socratics had various answers as to what was the ultimate constituent element or *arche* of the world. Thales of Miletus (ca 624-547 BCE) argued for water. This seems natural, since the Greeks were a maritime people, living in the Aegean Sea, ringing the eastern Mediterranean. Water also is found in all living beings, and even the ancients were aware of its necessity for life. Aniximenes (died 528 BCE) thought air was primary. Again, there are common sense reasons why this might be plausible. Air, too, is necessary, it is pervasive. It also is generally not seen, it is generally a clear medium (pollution being the exception). Anaximander (610-546 BCE) asserted that the Infinite was the primary substance. With this development we get a fully abstract concept emerging as a primary element of the world. The other two were observable physical quantities. Empedocles (fl. 450 BCE) gave us what came to become a consensus version the rest of Greco-Roman proto-science; the four elements of earth, air, fire, and water. These are retained as elements in the symbology of the Western esoteric tradition, also known as the occult tradition, and now known as the modern Pagan revival.

Another major dimension of philosophical discussion raised by the Pre-Socratics focused on the primary dialectical distinction between change and stability. Heraclitus (late sixth century BCE) took the position that the most real thing was the process of change itself. He gave us the famous aphorism that one cannot step into the same river twice, pointing to the on-going flow of water as metaphor for perpetual change. Parmenides, (b. 510 BCE), on the other hand, argued that those things which don't change are most real. Things that change and are evanescent lack the sort of solid reliable quality of those things which endure and persist and can be counted on. Thus, permanence and stability were his prime values for judging reality. Of course, we now recognize that a complete account of reality cannot be given without recourse to explanations of both change and stability. Yet their very opposition makes it so difficult to reconcile the sort of theoretical and conceptual structures that work best with one and those that explain the other.

Pythagoras (ca 569-475 BCE) is another pre-Socratic who deserves mention. We know him largely for his geometric theorem concerning the relationship between the lengths of the sides of a right-angled triangle. It is he who first articulates the idea that the universe itself could be modeled with numbers. Thus, all attempts to quantify the world owe him an acknowledgment for starting the dialog. One way the world as number can be heard is in the relationship of a length of vibrating string to the pitch of the tone. Intervals we term octaves in Western music which double the pitch are formed by fretting the string by half its length. The attribution of the discovery of this principle to Pythagoras is considered solid. He had a particular spiritual side, however, that is less well known, and was the founder of a religious and philosophical community in Italy. The Pythagorean society held itself apart from the rest of society, and might be termed the first secret society. Indeed, he is the first to use the pentacle, or five-pointed star, to articulate a sacred five-fold division. This symbol has persisted through the Western esoteric tradition and is current among modern Pagans. He is claimed, with some justification to be a major figure in this spiritual stream of thought.

For psychologists, the most important beginning point comes not from the philosophers but from the Pythia, the oracle of Apollo at Delphi. According to Plutarch, inscribed at the entrance to the temple of Apollo where the oracle provided divination is "know thyself" (Gk. *gnothi seauton*), an admonishment of great value. The whole of psychotherapy could be summed in that aphorism.

## The archetype of the teacher

For professional psychology the archetype of the teacher, the third of the four archetypes of healing by psychological means, is embodied more by the rhetors as the first professional teachers than the philosophers. They formed the discipline of rhetoric, the skill of persuasion and effective public speaking. The philosophical movement arising from their teachings is known as Sophism. Thus, to the extent that professional psychologists engage in teaching, either in academia, or in psycho-educational activities in clinical and counseling contexts, they are participating in the archetypal professional role begun here.

There is a very specific reason why the teacher is seen as a progenitor of psychotherapy. Entralgo pointed out the importance of the rhetors in general, but the particular Sophist, Antiphon, is the first clear example of healing by the word (Entralgo, 1970). In *Lives of the Ten Orators*, Pseudo-Plutarch recounts that Antiphon hung out a shingle in front of his house proclaiming his ability to cure mental troubles through words. What a shame that Antiphon did not think the cure of melancholy by persuasive speech to be worth his while. Had he done so he might have sparked a stream of transmission of therapeutic speech. The lack of a continuity from his singular bold claim had to wait many centuries for rebirth and fruition.

Rhetoric is now largely viewed as applying to public speech of a legal or political nature, and to the writing and literature. The leading Greek philosopher who wrote on rhetoric is Aristotle, who we will cover in more detail shortly. He pointed out that rhetoric has three domains, the legislative, or deliberative domain where public policy is shaped, the judicial domain where guilt or innocence is determined, and the ceremonial, or epideictic domain, where praise or blame is given to someone in a public speech. But clinical rhetoric is private conversation, not public oratory, so rhetoricians are loathe to see the parallels between the clinical and the other domains because of that.

The ability to speak effectively to both sides of an issue has been suspect to philosophers who seek a single truth. But the well crafted argument on any side of an issue raises the possibility of multiple truths. The phrase, mere rhetoric, displays an unease with regard to the nature of this skill and a tendency to dismiss it as a legitimate source of knowledge. History is written by the victors, so the writings of philosophers, the victors in this contest, tended to be dismissive of rhetoric. Rhetorical ability went against the goal of establishing true knowledge (episteme) from opinion (doxa). How could one establish firm knowledge if opposing positions could be skillfully laid out? This leads to a broader suspicion of relativism. Truth is absolute not relative.

Insincerity is another criticism of rhetoric. How can one tell the true belief of another if they can skillfully defend opposite points of view? To this day, part of the humor aimed against lawyers is fueled by this mistrust of someone who are trained to convincingly take opposite views. Another reason why rhetoric is not viewed positively comes from the field of literature, where rhetoric has often been viewed as synonymous with ornamented or flowery speech, as in florid oratory. So, overall, rhetoric has come out with a lot of bad press and unpleasant associations.

Yet the fact remains that this specialty, no matter how its social value is viewed, is the skill of using the most effective means of persuasion. All professionals who work by verbal means and seek to persuade others should have some explicit training in rhetoric. One of the major claims of this book is that the base or root skill in professional psychology is rhetoric (Larson, 2006). As noted in the first section of the book, modern professional psychologist has as its only tool the ability to be verbally persuasive. Despite forays into prescriptive power or some laying on of hands, our means as psychologists are characteristically verbal and own their skill component and competency in the tradition of rhetoric.

Sophism as a philosophical movement shares some of the characteristics of modern humanism. Of the Sophists, the most widely quoted is Protagoras (490-420 BCE). His most famous saying is *homo mensura*, and states an interesting point. "Of all things, the measure is man, of the things that are, that [or 'how'] they are, and of things that are not, that [or 'how'] they are not." (Quoted from Fuller & McMurrin, 1960, p. 104, see also Bartlett, 1968 p. 87A). His statement clearly places the frame of reference on the human experience. Protagoras suggests that the standard of comparison for reality resides inherently in the human realm not in some disembodied transcendental realm. The Sophist movement represents the beginning of a humanistic perspective on things which would be elaborated on later in the Renaissance.

Another point of disagreement between Plato and the rhetors especially was the bases of the warrant that justifies belief as knowledge and not opinion. Plato holds out reason as the sole arbiter. In rhetoric there are three bases of persuasion, reason, emotion, and character (Gk. *logos*, *pathos*, and *ethos*). Plato's point of view prevailed in philosophy, but the practice of counseling and psychotherapy inherently need to appeal to the client's feelings and personal sense of self (what we mean by character in this context). The purpose of clinical activity is practical, to bring about healing, so all means of persuasion should be in the tool kit, not just reason.

## Socrates, Plato and dialectic

Virtually all we know of the thought of Socrates (470-399 BCE) comes from dialogues written by his student Plato (428-348 BCE). His mode of teaching was dialog, or more technically, dialectic. Public discourse, discussion or debate was the means by which the free citizens of Athens or other city-states effected self-government. His philosophical style was not only dialogical, that is proceeding by way of discussion, but it also sought to find truth through the interchange of ideas, winnowing out the positions that when reasoned out, ended in contradiction or absurdity (Gk. *elenchus*, the process of correct reasoning. Since Plato recorded the dialogues it's often difficult to separate out Plato's views from those his teacher Socrates. They are, indeed, considered works of Plato and are cited as such. Nonetheless, one thing Socrates taught that is now recognized is that the life of the philosopher should exemplify the principles held; one should walk the talk (Hadot, 2002; Sellers, 2009). This will influence several Hellenistic schools of philosophy in a way relevant to modern psychologists.

Now we will take up the ideas of Plato. In Pepper's terminology, Plato is the first clear exponent of formism, the belief that structure is the most significant path to knowledge. For Plato, the abstract world of Forms was the ultimate reality, not the concrete objects that embodied these forms. He continued asking the basic metaphysical question as the pre-Socratics (what is the basic essence of things), but his answer was the transcendental forms of abstraction is most real and substantial. Every thing has an essence, a substance, a nature (Gk. phusis) that constitutes them as they are. He sides with Parmenides and asserts that only the most enduring things should be counted as real. The world of forms which gives substance and quality to existent thing is primary and ultimate reality because the realm of ideas does not change.

In his analogy of the cave, concrete reality is like a shadow cast upon the wall of a cave by a fire from behind the person. The object whose shadow is cast upon the wall is unobservable but knowable by reason. We mistake, however, the shadow for ultimate reality. We can only know the world of forms imperfectly and by reason. Thus the road to knowledge is reason, the sole sure path.

Plato also elaborated his ideas on society in a set of books titled the *Republic*. Here he also spoke of his social philosophy. Diversity among peoples is natural and their relative place in the social order should be governed by their innate capacities. You could not turn a sow's ear into a silk purse, though education also helps somewhat, people were caste into basically three molds, the philosophers, the soldiers and the workers. The capacity to reason was primary in the philosophers, the protective function paramount among the warriors, and productivity was the role of the workers. Everybody had their place and society was best when each fulfilled their natural function and did not seek to take on other functions. But there is a definite streak of social conservatism in Plato. Philosophers should be the ones who rule, because they are governed most by the life of reason and their judgment would clearly be superior. He went to the island of Syracuse when invited by the king to come teach. But since the king just wanted to hear Plato rather than let him become king, he came back to Athens somewhat disillusioned. His book *The Laws* is even more conservative. He believes that incorrect thought should be corrected, ultimately by segregating the people with bad ideas in a *sophronisterion*, basically a thought reform camp. This is the darker and autocratic side of Plato.

His contribution to philosophy came mostly from his basic idealist metaphysics. His view of the primacy of the abstract and their ultimate reality as objects in the world is still the first major synthesis of a tradition that continues today in one way or another. The philosophical position that an abstract order exists which is more fundamental than the world of phenomena is termed idealism and recurs throughout the history of thought. Many spiritual philosophies and religious movements have found in Plato's views compatible with theirs. Indeed, St. Augustine was an early Christian champion of Platonism as a philosophical tradition.

To know reality we must know its structure, how it is formed, literally and abstractly. Concepts and their relationships to each other have a reality that is more reliable than mere material form. Defining a structure is part of the formist epistemology. Those scientific theories which seek to identify a structure of the mind, the person, the group or community are inheritors of this emphasis on abstract conceptual ideas. It is one part the basis of modern science, even though most of the rest of Plato's ideas are not endorsed by the scientific world view.

## Aristotle

Following after Plato was Aristotle. He is sometimes called the first professor as he wrote on such a wide range of topics. He formally taught in the Lyceum in Athens. He also received an important private commission. Phillip of Macedon asked Aristotle to come to Pela, the Macedonian capital and teach his son Alexander all the best of Greek learning. Though Phillip did not live to see his vision come to fruition in a campaign against Persia, the old enemy of Greece, he did unify most of the warring Greek city-states after defeating their best army at Chaeronea (338 BCE), including the Theban Sacred Band. It fell to his son to throw his spear onto Asian soil, and then not to rest until he had become the master of much of the world, both Greek and non-Greek. Alexander took with him some of the ideas of Aristotle.

Aristotle's epistemology included a prominent role for observation, in contrast with Plato who distrusted the evidence from the senses. Since this cognitive ability is so crucial to the nature of the scientific enterprise, he is often viewed as the first scientist. His prolific writing encompassed many fields. He wrote not only on logic, but rhetoric as well; according each their role in human thinking and learning. Likewise he wrote extensively on the variety of living beings and the arts, too. His notion of catharsis is important for psychology, particularly for healing (Tick, 2001). His theory of the importance and value of watching drama was based on its purgative effects on negative emotions. Audiences would have these emotions stirred up by the play and the acting and then be able to discharge them in a cleansing release by the play's end. Good drama not only moves us, but allows us to vent indirectly all the psychological poisons we accumulate in social living. By venting it safely by watching others enact the feelings, we come away better people. Though the drainage hypothesis with regard to aggressive impulses seems to have not stood the test of time, particularly in modern studies of the effects of watching violent models and observational learning, the basic notion of the importance of catharsis, of letting go of the feelings that have been pent up, still holds true in a more modified form. Corrective experience as the psychodynamic theorists hold, begins with some catharsis or discharge of feeling, but it can't end there. There has to be a digestion if you will, a working through of the material before it is finally and harmlessly assimilated.

Aristotle is also known for his four-fold theory of causation. For him, all things are caused by four causal factors, the formal, the material, the efficient, and the final cause. The best analogy, and one often used in teaching, is that of the sculptor. The idea in the mind of the artist that he or she seeks to produce is the formal cause. It is the blueprint, if you will, the structure of the thing. The material cause, is literally the matter out of which it is made, in this case a block of marble. The efficient cause is the action of the artisan with hammer and chisel (or paint and brush, or flute and fingers) that give the idea specific shape. The final cause is the purpose for which the object was created. In the case of art, it is the enjoyment of beauty. This was a teleological cause, a sort of goal toward which the other causes were organized. As science became associated more completely with materialism and, especially with Comte's positivism (ca late nineteenth and early twentieth centuries), science came to reject all teleological explanations. Only material and efficient causes were allowed in scientific theory. The formal cause was a speculative metaphysical structure that smacked of Platonic forms, the final cause was some invisible hand pulling events forward to a goal. Neither of these were appealing to the hard nosed scientists who set the bedrock of our modern views.

## Alexander and the Hellenistic world

Alexander of Macedon, known as Alexander the Great (356-323 BCE) is even today viewed as among the greatest conquerors of history. He was a model for Caesar, Napoleon, and others in the West who yearned to establish a far-reaching empire. After setting foot on Asian soil in modern Turkey, he defeated one army after another sent by Darius, the Persian emperor. He defeated them in Anatolia, modern Turkey, dipped down into Syrian, Palestine, and took Egypt. He then turned back eastward and went on to Mesopotamia, seizing Babylon. Pushing westward, he sacked Persepolis, the Persian capital, and chased Darius and his successor into the heart of central Asia, defeating them all. He thought he might have conquered all, but learning of India, after digressing to conquer Sogdiana, he pushed on through Afghanistan, down the Khyber pass into the Indus valley. There his war-weary troops had had enough and at the point of revolt, he turned back toward Greece, planning campaigns in the eastern Mediterranean, but died in Babylon at the age of 33. Though his life was short and glorious, his empire was quickly divided among his generals, so the unity of his political achievement was soon lost.

The legacy of Alexander was his vision of a cosmopolitan world which was neither exclusively Greek nor Persian, but an admixture. To implement this, he took a Persian wife and had his leading officers also take Persian wives. He integrated the remaining Persian military units into his army. He had a broader vision, in part inspired by Aristotle, of a new world where old limitations were replaced by new possibilities. He did not live to see this manifested, but what was accomplished was an opening up in both his European and Asian empire to the influence of each other's ideas.

After Alexander's death his generals divided the empire and several dynasties (including the Ptolemies of Egypt, of whom the last was Cleopatra) continued to bring Greek influences eastward and Asian influences westward. Indeed, this period, known as the Hellenistic era, is characterized by a wide commerce in ideas across cultures. An example of this is the short dialog in the Buddhist scriptures between a monk and king Milinda (the Greco-Bactrian king Menander). Here a Buddhist monk and pagan Greek discuss the nature of human suffering and how it may be alleviated. Western and Eastern religions came into contact with each other.

The capital of culture in this era became Alexandria, Egypt, a city founded and eponymously named by Alexander. Here the great Library was the world's largest depository of learning. It has become legendary in its size and comprehensiveness. It went up in flames over a period of time when Marc Antony, Cleopatra, and Octavian (later Caesar Augustus) contended for the future direction of Roman rule. Its loss in incalculable. It would be like the loss of the Bibliotech Nationale in Paris, the British Museum in London, the Vatican Library in Rome and the Library of Congress in Washington.

The ancient world after Alexander was much more familiar with different religious traditions of East and West. This led to a period of religious syncretism, when the various deities of Babylon were identified with appropriate counterparts among the Greek pantheon. For example, the war god Marduk of Babylon was seen as the equivalent of Ares in Greek mythology, and later, Mars in Roman mythology. By the time Rome had supplanted Greece as both empire and cultural center, one of the most important shrines in the city was to the Egyptian goddess Isis.

It was also a troubled age, when the very uncertainties that come with being an insignificant speck of grain of sand in the large beach that was an empire, with dynastic wars which brought uncertain futures, all cast doubts about the previous stable beliefs and values of the ancient world. The response was two sets of solutions to an ancient crisis of meaning. The one, which was more popular with the educated elites, were the philosophical schools of the Stoics and Epicureans. The other, more for the common person, were the mystery religions of the ancient world. We now turn to those developments.

## Philosophical guidance for living

Life in Hellenistic and Roman times was full of uncertainties and insecurities much like our own (Grant, 1982). The role of fate, personified as the Greek Tyche, or Fortuna in Latin, became more prominent as people saw their world as very much outside their span of control. The uncontrollable aspect of the world was personified as three goddesses, the Fates or Moirae in Greek, the Parcae in Roman and the Norns in Norse mythology. This heightened awareness of the precariousness of life resulted in a search for a sense of stability in either one of two philosophical movements that focused on self direction and freedom from disturbance, or in the promise of salvation through participation in one of the great mystery religions of late antiquity. Two main responses were found, the philosophical schools of Stoicism and Epicureanism on the one hand and the mystery religions on the other.

Among the literate classes, the philosophical school of Epicureans and the Stoics provided a practical philosophy aimed at achieving the good life, well being, or *eudaemonia*. The means by which eudaemonia was achieved came from such concepts as *autarchia* (self-regulation), *ataraxia* (calm and equanimity), and *ascesis* (disciplined exercises, or regular practice). Living well was the result of philosophical work. These philosophies were more than systems of abstract understanding, their ethics, in particular were aimed at providing guidance for one's life. The classical scholar Nussbaum (1994) provides a detailed exposition of a medical philosophy by which the Stoics and Epicureans sought to address human suffering. With these sorts of philosophies as well as a variety of our solutions for normal human miseries, we see the beginnings of streams of ideas and the practiced of disciplined reflection and thought to improved well-being. We shortly will see how much earlier mental disciplines emerged in the Eastern context, but now we see it in its European garb.

The Epicureans, a school begun by Epicurus (341-271 BCE) articulated the concept of the atom, or most basic and indestructible unit of matter. With regard to life orientation, he advocated a retreat to the garden, the private pleasures of one's immediate home. Eudaemonia, living the good life, was the goal. But Epicurus did not advocate wild living, hedonism; instead, restraint was taught as a major human virtue. Pleasure comes from the gratification of desires, which are part of our nature, our *phusis*, but balance was important. Though pleasure is good, it is not good to be driven by our desires and to live life in excess. As one should seek out freedom from want, one should also live simply so as to experience contentment and imperturbability. The Stoics shared some of the same social philosophy as the Epicureans. The Roman emperor Marcus Aurelius's was an example of Stoic philosophy and his work, *Meditations* remains a popular example of this school. At the other end of social strata, Epictetus (ca 55-135 CE), a Stoic philosopher was reported to be a slave. Slaves were found with all degrees of oppression or comfort, those who were literate were highly prized and acted as major officers in large households and the courts of power.

Philosophy currently is taken up with analytic concerns about clarity in our use of language to describe various basic issues and to the average student seems quite removed from practical concerns, But not only Nussbaum but Sellers (2004) and Hadot (2002) that in Hellenistic times philosophy was seen as a practical guide to living one's life. Larson (2015) has argued that concepts drawn from Hellenistic philosophy, especially eudaemonia, autarchia, ataraxia, and ascesis, form a basis for integrating the various approaches to stress management.

Albert Ellis explicitly credits them with being a major influence on the development of his cognitive approach to psychotherapy. One of the central elements of Stoicism relevant to that period as well as to our own is the idea that there are limits to our agentic capacities, our ability to change our life circumstances. What we can change, and is under our more direct control, are our beliefs. We can change our minds. We can cultivate various beliefs and mind states. This is the basis of their therapeutic impact. They are disciplines of practice. History's first self-help revolution.

The type of mental state that was part of this combination of autarchia, ataraxia and eudaemonia, is a certain detachment. A detachment that comes from reflection and contemplation. This is the one component that was present in Greco-Roman philosophy at its cultural zenith in these trends that modern philosophy generally has lacked. Beginning with Scholastic philosophy in the middle ages, and continuing through most trends continuing through contemporary philosophy has been a divorce between thought and practice.

## Mystery religions and salvation

The other pole in the search for consolation in troubled times were the mystery religions of the ancient world. (Godwin, 1981; Meyer, 1987). Several cultures within the ancient world evolved a variety of esoteric initiatic cults promising a special wisdom (Gk. *gnosis*) often related to the mystery of life, death and rebirth. The mystery religions were different from the exoteric, or public and outward forms of religion, they were esoteric, semi-secret initiatic systems of spirituality. In Greek cultural context, the exoteric rituals were found in the temples of the Olympic pantheon of deities, now preserved in the Acropolis of Athens, and other major archaeological sites throughout the Mediterranean world. The major mystery schools of Greece included the Eleusian, Dionysiac and Orphic mysteries.

In Egypt, Isis became a central focus of a mystery religion. This goddess was imported into Rome when Cleopatra, Julius Caesar, and later Marc Antony struggled for how Rome and Egypt would come together. In the eastern Mediterranean the cult of the goddess Cybelle and her male mate, Attis were important from Asia Minor (modern Turkey) through the Levant (Syria, Lebanon, Palestine, Israel), even into Mesopotamia. By late Roman times, a mystery religion of Persian origin, Manichaeism laid roots in Europe and persisted into the Middle Ages as a heretical sect.

The Eleusian mysteries (Kerényi, 1976a) focused on the myth of Demeter and Persephone. The cyclical nature of life, the seasons, and rhythms of life are celebrated. Persephone, the daughter of Demeter catches the eye of Hades, lord of the underworld, and is kidnaped and taken down to his underworld kingdom from her ever bounteous and summer like Earthen home. All grows dark and living things die. Demeter asks Zeus to intercede and a compromise is worked out. Persephone spends 6 months on Earth with her mother, bringing spring and summer and their harvest of life-sustaining plants and animals, then she goes to her husband Hades and fall and winter bring dark, cold, and hardship. This myth of the origin of our seasons has as its core theme life, death and rebirth. Indeed, all the mystery religions have as a core doctrine a story, a mythic cycle of stories even, which are ways of understanding life and its end in death, with a larger redemptive vision of a life reborn. Salvation of the soul or person is a concept that pre-dated Christianity, indeed Christianity competed with the mystery religions for adherents in their early centuries before they got state sanction with Constantine in 350 CE

So as the individual seeks this redemptive knowledge, this initiation into an inner wisdom they are prepared by initiates in the outer teachings. The rite of initiation was an annual calendrical event. Applicants crossed the threshold, took their vow of silence and had the inner teachings revealed to them in the form of dramatic re-enactments of key mythic events. The whole process could last several days. In addition to the Eleusinian mysteries, another major focus was the cult of Dionysos (Kerényi, 1976b). This was a wild Thracian deities, the deity of wine (known as Bacchus in Rome). Though it would be a typical modern, even American, mistake to think of the meaning of Dionysos as solely hedonistic pleasure. Again, the altered state was a tool, as was the sexuality. Sacral or sacred sex is a concept now lost in the Western tradition, though it is kept alive in the Eastern Tantric traditions in Hinduism and Buddhism. Orpheus was also a focus of a mystery cult. The Orphic mysteries were built around the descent and return from the underworld, life reborn. So by the end of the pagan classical Greco-Roman world there were a variety of brands, traditions, or streams of thought and practice that offered some means of individual salvation through participation in the rites and teachings of these groups.

By the end of the Roman era, Christianity had suppressed and supplanted the various pagan cults, both exoteric and esoteric and set the future path of European civilization. Theodosius closed the pagan temples between 388 and 391 CE, and Justinian closed the schools of philosophy in 529 CE. The old ways were not entirely stamped out, particularly through the cultural chaos of the late Roman empire and Dark Ages when various tribal spiritualities intermingled Christian communities, who eventually converted the barbarians. This long process defined the beginning of the Medieval period and didn't end until Nordic peoples of Scandinavia converted in the eleventh centuries.

# 4

# Eastern World Views and Practices

RUDYARD KIPLING HAS A frequently quoted poem that is rarely quoted beyond the first line which emphasizes the difference between East and West and says they will never meet. Yet the two lines following that famous dicta emphasize the possibility of cross-cultural understanding. Kipling should know; he was a son of British colonial civil servants, a child of Great Britain's rule in India, known as the Raj. Even though he returned to England for school, he came back to India to ply his trade as a reporter. It is here that he saw and lived a sort of inter-cultural life, remaining British to the core, yet drinking deeply from the well of India. He has fallen out of favor because he was such a strident booster for British imperialism. In the last half of the twentieth century he came to be seen as gaudy and dated an ornament as any Victorian bric-a-brac. Kipling is an embarrassment in the current climate of multi-cultural sensitivity, something best kept out of sight. This is ironic given the depth to which he experienced and portrayed the East to the West.

A closer examination shows Kipling had a great reverence for India, her culture and peoples. His treatment of the Lama in *Kim* (1901 /1989) is an early and sympathetic view of Buddhism. But, by that time European scholars had already translated a large corpus of texts and knowledge of both Hinduism and Buddhism was available in Europe and America. Emerson and Thoreau in America and Schopenhauer in Europe were among the first Western thinkers to have available translations of Hindu scriptures such as the Baghavad Gita. Buddhism had begun to put down its American roots as well, with the first Parliament of World Religions coinciding with the Columbian Exposition of 1893 (Fields, 1986).

Inter-cultural experience comes in many flavors. The tourist or traveler is the most short term. Longer term stays are generally termed immigration. Short term immigrants are called sojourners in the literature on cross-cultural psychology. Longer term immigrants begin to take on identities and legal status, possibly even citizenship, in their new country. Some long-term movements of people are voluntary, some are quasi-voluntary (e.g. social circumstances make it advantageous to live abroad for an extended period, for personal or familial advantage). Others are non-voluntary, people who are fleeing the home country as refugees from some catastrophe and trauma. Natural disasters, such as floods, hurricanes, earthquakes, drought and famine are of one sort and the humanly inflicted ones, such as wars, political, religious or ethnic or other types of persecution are another an even more bitter forces pushing population migration. However it occurs, whether on small or large scale, temporary transit or permanent residence, people come into contact with each other and have to adapt to new cultural environments.

The new global environment of the twenty-first century is bringing East and West together even closer. Another divide is between the North and the South; meaning developed countries and developing ones. The world has been shrinking and now in America, particularly in urban America, our neighbor is likely to be an immigrant or recent descendant of one. The melange of cultures figures into their life experience and the professional psychologist must understand the client's cultural context. The archetypal dichotomy of east and west is deeply rooted in our thought even as our culture becomes more intermixed through the arrival of new immigrants.

We now touch upon ideas and practices such as meditation, yoga and the martial arts which are becoming ubiquitous in America. They come from Asia the large continental lump we associate with ancient wisdom, far deeper than our own perhaps. Mindfulness in particular has become extremely popular in psychology in recent decades, yet we know little of its origins. Yoga and martial arts studios abound, yet they are usually taught with little background as to their original cultural values.

It's time we explore those roots more deeply. Broadly speaking there are two large cultural areas that are part of the classical Orient, or East. One is the Indian subcontinent, the other is China. Other countries in east Asia are influenced by either or both of these larger domains, so we will turn our attention to each of them.

## Indian cultural sphere

The Indian sub-continent has been home to a variety of cultures and ethnicities. There is no better example of how geography effects culture than the Himalayas. They are a virtually impenetrable barrier to the north of India, making contact with China, the other large center of civilization difficult. The mountainous forests of Burma (Myanmar) also separate India from the Chinese sphere of influence to the east, cultural contact between the two large areas of early civilization in Asia, China and India, came late due to both distance and physical barriers. To the west lie mountainous Afghanistan and the deserts of Baluchistan which limits entry or invasion from the west, at least until Alexander.

There are several religions or spiritual world views which have their beginning in the subcontinent. The common root of all of them continues as Hinduism. Both

Buddhism and the Jain religion diverged from that core and developed as separate traditions in approximately the seventh through fourth centuries BCE. The Jains have always had only a small following and will not be considered here. The Sikh religion emerged much later, 1469 CE, in a part of northwest India, the Punjab, where Islam is strong to this day. It blends some aspects of each. All of these religious in one form or another cultivate meditative practices. There is a native Christian tradition in India as well, dating to the first century CE, by legend started by the Apostle Thomas. India, particularly northern India was strongly influence by Islam, which will be considered in a subsequent chapter.

The earliest layer of civilization in the Indian subcontinent is centered around the Indus river. Not a great deal is known about this pre-Vedic Indian civilization. The number of inscriptions is small enough that the language has yet to be deciphered. The graphic remains, however, show that this Indus culture had elements of the yogic tradition that was to become prominent in the succeeding Hindu and Buddhist spiritual traditions (Worthington, 1982). One key piece of evidence for the antiquity of yogic practice are two cylinder seals mentioned in Campbell's *Oriental Mythology* (1962). They both show a central figure seated in a yogic posture (badda konassana) flanked by animals or humans in postures of reverence. These seals show a long stream of continuity of the cultivation of mind-body techniques.

The Indo-Europeans, also known as Aryans, from the Sanskrit which means noble (victors always claim high culture and purpose) came into the area some time in the second millennium BCE supplanting the earlier peoples. Today, there are a variety of peoples in southern India who speak a variety of languages unrelated to their northern Indo-European neighbors. These peoples are known as Dravidians and appear to be remnants of the earlier pre-Vedic cultures, even though most have adopted some form of Hinduism for millennia. The classic civilizations of India has a cultural coherence arising from a pre-Vedic stock, while accepting the graft of the Indo-European ethnic, linguistic and spiritual stream. Recent evidence is emerging challenging the Aryan invasion theory, suggesting a greater degree of continuity of cultures. The matter is not resolved, and the Aryan invasion theory still holds many supporters.

The Vedas are earliest texts of Indian spirituality and arrive with the Indo-Europeans. Like all religions, the written text comes after a long oral tradition passed on from generation to generation. They are a series of stories in poetry and song (chant), as well as ritual and formal philosophy. The *Rig Veda* is the oldest best known element of the *Vedas*, as the whole collection is known. The main deity of this period was Indra. The *Upanishads* are the largely philosophical texts which date later than the Vedas. Their composition clearly reflects serious intellectual accomplishment by a body of scholars. They are a set of treatises commenting on the Vedas and aimed at setting out a coherent world view and theology. These works stand in a similar relationship to each other in Indian religion that the *Iliad* and *Odyssey* do for classical Greek religion. Included in the body of early writings are the national mythic epic stories, the

*Mahabaratha* and the *Ramayana*. The classical modern triumvirate of Hindu deities (Brahma, Shiva and Vishnu) emerges in the first millennium CE in the *Puranas*.

Hinduism can be seen as polytheistic, having many deities. Like other pantheons, the deities are both male and female, gods and goddesses. They are portrayed iconically as persons, often with multiple arms holding various implements and with variously colored skin. But as Vedanta became a major school of Hinduism, flowering also in the first millennium CE, a monistic tone began to emerge. That is, behind the multiplicity of deities was really one divine ground of being, or Ultimate Reality, identified as Brahman, to distinguish it from the deity Brahma. This synthesis was set forth by Adi Shankara (eighth century CE). The cosmic ground of being (*Brahman*) has embedded in each person a seed of that divine presence, known as the *atman*. The goal of spiritual development is the direct and sustained realization of unity of the individual with the transcendent.

## Yoga: Technology of mind-body

Yoga has become one of the most popular means of physical culture, rivaling sports in the number of adherents. Increasingly, the healthful benefits of regular practice of meditation and mind-body exercises in awareness are being documented. There is a continuous stream of transmission of this technology in Asia that was never developed in the Western cultural sphere. The West chose rationality over intuitive and contemplative activity. Some type of meditation is practiced in both Western and Eastern religions. Among the Western monotheist traditions, Judaism has Kabala, the Christians have a number of mystics, for example the desert fathers and mothers and ascetics, and in Islam the Sufi orders all use various means of entering ecstatic altered spiritual states for encountering the divine. But organized religion in the Western sphere generally viewed the mystical experience with scepticism. Even in many Asian cultures, only in the modern era have there been systematic efforts to teach meditation to lay practitioners. With the development of hypnosis, the use of altered states of awareness for psychological healing in the West was revived.

As yoga and meditation have become used in the West, they have become partially or completely divorced from their spiritual roots. For example, one of the most popular sources and traditions of meditation is Transcendental Meditation (TM), founded by the Maharishi Mahesh Yogi. Though TM is presented as a technology available without adherence to any particular creed or religion, it still is fundamentally grounded in Hindu roots. When the Beatles studied under him an immediate wave of interest rippled through America and Europe. Harvard cardiologist Herbert Benson, an early researcher of TM, found that his patients with heart disease benefit from TM as a relaxation technique. He also found, though, that many of his patients were reluctant to take the training and practice the technique because its visible trappings of Hindu religion was too far from their comfort zone (a brief ceremony with offering to Maharishi's guru, and initiation with Sanskrit mantras). He then took what he viewed as the active ingredients and packaged them in a completely secular version in his 1976 book, *The relaxation response*. This is but the first of several versions of meditation that have been presented totally free of religious or spiritual content and marketed as a mind-body technology. Whether one chooses to adopt the spiritual philosophy of these Indian technologies or approach their practice solely as healthful habits, it is helpful to know how they arose and how the spiritual values shaped the technologies.

The roots of yoga as a philosophy are encapsulated in the very origin of the word which refers to yoking or union. In this case the union is between mind and body or between the human and the divine, take your pick of world views. But the union is the result of practice, of finding the experiential link between mind and body through the postures and breath control exercises as well as the meditative calm. The goal of spiritual development in Hindu philosophy is to use the unity of mind and body to bring about the union of the individual to the divine. The goal across multiple life times is to grow that seed so that it blooms in union with the divine, losing all boundaries and merging with the One.

A big difference between East and West, philosophically, is in the conception of time and personal existence. In the West, time is linear. There may be seasonal cycles but the arrow of time moves forward and humans have but one life in which to complete their spiritual development. The Western religious views hold out the hope of an after life, however defined, but all agree that there is but one life span for each individual. In the Hindu and Buddhist versions of reality, an individual is on an endless cycle of births, deaths, and rebirths, known as the wheel of samsara. Reincarnation is the term generally used to describe the belief in an individual core persisting across multiple lifetimes. This doctrine very clearly makes it difficult for Western students to completely feel comfortable with Eastern thought and practices. However, Western thought has its own version of reincarnation. Though the origins are unclear the doctrine of metempsychosis, or transmigration of souls was taught by Plato and found in a number of other Greek schools of thought.

This doctrine of many lives, or reincarnation, can only be understood along with the concepts of dharma and karma, found in both Hinduism and Buddhism. We have referred to the divine life force and principle as Brahman. But it is also close to the meaning of the term dharma, which is usually translated as law, or ordering principle of the universe. Dharma is simply how things are in a metaphysical sense. Religious leaders are teachers and practitioners of dharma. We will see later that in the Chinese culture sphere, the term *tao* has a similar meaning. In monotheistic religions the divine is personified as god, but the concept of dharma or tao can be seen as the divine but impersonal ground of being.

Karma is principle of universal justice. Good begets good; bad begets bad, you reap what you sow. There is no escape. But unlike Western views of just one lifetime to practice good and reap the ultimate benefit, there are many. Indeed the quality of one's present life is the karmic sum of one's previous lives, both for good and ill. Whatever misfortune's befall one, are pay backs for past failures to get it right. This has culturally led to a certain passivity with respect to change of the external circumstances, people accepted misery as their lot and hoped for a better incarnation next time. Westerners have found it uncomfortable to think that a child's illness was pay back, since they are so young and couldn't possibly have sinned so badly to deserve such suffering. But, again, in the context of many life times it seems less unjust. Dharma, karma, and reincarnation constitute a core conceptual system in the Indian spiritualities.

One of the links between mind and body which is the breath. It is used in all Asian techniques, both those originating in India and those from the Chinese cultural sphere is the practice. Uses of the breath have been both in terms of naturalistic observation as a tool in concentrating awareness, and the use of systematic breathing exercises to accomplish certain mental-physical changes. Life force was long associated with the breath. The Greek *pneuma*, a major concept for the Stoics, is similar to the meaning of the Sanskrit *prana* or the Chinese *chi*, and *ki* in Japanese. In the West systematic use of the breath was limited even in the contemplative monastic communities of Christendom. But they were part of practice and teaching much more widely in Asia.

The breath is a nice link between body and mind because, though ordinarily our breath is automatic, without deliberate focus or awareness; it can also be voluntarily controlled. Breath control, or pranayama in yoga, is the key to being mindful of the body as one moves into, holds, and moves out of the various poses or asanas. If we just close our eyes and simply pay attention our natural shifting of awareness we will notice our breathing as well as other mental and physical activities, sensations, thoughts, and so on. This is basic mindfulness, which we'll come back to later. This natural flow of consciousness from an active and outwardly adaptive focus to an inward and self-referential focus is the basis of meditation. The breath is a natural focus of attention, it is physical, but it's control is mental, deliberate, and thus is a prime candidate for learning the yielding control skill (Shapiro & Astin, 1998) of letting go or more active control skill of deliberate breath modification.

The yogic philosophy embodied in the Yoga Sutras of Patanjali (ca. 200 BCE) developed these foundational beliefs and practices along with other ethical teachings into our modern yoga. Yoga was introduced to the United States at the World Parliament of Religions in 1893. Swami Vivekananda, from the Vedanta tradition came on behalf of Hinduism and immediately attracted a group of interested student. Now, the number of different styles, schools, teachers, and sub-types of yoga has proliferated.

An important complex of concepts within yoga comes from a pan-Indian school known as Tantrism. There are both Hindu and Buddhist forms of tantra, which developed in the first millennium of this era. It is the basis of Tibetan Buddhism in particular. Kundalini is the life force viewed as stored at a physico-spiritual center at the base of the spine. This life force is likened to a coiled snake, which when awakened unfolds ascending up the spine and passing through about seven chakras (some systems vary slightly in number). One can take this in a literal sense as it historically and even now is used, or as a guiding metaphor for therapy. The various centers represent various aspects of personhood, sexual desire, emotions, power need, and so on. Judith (1996) has adapted this system to psychology as a means of self understanding and development. Working with blocks to growth is part of either a spiritual or secular training system of self-improvement and growth. The ascent of Kundalini energy has been documented to create psycho-spiritual crises, Kundalini emergencies, as a particular transpersonal mental health syndrome, a generally culturally specific syndrome.

Indian medicine has begun to make inroads in Western practices as well. The Ayurvedic school of medicine has become popular as an alternative or supplement to modern Western allopathic medicine, along with elements of traditional Chinese medicine. The basic principle is harmony among the constituent elements of the human body. These constituent elements in imbalance, either excess or deficiency, cause disease states. Balance is restored through dietary and lifestyle changes. Vegetarian diet, for example, is a major part of Hindu religious practice; hence the phrase sacred cow, comes from a literal custom of not killing animals for food; they cannot be sacrificed as a sign of reverence to all living beings. The yogic stream is broad enough for many specific interests.

## Buddhism and the psychology of release

Buddhism emerged in the sixth and fifth centuries BCE from Indian philosophy. This stream begins with the historical person of Siddhartha Gautama, a prince in the Shakya clan in a northern Indian kingdom. His story unfolds when he renounced his kingly prerogatives and sought the life of a mendicant or wandering ascetic monk, like the modern sadhus of India. He gave up all sources of pleasure and lived at the very margin of life in austerity as a voluntary spiritual discipline. He practiced meditation for several years before realizing that whatever benefit this path of extreme renunciation or asceticism could deliver in terms of spiritual benefits it didn't quite take him all the way. When encountering a young girl herding cows at a river who offered him some milk, he broke his ascetic vow and drank the milk thus began the path of the middle way, between ascetic denial and hedonistic abandon. To accomplish ultimate realization, he simply sat down and determined to not arise until he had reached the ultimate state of enlightenment. So he sat under a bo tree, according to legend, until he achieved nirvana, or ultimate realization. According to legend he saw all his past lives and clearly perceived the very basis of suffering and the path out of it. Buddhists now celebrate the day of his realization as Veshaka (Sanskrit) or Vesak (Sinhalese).

As the morning light came he had doubts that people would understand his message and paused a long time before deciding he could teach and someone might benefit. He first taught the disciples who abandoned him when he took the middle path. In the deer park in Sarnath, India, near modern Benares he gave his first teaching, known as the first turning of the wheel of Dharma. In this sermon he identified the Four Noble Truths. The first being that suffering is universal; the second that the cause of suffering is the grasping attachments we have, the third truth is that there is a way out of the cycle of birth, death, and rebirth, and the fourth truth is that the way out is the Noble eight-fold path. They felt his power and became his disciples once again and the Buddhist community, or sangha came into existence. He then taught for many years dying at age 80, leaving behind a community of ordained monks and nuns who lived celibate lives dedicated to spiritual development, and lay practitioners who continued living in households as families.

By his death, the teachings of Buddha (the enlightened One) had generated a significant religious community. It spread beyond northern India where it originated and took paths both north and south. Early differences in both doctrine and practice emerged, then known as Hinayana and Mahayana. Those terms translate as lesser and greater vehicle. Hinayana is now thought of as a pejorative term, so the current major divisions within Buddhism are termed Theravada and Mahayana. A third path later emerged in Tibet, that is doctrinally closer to Mahayana, but is different in many ways because of its incorporation of a later pan-Indian spiritual movement known as Tantrism. Tibetan Buddhism is often known now as the Vajrayana path, or diamond vehicle.

The Theravada path went southward to Sri Lanka, than across the Indian Ocean to Thailand, Burma, Laos and Cambodia. The Mahayana path went northward, first into modern Pakistan and Afghanistan, over the high roof of Asia into the Xinjiang province of modern China where a number of Buddhist kingdoms existed until the arrival of Islam. From there it went to China, Japan, Korea and Vietnam. This describes the spread of Buddhism geographically. We will omit detailed discussion of doctrinal and cultural differences and focus on that aspect of Buddhism that has found a home in the West, especially in psychology, the practice of meditation.

Some scholars of comparative religion don't view Buddhism as a religion at all, since it lacks many of the key features of the Western monotheisms. Theravada in particular has little interest in supernatural deities. The Buddha was a human just like us and achieved a great deal, but he is not Divine. Tibetan Buddhism, like Hinduism has a whole panoply of deities; transcendental Buddhas, Bodhisattvas, and other spiritual beings. Even in Theravada Buddhism a god realm exists, but to become enlightened and released from the cycle of rebirth, even the gods must descend and take a human life. Across all forms of Buddhism it is a philosophy of transformation. The end point is nirvana or enlightenment, when one becomes totally awake, alive and knowing by direct experience the ultimate nature of reality, nonduality. This makes Buddhism a source of ultimate value which is a keystone for all religions and world views. Thus is clearly fills a spiritual purpose regardless of the degree to which it does not embrace a theistic ontology.

Among the gifts that Buddhism brings to current Western psychological practice of meditation is the specific technique of open-focused meditation, or mindfulness.

Modern psychological scholarship on meditation divides the techniques into two broad families, closed-focus and open-focus. In the former, also known as concentration meditation, when the mind wanders it is always brought back to the object of concentration, whatever that may be. In open-focused meditation once the person gets to a degree of stability of mind, that clear present-centered non-judgmental awareness is directed to all of the contents of the mind stream not just the original object of focus (traditionally the physical sensations of the breath). So one notices hearing as one hears, sensing as an itch or pain occurs in consciousness. One brings clarity to all the passing objects that come into the mind stream as they pass in an endless succession of momentary observation, bare attention as it is called. Buddhism has emphasized the benefits that come from those inner experiences, especially if practiced regularly.

Concentration meditation is practiced within both Hindu and Buddhist traditions. An example of concentration meditation is the use of a mantra as object of focus as in Transcendental Meditation (TM). The practitioner repeats the mantra silently to oneself and brings the mind back to the mantra when one notices the mind wandering. Chanting a mantra aloud in a group is also a part of practice. Buddhism spent more time and effort deepening the practice of open-focused style of meditation.

The stream of transmission for contemporary mindfulness meditation came from Zen in the northern transmission and through Vipassana, or insight meditation in the southern tradition (Goldstein, 1976). While third wave behavioral approaches such as Minfulness-based Stress Management (MBSR), Dialectical Behavior Therapy (DBT), and Acceptance and Commitment Therapy (ACT) have been the most widely researched, mindfulness meditation is not limited to those approaches and has been found in the transpersonal stream of humanistic-existential psychology as well.

One of the characteristic doctrines of the Mahayana tradition, is the emphasis on the role of the Bodhisattva, one who seeks enlightenment not only for oneself, but for all sentient beings. Consequently, compassion for all living beings becomes a central ethical virtue and guides many practical decisions regarding social relationships, not just with people but animals as well. Thus, many Buddhist monastics and some lay practitioners are vegetarians. The ethics of the southern tradition, or Theravada, also focus on concern for others via the concept of loving-kindness, or *metta* in the Pali language, though the role of the Bodhisattva is less prominent. In the film *Seven years in Tibet*, the concern of monks about injuring worms while digging the foundations of a new building show this ethical stance. Compassion coupled with skillful means are the path to enlightenment.

The Tibetan stream of transmission is unique in its blend of influences from Buddhism found in both China and directly taught by Indian masters as well. By the time of the great Indian sages who gave Buddhism to Tibet made their trek, they were bringing largely Mahayana traditions, though the early Tibetans who came down to India to study and later return had the benefit of university training at Nalanda, the great Buddhist center of learning, whose destruction by Muslim invaders is to Buddhist scholarship like the loss of the library of Alexandria was to Western scholarship. At that school students got the benefit of extensive study of both the Hinayana in its earlier flowering, and the Mahayana, and thus brought back elements of both to their homeland. A great discourse in the Tibetan canon records the debate in Lhasa between emissaries from India and China, the latter invited by the Chinese wife of the Tibetan king.

The particular type of Buddhism adopted by Tibet is called Tantrism. This entered Indian spiritual sphere late first and early second millennium of the common era. Tantrism was a pan-Indian spiritual movement in the Medieval period and there are both Hindu and Buddhist forms of Tantrism (Snelgrove, 1987). It is a blend of animistic magical practice with highly developed philosophical traditions of that period. In Tantrism, there is a dynamism of personal spiritual development based in a spiritual energy, kundalini in the Hindu version. This energy is spiritual, psychological, sexual and physical. This energy, when harnessed rises through a series of chakras in a ladder like the spinal column. For the professional psychologist, the practice of Tibetan Tantric forms of Buddhism offers a clear schooling in the uses of imagery and imaginative internal reconstruction of elaborate scenarios and alternate realities. The path of Zen is a plain and simple as the rock and sand gardens of the Japanese zen-do, or temple. The path of Tibetan Buddhism is as elaborate and variegated in its deities and practices as the complex brocaded tankas, or religious paintings, which are among the highest expression of Tibetan visual arts. These are wall hangings painted on paper mounted on cloth. They are visually very rich and busy, often with paisley and other intricate background. Tankas are used as tools for teaching the particular qualities associated with the particular deity of saint portrayed. A knowledge of the iconography of Tibetan deities is necessary to fully appreciate them and how they are deeply embedded in a complex spiritual system. From high mountain monasteries in Tibet, Ladakh and with the Tibetan diaspora now in northern India to homes of Western students of Buddha dharma, they serve as centers as Tibetan Buddhist spirituality spreads in the West.

## China and east Asian spirituality

Chinese culture developed mostly in isolation from its Indian neighbors because of geography. The mountainous region of Tibet separates the two cultural spheres and has influences of both. Indeed, the mountains of Tibet are the headlands of the river that feed both cultures, but those same mountains form a barrier. It is the roof of the world, the site of the world's highest mountain, and a broad expanse of mountain ranges that separate regions of the continent. The great Yellow and Yangtze rivers formed the earliest locus of Chinese civilization. In the south, the Pearl River drains the area around Guangzhou (formerly Canton), near modern Hong Kong and also became an early center of culture. In the South China sea the Chinese made maritime contact with modern Vietnam, Vietnam into the Gulf of Thailand and down the Malay peninsula. From there contact could be made in Indonesia and from the Philippines westward, around the Malay peninsula into the Indian Ocean itself. Contacts between China and India occurred through a sea route came later, after the earlier overland route brought Buddhism to China. Toward the northeast and east, China influenced the cultures of Korea and Japan as well.

The spirituality of China is quite different in many ways from that of India. Chinese forms of spirituality have family life as the central organizing principle. It begins with reverence for the ancestors. Many Chinese homes have an alter where pictures of recently deceased members of the family are honored with offerings of incense and prayers. The great sages of history are to be likewise venerated. Chinese deities are not treated in the same manner as the more theistic Western religions. This softening of the boundaries between gods and men comes from the fact that we're all mythically family. For example, the emperor of Japan is viewed mythically as a descendant of the sun god. In China the emperor, likewise, was viewed as linked through ancestry to the divine ones, receiving the mandate of heaven to rule. Many traditional cultures claim a lineage from the divine through the ancestors down to the present generation.

The philosophical elaboration and refinement of the veneration of ancestors was one of the major accomplishments of Confucius, (551-478 BCE). The ordering of the state and the cosmos must coincide, so the principle of obedience to parents and to emperor, or filial piety, was the basis of harmonious social life. The Chinese civil service system was influenced by the concept of meritocracy and exam. These are ideas that arise out of Confucian thought and practice, and this set of ideas, values and practices was transferred to Japan, Korea and Vietnam. The very organization to run a complex civilization requires systematic education of people.

As noted earlier, a basic Chinese concept is the pervasive life force energy, known as chi, now qi is the preferred spelling. But this energy divides into the polarities of yin and yang. This idea of harmony, especially with nature, is found graphically in the yin-yang symbol, also known as the taijitu symbol. Two mobile forces of light and dark circle around, and in the midst of the maximum of one there is a small dot representing the seed of change to the other. Chinese thought is suffused with this notion of the duality between light, active, masculine and the dark, receptive and feminine aspects of all things. All things, living or not, are an intermixture of these two principles. This has significant implications for Chinese medicine.

Lao-Tzu (ca fourth century BCE.) represents another major tradition in Chinese philosophy. He is the principle author of Taoism, a nature mysticism. He remains one of the teachers most widely read and studied in the West. Lao Tzu is, by legend, supposed to have so sought the comfort of solitude with nature that he walked to the border of China, left a bundle of sayings, at the border post, collectively known as the *Tao te Ching*, and walked off into the wilderness never to be seen again.

The Tao is like Dharma in Hindu or Buddhist thought, it is the very structure of the world, the way things are. So the wisdom of the sage suggests that one flows with the tao in it many changes, bringing one's life into harmony with flux. For the Taoists, harmony was sought particularly between the person and nature. The individual finds a sort of inner harmony by attuning the self to what is natural, to one's own nature and especially to the rest of the living world. Taoist sages often preferred living in high mountain caves or forests. But whether in the midst of an urban center or in the bucolic countryside, the Taoist sage sought to be in harmony with the Tao, the way of things, nature. Attunement was a basic skill, seeing through the complexity of manifest diversity and fluttering change, to the easy flow of the deep current that moves it all along. The Taoists were very much mystics, just as the Confucians were very much scholars; both poles of Chinese wisdom seek their harmony with life through different lenses.

The great teachers like Confucius, Lao Tzu and others were termed sages. The sage is the wise and learned person. The notion contrasts with the Abrahamic traditions where the prophet receives revelation from God about the ordering of human life by way of commandments. In Chinese thought there is no such revelation. Wisdom comes through observing the flow of life and arranging things so as to be in harmony with that very flow. How one lives and how society is structured is more influenced by the concept of harmony to the natural order of things than obedience to divine commandments.

Literacy was a high value in Chinese society. The complexity of a largely pictographic written language resulted in the elevation of calligraphy as an art. A corpus of classics emerged in China as it did in the West; poetry, history, medicine, religion and philosophy. But note the contrast between a sage and a prophet. Again, China, while having deities and a spiritual world view does not treat its great teachers as being the mouthpiece of a high personal God, rather they are human beings distilling a wisdom of living in harmony with the divine.

Traditional Chinese medicine (TCM) views the life energy, qi, as flowing in numerous channels throughout the human body, known as meridians. Health reflects smooth flow of chi throughout the body; illness stems from blockage of the flow. The flow may be restarted and the blockage removed by a combination of techniques, most dramatically, through acupuncture, the insertion very fine needles into the body at precise points where these meridians intersect in nodes. The flow of chi can also be influenced by massage or touch, known as acupressure. Traditional herbal remedies are integral to TCM, and most Chinese grocery stores have a wall with various herbal products that can be mixed into packets and taken home for consumption as teas primarily, but in other forms as well. Most stores have someone on staff with some degree of knowledge, who can dispense prescriptions from traditional Chinese physicians, or dispense preventative blends for the well. Specialists in TCM should be consulted for anything other than the same sort of common ailments that generally call for over the counter remedies. Dietary advise also follows a yin-yang theory in terms of the effects of various vegetables, meats, and so on.

One growing form of alternative healing in Western cultures is energy medicine, or even energy psychology (Gallo, 2005; Mayor & Micozzi, 2011). This is largely based on the Chinese concept of chi, the life force energy. This moves beyond the use of needles and meridians and looks to use other means of stimulating the flow of life energy for healing. Thought field therapy is one specific aspect of energy psychology (Gallo, 2005).

The physical culture aspect of traditional Chinese medicine begins with the gentle form of exercise known as Tai-chi. Westerners have probably seen pictures on TV of people practicing slow flowing movements in large groups in public parks or streets in China. This is considered a form of martial art, though in contrast the more forceful kung-fu, or two Japanese and a Korean version; karate, aikido, and tai-kwan-do respectively. The legendary beginnings of the Chinese martial arts stem from Bodhidharma, an early Indian Buddhist monk and missionary who came to China. He settled in a region with many bandits, and he need to train his monks at the Shao-Lin temple to defend themselves when on the road. Whatever the precise origins, the Shao-Lin temple continues as a training center, though it was closed in the cultural revolution of the 1960s. Its renewed existence and focus has been affected by public performances for entertainment as well as teaching.

Most cultures have their own history of martial arts, including Historical European Martial Arts (HEMA), but the Eastern forms have origins that are also spiritual in nature, as noted in the legend of Bodhidharma. The various martial arts of Asian origin, judo, karate, kung fu, tae kwan do, etc., came to the U.S. mostly after World War II. American servicemen in the army of occupation in Japan or from exposure to Korean styles during the Korean war, brought them back and invited Asian teachers to start schools. Now martial arts studios, like yoga studies, proliferate across America. For the Western student, particularly the professional psychologist, these Asian martial arts offer the possibility of blending sports and physical fitness training with meditative and mental discipline.

## Cultivating discipline

Indeed, to sum up the chapter, the relevance of the Eastern paths stems from their continuous stream of transmission of a variety of personal development skills. Both the spiritualities that grew up in the Indian sub-continent as well as the Chinese practices in physical and mental culture are helpful and health promoting activities which professional psychology is becoming increasingly involved with. The phrase culture here implies the sense of personal and disciplined practice, they are cultivated across time. The valued benefit is skill in controlling both mind and body through a set of mental and physical exercises using consciousness and movement. Each of the traditions we have explored has been based on one or more world views which differ from Western ones, but yet have a pull of familiarity in today's world where several decades of syncretism have blended east and west already.

We saw the beginning of the archetype of the teacher in the previous chapter where the Greco-Roman foundations of teaching began with rhetoric and philosophy. By the end of the classical ancient world, a number of systems, both philosophic and spiritual offered practical teaching of skills in living the good life. Ascesis, or disciplined practice of a variety of exercises, was the technique by which eudaemonia, or well-being was acquired.

The Eastern ways are now very relevant in living the healthy life. The habits of mental and physical culture which they embody are increasingly demonstrated to be associated with positive health in their practitioners. The acquisition of those skills also require disciplined practice. The cultivation of low arousal states through meditation is a sure antidote to the stresses of modern faced-paced living. Exercise both quiet and stretching, and active and martial, as well as the dietary values arising in those cultures all seem so relevant to modern American problems stemming from sedentary living and being overweight. From the standpoint of health psychology, the Eastern approaches show great promise. Psychotherapy has also benefitted from understanding the impact of the reflective psychology from these Eastern streams. So increasing our awareness of these techniques and the world views that brought them to our attention can only increase the value to us as persons and our clients. Studying these ideas, living and teaching the disciplines that embody them can only add to our professional skills and practice.

# 5

## Emergence of the Modern World

### Our global world

WHETHER YOU VIEW IT a boon or a bane, we live in a truly global world. I'm not just talking about the economic integration nor the media which brings us instant news of far away places. Nor am I talking about the hegemony of Western culture or languages. All of those put together as well as the fact that we all inhabit this one planet makes for a degree of connectedness unknown before. How did this come about? What does this have to do with the practice of psychological healing? It is easier to answer the last question first. In most American cities we find minorities, many of whom may have themselves come from abroad, many are second generation immigrants. Some, like African-Americans have been here for many generations. Native American are indigenous to this land, and many Hispanic-Americans share indigenous ancestry with European ancestry. As noted in the first chapter cultural competence is an important element in professional practice. To know the impact of race, ethnicity, language, religion, gender and other factors is clearly important. The aim of studying world history is to be able to fit the individual, couple, family, group or community with whom we work into their cultural matrix so we can more competently serve them. This brings us now to answer the first question about how this multi-cultural world came about. Because it is in the answer to that question that beginnings of cultural competence lie.

We will now trace how Europe came to be what it was between ancient Rome and the modern era and how the subsequent centuries of colonial expansion and empires spread European genes, languages, memes, and culture throughout the rest of the world. The reaction to that history of European dominance now shapes the tensions that boil over into today's various conflicts, creating new waves of immigrants and refugees, veterans of foreign wars, and victims of terrorism. Let us examine how this unfolds. Along the way we will also look at how ideas of mental health and treatment change as well as how our modern intellectual heritage leading to psychology as a discipline develops.

Three major changes take place in the first six to eight centuries of the common era which provide the basis for European cultures in the Middle Ages. The first is the rise of

Christianity as a major world religion which became the dominant religion of Europe. The second change was the wave of migration of peoples coming into Europe and becoming the ethnicities which later became nationalities we now know. A third change which occurred in Arabia would dramatically affect Europe as the new monotheistic religion of Islam swept across North Africa into Spain, into the Balkans, and through the Middle East, including converting the Turkic peoples already settled in Anatolia.

## Rise of Christianity.

As noted in the previous chapter, Christianity shared one of the same goals of the other mystery religions of classical antiquity – it offered a means for salvation of the individual human soul, a way by which life triumphs over death. It sprang from Judaism through the life and mission of Jesus of Nazareth. The ministry of Jesus was short-lived, and the fundamental message that the early disciples, the Apostles, took as they spread their good news, or Gospel, was the resurrection of Jesus after he was put to death by crucifixion. His individual death was seen as paying for the sins of all humans through his personal sacrifice. The individual soul could be saved by grace through faith in the message of Jesus, and baptism into the community of faithful.

But it was the efforts of two great missionary Apostles, St. Peter, one of Jesus' early disciples, and Saul of Tarsus, who later became known as St. Paul that made Christianity a world religion. St. Paul's story is dramatic. Originally a persecutor of Christians he experienced an encounter with the Divine and converted. He traveled throughout the Roman world, starting churches in many cities of the empire, Corinth, Ephesus, in the province of Thessaly were some of his congregations. His letters to the various early churches comprise much of the New Testament of the Christian Bible. The other books are the four gospels, or main narratives of Jesus' ministry, the Acts of the Apostles, and letters from other Apostles as well. The canon of the next testament was not fixed for several centuries so a much wider body of Christian literature circulated. The Gnostics were a syncretic sect that integrated much of Christian and Jewish mythology and symbols, though it was recognized as perhaps the first heresy. A major issue of contention in the first century was to what extent Gentiles (non-Jews) could become Christians, and whether males needed to be circumcised in order to convert. Paul favored the open approach which was adopted, thus making it easier for non-Jews to become Christians.

Christianity found particular favor in the lower classes, including slaves, which made it suspect to Roman rulers. The biggest problem from a Roman perspective, was their refusal to respect the state religions, which involved making reverence to statues of the gods as well as sacrificial offerings. Christians viewed making such offerings as idolatry, long prohibited in Judaism and retained by Christians as a cardinal sin. Persecution of Christians occurred with some regularity until the time of Constantine in the early fourth century CE when his patronage led to its triumph as the official religion.

The emperor was converted and promoted the Christian faith. By 390 CE, one of his successors, Theodosius, made Christianity the official state religion and began prohibiting the various pagan religions, closing their temples and schools of philosophy.

Originally all bishops were more or less equals, but soon several important sees (seats of episcopal authority) had come into prominence and were accorded the additional rank of patriarchs. There was a period of time when there were five relatively equal patriarchs presiding over Christian orthodoxy; in Rome, Constantinople, Antioch, Jerusalem and Alexandria. As the twin capitals were rivals for political power so the two patriarchs became rivals for spiritual authority in Christendom. The patriarch of Rome took the title of Pope, whereas the Patriarch of Constantinople retains the title of Patriarch. He is revered as spiritual leader, first among equals among the patriarch of autonomous Eastern Orthodox Churches in Russia, Ukraine, Bulgaria, Serbia, and Romania. The Oriental Orthodox branches broke with the main body from the Council of Chalcedon in 451 CE. They include the Copts in Egypt, the Church in Ethiopia, several Syriac Christian denominations throughout the Middle East, and including the Malabar Christians of India.

Different doctrines between the Western Roman Catholic and the Eastern Orthodox emerged regarding the Trinity, different liturgies, or worship services, emerged. Over the course of several centuries a number of Ecumenical Councils were held to decide matters of doctrine. Beginning with the First Council of Nicea in 325 CE, convened by Constantine himself, several losers in the theological debates were declared heretics or separated themselves from communion with Rome. The Roman Catholic and Eastern Orthodox branches of Christianity recognize about seven Ecumenical Councils as authoritative, but the Oriental Orthodox, the Assyrian Orthodox, Nestorians, Arians, Gnostics, and others also fell away or were pushed out. The cultural divide between the Greek speaking east and the Latin speaking west wound up dividing Christianity. The final break between Eastern and Western Christianity did not become official until 1054, when the Pope and the Patriarch of Constantinople excommunicated each other, an event termed the Great Schism.

The first through third centuries of the common era is known as the Patristic period of Christian history, because the works of several Church Fathers like Clement of Alexandria (150-215), Tertullian (155-222), St. Augustine of Hippo (354-440 CE), St. Jerome (347-420), St. John Chrysostom (347-407), Gregory the Great (540-604) and many others. They articulated the basics of Christian theology. Of those St. Augustine was perhaps the most significant, as he sought to adapt Platonic philosophy to fit Christianity. His *Confessions* is recognized as the first autobiography. The Catholic Church officially adopted Augustine's position until the Middle Ages, when it was influenced by St. Thomas Aquinas (1225-1274) to switch allegiance to Aristotle.

Christianity is a religion with active outreach to convert others. Central to its doctrine is the belief that adherence to the teachings of Jesus is necessary for salvation. So missionary activity continued as waves of new peoples came into the empire. The history of the emergence of modern Europe has in each country a date or period when they were Christianized and gave up their indigenous Pagan religions. Among the first, of course, were those geographically closest to the Mediterranean world where it originated. But far flung places like Ireland and England had monastic communities that were centers of art and learning. The Germanic and Scandinavian people converted later. In the east, the Slavs were converted by saints Cyril and Methodius. Cyrillic alphabet for writing Slavic languages was originated by St. Cyril. The Baltic countries, Lithuania, Latvia and Estonia were among the last European peoples to convert.

## Era of migration

The very concept of the Middle Ages is not only a Eurocentric one, but a western European one at that. The concept applies best to those areas of Europe that were part of the western Roman empire. In 330 CE, the emperor Constantine saw the weight of empire shifting toward the east as Rome acquired more territory in Asia. He renamed the older Greek city of Byzantium on the Bosporus between Europe and Asia after himself. Constantinople became a new administrative capital, an eastern equivalent to Rome. The empire was so large it needed a more distributed administrative structure. But this act sowed seeds of disunity that was to have significant consequences for the western part of the empire. Soon there were two emperors, one in the east and one in the west. Behind these political changes, there were some real cultural differences which shaped the history of Europe. The eastern part of the empire spoke mostly Greek while the western part spoke mostly Latin. These cultural differences promoted further parting of the ways of a once unified Rome.

The most shattering development in terms of continuity of Western Europe from the older world of the Roman empire to modern Europe was the succession of invasions by nomadic peoples out of the vast Asian heartland. These barbarians, as they were called by Romans, represented new tribes that were in part lured by the great wealth of Rome. Indeed many were paid from Roman treasury to perform military service against other barbarian tribes (Pohl, 1991). Many of them spoke other branches of Indo-European languages and settled across northern Europe. Some were replaced by later waves of migrating peoples ultimately pushed westward by movement of the Turkic peoples in Central Asia. Indeed several Turkic tribes settled in the Anatolian peninsula and ultimately grew in strength to replace the Byzantine or eastern Roman empire and give Turkey its modern ethnic composition.

The Roman empire had earlier expanded to ring the Mediterranean Sea from the Iberian peninsula in the west (modern Spain and Portugal), northerly through France, Britain, Belgium and parts of Germany up to the Rhine river. In the east they controlled the Balkan peninsula down through Greece. The Roman empire controlled the north African coast from west to east through Egypt and up the eastern shore of the Levant (Israel, Lebanon, Syria) and the Anatolian peninsula (modern Turkey).

The Gauls, Franks and others were allowed to become Roman citizens by serving in the military. Even newcomers like the Goths, Visigoths, and Ostrogoths also served Rome as mercenaries. The legions were sometimes comprised of multiple ethnicities with some divided loyalties to Rome or their tribal cousins. The various tribes rose in revolt and poured across the frontier. Rome was first sacked in 410 CE, by Alaric, a Visigoth. Many historians date the fall of the western Roman empire to 476 CE, when the last Western Roman emperor was deposed by a general of Germanic tribal origins. Some put it later at 1453 CE, the date Constantinople fell to the Ottoman Turks, ending what is now known as the Byzantine Empire, which succeeded Rome in the eastern provinces.

With the fall of Roman power in the west, there were dramatic changes which do, in fact, mark a watershed in European cultural history. The degree of urbanization declined, the infrastructure which promoted civilization and urban life such as roads, aqueducts and so on fell into disrepair. Literacy declined dramatically. The small middle class of merchants and civil servants to administer large areas of territory vanished as well. Government devolved to the local level and with the decline of literacy the communication of ideas became extremely limited. The monasteries and convents of the Christian religious orders were the only thread of continuity for reading and writing. Europe, once again, became an oral society. With this cultural decline the learning of classical Greece and Rome was lost for many centuries, only to become reborn or reclaimed in the Renaissance. This is what is termed the Dark Ages in European history.

The Germanic branch that evolved out of the Proto-Indo-European (PIE) peoples and languages came to dominate the lands of Germany and Scandinavia. Tribes from north German plains and Denmark, the Angles, Saxons, and Jutes replaced the earlier Celtic population of England, though the Scots and Irish retained their lands for the time being. Another set of Indo-European peoples, the Franks and Burgundians settled in France. The Visigothic kingdom in Spain remained until the Arab invasions of the eight century. Various Slavic peoples followed the migration of the others and settled in central and eastern Europe. From the Pannonian plains in modern Hungary through the Ukraine and into the Pontic steppes beyond the Black Sea there arose a variety of kingdoms and principalities that are of poly-ethnic makeup such as the Avars and Bulgarians (Pohl, 1991). By the end of the first millennium of the common era the bases of the current ethnic make up of modern Europe were in place with one exception. The Magyars were among the last of nomadic horsemen to sweep in from the steppes of Eurasia and settle in the Pannonian plain of the Danube River in modern Hungary. Indeed, the history of Eurasia is marked by waves of movement of peoples skilled in horseback riding and archery from the first groups of Proto-Indo-Europeans in the second millennium BCE to the Mongol invasion of the Levant and eastern Europe in the thirteenth century of the common era.

In the early Middle Ages, the Norsemen from Scandinavia conducted extensive raids on Britain, France. They were among the last peoples to make raids into Europe. The Vikings, as they were also known, ruled over northern Britain (the Danelaw), parts of northern France (Normandy), coastal areas of Ireland, and settled Iceland and Greenland. Though they visited North America, only a small archaeological remnant of their colony survived into the present day. They, too, were soon converted and became part of a Christian Europe, though several Baltic peoples in eastern Europe did not convert to Christianity until well into the fourteenth century.

Other parts of the world did not suffer such a dramatic cultural shift. As noted above, the Eastern Roman empire morphed into the Byzantine empire which lasted until 1453. In China, India and the Middle East various dynasties came and went without the same drastic loss of prior learning and literacy. The Silk Road flourished as a trade route from other parts of Asia into China. In the Middle East there was a dramatic shift in culture with the rise of Islam in the seventh century CE, but unlike the situation in the West, there was no loss of prior learning. Indeed, it was in the libraries of the Muslim world that the heritage of Greece and Rome were preserved until Europe was once again ready to receive it.

## Islam

Islam is the religion founded by the prophet Mohammed (570-632 CE). He was a merchant in the Arabian town of Mecca who made a fortunate marriage to a wealthy woman. In his middle years he was troubled by a spiritual vacuum and sought consolation in retreat. It was there, according to tradition, he was visited by the angel Gabriel who told him to write, though he could not; and the *Q'uran* (*Koran*), the Muslim scripture, was dictated to him. He taught monotheism, the worship of one god, in opposition to the polytheism which then existing among the tribes throughout the Arabian peninsula. He saw himself as a final prophet in the line of Abraham, Moses and Jesus; well, next to last, since the Mahdi is the prophet yet to come. The people of Mecca rejected his teachings and became hostile. In 622 CE he fled Mecca finding refuge in Medina. This is known as the Hejira, and is the beginning year of the Muslim calendar whose years are numbered AH. In Medina, he was more favorably received, especially after settling a dispute. This conflict resolution resulted in acceptance of Mohammed as a prophet by Medina's population. They became the first Muslim community, the ones who surrender themselves to the will and governance of God, which is the meaning of the term Islam in Arabic. It was also in Medina where the link between religion and state was forged. Unlike Christianity, which was an outcast faith for nearly three centuries before it found a patron, Islam was founded on the use of its spiritual teachings to set out a law for social living and enforced by at least a small foothold of believers.

From his base in Medina, Mohammed lead armies which reconquered Mecca and then united the various Arab tribes. He established his headquarters in Mecca, which now is the most sacred place in the Islamic world. A pilgrimage to Mecca is one of the obligations Muslims must strive to fulfill during their lifetime. From the very beginning, Mohamed was called upon to settle disputes and organize the social structure of his new flock of believers. So Islam was from the beginning, not just a religion, but a way of ordering human communities; law and governance of a society in accordance with the divine will are as much a part of the Koran as personal piety.

The Muslim cleric, or religious professional, is a student, above all, of Islamic law, or Shariah. There is very little emphasis on ceremonial or ritual functions in Islam, in contrast with the Christian High Mass, for example. The imams lead prayers, they teach, but above all they rule on matters of human conduct. This is very similar to the role of rabbis in Judaism after the destruction of the second Temple with the crushing of the Jewish revolt by Rome in 73 CE. They are primarily teachers and judges of Jewish law. This is different from Christian priests whose sacerdotal role is exemplified in the sacrament of the Eucharist, a mystical re-enactment of Christ's sacrifice.

Beginning in Mohamed's life time and continuing after his death, Arab armies spread out and rapidly conquered their neighbors and converted them to Islam. Indeed, the spread of Islam was among the most rapid for a major religion. At its greatest extent, Muslim influence penetrated into Europe, where north African caliphs ruled from Seville and Cordoba in Spain; and Islam expanded eastward conquering Persia and continuing eastward into central Asia. Modern Xinjiang province in China was settled by Uighurs, who converted to Islam, marking the far north easterly boundary of the modern Muslim world. Later Mughal dynasties from Afghanistan moved into northern India. Islam also spread to Indonesia, replacing the earlier Hindu, Buddhist and animist religions.

Division within Islam began very early. There are four rightly guided caliphs, or successors, who are recognized by the Sunnis, the largest group within Islam. The Shia believe that the succession to the prophet should have gone first to the man who became fourth caliph, Ali, the cousin and son-in-law of the prophet, and view the other three as usurpers. Hussain, the son of Ali was killed along with all his followers at the battle of Karbela in 680. In Shia communities, this event is marked as a holy day of mourning, Ashura, for Ali and his followers as martyrs. The prominent place of martyrs in the growing suicide bombing tactic in the war in Iraq is reinforced by this bit of religious history.

That victors of that battle, the Ummayad caliphate, ultimately was succeeded by the Abbasid caliphate, which was the first major unifying political center in the Muslim world. It ruled from Damascus, Syria, over an empire that stretched across north Africa and as far east as Persia and sponsored a growth in culture. Early Islam was quite tolerant of other religions after its political conquest, which was, like all conquests, taken by force of arms. Jews, Christians, and others except were allowed to practice their religions, though they were levied a special tax, the jizya. There was a certain freedom of thought and religious that, though not exemplary by modern standards, was relatively tolerant. The fanaticism of present Islamic extremists arises out of complex factors influenced in part by European colonization of Muslim countries.

Culture and learning flourished in the Arab world. Great scholars in philosophy, astronomy, mathematics as well as Islamic law flourished with royal patronage and a cosmopolitan and thriving economy. In the West, the Islamic kingdoms of Spain were a major center where Muslim, Jewish and Christian scholars could dialog and pass on the remains of classical antiquity. When western Europe had forgot its own Greco-Roman past, the libraries Seville, Cordoba, Cairo, Constantinople, Damascus and Baghdad kept the books and scholarship alive.

For psychology, the great scholars are Ibn Sinna (known in the west as Avicenna) and Ibn Rushd (Averroes). They kept alive the faculty psychology of Aristotle with some modifications. Classical learning was passed on through these Arab scholars. It is still with us in a much elaborated version in modern cognitive psychology with its emphasis on the separate cognitive and affective abilities and structures. In psychiatry, as well, the works of Galen and others scholars of late antiquity were added to by Arab physicians. Baghdad had a hospital with a unit for mental problems long before Paris or London.

There was resistance in the West in response to Islam. The initial conquest of Spain and parts of France was halted at the battle of Tours in 732 by Frankish forces. They retreated to Spain and kept a hold there until much later when Ferdinand and Isabella of Leon & Castile pushed the last of the Moors, as the Muslim peoples were known, out of the Iberian peninsula. These were the patrons of Columbus. The *reconquista*, as it is known also brought on the expulsion or forced conversion of not only Muslims but Spanish Jews as well. The tolerant climate of *el Andalus*, as the Muslim part of Spain was known, vanished and in its place came the Spanish Inquisition, a most brutal repressive apparatus.

But the part of the military struggle between Islam and the West that is more widely known are the Crusades. These were a series of invasions of the Middle East by French, German and English nobles and soldiers, begun in 1095 CE and continuing until 1291. The first Crusade sacked Constantinople, a Christian city before it reached Jerusalem. The Christian armies plundered and sacked that holy city and established several kingdoms along the coast stretching from modern Israel up to Turkey, collectively known as Outremer (from the French *outre mer*, beyond the sea). The great Muslim general, Saladin retook Jerusalem in 1187. The last of the Christian kingdoms was defeated and the European armies withdrawn with the fall of Acre in 1291. Over the course of European occupation of the Levant, many Islamic influences were adopted by Europe. The lute, for example, became a staple in Renaissance music, but it's origins are the Arabic 'oud.

The rise of the Ottoman empire brought Islam to the Balkan peninsula in Europe. All of Greece, Bulgaria and Serbia, much of Romania and parts of Hungary were under

Turkish rule for a number of centuries. The Turks laid siege to Vienna, Austria, as recently as 1683. During the nineteenth century, first Greece, then other countries in the Balkans gained their independence. Part of the Balkan wars of the 1990s was conflict between those Serbs who remained Christian and those who converted to Islam, largely in Bosnia, as well as the nation of Albania and their ethnic cousins in Kosovo. The long history of relations between the Muslim world and the West have been fraught with military conflict from the first arrival of Muslim armies in Spain. The presence of American and European forces in the Middle East and the Balkans is still viewed in light of this long history, though the current conflict has additional roots.

We think of the Crusades as directed against the Islamic Middle East, but there was a similar zeal to convert non-Christian peoples of northern Europe and Christianize these peoples as well. In the northern Europe, the Teutonic knights pushed pagan tribes back in areas from eastern Germany through Poland, Latvia and Estonia, ringing the Baltic sea with forts and then trading centers. The Albigensian crusade (1209-1229) was a crusade within Europe against a heretical Christian sect known as the Cathars. The Crusades, despite their violence and intolerance, nonetheless brought some things of value based on cross-cultural contact.

In summary, the roots of the modern world were planted with the fall of the Roman empire and the arrival by a number of waves of people who supplanted and/or intermarried with the earlier tribes living in northern and western Europe. All of these peoples converted to Christianity within the first millennium of the common era. The rise of Islam set a religious and cultural boundary in the Mediterranean world. Spain was divided between Islam and the West until the late Middle Ages; much of the Balkan was part of the Muslim Ottoman empire. The learning of classical antiquity was preserved in Muslim libraries and when translated into Latin became fodder for the Renaissance and the burst of artistic and intellectual ferment that followed. Europe was divided religiously between the Catholic west and the Orthodox east, including Russia.

## Universities and scholastic philosophy

The modern university as a place of universal knowledge takes shape in the Middle Ages. The roots of the university lie in the Academy of Plato (387 BCE), hence the term academia. In Islam, Al-Azhar University in Cairo, ranks as the oldest (988 CE). Nanjing University claims descent from an academy founded in 258 CE by the King of the Chinese state of Wu. Also as noted earlier, Nalanda was a Buddhist center of higher learning from the seventh to twelfth centuries. The first European universities were founded in Italy at Salerno in the ninth century, and Bologna (1088). Soon the Universities of Paris (1100), Oxford (1167) and Cambridge (1209) joined them, and by the end of the Middle Ages, most European countries had several schools. The training of the clergy was the prime goal and organizing task. The clergy, being literate, were also used by secular leaders for these skills as well.

Philosophy was the first purely academic discipline to evolve, with no immediate practical goal but thought abstracted. The universities evolved with teachers of particular subjects which over time evolved into faculties teaching coherent disciplines. The faculties of theology and philosophy were often supplemented by faculties in medicine or law, either canon or civil. One of the major developments in education occurred toward the end of the middle ages with the establishment of the liberal arts curriculum. There were seven basic disciplines, or coherent bodies of knowledge, divided into two major sets. The trivium included grammar, rhetoric and dialectic, and the quadrivium included arithmetic, geometry, astronomy and music. Modern thought, and consequently, the bureaucratic divisions within a university, divide between the arts and humanities on the one hand and the sciences on the other.

The whole period of Medieval European philosophy is known as the Scholastic period, from its close association with the universities. Christian philosophy, especially that of St. Augustine (354-430 CE), adopted Platonism as its central organizing structure. The gospel was to be harmonized with the realm of logic. Christianity, after all, had to contend with secular and pagan Greek philosophy as an alternative for the hearts and minds of both the laity, both illiterate and literate. Modern Catholic philosophy really emerged with the work of Thomas Aquinas (1225-1274). He shifted the allegiance of the Church over to Aristotelianism. There it has mostly remained until the present.

In terms of philosophical psychology, the theory of the human person, Aquinas retained the various Aristotelian mental faculties as distinct types of our cognitive structure. He accepted a generally three-part division of the soul into the biological, emotive- perceptive, and the cognitive. This began with Plato and was further refined by Aristotle. Implicit is a hierarchical arrangement of capacities or abilities from passive and receptive to active and initiating. This *scala natura*, or ladder of nature, is an ancient idea. It can be applied to the psyche, soul or person, as in psychology, as well as to the human classification of the natural world. Indeed, the abstract objects of human thought are the representations of sensory impressions passively received coupled with the active biological, emotive and active cognitive level. The latter he identifies as *voluntas* or will, which plays an important place is later philosophy and psychology. The particular ladder goes from the biological activities that keep us going as living beings, through our external senses as a basis of realistic understanding and acting in the world, through the abstractive and deliberative capacities by which we affect the world and act ethically or not.

The concept of natural law was part of Aquinas' ethical theory. He saw the possibility of universal moral principles known by reason. At an individual level, the person should comport themselves in accord with reason and faith. Reason informs us of natural law and our volition, or will guides the choice or selection of actions.

Faith gives us the grounding of ethical activity in a spiritual framework. The appeal to natural law as a basis for civil laws is at the heart of Catholic jurisprudence as well. The just society should operate in accordance with natural law and God's revealed standard as well.

The problem of universals was an important one in Medieval scholastic philosophy. Obviously if there are universal ethical standards as well as universal concepts which are assented to as true by every reasonable person, then one can hold people accountable for their actions and beliefs and expect them to change their beliefs to bring them in accord with reason. Thus realism and nominalism were the twin poles around which a debate swirled about the metaphysical status of abstract concepts as objects of intellect, or reason. The realists held that such objects existed and could be known, the nominalists questioned their existence and said they were just linguistic names devoid of substantial independent existence.

The status of abstract ideas which was the subject of that debate bears on current issues within cognitive psychology. Do concepts have a reality or are they merely names of non-existent things?. Concrete words point to concrete objects, but what is the reality of abstract words? What is the metaphysical status of truth, justice, or the good? It speaks to whole nature of theory, since theories are made up of concepts. This debate continued into the twentieth century with Wittgenstein, Ayer, and others championing a nominalist position based on how language is used as social tool, a game based on shadows. This implies a relativity about concepts or universal rules and principles.

Another important scholar was William of Ockham, an English monk. His statement of the principle of parsimony has become known as Ockham's razor for its ability to pare away unnecessary layers of objects in an explanation. The principle simply stated holds that when two accounts will accord with the facts equally well, the account that requires the fewest concepts is preferable. This has become a foundational concept in science. Particularly during the early modern era the principle was used when the complexities of the patch-jobs on the geo-centric theory espoused by the late classical Ptolemy became trumped by the simplicity of the helio-centric view of the universe which was supported by newly acquired observational data of Kepler, Galileo and others. His other major contribution toward an emerging psychology is his view that all human habits are acquired and represent a disposition to act toward the object of the habit in a more smooth, easy, and fluent manner (Robinson, 1981).

## Guilds and occupational regulation

While the Medieval universities are the source of our modern system of higher learning, the guilds for crafts and other skilled occupations are the source for our modern system of occupational regulation. They are the earliest forms of professional organization. Intellectual work was not professionalized in quite the same way as producing goods. The ordinary objects of life were all made by skilled hands; barrels were made by coopers, jewelry was fashioned by goldsmiths, clothing was made by weavers, milliners, furriers, and so on. It took skill to produce the products, and time and training to develop the skill. Collectively, the skilled artisans formed guilds. The crown or local prince would charter these bodies and give them both standing and authority to govern who practiced the occupation and what training was required to enter into the trade. The apprentice-ship model started here, setting out our modern path from apprentice to journeyman to master. Supervised experience became the mode of training. The skill of the master was passed on to the pupil through apprenticing in the workshop.

The guild halls were an important social nexus where conviviality and good com-radeship cemented the bonds among fellow craftsmen. While the high gothic arches of the Medieval cathedral embody the spiritual yearnings of medieval society, the guild halls were also generally works of pride and influence. City life emerges once again in the Middle Ages, and the burghers, the townsfolk, begin to find work and live within urban centers. By the end of Medieval and Renaissance periods, urban life and some forms of secular self-government and regulation emerges. The guilds as social organization expand beyond the initial definitions of skilled trades organization and involve more retail commercial networks.

Today when we speak of guild issues we are referring to those issues of central importance to our professional group. Compensation, advancement in career, ben-efits, and participation in the community of practitioners are all part of what each pro-fession, including that of psychology, must now contend for. Control and autonomy of practice is a prime guild issue. This is the basis of all self regulation. That is why the American Psychological Association has a code of ethics and enforces it. Self regula-tion requires some measure of quality assurance to the consuming public.

## Madness in society, art and law

The importance of visual communication is magnified in cultures with low litera-cy. The study of visual symbols and their meaning is known as iconography. Thus, learning about how people viewed mental illness and how it was treated requires a deconstruction of the iconography of madness. Sandor Gilman compiled a large col-lection of visual images of madness (1982) which remains an important source for the graphic history of mental illness.

In this book Gilman notes how the sculptural friezes over the doors of early men-tal hospitals reveals much about the continuity of thought from classical antiquity. The polar images of mania and melancholia are repeated in a number of different locations. One of these was installed above the entrance to St. Mary of Bethlehem Hospital in London, England, which came to be known as Bedlam. Indeed, the very word is now synonymous with agitated chaos. The figure for mania is portrayed by outward gestures and frantic appearance, whereas melancholia is portrayed with a bodily posture turned inward with a brooding expression. Besides these two polar types, madness was also associated with the wild and untamed aspects of human experience.

The unruly nature of madness was physically linked to the margins of society. Consistent with Aristotle's three parts of human nature, the vegetative, appetitive, and the rational; if the rational is lost then only the animalistic parts of the human remain. Thus, the mad were seen as closer to animals. In many asylums, even into the nineteenth century little care was given to the comfort of the inmates in part because of this view, that like barn animals, they could withstand the cold better than their sane counterparts. Gilman shows how madness was likened to a stone embedded in the head. He also features the esoteric figure of the alchemist or physician is removing it with a lancet. Another rendering, a lithograph by Durer, shows the link with alchemy. Alchemy was the high art of creating physical combinations and transformations. Several of the drawing selecting by Gilman show how ridding people of their hidden demons was likened to removing the philosopher's stone or flaming away impurities of the mind. Jung, especially, was later to draw from this and use alchemy as a metaphor for the symbolic transformations of psychotherapy.

Michel Foucault (1926-1984), an important figure in late twentieth century thought, wrote a history of the medicalization of madness from the seventeenth century onward. His book *Madness and civilization* (1961/1973) chronicles the ways in which the problems of mental illness become enmeshed with the mechanisms of social control. He points out that the mad were generally left to the care of their families, and when the families did not have the means to look after them, they were allowed to become homeless. The possibility of unrest from groups of people who were either mentally ill, physically disabled, unemployed, or otherwise not part of the mainstream of society was a rationale for the increasing use of institutions for the confinement of all manner of socially different persons.

Foucault calls attention to the fact that the mentally ill were often left to wander from town to town begging for their sustenance. He recounts the work of the German writer Sebastian Brandt (1458-1521), who in 1497 wrote a novel, *Das Narrenschiff*, translated as the *Ship of Fools*. Few read the book today, but many are familiar with the painting of the same name by the Dutch painter Hieronymous Bosch (1450-1516). This shows a motley crew of figures both within and outside of the boat, drifting downstream in life. The existence of several nuns and clerics is often seen in context of satirical critique of the corruption in the Medieval and Renaissance Church. Bosch was also probably involved in an esoteric study group. His use of vivid and shocking imagery puts him at some distance from the otherwise more restrained and conventional images of piety and faith.

Folly was often synonymous with madness. In French, la folie, was the colloquial term for madness. Folly is a wonderful word in its range of meanings, for it implies a degree of willful activity, bad choices, not just unfortunate circumstances. Madness is so often viewed as something (the mind) or someone out of control, but another

aspect is the reflexive and obsessional nature of delusion and the acts done with exqui-
site planning and rumination, or its opposite, acts done heedlessly with little thought
of consequences. Folly encompasses behaviors we know would view as impulsive,
compulsive, or even addictive; those bad things we do to our self knowingly.

However, the graphic representation of madness was but one aspect of the social
situation of the mentally ill. Another perspective comes from the preserved legal records from the English Medieval court system. As Neugebauer (1979) found, the records of the courts for adjudicating wards or dependents of the crown reveal a variety
of theories of mental illness, some of which are naturalistic. The history of psychiatry
has often advanced the idea that the medieval world saw only demon possession as
the source of madness, with exorcism as its cure (Cf. Zilborg, 1941). Such accounts
were self congratulatory stories of advancement of science and away from superstition. The reality revealed in the records show they recognized that old age brings on
a dementia and that some people are born with grow up with a more permanent and
profound cognitive incapacity. These individuals, termed natural fools in the Middle
Ages, would now be identified as mentally disabled. Their estates would be forfeit to
the crown, since there was broad recognition that the person would never be likely to
assume the normal social roles involved in managing one's affairs and property. The
estates of those who were termed lunatics were kept in their name with the possibility of return to them if their sanity was restored. These individuals we would now
recognize as suffering from some type of mental illness. It is known that many diagnoses, for example, bi-polar disorder have a cyclical course with periods of lucidity
interrupted by periods of madness or psychosis. Both Kroll (1973) and Neugebauer
(1979) combat the view that our predecessors were utterly superstitious and unable to
recognize non-spiritual sources of human suffering.

If the wealthy cared for their ill family members in the home, and destitute allowed to wander homeless and uncared for, were there no other alternatives? Yes, the
beginning of modern hospitals also starts in this period. According to Rosen (1968), at
Elbing, Germany, in 1326, the Dollhaus, or madhouse was founded. We have spoken
earlier of Bedlam Hospital, but this was formally known as the Hospital of St. Mary of
Bethlehem (1403). The Hotel de Dieu in Paris began serving the mentally ill in 1316.
Fr. Jofré founded the Hospital of the Innocents in 1350 (Rumbaut, 1972). These early
examples of major institutions for the care of the mad or others in suffering exemplify
the best at the time of the ethic of charity. Charity was the dominant motive for helping in Medieval society. There was no formal governmental support and commercial
asylums as businesses did not come into being until a couple of centuries later. Staffing
the hospitals was the business of the monks, nuns, and priests. The laity supported
those charitable activities but generally did not personally participate, Gheel being a
notable exception.

The term hospice was used to refer to the way stations on a journey of pilgrimage. As we noted earlier about the Asklepian tradition, finding healers often meant

traveling long distances to get to the places where they practiced. Medieval Christianity also sponsored pilgrimages to places holding the relics, or bodily remains of saints. A veritable market emerged in real or constructed holy relics. So for both spiritual reasons as well as practical and often urgent need for healing, the pilgrimage was a major feature of life. In Catholic and Orthodox Europe, the veneration of the saints was an important part of the spiritual and social fabric, and each human activity had its patron.

St. Dymphna is the patron saint for those suffering from mental illness. She was daughter of a pagan Irish king and she had converted to Christianity. When her mother died, her father went mad with grief and pressed Dymphna to marry him. She resisted, but he persisted. Ultimately she fled and found refuge in Gheel, Belgium. Her father pursued her there and in his jealous rage killed her, making her a martyr to the faith. At a very early time she became a patron for the mad, as her father's actions came to be seen as the result of madness, and her faithful resistance a sign of connection to those so afflicted.

Gheel became a site of pilgrimage. As we noted with the Asklepian tradition, there was a popular tradition of pilgrimage, of travel to a distant site which specialized in healing. The journey served as a preparatory period to heighten motivation and focus attention carefully. Gheel saw many mentally ill come into their town to seek healing at the chapel dedicated to St. Dymphna. They took them in based on an ethic of charity and cared for their physical needs while the priest and other religious associated with the shrine attended to the spiritual aspect of the healing. It is arguably plausible that the whole community took on a mission to serve the mentally ill who came to the shrine of St. Dymphna. Even today, there is a substantial residual shrine in an era of primarily secular medical or social services, and there still is a strong component of community volunteer facilitation of the historic venture as a point of civic pride.

Rites of healing in Christianity often made use of the laying on of hands. Therapeutic touch does not begin here, for it was used in classical times, but in terms of the modern Western religious or spiritual and even secular world views and healing practices, it certainly gets a big boost in a Christian context. This ultimately led to others, non-clerical people to become known for healing by touch. The royal touch was that power exercised by a sovereign to heal by touch. In seventeenth century England, Valentine Greatrakes was a widely popular healer by touch (Bromberg, 1937). We will later see how Mesmer picked up on a tradition of transmitting healing energy by touch and how his successors removed touch from what then became hypnosis

## The Black Death.

One of the turning points for the Middle Ages was the Black death. Its relevance for us is the social psychology of epidemics. The current world wide worry over a variety of infectious agents that threaten to create widespread illness. The Ebola virus, H5N1 avian influenza, SARS, HIV, Zika virus, or other contagious diseases are but the latest wave of concern about epidemics. From the standpoint of professional psychologists, we should look to this event as a model for the psychology of trauma. The Black Death struck fast and hard and swept away an estimated one third of the population of Europe. It may well have been a result of an early act of biological warfare. The bubonic plague had spread westward from China across Asia; during a siege of the Crimean city of Caffa by the Mongols of the Golden Horde in 1347, infected corpses are reputed to have been catapulted over the walls in an effort to bring the siege to a conclusion by devastating the population. Caffa was a Genoese trading post, and the Genoese escaped by sea, bringing it to Italy.

Once the disease got a foothold in Europe it changed its vector of transmission. Bubonic plague was spread by fleas from rats which existed along side people in medieval village and city life. It was a blood-born disease, and required closer physical contact for transmission, and thus its spread was slower. But it soon an air-borne form of the bacteria emerged and the pneumonic plague then rapidly spread in crowded urban populations. This new form was transmissible by coughing or sneezing, just like the flue or common cold. But it was much deadlier. By early 1350's it even reached into Scandinavia and Russia. Again, the estimate of the toll over the short period of about two years was enormous, one third of the population gone. Imagine the psychological impact of disease causing the death of one of every three people in us in the modern world. In many areas, entire communities were wiped out, and the remains of abandoned villages still can be found in the European countryside.

Scapegoating was a major social response to the trauma, loss and uncertainty of continued life itself. Jews were the main targets of fear; they have long been Europe's easy victim since due to persecution they existed in small easily identified communities embedded in a larger, usually urban society. Vicitimization and pogroms have been cyclical reactions of de-stabilizing forces in the larger community.

The uncertainty of life and the grim equality of death was played out in artistic visions in both literature, music and the visual arts. The children's rhyme "ring around the rosey, pocket full of posey, ashes, ashes, we all fall down" is a cultural remnant of the plague years. The ring refers to the usually circular bubo, which was the sign of its less transmissible form. St. Roche, the patron saint of plague is portrayed with leg splayed outward and tunic lifted to reveal the black nodule which gave the Black Death its name.

The major impact of this mass death was the emergence of wage labor as we now know it, and the death of feudalism as a way of life, except in Russia. Serfs, in the feudal society were tied to the land and could not move about without permission of the landlord, who was literally a lord, part of the hereditary nobility. Feudal society was a set of alliances among local knights, lords of various ranks and ultimately, kings. Medieval society was quite hierarchical in natures, each layer, theoretically owing allegiance and loyalty to the higher one. The lowest level was the common peasant, or serf. Some serfs could become free peasants and over time small property holding emerged, but the largest number of people were attached to the land where they were born. With one third of the population gone, landlords had fewer people to raise the grain and other raw agricultural products upon which their wealth depended. Landlords had to compete with life in the city, which renewed itself, as well as the possibility that another landlord just over the ridge, or beyond the next river might offer a better deal. Social inequality and stability of residency still persisted, but there was greater play in the system, greater opportunity for the adventurous, entrepreneurial, or knavish.

The lesson of the Black Death for psychologists is the power of fear of contagion during an epidemic. There will undoubtedly be outbreaks of rapidly spreading illnesses in the future and the psychology of contagion, panic, fear and scapegoating will require careful and compassionate intervention by mental health professionals to supplement the work of biological medicine.

## The Renaissance

Cities began to flourish again in the late Middle Ages and with them came a greater opportunity for relationships not governed by solely religious authorities. Trade, commerce, and exposure to the world beyond Europe's borders brought both goods and ideas from other societies, often from the Islamic world which was closest to Europe. The transmission of the classic books of the Greco-Roman world via these inter-cultural contacts, coupled with the scholarship that began to flourish in Medieval universities, ultimately led to the translation and dissemination of the works of the classics into wider circulation.

The recovery of the heritage of ancient Greece began in the late middle ages as scholars from the West who read only Latin visited such places as the libraries of Seville and Cordoba in Spain. In the areas controlled by the Moors, the Muslims who ruled southern Spain, there was a fairly modern degree of religious tolerance; Jews, Muslims and Christians coexisted, and scholars from around Europe found both manuscripts and the time to translate and discuss them. Scholars could also visit libraries elsewhere in the Eastern Byzantine world, or even in Egypt or the Levant.

The invention of the printing press would have a profound impact on the accessibility of works from classical Greece, from which humanism began, as well as the availability of the Bible in the vernacular languages of Europe, which sparked the Protestant Reformation. This single technological invention made possible wider education and literacy through the more available copies of books. The importance of this invention in human history is primary. Newspapers and magazine emerged later, in the modern era. But the dissemination of knowledge through printing enabled the growth of an intellectual culture, a common discourse of those who were well read to one degree or another. This flowering of an intelligentsia in the Renaissance period marks a major prelude to the modern era.

One of the most important consequences of this dissemination of knowledge and commentary is the emergence of humanism as a world view. Humanism shifts the focus of intellectual concern from the salvation of the soul in the after life to the here and now conditions of human existence. It was both a movement in art and in ideas. In art, the human form was once again portrayed with naturalism, dimensionality and even nakedness. In the realm of ideas several thinkers of the Italian Renaissance moved philosophy toward an emphasis on individual dignity and freedom of choice. Giovani Pico della Mirandola (1463-1499) wrote a famous essay, *Oration on the Dignity of Man*, which begins a long tradition leading to the Enlightenment idea of individual rights at the end of the eighteenth century. His views were declared heretical in part, and he had to flee Rome. Humanism had to struggle against the power of the Catholic Church to enforce orthodoxy and dissuade ideas that threatened the existing order. Desiderus Erasmus (1466-1536) was a Dutch scholar whose work *The praise of folly* (1511), used satire to critique the Catholic Church. Though we now associate humanism with agnosticism or atheism, in the Renaissance most of the leading figures who are considered humanists are spiritual men who just challenged the rigid enforcement of narrow orthodoxy. Only in recent decades was the epithet, secular humanism, coined as a pejorative phrase in the current debate between religion and science.

The Renaissance was the last period in European history when a magical or animistic world view was still part of the mainstream of acceptable thought or practice. Mirandola (1463-1499) translated the Hermetic Corpus, a body of classical magical writings as well as the works of the Neo-Platonists like Plotinus, Porphyry and Iamblichus. Beyond this period the modern world begins, with the emergence of science and the rejection of spiritual world views and the co-emergence of completely secular set of world views and philosophies emerge in concert with the technological advances with which had co-evolved.

The best example of how magic was still a part of healing comes from the diaries of Rev. Dr. Richard Napier, an astrological physician (1559-1643) as told by the British scholar Ian MacDonald (1981). Napier gave his casebooks to the Ashmolean Museum at Oxford University, where they lay in dusty neglect until recently. The log of cases provide an penetrating insight into Elizabethan and Jacobean English thought and practice of healing for disorders which now would be recognized as psychological. He practiced medicine in Oxfordshire, and drew from all classes of society, though mostly the gentry, an early middle class between the peasantry and aristocracy, though he had both as small elements in his overall experience. In short, he was an independent practitioner of the healing arts for all sorts of local complaints by people of the broad middle of English society. He seems to have specialized, however, in the more psychological or emotional ailments. Women were more numerous than men as clients, even as now there were gender differences in utilization of psychological services. The stresses that precipitated the visits to Dr. Napier were remarkably modern in nature,

24% had troubled courtships, 18% had marital problems, 18% were suffering bereavement, and 13% had economic problems. Individual private general practice seemed to focus on relationship issues or circumstantial issues in large part for Dr. Napier, and this parallels modern practice. The nature of human problems then do not differ that much from our modern understanding, the basic causes of suffering are shared across the ages. He did not specialize in the very disturbed, though he had some in his practice who were clearly mad, but the bulk of his concerns were those of the ordinary person with unhappy human connections.

His conceptualization of the clusters of symptoms and signs have some similarities and some differences from now. Their categories were abstracted from symptoms reported in 2, 483 consultations. Melancholia, or depression were part of 493 cases, grieving was found in 328 cases, fears accounted for complaints in 305 cases. But some of his categories are less clearly related to modern ones. *Mopish* was a symptom in 377 cases, *light-headed* was noted in 372 cases, and *distraction* was found in 134 cases, though the meanings of these terms are different from modern usage. The entry in his case book for *troubled in mind* was found in 794 cases, a fairly general description of distress. Clusters which correspond to the ancient designation of mania accounted for the most severe cases. These would probably be a combination of bipolar and schizophrenic diagnoses in the modern formulation.

Astrology constituted one his most frequent bases of diagnosis and conceptualization. As noted above, this was probably the last time when this was the cutting edge, and from here it declined as an explanatory system for understanding the human condition. It remains, even now, as a expression of minority esoteric Western thought. Despite popular newspaper horoscopes, astrology ceases to have mainstream credibility as a symbol system of importance. Yet the system of astrology in this period represents a continuous refinement of a stream of symbolic meanings and categories originating in ancient Babylonia and other societies filtered through the Western core of both exoteric and esoteric mythic structures. His treatments were based in Galenic theory, using herbal medicines, and Paracelcian theory, which embodied the new esoteric theory of metals and magnetism. He also used magical means, using amulets and talismans and the even performing healing rituals, including formal exorcism. So he combined a series of natural and supernatural means communicated through his personal consultations and conversations with his clients. As we shall see in the next chapter, the basis of modernity is the rise of empiricism and science as epistemologies coupled with technological innovations in sailing and weaponry that open up the globe to exploration and colonization by European countries.

## The Protestant Reformation

The problems of defining orthodoxy is a problem for any large religion where belief is a big part of the glue that holds it together. Defining orthodoxy, and its dialectical opposite, heresy, had taken up time and energy in Christianity since the early Ecumenical Councils from the fourth through eighth centuries of the common era. Movements aimed at reforming the Catholic Church grew over the course of the Middle Ages, several themes come together and create another major fracture point in Europe history. As the Church had consolidated its position of both spiritual control and secular hegemony of influence, it had also grown rich and bureaucratic. It controlled the rents from large tracts of land to support monasteries, bishoprics, and the ecclesiastical structure growing up around cathedrals. Moral discipline among clergy was often lax, which was lampooned by the bawdy literature and songs of the era. Voices of protest rose against the Church. This reform movement rapidly spread in the fifteenth and sixteenth centuries. It became not just a heretical sect, but a whole new type of religion. This was the Protestant Reformation.

Martin Luther (1483-1546) was a German priest who first posted his theses disputing the prevailing orthodoxy in Catholicism on the door of the Wittenburg castle church in 1517. Several other reformers had surfaced previously, but had usually been put to death or otherwise silenced. So Luther was not the beginning of the religious ferment we call the Reformation, but he was the catalyst to its rapid growth. Fortunately, Luther found sufficient followers, among the people and among powerful princes in Germany. This allowed the movement to survive and go forward as a major social force across northern Europe. The Protestant Reformation eventually split western Europe but there was less influence of reformers in areas where Eastern Orthodox Christianity prevailed, among the Slavs of eastern Europe.

A key to the success of the Protestant Reformation, unlike earlier schismatic movements, was the invention of printing by press and movable type. This made possible much more rapid dissemination of information in the form of printed material. The Bible was the first book printed by Gutenberg, who is credited with invention of a practical printing technology in 1440 CE. In the late Middle Ages people started to write in the vernacular languages, French, German, English, rather than exclusively in Latin. There was also strong pressure to translate the Bible into the vernacular and made it widely available to all. The quantum leap in the availability of books that resulted from the invention of the press suddenly made literacy a key to independence from the church. If you could read the Bible yourself rather than hear only what the priest teaches you, then you could form your own opinion of what it means to follow God's will. The genie was out of the bottle, Pandora's box had be opened.

The availability of the Bible in the language of the people led to the modern forms of Protestant Christianity. The newly acquired access to Scripture resulted in preaching and hymn singing dominating Protestant worship, whereas the earlier Catholic worship, the Mass, was a drama with high ritual. But the form of modern evangelical Christian worship was slow to catch on. People were reluctant to abandon practices that had stood the test of many centuries, so some Protestant denominations even today are more liturgically oriented and have the Eucharist, or sacred meal and communion, as a central feature of worship. Anglicans, the Church of England disagreed only on matters of governance at first, with Henry VIII's need for a divorce. Lutherans still keep the liturgy of Eucharist as well. With Presbyterians and Methodists you get more of a feel for the dominance of preaching, even though a Eucharist is still used. There is a continuum between more or less ritual and use of colorful vestments, incense and so on that marks the boundary created by the Reformation.

Another major doctrine was the priesthood of all believers. The central role of priest as mediator between God and individuals through dispensing grace through the sacraments, especially Eucharist, was rejected. Not only was the mystery of the Mass abandoned, but the role of the ordained priesthood shifted as well. The initial movement was for more independence from Rome and papal control, but increasingly even local hierarchies were challenged. So some Protestants, Anglicans and Lutherans retain bishops, but others rejected that type of governance. More governance by laity also became the norm. John Knox founded the religious movement in Scotland known as Presbyterianism. Presbyterians rejected bishops and vested governance in a council of elders, or presbyters. The initially much smaller movements like Anabaptists were completely local as organized groups, there was no formal hierarchy and often had clergy with no formal training as priests, but who had a Bible and could attract a following with their preaching. Not only was the governance becoming more democratic and decentralized, but the clergy could marry and have families. This opened up religious leadership to a larger number of men. Priestly celibacy was actually relatively recent in Roman Catholic tradition, but the pressure to open spiritual leadership up to men with wives and families was quite radical, but met a need.

By the 1600s the conflict Protestants constituted a majority of the population across many areas of northern Europe. Pockets of Catholics in Protestant areas, or vice versa made for many flash points between Protestant and Catholics. The conflict became quite bloody, with waves of persecutions and wars of conquest and/or rebellion, depending on who is telling the story. The princes of northern Germany, Holland, and Scandinavia were supporters of the Protestant cause, whereas the Kings of France and Spain, and the Holy Roman Emperor, dominated by the Austrian Hapsburgs were the major forces for Catholicism and the Counter-Reformation. In France, persecution of Protestants (Huguenots) took a particularly nasty turn on August 24, 1572 when the St. Bartholomew's Day massacre of Huguenot leaders precipitated a periodic of mass murder leaving an estimated 100,000 dead by the time it spread from Paris wreaking death through the rest of France. The height of the religious wars in Europe was the Thirty Years War (1618-1648). The German princes and their territories remained divided between Protestant and Catholic, the Dutch won their independence and remained largely Protestant. The end result was a religious stalemate where Protestantism and Catholicism predominate in a generally north to south geographic boundary in Western Europe.

# 6

# Modernity

WHAT IS MODERNITY? WHAT does it mean to say we are in a post-modern period? We focus on four developments in this chapter that define modernity: First, the basis for today's globalization of our lives via the history of European colonial expansion. Second, the spread of a secular world view, a way of looking at the world independent of any spiritual or religious framework. Third, the shift in philosophy toward the importance of epistemology, and the dialectic between rationalism and empiricism as a necessary step in the development of science. Fourth, the emergence in the Enlightenment of a broad understanding about the nature of individual human rights along with the reform movement in the treatment of mental illness which arose from those ideas.

## The age of European colonization

What has been termed the Age of Discovery is the European view of the beginnings of colonization and empire. The native peoples of the globe might view it as the Age of Subjugation. Those are the twin sides of the reality that large parts of the world became parts of European colonial empires. We are now in a post-colonial era and those of us in countries that had empires, however lately acquired, now look back with some mixture of shame, anxiety, and nostalgia, about what was proudly held up as the best gift of civilization. Voices that praised spreading civilization to backward natives for their own good now seem completely out of place.

We are generally familiar with the received version of this story. Spanish and Portuguese mariners paved the way with trans-oceanic voyages making use of two new technologies, the stern-post rudder and square-rigged sails. First they traveled down the coast of Africa to the Azores.. One route went around the tip of Africa into the Indian Ocean, to India, Indonesia and into the Pacific. The other route went westward across the Atlantic to the Americas, and soon Magellan's expedition circumnavigated the globe (though he did not survive it). Finally, even the vast Pacific Ocean yielded its secrets to other European navigators. The Dutchman Abel Tasman charted parts of Australia. Englishman Capt. James Cook further identified various islands; his voyages followed the routes of the Manilla galleons when Spain alone sailed the Pacific Ocean. The beginning of our global world does not date from 1492 when Columbus discovered land in the Caribbean, rather it begins in 1522 when the remnants of Magellan's global circumnavigation return to port, without their leader.

One institution that developed in that era is the multi-national corporation. The first one was the British East India Company, founded in 1600, followed by the Dutch East India Company, founded in 1602. European countries varied greatly with respect to how they exploited the riches they encountered. Spain and Portugal found the lure of gold enchanting. The Spanish economy, in particular, was dependent on gold from the new world. The various countries differed in the harshness with which native peoples were treated. The Spanish earned a reputation for blunt force, whereas the French and Dutch emphasized trade and formation of alliances as means to spreading their influence. Christianity and European ideas about private property, morality, propriety and individualism were passed on along with the European languages. Much of the current distribution of languages throughout the world is related to the European country which was the colonial power. Latin America speak Spanish or Brazilian, a variant of Portuguese. Elsewhere English or French became a second common language linking other smaller tribal languages in a national or regional commonwealth.

The opening salvo in the wars of independence, launched by colonial peoples against the mother land, was the American revolution. Haiti was second to succeed, throwing off their colonial masters, but slave owners in the U.S. south prevented America from supporting what was seen as a slave rebellion in Haiti, allowed French forces to retake the island. Then the revolutionaries, Simon Bolivar (1783-1830) in Venezuela, and José de San Martín in Argentina broke with Spain. Mexico also asserted its independence from Spain under Miguel Hidalgo (1753-1811) and held on to it under Augustín de Iturbide (1783-1824). Spain became the first big loser in the era of European colonialism and began to suffer the profound changes both economic and in terms of national self perception.

Late entries into the scramble to gobble up parts of the globe were the Germans, who did not begin building an empire until they unified in the late nineteenth century. They claimed some parts of Africa and some islands in the Pacific and the United States. Those islands passed to Australia, the United States and Japan in the wake of World War I. The United States entered the game of empire even later in the Spanish-American war in 1898. America seized the Spanish colonies of the Phillipines and Guam in the Pacific, and Cuba and Puerto Rico in the Caribbean. Native Americans, however, see the whole of the continental United States as simply a continuation of the colonization by Europeans begun centuries before. Russia established a land based empire, spreading across the northern reaches of Siberia to the Pacific, then taking over various independent central Asian khanates over the course of the nineteenth century.

Britain maintained, even expanded its empire after the loss of the United States. It's decline began in 1947 when India, the jewel in the crown, gained independence and was partitioned into modern day India, Pakistan and Bangladesh. The end of World War II brought on the independence of most of the other former European colonies in the 1950s and 1960s. Among the last handovers was Hong Kong, which was returned to China in 1997.

The boundaries of the nation states that emerged in the twentieth century out of the older empires were often arbitrary and an uncomfortable amalgam of ethnic groups. Mesopotamia, now Iraq, was a province of the Ottoman empire. In the wake of World War I, it was carved up between British and French spheres of influence in the Sykes-Picot agreement. Modern Iraq is a painfully open sore spot where European powers imposed national boundaries and it is an open question whether a sense of national identity among its disparate communities can be sustained. The split between Shiite in the south and Sunnis in the north and west result in fodder for sectarian conflicts. The Kurds are split between modern Turkey, Iran and Iraq. Unfortunately, autocracies (dictatorships) and kleptocracies (government by thieves) have been the rule rather than the exception for so many countries' first or early post-colonial independent governments.

The economic and cultural dominance of the West is still strong, even after the political bonds of empire and colonialism have been reshaped a number of times. Following World War II America rose to its dominance as a world power not only politically and economically, but culturally. Hollywood movies have influenced global popular culture. We now turn to the intellectual developments that lead to modern thought in general and professional psychology in particular.

## Secular world view

One of the major markers of modernity is rise of the secular viewpoint, that is, a view of the world through lenses not grounded in a religious or spiritual philosophy. A secular world view is both pervasive, coming with science and Western culture, and the focal point of resistance. Indeed, many of the sources of present day conflicts are based in a type of fundamentalist rejection and reaction to some aspect of the secularism of modern developed societies. Whether it is the teaching of evolution in the public schools of Kansas, or the blind eye that continues to be turned on the subject of honor killing of young women in traditionalist societies of the Middle East and Indian sub-continent, modernity has its foes.

As noted in an earlier chapter, even in the Middle Ages when European culture was so clearly dominated by the Catholic Church, there was secular life. Songs of love, spring, and youth are preserved from the middle ages in the collection known as *Carmina Burana*. Yet, much of intellectual life in the Medieval period was still dominated by religion. As Europe divided between Catholic and Protestant, the importance of religion intensified. Certainly the distinction between the sacred and the mundane go back as far as antiquity, but what distinguishes the modern period is not the growing presence of secular life, but the shift in intellectual authority toward multiple sources of authority.

Secularism as a way of thinking, arises out of the awareness that there are other sources of authority than religion for ideas and practices. Authority comes in many forms. The most clear cut is force of arms under pain of death. Below that level we have police power for civil order, with power to arrest, question, detain, and charge with crime. Thus, law and physical, raw, power go hand in hand. Social power comes in many additional forms. In the family, power is interactional and emotional in nature. Home is where the nurturant power of support is most concentrated.

The marketplace defines the broader economic context of authority. Foreign trade whether it be between equals or forced by colonialism clearly sets the context in which families can function. Other social powers such as education, class, religion exert other types of social power or authority. All forms of social power and authority have in common the power of persuasion, motivating people to go along with the norm. The market for goods expanded with the Industrial revolution in the nineteenth century so that people today often define themselves by their possessions.

Intellectual or ideological authority comes by control of the discourse, the conversation, the buzz. Foucault (1970) has emphasized how the control of discourse, especially the categories by which we think and talk about a problem, support the current prevailing social structure. He draws our attention to this fact as a critique of society. But no discourse is completely value neutral, no way of looking at the world is divorced from the concrete social structures which embody the power relationships between groups of people. He applied this thesis to the analysis of the rise of mental hospitals, prisons, and even the medical definition of sexuality.

One of the synergistic effects of the coffee house was the development of our modern mass media. First, newspapers were quickly printed and distributed, posted to buildings and circulated among coffee house patrons. By the end of the eighteenth century, Benjamin Franklin had begun to pen advice and aphorisms which he then distributed to his readers in Philadelphia. The very existence of an informed public which could make its voice known, peacefully through written essays or through muscular mob action was made possible by the development of this means of disseminating knowledge and opinion. The internet has now so democratized discourse that the distinction between facticity and falsehood becomes blurred in the minds of many.

Yet another major alternate source of authority was the power of the state to control civil affairs. The modern nation state based on the principle of sovereignty emerges in this period. People of the Middle Ages were Burgundians, or Piccards, their identities were regional. Under Louis XIVth, the Sun King, they became French. Nationalism as an ideology became increasingly important, merging many regional differences in a common sense of patriotism. England, coalesced into Great Britain as they incorporated

Welsh and Scots into one kingdom. The Germans remained politically disunited as did the Italians. Cultural nationalism often preceded political nationalism. The period of German idealism as a philosophical and artistic movement in the early part of the nineteenth century certainly facilitated the rise of one dominant kingdom, Prussia, to form a second German Reich, or unitary government, the first being the Holy Roman Empire. But, however early or late, nationalism brought further economic, political and social integration from regional allegiances to a sense of nationhood.

## Epistemology

A fundamental revolution in philosophy took place during the early modern era. Up to the sixteenth and seventeenth centuries, the primary questions were about what exists, the nature of the world, a branch of philosophy called metaphysics. Epistemology is the branch of philosophy that deals with questions of knowledge. How do we know and how do we justify our claims to knowledge? The twin schools that offered different answers to those questions were rationalism and empiricism.

Joseph Rychlak (1977) noted these competing epistemologies as a watershed for developments in psychology. There has been a great divide in philosophical traditions within European philosophy. The contrasting views of British empiricism and continental rationalism set the stage for the development of the two views of psychology that would arise. American psychology has been heavily influenced by the Anglo-American empiricist stream, resulting in behaviorism. European approaches to psychology, psychoanalysis and phenomenology, were born from rationalist roots, though modified by Kant's attempt to synthesize the two viewpoints. They have attracted relatively minor followings in America. Rychlak sees the fundamental dichotomy in American psychology as one between a Kantian and a Lockean perspective. The psychodynamic theories of Freud as well as the entire humanistic stream which includes phenomenology, gestalt, and existentialism, they all owe much of their philosophical underpinnings to Kantian perspective.

Rychlak emphasized the importance of the difference between demonstrative and dialectic reasoning for defining the two main streams within psychology. Dialectic reasoning, the Kantian approach, gives meaning by the relationship of one thing to another. For example, we know the meaning of night by its relationship to day, and vice versa. Lockean psychology emphasizes demonstrative reasoning, pointing to the concrete and specific manifestation of a concept to show its meaning. Lockean psychology is more object focused, treating psychological subject matter in a social, consensual manner seeking consistency of accounts across individual observers, and grounding it in mathematical rigor and precision where possible. Kantian psychology is more subject focused, treating the personal, subjective perspective as a central determiner of human experience. Neither can be a sufficient foundation for a comprehensive psychology, since we straddle the boundary between self and other, between subjective and objective perspectives. Rychlak's narrative sees the history of American psychology based in the tension between these streams. Each are the sources of both psychodynamic and humanistic-existential thought on the one hand and the behavioral stream on the other. The challenge is finding ways of both perspectives co-existing in the overall enterprise of psychology.

Rene Descartes (1596-1650) was the first in a line of thinkers who advanced a position now known as rationalism. After Descartes came Benedict Spinoza (1632-1677) and Gottfried Wilhelm Leibniz (1647-1717). The rationalist stream of thought moved on through the work of Immanuel Kant (1724-1804) who sought to integrate the ideas of both schools. He was another of those towering figures in philosophy and much of German philosophy in the nineteenth century was in reaction to his ideas. The German idealist philosophies came after Kant in the nineteenth century. Georg W. F. Hegel (1770-1831), Arthur Schopenhauer (1778-1860) and Friederich Nietzsche (1844-1900), all carried forward or modified aspects of Kant's positions.

The empiricists begin with Sir Francis Bacon (1561-1625) who emphasized the role of induction in scientific reasoning. He was followed by Thomas Hobbes (1588-1679) who is best known for his political theory. John Locke (1632-1704), articulated perhaps the best known position among the empiricists. The stream continues with George Berkeley (1685-1753) and David Hume (1711-1776). It should be noted that the empiricist tradition is often called British empiricism, since it originated in Great Britain (Lock was English, Hume was Scottish, and Berkeley was a professor at Trinity College, in Dublin, Ireland, all of which were under the British crown at that point). The behavioral stream of thought descends from British empiricism.

Descartes, sought to find a sure foundation of knowledge, something that could not be doubted. He began by examining his own mind, using introspection as his method. That method influenced the selection of method for early experimental psychology. Reflective self-examination was a way to find knowledge based in experience. He came to bedrock and could not doubt that his awareness of his own thought was something he could not doubt. He is famous for the saying *cogito ergo sum*, Latin for I think, therefore, I am. This places thought itself in a place of psychological and philosophical primacy. The whole basis of the cognitive revolution in psychology owes a debt to Descartes for focusing us on the nature of human cognition itself as an object of study. Though at this time the study was by reason alone and only drawing on some common sense observations.

He also gave us a systematic form of mind-body dualism. This was a restatement of much of Western philosophy which incorporated Plato's, or more generally, the Greek view that there were two different substances, mind and matter. He emphasized the importance of the innate structuring capacity of the mind to shape experience. Descartes also gives us an early account of the stimulus-response reflex arc. His belief in the power of reason was embodied in his work in mathematics. His psychology was in part organized around his understanding of primary and secondary qualities.

Primary qualities, such as being one or many, being round or square, inhere in the object. Secondary qualities, like color and texture exist in the mind of the perceiver.

Descartes' views were in contrast to Locke's view on mind. At birth mind is a blank slate, or tabula rasa, upon which experience writes and creates learning. To Locke experience is grounded in sensory experience; the mind was more passive and received impressions through the senses which then were further processed with memory. Berkeley's famous dictum is *esse es percipi*, to be is to be perceived. He thus takes Locke's emphasis on perception and observation to an extreme, which led him to idealism, that is, everything exists in mind. Berkeley is most remembered in psychology for his theory of vision.

Rationalism emphasized the power of mind to grasp reality and the primacy of reason, especially in its more structured paths as logic. That component of modern science which embodies the abstractions of mathematics and the logical derivation of propositions arises out of a rationalistic set of assumptions. Reason may need to be specified in numbers, but reason can be advanced linguistically as well. Empiricism, by contrast, emphasized the power of observation. This, despite the growing awareness that naive sensation or perception can be fallacious, and that perception aided by telescopes and microscopes can yield powerful visions of worlds greater or smaller than the unaided eye. Empiricism found a key concept in the term idea which it saw as the raw impression of the outer world on the mind via sensation. Locke stated the notion that the idea was the basic unit or element of mind. All simple ones could be combined into more complex ones, thus accounting for the panoply of complicated thoughts we experience.

Rationalism and empiricism both put great stock in the concept of experience, though each emphasized different aspects of it. Continental rationalism would lead, ultimately to phenomenology, the examination of subjectivity, and the human science perspective; British empiricism would lead to a logical positivist view of science, and a materialistic reductionism. The difference between innate mental structures and acquired mental structures, between nature and nurture is a convenient way of summarizing the tension and differences between these two schools of philosophy.

One development of interest for psychology comes from Leibniz (1646-1716). His doctrine of the monad is of particular relevance for personality theory. The monad was like an atom, it was a thing of matter than was indivisible, a primary unit. But it differed in one important way; it was a source of activity and capable of experience. He adopted a position that to some degree or another, all things have a type of consciousness or awareness; this has been termed panpsychism (Skrbina, 2007). The quality of the experience of a unit of matter is quite different from human experience in degree and quality, but the two share some common thread, not only as objects, but as subjects. While a literal interpretation of this idea may strike many as ludicrous and mentalistic (indeed such has been a criticism), yet we can see in our modern understanding of the self a chord of resonance. The self is the model for the monad;

the self experiences organismic unity and active interaction with the environment. Leibniz' idea of monad expresses what it would be like if personhood were found, albeit attenuated at other levels of organization that the human individual.

The movement in philosophy from Descartes to Kant gave psychology competing paradigms of how one can be confident in knowledge. These differences between Anglo-American empiricism and continental rationalism persist; though the continental stream has now been filtered through German idealism of the nineteenth century and is better termed phenomenology.

## The Enlightenment and the doctrine of human rights

From about 1730-1800 developments in European philosophy formed a body of thought that is called the Age of Enlightenment in which reason was elevated as the chief source of wisdom and, in particular, of sound principles for organizing society. Reason was not solely equated with the rigor of logic or mathematics, but a broad approach to all forms of human activity. It is no accident that the principal bequest of this time period is found in political and social philosophy.

This political and economic ideas of the Enlightenment came to be known as liberalism (not necessarily related to the current use of that term in American politics, nor with the more recent concept of neoliberalism). The modern concept of the liberal/conservative dimension, particularly in America, is based on some but not all of the ideas of classical liberalism. Indeed, most of the elements of classical liberalism are now part of the basic assumptions of modern politics. The general goal is to maximize liberty. There are several elements in this world view, 1) rule of law, 2) representative republican government created through elections, 3) open and free markets for both ideas (freedom of thought and press), as well as in goods and services (economic) and, 4) a doctrine of individual rights recognizing individual dignity and emphasizing personal choice (decisional autonomy) as a general rule.

A professional code of ethics governing the relationship between client or patient implies some form of contract as the basis of the relationship, some sort of mutuality of obligation and expectation. This is but one aspect of the broader concept of the social contract that came to prominence in the political thought of the Enlightenment.

The idea of a social contract stems largely from the conflict between the British monarch, Charles I, and Parliament. He championed the idea of the divine right of kings, but Parliament thought otherwise, seeing sovereignty resting fundamentally with the people who were governed. Society is formed implicitly in a grant of rights to those who govern in exchange for certain benefits such as protection from foreign invasion and the provision of some of the infrastructure like roads and markets aimed at promoting the common wealth. Thomas Hobbes (1588-1679) then John Locke (1632-1704), articulated these ideas with the English civil war as the context. Hobbes likened government to a monster, *Leviathan* (1651) which is composed by all of us together and is in a perpetual state of war, each person jostling and jockeying for advantage. Peace is only obtained by social contract, be agreement. Locke elaborated on the idea of a tacit agreement underlying the legitimacy of government. We each seek our own benefit but allow government because it provides some important benefits. Those who govern do not do so by divine right, but by the consent of the governed. These ideas were later embodied quite clearly in the Declaration of Independence for the United States of America. When a government violates the social contract it can be changed or repudiated by the people.

The market place became a central element of classical liberal thought. The ownership of property was a fundamental right in Locke's philosophy. Adam Smith (1723-1790) then elaborated on how the market itself is governed by the natural forces of supply and demand. His version of modern capitalism has been recognized as seminal and a foundation of modern thought. By the mid nineteenth century, however, the effects of both industrialization and early free market capitalism resulted in a dialectic opposition. Karl Marx (1818-1883) introduced the idea of class conflict and made the first statement about both the economics and the psychology of modern industrial capitalism. His theories of social organization are grounded in the alienation of the laborer from the product of his labor. Modern Marxist psychologists such as Marcuse (1964) have seen the psychological alienation of the worker as linked to the psychodynamic theories of Freud.

The political enumeration of rights came from the philosophies of the American and French revolution. Such statesmen and thinkers as Thomas Jefferson, Tom Paine, James Madison, Benjamin Franklin and John Adams set the tone for the new order of things, a *novus ordo seclorum* (McDonald, 1985). The French followed up the American Bill of Rights with their own declaration of human rights. Each individual was constituted as a free person to seek their life, liberty and pursuit of happiness; at least that was the aspiration.

## Reform and active treatment

The philosophy of human rights had one practical implication with regard to mental illness. These ideas brought about reform efforts in both France, Britain, and later, America. Dr. Phillipe Pinel (1745-1826) was appointed head of the Salpetriere and Bicetre asylums in Paris during the French Revolution. He found the situation typical for asylums, conditions were deplorable. The patients were confined and warehoused in a pitiable condition. In the age of reason, to have lost one's reason reduced one to the level on an animal. Like animals, their needs could be more easily managed. There was no heat or adequate ventilation. Good care was measured by minimally adequate food of soup or gruel and bread, bedding was straw, and as in barns it was raked out and replaced as it got soiled with human waste. The most violent were chained to the wall. Many were manacled as well, though allowed to walk about. There was very little in the way of active treatment or care, except as wealthy family might pay for medical care. Bleeding and herbal remedies that induced vomiting or diarrhea (emetics and purgatives) were the order of the day. There was little attempt by staff to do more than control the level of behavioral disturbance by verbal or physical means.

This is not to say that there were not verbal or social interactions between staff and patients, but there was no theory or sense of how or why it might work better than meeting out punishments for misbehavior and encouragements to think clearer. Pinel came into this situation with a generally positive frame of mind, inspired by the optimistic ideology of revolutionary France. Pinel was painted by Robert-Fleury in the dramatic moment of unshackling the patients of the asylum, this scene has become iconographic of reform in the treatment of mental illness. This image has been used by psychiatry as its founding moment. Science and humane practice step in to end a period of barbarism.

Across the English channel, a more systematic approach to treatment was implemented by William Tuke (1732-1822) a wealthy Quaker merchant in York, in the north of England. He was appalled at the conditions in the asylum in his area, so he founded a new facility, the York Retreat. His son, Henry Tuke (1755-1814) and his son, Samuel Tuke (1784-1857), continued the operation of the facility. Their approach to treatment was called *moral treatment*. Samuel's sons James Hack Tuke (1819-1896) managed the Retreat and his brother, Daniel Hack Tuke (1827-1895) wrote a leading treatise in 1858, *A manual of psychological medicine*. The Tuke family thus appears as a veritable dynasty of philanthropists and physicians who specialized in care for the mentally ill.

Unlike the run of the mill custodial care for the mentally ill, this was a very active approach. It was based on the use of reason and correction. The staff would maintain surveillance of the activities of the patient and would encourage them and correct them in their thinking and activities. Being a Quaker center, prayer and religious observance were important parts of the experience. It was all conducted in a family like atmosphere, where the staff were encouraged to take on a more caring attitude, as if the patient was a family member. Benign paternalism is a good description of the dominant attitude taken by staff towards their charges. Civilized discourse was encouraged. Dinners would be opportunities to engage in polite and elevated conversation and decorous manners. All of this was aimed at increasing the self control of the individual patient.

This was considered quite a forward looking institution in its day. Several visiting American Quakers brought back these ideas to the United States and founded asylums on this model. The first American asylum was located in colonial Williamsburg in Virginia, and was unrelated to these developments, but Bloomingdale's asylum, the Hartford Retreat, McClean Hospital and others sprang up using variants of the moral treatment approach (Bell, 1980). The York Retreat continues its existence today, though its approach is more contemporary and conventional. Moral treatment was a promising application of Enlightenment ideas about the possibilities inherent in a view of humans as rational or potentially rational beings. It stands as a clear cut advance over the general attitude of neglect and confinement which was the rule. This was a beneficial application of notions of human rights to mental health care.

This was part of a much larger movement for reform tackling a much graver problem. Slavery became a moral issue in Britain and American. Abolitionist movements were spurred in, part, by a great wave of evangelization that spread across America in the 1820s, the great awakening. This became the dominant issue in America by the 1860s, leading ultimately to a civil war as a resolution of this controversy. A nascent temperance movement got started in America which underwent a wave of heavy alcohol abuse, a great binge in ante-bellum and in particular, Jacksonian (1830s) America.

Dorothea Dix (1802-1887) championed the cause of the mentally ill. She had traveled to Britain and saw the work being done there with such places as the York Retreat and others, and brought the message home to America. She agitated in her home of Massachusetts and began making headway in improving the care to the mentally ill. She was most helpful in setting up public mental hospitals that would take people who otherwise would wind up in the county jail. The jail was a multi-purpose repository of the unruly, dangerous, and the disabled. Little provision was made for separating out people by nature of their condition, they were sources of civil disorder by their very existence as well as behavior. This wave of reform begun by Dix resulted in the emergence of the modern state mental health bureaucracies. It led to an almost universal sponsorship by the government of large institutions separately segregated by class; criminals went to prisons and penitentiaries, the mentally ill went to asylums, the congenitally deaf or blind and the mentally retarded often had separate institutions.

In America, the dominant legal structure for handling dependent adults was the Elizabethan Poor Law of (1601). This gave the British shires, or translated into the American political idiom, the counties, the responsibility for caring for those who could not care for themselves. This meant that the problem was kept local. The sheriff of the county would often house mentally ill, disabled, and others in the same facility as criminals. It was this prevailing practice that spurned Dix and other reformers on, forcing larger political entities, the state, in the American case, to take responsibility for maintaining facilities that were specialized for the treatment for the mentally ill, the sensory impaired (blind, deaf or mute). The county poor farm was often used as a way of housing the indigent poor or disabled as well.

Bell (1980) noted that in the first half of the nineteenth century when moral treatment was popular there was an optimistic tone about the possibility of human change and the ability of reason to bring about. These hopes were soon overwhelmed in America by two demographic events. One was the increased waves of immigrants adding to general growth of population, the second was emancipation of the slaves in the south which allowed internal migration and the expansion of African-American communities in the north. Since education for African-Americans was limited, illiteracy was high. Thus, the mental hospitals not only had to deal with relatively well educated whites, they also had to deal with a population of immigrants and poor blacks. The sheer numbers as well as language and cultural barriers led to a regression in care by the end of the nineteenth century and a replacement of optimism with pessimism as to the possibility of active treatment of mental illness.

Total institutions are now out of fashion. The pendulum of public policy has now been going the other direction and de-institutionalization is an on-going public policy goal. We will consider that story later. The large state operated institutions which were founded as part of a reform movement represented at the time were a step forward in mental health care, but over time abuses and neglect would creep in and eventually dominate public perception. The movie *Snake Pit* (1948) is an example of how Hollywood looked back at the not too distant past at that time, and sensationalized the shoddy care of the mentally ill.

But total institutions had a positive side as well. Since people were generally there on a long-term basis, sometimes even for life, there was a sort of community. This led many hospitals to be situated in the country as opposed to the city. The concept of asylum, literally, meant retreat from the challenges and stimulations of the city and civilization. Self-sufficiency and the therapeutic value of work, values started in the earlier moral treatment, continued. To support these large institutions, the principle occupation of many of the patients who could work was farm labor. Work was considered a therapeutic activity and it contributed to sustaining the institution. The film from Longview State Hospital (Larson, 2005) highlights the self-sufficient nature of the institution. Medical leadership dominated the institutions. By 1844 there were enough institutions and enough momentum for organizing The Association of Medical Superintendents of American Institutions for the Insane, which later became the American Psychiatric Association. Over the course of much of the nineteenth century, and as a result of the reform efforts many states began setting up separate facilities for prisoners, the mentally ill, and also the blind, deaf or developmentally disabled. This was the real era of confinement and containment (Bell, 1980).

In France a similar reforming trend was applied to other sorts of disability in addition to mental illness. Children with sensory disabilities or what we now recognize as developmental disorders were given some new attention. The foundation of special education facilities and concepts for dealing with sensory and developmental disabilities emerged in France. Jean-Marc Itard (1775-1838) was a French physician who produced an early book on diseases of the eyes, ears, nose and throat (otorhinolaryngology), and pioneered means of educating the deaf. He is best known for his work with the so-called wild boy of Aveyron. This young child of 11 or 12 was found in the woods. Eventually, he was brought to Paris and placed in Itard's care. While Pinel declared him an idiot, Itard had hopes he could raise the boy's functional condition. He was superintendent of the National Institution for Deaf-Mutes, and spent five years educating this young man, who he named Victor. Itard was able to improve

Victor's capacity to interact with others and his social skills, but he would never be normal, as Itard had hoped. He was now what we would term pre-lingually deaf, that is, he had trouble learning the connection between sound and language (phonemes) so his entire language acquisition was seriously impaired. Plucker (2003) sees him as the first person to devise an Individual Educational Plan (IEP), and a patron of special education. An important figure was Jean Itard (1775-1838). Itard's students, Eduard Séguin and Maria Montessori went on to extend his pioneering efforts in education and especially for children who had sensory disabilities or developmental problems.

# 7

# The Sciences, Natural and Human

IN THIS CHAPTER WE chronicle the emergence of the fourth archetype of professional psychology, the scientist. The chapter deals primarily with the development of the sciences into the nineteenth century. Over the span of about three centuries the sciences as we know them developed, including psychology. A major thesis of this chapter is that the scientific underpinnings of psychology encompass both the natural sciences and the human sciences. Most students have just heard of science without any modifying adjectives. Scientific method is often considered broadly similar across specific disciplines. While there's broader agreement about the nature of the physical and life sciences, there are two contrasting views of how best to study human behavior and experience. The natural science approach takes the stance of an observer viewing an object from the outside, the human science approach takes the stance of the experiencing subject. The natural sciences grow out of an empiricist philosophy, whereas the human sciences grow out of the rationalist tradition, as filtered through Kant, and German idealism as proximal sources for phenomenology. This distinction is rooted in the much older one in Greek philosophy between the two understandings of law, between *phusis*, or the law of natural objects, and *nomos*, the constructed laws of human beings in culture.

One of the fundamental aspects of human experience and behavior is choice, agency, and purpose. People organize their behavior around goals so some account of teleology or purposiveness is necessary. As we shall see, the positivist philosophy of science which was adopted by the behavioral approach to psychology sought to banish purposive explanations as beyond the scope of science. But such a fundamental fact of human life could not be ignored or dismissed for long without being revived and given a place at the table of science.

## From natural philosophy to the natural sciences

Science, like most disciplines, evolved out of philosophy. It was first termed natural philosophy, or the philosophy of nature. The earliest layer of philosophy, the Milesian school of Greek antiquity first sought to describe *phusis*, the nature of things. Physics is derived from this etymological root. Aristotle covered what we would now call the natural sciences in the magisterial scope of his philosophy. Although he emphasized the value of experience, including sensation, more than Plato, his descriptions of natural phenomena clearly were lacking in observational basis and were largely speculative.

There were early versions of materialism, the doctrine that all that is fundamentally real is matter; also early versions of atomism, the doctrine that all matter is composed of minute indestructible units; called atoms. The best statement of that position in antiquity comes from the Roman Epicurean philosopher Lucretius (99-55 BCE), who wrote *De rerum natura*, roughly translated as *On natural things*. He gave us the etymological source of the term natural as applied to philosophy, or science. Increasingly over the course of philosophy, the terms and language by which basic questions about the natural world were put shifted toward impersonal, non-living naturalistic forces and factors. This has become developed as part of our very structure of thought in an almost unconscious manner since we do not think that tables have spirits and intentions; they are inanimate inert matter.

Part of science is the acceptance of matter as inert, passive, acted upon rather than acting. Science begins with the denial of animism as a doctrine and continues to seek non-personal concepts and forces as determinative of physical and living beings and their actions. Many living beings, and especially humans, show signs of agency, will or deliberate choice, but the sun, moon, stars and planets all move in very regular paths. Empirically, ancient astronomical observations were quite detailed. It was in part the application of mathematics to the explanation of observations that led to the triumph of the heliocentric view of the world. We accept mechanistic explanations of the interaction of inanimate objects accounted for by energy arising out of matter (as in thermal energy) or transferred from one object to another (as in kinetic energy).

Thomas Kuhn (1970) set out a major theory of the history of science based on paradigms, the collocation of both theories, procedures and instruments that define the consensus of normal science at a given point. Science does not change by small degrees. A paradigm prevails for a period of time, shaping what questions are asked and how they're answered. When a body of anomalous data accumulates there comes a tipping point where a new paradigm gains acceptance, not so much modifying the old paradigm, as replacing it, hence the concept of scientific revolution in general or several revolutions across time within a science.

The first struggle for a natural science making claims independent of spiritual authority began in the late Renaissance and early modern period and brought about the foundations of modern astronomy. Nicolas Copernicus (1473-1543) and Galileo

Galilei (1564-1642) challenged the geocentric view of the world with observations and calculations of planetary orbits that put the sun at the center of our local part of the universe (the heliocentric theory). The struggle between Galileo and the Roman Catholic Church exemplifies the early tension between a secular and naturalistic world view and a spiritual one.

The power of mathematics to explain the motions of the celestial bodies was convincing. The invention of the calculus by Isaac Newton (1643-1727) and Wilhelm Gottfried Leibniz (1646-1716) allowed significant advances in all manner of science. Newton's *Principia Mathematica* (1687) set out a magisterial body of mathematical theories of physics, force (mechanics), optics, dominating physics for nearly two centuries. Only with Albert Eienstein's theories of relativity in 1905 did a new paradigm come along to replace the mechanistic universe of Newton. Recently, Newton's alchemical and mystical diaries have been published, so he was not entirely taken up with materialistic reductionism as much of science has become.

Pepper's (1942) world hypothesis theory set out 4 such hypotheses which were minimally acceptable. The sciences have been involved in all four of them. The formistic part of the sciences developed directly out of the desire to classify the wide range of objects in the natural world and a variety of taxonomies has been the product of those efforts. From rocks to plants and animals, field science from the seventeenth century onward was a rush to collect, examine and describe the world's diversity of things. Carolus Linnaeus (1707-1778), a Swedish botanist, produced the first major classification system for plants and animals. His hierarchical taxonomic system of kingdoms, phyla and so on down to genera and species survives with modifications (e.g. modern cladistics) as the basic structure of understanding the amazing diversity of living beings on the planet. Early scientists sometimes accompanied or led expeditions of exploration. Alexander von Humboldt (1769-1859), for example, is known for his extensive detailed descriptions of geology, flora and fauna on his expeditions to the Americas, Africa and Asia. The mechanistic world hypothesis was advanced in the realms of astronomy, physics and chemistry, where the metaphor of the clockwork universe seemed to account for phenomena quite adequately. The world hypothesis of organicism derives from the advances in biology, and contexualism from the human sciences. Those stories follow in more detail.

One can't talk about the emergence of the sciences in the nineteenth century without talking about the broad movement in evolution. While we typically associate evolution with the emergence of biology, in fact, preceding and contemporary work in geology and the problem of the age of the earth were already in discussion among learned circles before Darwin advanced his major thesis in 1859. James Hutton's (1726-1797) paper in 1795 titled *Theory of the earth* put forth the idea that the earth was much older than we thought. Up to this time only a literal reading of Biblical chronology was used to estimate the age of the earth, several thousand years at most depending on whose version one relied on. In his notice of the time involved in both sedimentation, the laying down of layers by deposition, and erosion, or wearing away of layers he argued many thousands of years might be needed for present formations to come about. Charles Lyell's (1797-1875) 1830 *Principles of geology* further advanced the idea of stratigraphy, the deepest layers of the earth contain the oldest rocks and the surface shows recent geologic action. Thus a time line was inherent in the physical evidence of rock formations.

Charles Darwin (1809-1882) published his major book in 1859, the title was *On the origin of the species*. This becomes a watershed year in the history of science. He stated for the first time that humans were descended from lower animals, thus sparking an enormous cultural debate around religion and science which is still going on. As science took over the primacy in explanations of the inanimate and the animate realms, the human realm remained subject to explanation by religious or supernatural forces. Now Darwin challenged that and further more set out a mechanism by which change occurs. Natural selection of biological variation with respect to the demands of the environment was the mechanism by which species emerged and changed. Ultimately more species are created by on-going variation. Each organism is in some way different, and in many ways the same as the parent and home population of organisms. But over time certain variations have adaptive advantage and tend to persist, whereas others are either clear disadvantages and died out as the organisms with them are less adaptively suited to their environment. There is, of course, a normal range of variation of phenotypes within a species. Having stated a major thesis and provided a clear mechanism, he set out his evidence which came from years of observation as a naturalist, a field biologist. His famous trip to the Galapagos Islands on the HMS *Beagle* provided important specimens which aided development of his theory. After the genie was out of the bottle, several scientists adopted and championed his ideas. Among the most important defenders of Darwin was Thomas Huxley (1825-1895). His earlier work on taxonomy made an important contribution as well.

Herbert Spencer (1820-1903), however, took evolutionary ideas in a different direction. He was primarily a philosopher and interested in economic and political thought. His work most closely bears on the developing psychology. Unfortunately, his reputation is tainted by a trend he helped foster known as social Darwinism (Hofstader, 1944). This theory applied the principle of fitness of a species to the social standing of various peoples, races, ethnicities, and conditions. It was used to justify the view that non-European peoples were inferior, and that those with particular developmental challenges were likewise suffering from a biological taint that made them inferior. The eugenics movement came from this trend, which we'll detail later.

The science of human beings was first localized in physiology and medicine, the archetypal healer by natural means. Medical theory evolved out of Galen's synthesis of the Hippocratic beginnings. A greater empirical knowledge of anatomy preceded growth in physiology. A major barrier that needed breaching was anatomical knowledge through dissection. In Christian countries the doctrine of the resurrection made preservation of the intact body more important to the faithful, so access to internal anatomy was limited to what was revealed through wounds of war and accidents. Dissection of cadavers was otherwise generally prohibited as desecration. Condemned criminals were sometimes sources of fresh corpses for anatomical study. Throughout the nineteenth century body snatchers earned money by digging up fresh burials and selling the body to medical schools. Despite all this such advances as the understanding of the heart as the basis of circulation by William Harvey (1578-1657).

More importantly, advances in chemistry and microscopy allowed the germ theory of medicine to emerge as the role of bacteria in illness was demonstrated. Theodor Schwann (1810-1882) established cell theory in biology and physiology. Such advances as the need for cleanliness (sepsis) in surgery by Joseph Lister (1827-1912), or vaccines by Louis Pasteur (1822-1895). The precise relationship of causation of illness by microbes was established by Robert Koch (1843-1910) and Friederich Leffler (1852-1915) in 1884. Advances in chemistry facilitated those in pharmacology as first synthetic compounds refined from herbal preparation were made purer, but new compounds could be created and tried for their therapeutic effect. The growth of public sanitation came during this era, prompted by such medical innovations as mosquito control for malaria reduction, and the importance of refrigeration for food safety. So our modern framework for understanding health emerged in the late nineteenth century.

As the sciences, both physical and biological or physiological made rapid advances, so too did engineering and technology advance. By the mid nineteenth century there was a sense that this new age offered much promise. The French thinker August Comte (1798-1857) coined the term sociology and laid out a place for science as the pinnacle of human advancement. He summarized human intellectual development as a progression from an age of faith, an age of speculative thinking and the now arriving modern era, an era of scientific, or positive knowledge. He saw a sort of hierarchical ordering of the sciences, not unlike our modern understanding of the physical and life sciences. Sociology, was the apex of the sciences.

## The age of industrialization

While the development of the sciences is a theme of intellectual life in the nineteenth century, the whole fabric of life shifted with the advent of industrialization. Science helps develop technology. The laws of gasses was explained by Newton and Boyle, but it was the harnessing of steam under pressure to move people that heralded the beginning of industrialization. The power that drove society up to that point was human or animals, beasts of burden. But steam allowed railroads, steamships and suddenly the world shrank. The fastest a message could travel at the beginning of the 1800s was the distance of a mounted rider could travel with relays of fresh horses. Ships powered with steam were less dependent on the fickle strength of the winds. Railroads knit the world together; the first transcontinental railroad in the United States was completed in Utah in 1869. Mills to grind flour were powered by oxen, water wheels in rivers, or wind. But once steam had been put to use in engines, then the use of power to drive machines in factories quickly followed.

Steam engines required iron and used that mineral resource extensively. The engine itself as well as that which it was hitched to were all made of iron. Advances in metallurgy brought steel into large scale production by the end of the 1800s. But steam had to be generated in boilers, so first wood, then coal came into prominence as a fuel for industry. By the end of the 1800s the development of the internal combustion engine ushered in our modern use of petroleum based fuels.

Factories required labor, so jobs became available in the cities where manufacturing was a main industry. Labor was cheap, and conditions were squalid in the rapidly industrializing cities of Europe and America. The pollution in Los Angeles in the 1960s was nothing compared to the haze of coal smoke and soot that hung over London in the nineteenth century. Claude Monet's painting of the *House of Parliament, London,* (1871) was true to the environmental degradation which had already taken place. Sanitation did not significantly improve until the end of the nineteenth century when indoor plumbing and water purification became matters of public health. Even with steam ships and railroads, horses continued to provide most urban transportation until the twentieth century. But slowly over the course of the century industrialization worked its effects on the society and on the mind of those living in those changing urban landscapes. Industrialization was, of course, mostly an urban phenomenon.

The modern wage labor system began after the Black Death broke the back of feudalism as a shortage of workers put labor in a more favorable bargaining position. But the labor market of a mercantile society changed with modern industrial capitalism. Though his work preceded the industrial revolution, Adam Smith (1723-1790) laid the basis for our modern understanding of capitalism. The competition for goods and services in a market were the root ideas, and the struggle for individual gain was the basic motive for exchange. Thomas Malthus (1766-1834) raised concerns about the limits of production and our ability to provide food and other necessities to a growing population.

Karl Marx (1818-1883), the German political philosopher, offered a philosophy of dialectical materialism, which became the basis of much socialist thought and all communist political theory. Influenced by Hegel's dialectical theory, which we shall discuss below, Marx formulated an economic theory based on social class. The course of history is a dialectical one as the social classes struggled. From the feudal era when the aristocracy owned the land and means of production society moved to the industrial era and capitalism emerged. In that system the bourgeoisie came to own the means of production; the workers, or proletariat, experienced alienation as the products of their labor were outside their use or control. His colleague Friedrich Engels

(1820-1896) emphasized the importance of ideology and the notion of false consciousness, how the working classes are deluded and hoodwinked into compliance.

Socialism was a broad movement that also arose during the same period of time. There were roots to socialism reaching back into the Enlightenment with experiments to create utopian communities, sometimes based on spiritual philosophies. Such thinkers as Charles Fourier (1772-1837), Robert Owen (1771-1858) inspired idealistic communities in the United States as well as Europe. But they were largely agrarian utopias. The labor movement that arose in the nineteenth century was primarily urban and drew from manufacturing. Ideas of collective ownership and/or use of economic assets grew in popularity and in Europe even today socialist ideals and parties influence politics. The United States was dominated by the industrial capitalists who kept organized labor marginalized until the early 1930s. By the early twentieth century European countries, and others like Australia and New Zealand had social welfare reforms such as work place safety, social welfare programs and regulation of commerce, retirement income and health care.

One of the consequences of the defeat of the Prussians and other German armies by Napoleon, was a period of educational reform. In the medieval universities the master's degree was generally the ticket into teaching, and doctorates were awarded in medicine, theology and law. But in the nineteenth century Prussia, then other countries began offering the doctorate in philosophy, the Ph.D. as a pinnacle of achievement in scholarship. By the end of that century the Ph.D. was established in most of the world as a degree based on original research, and led to careers in the sciences and humanities. As each science broke away from natural philosophy and established a basis in empirical research, separate departments or faculties emerged for each such domain of scholarship. Thus, it was not surprising that as new disciplines like psychology emerged, that degree became the chosen one for establishing credentials. Although, as we shall see, there were early attempts to establish psychology as a profession, it was almost exclusively viewed as a science.

## Romanticism and German idealism

We now turn to broader cultural developments which lead to the human sciences and impinges upon a number of different aspects of society, romanticism. It is connected with German idealism as a philosophy. Romanticism is mostly linked to the arts, and was a major movement in both literature and music. The general thrust of the Romantic movement was a reaction to the elevation of reason in the Enlightenment. Emotion was now seen as more important. Feeling, sentiment, all were elevated as a source of meaning and a common theme of social interaction. People expressed their feelings quite deeply and sincerely in writing and fact. The letters of people to each other from this period were framed in a quality of emotional expression we find somewhat foreign. Men expressing tender feelings to men, would now be viewed through the lens of eroticism and sexuality, but up to the mid to late nineteenth century, it was quite common for persons of all sexes to communicate to each other with expressions of strong sentiment. Gay history struggles with the boundary between the rhetoric of affectionate male bonding and the identification of threads of a gay sensibility. Feelings were more acceptable as part of the totality of human experience. Reason found its match in the human sentiment of common bonding, one to another by feelings, by connections, by attachment.

The significance of romanticism for psychology, particularly professional psychology should be plain. One of the major ways in which we talk about mental illness is as emotional problems, whether the unwanted feelings are active and anxious or quiet, depressive and brooding, or even whether they shuttle between the two poles of emotionality. Either our emotions have been suppressed or repressed, which according to psychodynamic thinking causes neurosis, or they rage unchecked causing havoc in the life of the person experiencing these powerful feelings. In short, the general focus on a healthy or unhealthy emotional life in psychology comes about as a result of this cultural and artistic movement called romanticism.

German idealism is the philosophical movement that develops at the same time as the Romantic movement in arts and culture. Romanticism and idealism were counter currents running against the rule of reason which epitomized the late 1700s as the period of Enlightenment. Idealism as a technical term in philosophy does not mean having lofty goals and aspirations, rather it means the emphasize on the realm of ideas, the non-physical aspects of the world and of human experience. The epistemological controversies covered in the previous chapter ranged back and forth as to whether reason or sensory experience was a sounder foundation of knowledge, the debate in the nineteenth century focused more on the subjective phenomenological point of view versus the objectivist point of view. This, of course, is the subject / object dichotomy which sets the difference between the human sciences and the natural sciences.

Immanuel Kant (1724-1804) came at the peak of the Enlightenment and formulated his philosophy having read both the rationalists and the empiricists. His philosophy became the starting point of German idealism. Kant, sought to synthesize these two positions of empiricism and rationalism. Knowledge began in sensory experience, but the very nature of that experience, the very meaningful quality of it, was shaped by the inherent structures of the mind. Unlike Locke's blank slate, or tabula rasa, the mind has built in wiring that creates the experience of space, time, causality and other qualities. The categories of understanding, such as space, time and causation, were part of how the mind made perceptions into understandable experience. The categories are the framework which makes any knowledge possible at all.

Johan Fichte (1762-1814) continued the stream of German idealism. For Kant, *noumena* or things in themselves, as opposed to things as experienced (phenomena), could be known through reason alone. Fichte took a more skeptical turn and held that consciousness arises in the dialectic between self and non-self. We can only be reflectively aware of our self because there are other conscious beings, so we co-create our phenomenal world. He took the position that our consciousness of self is made with others through discourse, anticipating some aspects of modern constructivist positions.

Arthur Schopenhauer (1788-1860) continued the idealist tradition in German philosophy. His major work, *The World as will and representation* (1818, 1844, 1859), emphasized the importance of the human capacity for choice. The argument for will, agency, the capacity to act in the world and shape one's destiny as opposed to being determined by external forces has been shaped by Schopenhauer's work. He was also the first European philosopher to have available to him translation of the Vedas as well as Buddhist works, the early font of Indian spirituality. His theory of will links into his theory of ethics and esthetics and his theory of representation constitutes a metaphysical division of the universe as set of dichotomies (will/representation, subject/object, ideas/objects, body/external objects). In terms of modern psychology, Schopenhauer is important in understanding volition, the capacity to initiate behavior.

Perhaps the most important of German idealists is George Wilhelm Friedrich Hegel (1770-1831). He is chiefly cited today for his popularizing the three-part statement of dialectic; thesis, antithesis and synthesis (originated by Fichte, however). This was part of his philosophy of history. For Hegel, history had a particular dynamism to its development, it was moving in a certain direction. That direction was defined by the dialectical movement of certain historical forces. First the pendulum swings in one direction then seemingly in another, yet behind the changes there is a tide to human development. As noted above, Karl Marx took this general idea and developed in terms of a theory of social class conflict as the basis of history. Hegel was also influential, through his friend Friedrich von Schelling (1775-1854), whose lectures were heard by Søren Kierkegaard, one of the founders of existentialism. Indeed, Hegel is one of the points of reference for most of continental European philosophy in the last part of the nineteenth century and into the twentieth century. Sartre, another major existentialist thinker found in Hegel an important source of ideas.

## Human science and culture

Pepper's last acceptable world hypothesis is contextualism and the root metaphor is the text or the historical event. Both are particular, that is, they are situated in a context of time, place, and culture. The goal of the natural sciences was to discover laws of complete generality, independent of the contextual factors of time and place. But history is deeply rooted in the particularities of context, and human beings are deeply embedded in their cultural context, which is also based in time and place. As the natural sciences advanced with improved mathematical modeling of relationships between objects, the human sciences advanced with a deeper understanding of language. What is now called linguistics was in earlier time called philology, and many of the initial contributors to the human science perspective wrote extensively about language.

In the modern era, the distinction between humans and other subjects of science still seemed to be focused on the human capacity for consciousness and choice or agency as markers of a particularly high level of development. Those capacities are now termed our cognitive capacities or abilities. The cognitive capacities manifest subjectively as experience and objectively as communication in the social network of humans. In Pepper's schema, the human sciences represent a contextualist position just as the life sciences represent an organicist position and the physical sciences represent the mechanistic position. All partake in a classification scheme for the basic elements and their relationship, so in this sense all sciences require a formistic position as well. The human science perspective is grounded in three concepts; language, culture and history. We shall take up each of these streams that feed into the broader movement.

Gottfried Wilhelm Herder (1744-1803) was perhaps the founding figure in this movement, though he may not have seen clearly where his initial ideas would lead. Herder focused attention very early on the importance of language. His essay, *Treatise on the origin of language* (1772), won a prize from the Berlin Academy. He challenged Hume and Voltaire's idea that humans were the same everywhere, and emphasized the variety of difference and the fact these differences are embedded in a social and linguistic context which require interpretation (Forster, 2001). The relation between linguistic diversity and diversity of thought was clear to him. This argues for a poly-vocal science of the human. Indeed, the whole discipline of hermeneutics, as a scholarly endeavor derives from Herder's philosophy of interpretation. He stressed a secular and empirical approach to the interpretation of Biblical texts.

One of Herder's students was Friedrich Schleiermacher (1768-1834). Like Fichte, he also emphasized the importance of the duality of self and not-self as a primary aspect of our reality. He is best known as the father of hermeneutics, the discipline that seeks to lay out the canons of interpretation of texts, which is important to human sciences. He originated what was known as higher criticism of the Bible, interpreting the texts in light of knowledge gained from the revitalized study of languages, especially as early European exploration led to uncovering long dead civilizations and their artifacts and texts. From Napoleon's campaign in Egypt 1798, the Rosetta stone lay waiting for someone to decode the ancient hieroglyphic writings. Exploration and empire brought Europeans into India, the land of the Vedas and Upanishads, and also the Middle East, home of the Biblical Ur, Assyria and other civilizations. The basis of hermeneutics is the circle of understanding which allows interpretation, a deepening of our understanding of text, especially the Bible, by reference to the archaeological context, and a use of that added textual knowledge to further clarify the meaning of artifacts as cultural markers.

Part of the intersection between German idealism and the study of human beings was the concept of people as a group, which emerged during this period, especially from Herder's writings. In German, *volk* became a basis for growing national and ethnic identity. The brothers Grimm, for example, found an audience for collections of folk tales, beginning the whole study of folk lore as an academic discipline. The importance of this development to psychology was not to be fully realized until Jung in particular saw noted how mythology, folk lore and cultural symbolism is deeply involved in our collective unconscious.

Wilhelm Dilthey (1833-1911) continued Herder's ideas about the importance of context and went further in applying it to history and to the human sciences. Indeed his 1883 essay *An introduction to the human sciences* is where the term was first used to describe a coherent position with regard to the study of the human condition. Dilthey contrasted *geisteswissenschaften* with *naturwissenschaften*, which is now translated as human science and natural science. The natural sciences studied inanimate beings or living beings as objects; the human sciences studied the meanings humans ascribe to their lives and historical events.

He saw that the evolving disciplines of history, philosophy, art, psychology, sociology, anthropology, economics and political science had features that were interpretive in nature. They were different from the characteristics of the objects of natural science. They were expressions of the meanings that humans impart to events. The goal of the scientist was to gain an insider's understanding of the particularities that gave rise to specific human events; this required the interpretation of meanings. This special understanding bears a resemblance to our modern concept of empathy, and would also be congruent with the emic/etic distinction when applied to group differences. Dilthey held that the meaning of data concerning inanimate objects, the focus of study in the natural sciences, were more apparent and straightforward. But with human events, the context was crucial for understanding and the process of gaining understanding was the hermeneutic circle, shifting back and forth between person and environment, historical event and context, text and historical context.

Since the study of language became so central to the arguments about the ability to scientifically study human behavior, it is natural that a formal theory of signs would emerge, as language is but one particular type of sign. It also was important from the standpoint of evolutionary theory to link human languages with the signing behavior of other animals. Semiotics is the general theory of signs. The term was coined by John Locke (*semeiotike*), but it was not until the end of the nineteenth century that there was sufficient development to move from an isolated word to a discipline of scholars. We shall see in a later chapter how this discipline can be integrated into a systems perspective.

The two founding figures in the theory of signs, or semiotics, were the Swiss linguist Ferdinand de Saussure (1857-1913) and the American philosopher and logician, Charles Sanders Peirce (1839-1914). Peirce is also one of the founding members of a uniquely American philosophical movement known as pragmatism, which will be discussed later. The theory of signs addresses the relationship between the sign, the meaning conveyed by the sign, and the interpretant, the one who decodes the sign for its meaning.

## Neurology and nervous maladies

No introductory psychology textbook would be complete without a few paragraphs on phrenology as a pseudoscience along with a picture of a phrenology bust marking out the regions of the scalp and the underlying traits. Phrenology was a misdirected theory of localization that would be supplanted by more solid evidence and more cogent reasoning, but it illustrates the desire in the nineteenth century to tie psychological characteristics to underlying brain mechanisms. Despite its flawed theory, however, phrenology became one of the first attempts at the talking cure. Phrenological diagnosis of personality traits were used by people to check compatibility for employment, marriage or other issues as well as to better understand themselves (Sokol, 2001). It was one of the earliest uses of skilled use of non-trance types of communication to improve client well-being.

Phrenology was devised by Franz Joseph Gall (1758-1828) and popularized in the United States by Johann Spurzheim (1776-1832). It was based on an early and incorrect understanding of brain localization, coupled with Aristotelian faculty psychology. The reasoning went that the more an area develops the larger the underlying brain structure, just like muscles. This growth would create subtle deformations of the skull palpable by the sensitive hand and capable of defining the individual's strengths and weaknesses on the basis of the location of the raised surface and the psychological function beneath it in the brain. A profile of various abilities and characteristics was created and was then given to the subject of the phrenological reading along with advice on personal problems.

Phrenology, like mesmerism suffered from a theory that turned out to be grossly untrue. Each, however, led to techniques and practices that were fundamentally sound. Mesmerism led to modern hypnosis, phrenology led to the modern practice of giving advice on such things as marriage, employment and other decisions on the basis of an assessment of personality characteristics. Sokol (2001) observed that by using a mixture of common sense, the advice given was often found to be helpful.

The aspects of early neurology that have endured began in the late nineteenth century as the brain and nerves were coming to be seen as the seat of human experience and consciousness. The various mental disorders were becoming the province of neurology and psychiatry branches out from neurology beginning with such seminal figures as Jacques Charcot, Sigmund Freud and others. The basic distinction between sensory nerves and motor pathways was jointly discovered by two physicians, one British the other French; Charles Bell (1774-1842) and François Magendie (1783-1855). Localization theory became more widely accepted with Paul Pierre Broca's (1824-1880) discovery (1861) of site of damage in the frontal lobe of the brain leading to expressive aphasia, followed by Wenicke's (1848-1905) discovery (1874) of the locus of pathology for receptive aphasia. Countering localization theory was equipotential theory which was championed by the British neurologist Hughlings Jackson (1835-1911), though his contribution was less recognized in his day than now. With the localization of language functions it became possible to predict human neuropsychological deficit from location of medical lesion, though that story comes later.

Up to now the history of mental illness had focused on the serious forms of illness termed madness; what we now would call psychosis. Little attention was paid to the garden variety unhappiness of ordinary people. This began to change in the nineteenth century. Caplan (2001) chronicles the relationship between the new technology of the railroad and the birth of the concept of neurosis. With the many accidents that came with railroads, ordinary people began to complain of chronic back pain, partial paralysis and so on subsequent to being involved in these accidents. Much efforts of railroad surgeons went into trying to find an organic basis for what came to be known as railroad spine. Eventually, though hope was maintained that at a microscopic level, some organic cause would be found, increasingly the medical community began to see that these complaints were primarily psychological in the mechanism by which they were sustained.

Hysteria became the major neurotic diagnosis, and the concern of several leading neurologists. Hysteria was the complaint of symptoms of disorder of sensation or movement. Anesthesia, paralysis, often accompanied by histrionic presentation became a major focus of attention. The condition appeared mostly in women. The very name is derived from the Latin for uterus, or womb. So there was, what we now would recognize, a significant socially modulated set of reactions to the social situation of women in that era.

Another major category of mental and physical illness was neurasthenia. The popularity of this diagnosis and its subsequent eclipse illustrate the rise and fall of fads in medicine and popular culture. The other part of the story, however, tells how this disease sparked an understanding of the connection between social factors of modern life and health. Neurasthenia, or nervous weakness, was propounded in 1869 by Connecticut physician George M. Beard (1839-1869). He held that nerves, like all cells in the body can be weakened by overuse. Additionally, some individuals had a particularly vulnerable constitution (diathesis) and predisposition to maladies of a particular organ or type. Weakened nerves tend to cause symptoms of nervousness, including fatigue, exhaustion, and ultimately collapse. The modern phrase *nervous breakdown* draws from this theory of nervous energy as a source of bodily health or illness. It drew on the earlier physiological theory of sensitivity, readiness to be reactive.

There was a particular suspicion about the role of sexuality in the depletion of nervous energy. This was the era when masturbation was considered self pollution. For males in particular, ejaculating literally drained one of energy that the healthy man who was continent experienced in abundance. Shame tinged with medical concern added to the problem. Then, as now, concern with male erectile dysfunction spawned a variety of cures, nearly all of which were off base.

Civilization, itself was seen as a cause of nervous exhaustion. The stress of industrial societies was thought to drain vital energies. Beard saw neurasthenia as most likely to occur with what he called brain workers, the modern occupations using the mind not the body (Caplan, 2001). It was the cost of the march forward toward progress and betterment. Rousseau capitalized on the filth and squalor of European cities in the early modern era and talked about how indigenous peoples untouched by civilization were morally better off than their civilized counterparts. The idea of living in harmony with nature was had become a major force after several decades of Romanticism. The notion of the polluting and corruption power of urbanism and industrialization was an ideology seeking to counter the overwhelming march of modernity and its doctrine of inevitable progress. It harkened back to simpler times when values were clear and harmony prevailed. Our modern era is corrupt, poisoned and degenerate. Neurasthenia captured this darker view of the value of civilization and melded them into modern American industrial productivity (Lutz, 1991). One must avoid the debasing habits which lead to weakness and bolster our health to be productive workers in a modern industrial giant, just coming alive. American expansion and commercial development was moving ahead and needed strong people, so just at the very time when we were building the industrial might that would later make it a world power, there was a cautionary movement identifying the cost of civilization to health and mental and emotional well-being

Nature was seen as healing. S. Weir Mitchell (1829-1914) developed the rest cure. The 40-hour work week and paid vacations were rare, so any opportunity to take time off from work for rest and recreation was highly valued. To facilitate periods of extended restorative rest, new clinics and sanitariums sprouted. The prototype was the one built in Battle Creek, Michigan, by John Harvey Kellogg (1852-1943), who with his brother developed corn flakes as a commercially successful cereal. The spa was a place not only of peace, but of solid country values. Railroads facilitated this development by constructing lines to thermal springs, sometimes building the resorts as well. Furthering opportunities for leisure time and travel, in the early part of the century under the administration of Theodore Roosevelt, the first national parks were set aside and an early conservation movement launched. The designer of New York City's Central Park deliberately arranged the park to seem wild, natural, uncivilized. Getting into contact with nature was seen as an important part of mental hygiene. Many of the large mental hospitals as well as prisons were located in rural areas in order to remove the patient from the stresses of urban life.

This was also the first period in American history when physical fitness or physical culture became a popular recreational opportunity (Green, 1986). Bicycles were invented, exercise equipment was marketed through mail order catalogs to the average

American. Organized sporting events became more common, including foot races for money prizes (Algeo, 2014), as well as team sports such as baseball.

In short, despite its theoretical and empirical mistakes, neurasthenia as a disorder was a major force behind several developments which have proved beneficial for a healthy life. Good nutrition, vigorous exercise (preferably outdoors), recreation in nature and away from stresses of ordinary life, and, of course, rest. These are all the province of health psychologists as consultants to individuals and groups, how to incorporate healthy habits into a daily routine. The emergence of behavioral medicine that addresses the relationship of lifestyle to health comes directly from this beginning.

## Mesmerism and hypnosis

We will end this chapter by considering the first technique for psychological healing to develop in the West in modern times. While the therapy of the word had mostly been lost after classical antiquity except through spiritual activities like prayer and preaching, this new approach became the foundation of hypnosis. Ellenberger's (1980) *Discovery of the unconscious* chronicles the history of what he calls dynamic psychiatry, those approaches to illness and treatment that rely on th concept of the unconscious in some manner. He begins his work with Mesmerism. What we now call hypnosis emerged out of Mesmer's work. Though there are a variety of theories of what makes hypnosis work, the unconscious is still among the ideas that are held by contemporary practitioners. Hypnosis is another of those approaches to healing by psychological means that started out with a misguided theory but nonetheless were effective. Hypnosis, like other techniques in counseling or psychotherapy, uses only verbal social interaction, usually live, face to face and spontaneous.

Franz Anton Mesmer (1734-1815) completed his doctor of medicine degree at University of Vienna. After graduation Mesmer made his way to Paris where he became quite popular. He theorized that magnetism was like a fluid, albeit extremely fine and invisible, and could be transmitted by healer to patient. He initially used tubs, or bacquets, filled with water and iron filings out of which rods emerged which patients seated around the tub would grasp onto for periods of time. People holding on to the rods reacted with strong emotionality; having fits, convulsions, and entering a trance. Mesmer, with a sense for the dramatic, conducted these seances or group therapy sessions in a lilac robe.

Trances had always been the province of spiritual visionaries and mystics, whether Catholic, Protestant or Jewish (Taves, 1999), and Ellenberger (1970) finds the origin of Mesmer's practice in the faith healing that took place in the part of Austria where Mesmer grew up. The spiritual crisis became a characteristic state of excitement where healing took place, or at least began. We now would recognize these as ecstatic trance states (Fischer, 1971). These, of course can be both psychologically positive (as in healing activity) or negative (as in hysterical crises, which dominated the interest of neurologists and psychiatrists at the end of the nineteenth century and into the twentieth.

Later, he recognized that the tubs cumbersome and discovered that he could accomplish the same end, the induction of a trance, by making passes with the hands across the body of the patient. Thus began the next phase of mesmerism. Shedding the bacquets, the process became one of interaction between the healer and the patient. Some physical stroking or massaging was permitted, but the process was mostly non-verbally induced. This a bit of contagious magic, the belief that the magnetic fluid could be transmitted through touch. It was a close personal ritual of induction and healing.

Mesmer became quite popular in salon society in Paris. He had one powerful patron in the Queen of France, Marie Antoinette. King Louis XVI, her husband, however, was influenced by the leading French physicians to set up a commission to investigate the soundness of Mesmer's practice and theory of animal magnetism. Among the leading intellectuals who happened to reside in Paris at that time was the eminent French chemist, Lavoisier, and the equally eminent natural philosopher and inventor, Benjamin Franklin, who happened to be ambassador from the American colonies seeking independence. Louis appointed Franklin as its chair. After investigation they concluded that the theory of magnetism was not established and the effects were done by manipulating the beliefs of the people. Mesmer was essentially called a quack, and the theory of magnetic fluid was discredited. Mesmer left Paris in disgrace and lived on but in more modest circumstances for a number of years. The irony was that the Franklin commission got it right by asserting that the mechanism for cure was the powerful force of human persuasion and psychological means. That development came later.

The theory of animal magnetism is very similar to the concept of that of vital energy. A variant of the same notion is found in Eastern cultures, the *prana* of Indian medicine, *chi* or *qi* in traditional Chinese medicine, and *ki* in the Japanese version. The link within European cultures was the Greek *pneuma* as taught by the Stoics. In the nineteenth century Karl Ludwig von Reichenbach (1788-1869) a noted German chemist labeled this concept the Odic force. As noted in the chapter on Eastern approaches, the alternative healing approach of energy medicine and psychology uses this concept still. So it's not quite a dead idea, though it is viewed with skepticism by mainstream medicine and psychology.

But mesmerism didn't die out with Mesmer's fall from popularity and the discrediting of animal magnetism as a theory. Mesmer had developed followers who took the original idea and transformed it. The Marquis DePuysegur (1751-1825) hitched the practice of mesmerism to the concept of somnambulism, or sleep walking. DePuysegur saw the connection to trance, and likened it to sleep, seeing the link to states of consciousness induced by personal interaction. A decade or so later, José Custódio de Faria, known an Abbé Faria, continued the association with sleep with his theory of lucid sleep. He emphasized the importance of the concentration by the patient;

all active mechanisms were in the mind of the patient. James Braid (1795-1860), a British physician, coined the term hypnosis, which is the modern term for induced trances. James Esdail (1808-1859), another British physician first used mesmerism in surgical anesthesia. He was in the British army in India and found the native troops, or Sepoys, particularly amenable to entering altered states of consciousness. This is natural, because of the continuous cultural history valuing trances and meditation as a regular practice within a spiritual tradition. In the West, trances were banished from mainstream practice and kept at the margins. Even religious trances, or *enthusiasm*, though common among a number of Protestant sects, were still treated skeptically by the establishment (Taves, 1999). By mid century, however, the London Mesmeric infirmary, established 1850, kept 4 full-time mesmerists employed. So even within the heart of industrial development the public was willing to support hypnosis as a healing technology. The leading professional publication was *The Zoist*, published from 1844-1856. Both lay and medically trained magnetizers contributed case histories and systematic, if uncritical, treatment recommendations.

Magnetic healing or hypnosis fell out of favor, but was given medical credibility by Jean Martin Charcot (1825-1893). As a neurologist and teacher he attracted many students, including Sigmund Freud and Pierre Janet. His legacy for hypnosis, however, is unfortunate. He viewed the ability to go into the hypnotic state as a sign of psychopathology; only hysterics could do so. In addition, the novel *Trilby* by George DuMaurier in 1894 introduced a character, Szvengali, who was a manipulative hypnotist. This didn't help public trust in hypnotism. The idea that hypnosis is a result of mental weakness and the stronger will of the hypnotist can impose it on the weak minded is a myth largely influenced by Charcot's theory.

Among those who opposed Charcot's theory were two physicians associated with the medical school in Nancy, France. Ambrose Liebault (1823-1904) and Hippolyte Bernheim (1837-1919) are known for their position that suggestion was the active mechanism in the hypnotic process (Bernheim, 1884/1964). This was a critical development. It firmly put the nature and therapeutic power of trance as a purely psychological phenomenon without reference to vital energies or fluids. They also taught that the ability to go into the hypnotic state is part of normal cognitive abilities and not associated with psychopathology. They also applied its use to a wider range of conditions other than hysteria. This is really the birth of modern hypnosis. Suggestibility was used in mid twentieth century research on personality characteristics that accounted for variations in depth of hypnotic trance. Several measures of hypnotic ability were constructed based on responsiveness to suggestion.

Pierre Janet (1859-1947) was the leading exponent of hypnosis during the era of Freud's early work. While Freud had earlier used hypnosis, which he learned from studying with Charcot, he subsequently abandoned it. Janet, however, never abandoned or disavowed hypnosis, though in his full statement of the nature of psychological healing (1925/1916) he describes the status of a wide range of psychological and educational approaches to healing. Janet's major innovation on hypnosis theory was the concept of dissociation. This places him in the stream of psychodynamic theorists, for dissociation is a splitting of consciousness into two or more relatively independent activities. Dissociation allows disturbing material to be put out of awareness. It is a result of trauma and leads to neurosis. But there is also a therapeutic use via hypnosis to recover those repressed memories. There is a dynamic between conscious and unconscious forces in human experience. A splitting of consciousness into functional units was both helpful and baneful, depending on the particular combination with other factors.

# 8

## Founding Psychology: Science and Profession

### The new field of psychology

WE ARE NOW AT the beginning of the science of psychology as an independent discipline among the sciences. The profession of psychology has its beginnings in this period as well, though the number of psychologists doing any applied practice was minimal. That story will be told in the next chapter. Research and teaching were the dominant activities. Acceptance of professional roles within psychology was much slower both among psychologists and the public. Psychology as a science emerged in the latter half of the twentieth century as the natural sciences were in their great period of branching off into specific disciplines. As noted in the previous chapter, German educational reform led to the Ph.D. being the major degree for scholarly research, so American universities began granting the doctorate, and newly minted Ph.D. in psychology from German universities became professors at American universities.

There are three paths that led to the emergence of psychology as a separate discipline. One was from philosophy, another was from education (pedagogy), and the other from physiology and medicine. Education as a discipline was emerging as well, but at this time the philosophical roots more evident than empiricism. For our purposes here education and philosophy can be taken together as they fit the archetype of teacher and both use words as the primary medium for conveying knowledge through dialog. In many ways these still represent two poles within psychology, the natural science tradition from physiology and the human science tradition from philosophy. Most of the early psychologists came from one or the other of these fields and found the new discipline the place where there interests were better served than the discipline of the formative parts of their careers. Within psychology, it was quite clear from the start, that the new discipline was to be an experimental science. To the extent that someone wanted to work with patients in a clinical context, you still had to get training as a physician.

The career of Pierre Janet can be used to illustrate the shifting opportunities opened up for different advanced degrees (Ellenberger, 1970). He took his first doctorate (doctorat ès lettres) in philosophy. His subject was psychological automatism, a topic arising out of hypnosis. His committee congratulated him on avoiding getting into medical issues or domain, and keeping his analysis strictly philosophical. It was in many ways a very psychological dissertation, based in a study of consciousness, in this case the type of dissociated consciousness exemplified by hypnosis. Janet would continue to study altered and dissociative states throughout his career. However, his access to patients, particularly hysterics, who were the prized objects of study in both hypnosis and psychiatry research, required a medical degree. While still involved in teaching psychology, he also undertook his medical education and received his M.D. in 1893. This allowed him continued access to hospitals and to be able to treat patients. These were opportunities not open to holders of the Ph.D. in psychology at this time. Treatment was the exclusive domain of medicine. Another early psychologist who had a medical degree was William James (1842-1910). He got his M.D. in 1869 but never practiced that profession. We will cover his contribution in more depth later.

Many textbooks credit Wilhelm Wundt as the founder of the first psychology laboratory, though recent evidence shows that James helped establish a lab earlier (1875) at Harvard, despite not being personally involved in experimental science. Yet another claim for an earlier founding of psychology could be made for the work of Johann Friederich Herbart (1776-1841) who we encountered earlier. He even used the word *psychologie* in his writings and is also considered a founder in the field of education or pedagogy. He believed that psychological laws could be discovered by observation of nature and foresaw quantification (Heidelberger, 2004). All of these thinkers and several others could also be mentioned depending on what aspect of the study of human experience is chosen. Let us at least look at these three.

Herbart's psychology was more on educational considerations whereas physiological considerations would be paramount for Fechner and Wundt. Herbart was the first to systematically explore the difference between pedagogical method or process and content area. He also focused attention on the abilities or aptitudes of the students in different areas. He was clearly interested in the psychology of learning, but the learning he was most concerned with took place in a class room not a laboratory. This is not surprising. Though the concept of experimentation had been introduced as early as Bacon, it was really the flowering of experimental physics, chemistry and physiology through the nineteenth century that served as a model for a new psychology to adopt in emulation. Herbart emphasized the reality of volition, desire and impulse to act; the person or psyche was active, though there is an implied receptive influence by other real psychological forces to create a dynamic balance of like and not-like elements (Fuller & McMurrin, 1955).

Gustav Fechner (1801-1887) can also be considered a founder of psychology. He coined the term psychophysics. He was one of a number of physiologists who were interested in mind-body relationships, focusing on the area of sensory physiology. He sought to bring the measurement of the two together. He refined Ernst H. Weber's (1795-1878) method of just noticeable difference (AND), or limen of perception, and added two new methods, right and wrong cases, and average error. These tools helped to measure the relationship between sensation and perception; that is, between the physical stimuli which carry the signals, to the psychological processed meaning of the signal. From his research in both visual and tactile sensation he formulated a law; the stimulus intensity as experienced is a log function of the physical intensity of the stimulus. Fechner had a metaphysical side and, like Leibniz, argued for a unity of consciousness and objectivity embedded in individual active elements (similar to Leibniz' monads) interacting with each other. He has become known for his experimental contributions, though his other views bear some consideration in light of a theory of personality.

Wilhelm Wundt (1832-1920) obtained his medical degree in 1856. We will see that many of the pioneers in psychology had degrees in medicine, as the Ph.D. in psychology was the result of their efforts and those who came later would train in that manner. Both James, Helmholtz, and Janet also had medical degrees. Watson (1977) notes that they combined in a single person the role of psychologist and physician. Wundt taught in physiology, and like James, was the first at his university to identify as teaching the new discipline, psychology. Ultimately James took a chair in philosophy later in his career. Wundt trained under two of the greatest physiologists of their day, Johannes Müller (1801-1859), who developed a theory of specific nerve energies, what we now refer to as the dual classification of neurons as sensory or motor, and Herman von Helmholtz (1821-1894), who did major work in the acoustics of hearing. Wundt sought to link the mind and body through sensory means, and was influenced by Fechner. Wundt viewed psychology as the study of consciousness. Consistent with the physics of his day, he was atomistic and elementaristic, in the sense that he was seeking to uncover the individual elements of mental life. He sought to break down the ordinary holistic consciousness we experience into its constituent elementary particles, the bits out of which experience is stitched together. He used introspection as a method, which links him with Descartes, though his lineage proceeds more through experimental physiology rather than through the philosophical phenomenological stream, at least initially.

His experiments sought to find the basis of mental life in the objects of perception as received and reported by trained observers. An interesting problem lead to Wundt's paradigm as set out by one of the first historians of psychology, E. G. Boring (1950/1929). Wundt's early interest in the psychological problem of visual perception came from astronomers concerned about the problem of the human observer. The problem, called the personal equation, attributed the source of error of observations to human processing differences between input and output. Two observers had differences in the time lag between hearing the click of a clock marking the time and marking the visual transit of stars past a cross-hair in the eye piece. Careful observations of transit time were essential to astronomy. Wundt inherited the task of describing the parameters of the human equation, the observer was now the subject of observation.

He accepted many students and produced a fair number of new Ph.D.s in psychology, many among the founders of American psychology. One who was a major influence in U.S. psychology was Edward Titchener. He was born in Britain, but wound up teaching at Cornell University in New York. He called his version of experimental psychology, structuralism, and the name stuck as a label for the earliest school or stream of thought in experimental psychology. Criticism and elaboration led to a broadening of the realm of experimental psychology to include other scientific frameworks, including functionalism and behaviorism. But the early experimental positions were largely responses to or critiques of the Wundtian tradition. When the field was moving away from the classical methodology involving introspection, Titchener held the line. Consequently, he became increasingly by-passed by other modes of experimentation which were more behavioral in tone and by the 1920s his influence was declining.

Wundt, later in his career, came to shift his position and focus more on social psychology. He adopted the human science concept of culture and ethnicity, the German *volk*, and began to shift his attention to the symbolic, cultural, and linguistic as opposed to the elemental and experimental. His methodology shifted to ethnography. *Volkerpsychologie* ranged over the various levels of organization of human societies and their impact on the individual. Thus Wundt's career shows a trajectory, beginning in medicine and physiology and ending up in psychology and ethnography, or social science. James, too, had the same trajectory, though his involvement in the physiological pole was briefer and he moved into philosophy, the most abstract of all scholarly disciplines.

Wundt and Titchener were not the only experimentalists. Herman Ebbinghaus (1850-1909) was another significant early psychologist. His work was principally on memory. He used the nonsense word and syllable as a stimulus item. The goal was to get the pure process of memory, unaffected by meaning. His work gave us the concepts of a learning and forgetting curve when results were plotted out.

## Functionalism and American pragmatism

America made its first major contribution to psychological theory with the school known as functionalists. Leahey (2000) termed this group the psychology of adaptation. As with Wundt, they defined psychology as the science of consciousness (rather than behavior). The term functionalism refers to their emphasis on the adaptive functions of consciousness. Darwin's ideas on the evolution of life made the idea of adaptation of organism to environment the leading meta framework which the functionalists adopted for the new science of psychology.

The functionalist school of psychology was linked to the philosophical movement called pragmatism. It embodied a particularly America emphasis on practicality.

Earlier British philosophers like Jeremy Bentham (1748-1832) and John Stuart Mill (1806-1873) had emphasized utility, or usefulness as a principle, but it was this group of Americans who put the root idea into psychological theory. The leading figures in the development of this approach to philosophy were William James (1842-1910), John Dewey (1859-1952), and Charles Sanders Peirce (1839-1914). James taught all his career at Harvard, Dewey had a more varied academic career and Peirce worked at the U.S. Coast and Geodetic Survey. They are the first set of American philosophers who reached world class status through the influence of their ideas. Peirce, besides being a founding figure of pragmatism, was also one of the two founders of the discipline of semiotics, the theory of signs, along with French linguist Ferdinand de Sausurre (1857-1913). We will explore semiotics and its implications for psychology in a later chapter.

William James is a major figure in the development of psychology, despite the fact that he spent much of his career as a professor of philosophy. As such he is recognized as the main figure in Pragmatism. Many biographers view him as being primarily a philosopher, and only secondarily a psychologist. This is probably true, but his commitment to psychology was recently noted by Heft (2001), as he traced the use of James' psychology of radical empiricism by his student Edwin B. Holt, who passed it on to his student, James J. Gibson, a founding figure in ecological psychology. James' pragmatism was deeply grounded in evolutionary theory. The role of habits as adaptive tools for humans became a defining feature of functionalism.

To James, psychology was the study of consciousness, and it was the last major psychology of consciousness to be entertained widely in American psychology for some time. Over the decades following World War I, American psychology became dominated by behaviorism, which re-defined psychology as the study of behavior only. This very dispute of how to define psychology marks a turning point in the history of psychology. The focus shifted from conscious experience to only observable behavior. Mental constructs were kept alive in the intervening decades of behavioral dominance by the psychodynamic and humanistic-existential streams. Now, the pendulum has swung far enough in the other direction that behaviorism has adopted a version of mentalism in the form of cognitive behaviorism, which will be touched upon in an coming chapter.

James' magnum opus in psychology was his 2 volume *Principles of Psychology.* It is among the classics of psychology. William James was called the psychologist who wrote like a novelist, and Henry James was the novelist who wrote like a psychologist. The James brothers shared a similar perspective, a psychological one, a subjective one based in human consciousness, but they had different modes of expression. Henry worked in literature, William worked in philosophy and psychology. The work sets out an eloquent statement of the nature of consciousness and its relationship to human action. He gives us such important phrases as stream of consciousness to describe the on-going experience of awareness.

James suffered from periods of depression throughout his life. From 1869-1872 he found it difficult to function. After reading a book by the Frenchman, Charles Renouvier, he became convinced that he could change his mental state by deliberate will. This led to a recovery. He was always a booster of self-help approaches to mental health thereafter. Later, he become a patron of Clifford Beers, who published his own memoirs of recovery from mental illness and founded the mental hygiene movement. He supported the Emmanuel movement in Boston, pioneering in self-help group therapy.

He also wrote the first major book in the psychology of religion. *The Varieties of religious experience*, were delivered as the Gifford lectures in Edinburgh in 1901 and 1902. In his introduction he was quite clear that he was not writing as a theologian, but as a psychologist. His focus was on the study of religious experience, not the beliefs that come out of it. Whatever one comes to believe about the divine is filtered through the experiencing person and thereby stamped with a certain personal as well as cultural marker and matrix. His own conflict between skepticism and belief was the engine that drove much of his interest. He sought to set forth the ways in which religion could cure the sick soul and lead to healthy mindedness. He also covered the experience of conversion as well. But as the title suggests, his emphases was on religious experience rather than dogma or belief.

Another major figure in functional psychology was John Dewey (1859-1952). His critique of the reflex arc concept (1896) is still a classic piece of early American psychology. He also emphasized the distinction between the molecular and the molar. He contrasted his approach which emphasized the larger units of behavior and experience, the molar ones, with Wundt's attempt to get at the molecular level of consciousness. Dewey taught at the University of Chicago and while there he also had a significant influence on education. He founded a laboratory school to implement his ideas on pedagogy. Dewey was an important influence in teaching as a profession. His influence was both pedagogical, in the sense of practical instructional techniques, and formative, in terms of the philosophy of education and what social values the process should be organized around. His theory spread and progressive education became a major influence in American educational policy. The goal of education was not just technical competence in the basics of reading, writing and arithmetic, but should also include education to become an informed citizen in the community. It should have the practical or pragmatic value of creating people who could not only succeed in terms of their individual adaptation to the environment, but that they would be effective in contributing to the whole, the common weal, the common wealth.

Another important figure, indeed, often considered the last of the functionalist psychologists, was Robert Woodworth (1869-1962). He has been considered by Hilgard (1983) a true generalist. In this sense he was a synthesizer, like Galen of the ancient medical corpus. Woodworth brought forth a position that sought to bridge the stimulus-response psychology that began with Ivan Pavlov in Russia with the experimental work of Wundt and Titchener. He sought to integrate the experimental and the non-experimental, the introspective and objective. He noted the importance of organismic variables, putting the *O* in between the *S-R* equation (*SOR*), which was the basis of mechanism as articulated by the reflex arc physiologists. His *Dynamic Psychology* (1918) is his major statement of position. He added drive as a concept and later elaborated this (Woodworth, 1958) to *Ow*, the *w* being the situation. (Hilgard, 1983). With the introduction of terms for the inner processing of the organism (organismic variables) and the situation as a set of environmental conditions, we have a nascent ecological view point in psychology.

By the 1920s the ideas of functionalism were absorbed into generic psychology, and functionalism as a distinct school lost out through winning. It's emphasis on the adaptational model became an assumptive framework within which American psychology was to develop, though with an overlay from the next paradigm, the behavioral one. John B. Watson is recognized as founder and major advocate of behaviorism, which is the third classical school of psychology. The Gestalt psychologists constituted the fourth and last school of psychology.

After this American psychology became too diverse to encompassed within the concept of school, or coherent systems of psychology. The poly-vocal situation of theories, methodological paradigms, and concrete applications had become too diverse, and the whole scientific zeitgeist (spirit of the times) for big thinking had disappeared. More local theories of specific phenomena in specific circumstances became the norm. Psychology divided into division as an organizational structure later, but after the articulation of behaviorism and gestalt psychology, the era of systems ceased and the growth of psychology, both as a science and as a profession challenged that easy sense of unity embodied by the word school or system. The remnant of this period is the title this course often takes, *History and systems of psychology*. Systems theory, however was yet to have in influence on psychology because that stream has a very different origin to be taken up later.

The thumbnail sketch of the first half century of psychology as an experimental science begins with introspection of conscious experience as basis of method of exploration of mental phenomena. Wundt and Titchener with his structuralism represent a more atomistic approach to the object of study, human experience. The functionalists represent the strong influence of the evolutionary biological principle of adaptation of organism to environment. Adaptive being the key word here. How does one's already organized mechanism of sensing, selecting, and acting in the world match up with what will accomplish survival and growth? By the 1920s the Gestalt psychologists would echo the organismic perspective of functional psychology and its ecological implications. Behaviorism, however, clearly won the day by the 1920s and 30s in America. Despite influence of German immigrant psychologists and psychoanalysts in the 1930s American psychology had become dominated by learning theory. Most other perspectives were less well situated.

## Diversification of areas of interest

As the various sciences emerged as separate academic disciplines in the nineteenth century, each had to define its scope and domain distinctly from the others. Psychology was no exception. We have already established that its triple roots were in physiology, education (pedagogy), and philosophy. We will later see how systems theory developed and gave us the conceptual tools for understanding boundaries between disciplines. If we take the study of the individual person as the system of focus, for example, the physiological substrate of the organism are the subsystems of the person. The person is a subsystem of various social networks or systems, and they are a suprasystem to the individual person or organism. Psychology has two basic links then, one upward in a sense to the broader social and cultural systems in which individuals are elements, and the network of organs, tissues and cells that make up the individual organism, the biological basis of the person.

From the beginning a variety of people began investigating topics that linked the various levels of systems as well as other questions about the nature of the person or individual organism. It is clear, however, that psychology took that initial focus on the individual. As noted, many early psychologists got their initial training in physiology and medicine and focused on neuro-sensory and neuro-motor activities of the individual. Others came from philosophy and education and took different questions in hand. Among the disciplines broadly termed social and behavioral sciences, anthropology and sociology had a clear focus on the group level. For sociology the label that seemed to fit for the collectivity was *society*, for the anthropologist it was *culture*. Sociology dealt mainly with developed European or American examples, while anthropologists focused on the exotic foreign and primitive groups. Psychology was focused on the person but with linkages up and down the levels of systems, so though it took some decades, there was early recognition for the need of a bio-psycho-social approach if the discipline were to be comprehensive in nature.

## Developmental psychology

One of the roots of psychology is pedagogy which is concerned with the means by which to best educate children, so this stream that fed into psychology highlights developmental psychology as a key area of inquiry. The early scientific writings dealing with children are theories of education by Froebel, Montessori, and others. The kindergarten and infant school movement likewise contributed to understanding early childhood. Infant diaries in which parents (usually the researcher) write about their observations of their children's development. Darwin wrote in this vein himself. G. Stanley Hall (1844-1924) was among the first developmental psychologists, conducting pioneering work on adolescence. He introduced the questionnaire method into developmental psychology, seeking information from parents and others who observed the child regularly. He was also the convener of the founding meeting of the American Psychological Association in 1892, and served as its first president. He was also president of Clark University, an early free-standing graduate school.

One important method of developmental psychology is the longitudinal study. Most laboratory experiments are only concerned with the behavior of interest in the present moment, but the developmental psychologist is inherently interested in change processes over time. Lewis Terman (1877-1956) spent much of his career at Stanford University and is perhaps best known for his version of the Binet Scale, the Stanford-Binet ©. But he also conducted one of the earliest and most successful longitudinal studies. His work on gifted children watched and measured key aspects of their abilities as they moved into adulthood. In addition several other longitudinal growth studies were conducted in the period between the two world wars.

## Personality

If psychology reached both downward to the physiological base and upward toward group life, it also looked inward into the individual psyche. This became the domain of personality theory. Broadly speaking this touches upon many current domains. Clearly cognitive psychology deals with the thought processes of the individual. The psychology of motivation deals with the primary forces that create behavior. Here also is lurking the philosophical dilemma between causation versus agency. We experience choice, an ability to select and choose among alternatives. This agentic capacity is challenged by the basic scientific assumption of causation. So how then does the experience of will or choice square with the belief that every event has a cause. Can the individual psyche be a source of causation itself? The philosophy of mechanism says no. Psychology has had several periods when lively debate about mechanism or will have been active or fade into ennui as an insoluble paradox. Epiphenomenalism is the belief that our experience of choice is illusory. It simply means we don't yet know all the factors and details or have the computational power to predict the event by naturalistic means. But common sense and lay understanding gives the individual a range of selection, albeit limited by many factors.

Mary Whiton Calkins (1863-1930) was a pioneer in self psychology. She had a strong background in Classical Greek and taught that at Wellesley College. The President of that school asked her to teach psychology as well, and she asked to study it a year. She applied to nearby Harvard but the President of that institution firmly opposed women as students. She attended lectures by Josiah Royce and William James but could not register as a student. Later she would also study with Hugo Munsterberg. She would do her doctoral dissertation under him in 1896, but the degree was again denied because she was a woman. Nonetheless she continued research and teaching. She was not the first woman psychologist, but she was the first woman president of the American Psychological Association (APA). Her view of self sought to combine both an introspective components and behavioral. She developed the idea of the self concept. It came out of the experimental introspective tradition, as a basic awareness. Titchener denied this and they sparred, though she always sought to harmonize structural with the functional position. Her basic dimensions of personality included, active/passive, determined (compelled)/free choice, egocentric/allocentric (other centered), and its capacity to generalize/particularize (individualize).

William McDougall (1871-1938) was best known for his purposive or hormic psychology. The term was derived from a Greek root meaning purpose or motive. Hilgard (1983) calls the concept the primacy of purpose. His was an instinct theory and it was later eclipsed by Freud's psychodynamic formulation of instinct theory. He also was a part of several ethnological expeditions, so his views encompassed what would not be considered cross-disciplinary activities. Hilgard also credits him with making the case for the three-part division of psychological capacities, emotion (affect), reason (belief), and will (conation), the ABCs of psychology.

## Biological psychology

The neural basis of sensation was examined in the nineteenth century and the field of psychophysics emerged from the pioneering work of Gustav Fechner (1801-1887). Efforts by Christine Ladd Franklin (1847-1930) advanced our understanding of the basis of color perception. Many of the early mental tests were in fact psycho-motor tasks. But there's more to the biological bases of behavior than sensation and movement.

Keep in mind that psychology was defined at the time as the study of mental life. So the domain of what is now known as comparative psychology took as a serious question the nature of animal consciousness. With the dominance of behaviorism study of animal consciousness, like all foci on mental life, was deemed unscientific. But the use of animals in psychology laboratories became dominant in another manner. The white rat became the winner in laboratory popularity. They were small, easily housed and cared for, and with careful apparatus their ability to learn was investigated. Pavlov had his dogs, and Skinner preferred pigeons, but the rat was the subject of most studies of learning from the 1920s onward.

Observational studies of other animals continued as well. Primates were acknowledged to be our closest relatives in the animal kingdom so psychologists like Robert Yerkes (1876-1956) set up primate research facilities. The Gestalt psychologist Wolfgang Köhler (1887-1967) also spent time at the primate facility in the Canary Islands and published important studies on insight learning in chimpanzees.

## Social.

Our life is embedded in groups of others, and the broader concept that covers the many humanly invented symbols and artifacts is culture. The material substrate is the humanly created environment of places and objects; the social substrate is the interactional patterns and realm of communication that structures human society.

August Quetelet (1794-1874), a French scholar, is known as the father of demographics and instituted some of the earliest population surveys. He also invented the Body Mass Index (BMI) as a means of studying body size and composition. His aspiration was to apply the newly emerging mathematical tools of probability theory and statistics into what he called social physics. Like Fechner with sensation, physics became the model for science. All disciplines sought to relate themselves back to physics as the basis of all science. The human science perspective, however, challenged that reductionism. For now, the lesson is that the natural science perspective on social phenomena emerged at a similar time period and with similar hopes.

Though Wundt is most remembered for his physiological psychology, it was earlier noted that in the latter part of his career he shifted toward what he called *Völkerpsychologie*, or cultural psychology. Also influential in this time period were the French sociologist Émile Durkheim's (1858-1917) study on suicide and Max Weber's (1864-1920) study on the Protestant work ethic. Anthropology likewise began contributing both field work in ethnography as well as theoretical concepts such as culture itself.

In American psychology social psychology gets its most widely known proponent with Floyd Allport (1890-1978). His 1924 textbook established this course in the curriculum (Hilgard, 1983). His brother Gordon Allport (1897-1967) also contributed an early study on the psychology of prejudice (1958/1954).

## Conclusion

Psychology has focused on the individual person and studied the person in a laboratory through experimental methods. We soon broadened our scope to develop the techniques of formal psychometric assessment instruments to describe the rich diversity of human attributes, their thoughts, feelings and motives. Now we have begun to make the links down toward our physiological roots and upward toward our various groups.

Psychology emerged as a science and an academic discipline in the second half of the nineteenth century, independent from its roots in philosophy, education, and physiology. This new discipline saw itself as striving to become an experimental science. The locus of such sciences was the laboratory. So most of the narrative around the development of how psychology sought to gain knowledge about human experience and behavior was generated by laboratories. Sociology and anthropology have a long history and rich tradition in field studies, going out into the world and observing things as they occur in nature. Psychology has had almost nothing in the way of a tradition of field research. Barker's (1968; 1978) works on ecological psychology are the rare exception. Likewise the locus of study of healing and medicine is the clinic and the hospital. While psychologists were employed to do research and assessment in those venues, therapy was still seen as a medical activity and outside our scope of competency. So the thrust of American psychology from its first decades in the nineteenth century through nearly mid twentieth century was the laboratory where subjects were put through experimental conditions to find laws of behavior. As noted in Chapter 1, the locus of practice has a great deal to do with the nature of practice, as it embodies the goals, values, and methods of the dominant cultural force in the locus. We will see later where professional psychology gets its own locus.

Though the laboratory and the academic department of psychology were the modal loci of occupation, it wasn't the only one. From very early in its development, there was interest in applying the findings of the laboratory to concrete human problems and needs. The application was brought psychologists in contact with situations where the degree of control in the lab were impossible to achieve, so new tools had to be developed. These new tools involved interviews with subjects to learn more about their life circumstances, and specific procedures aimed at measuring certain important functions.

Eventually, a body of data emerged about how individuals differed on a variety of measures. The field of differential psychology flourished for many decades, and in the process, mental testing of all sorts became a major specialty of professional psychology. The psychology of individual differences was, in its own way, a progenitor of the modern course on cultural differences.

# 9

## Measuring the Mind

### Psychometrics, testing, and early professional activities

How do we match up mental life with numbers? The movement toward quantifying, assigning numbers, to human functions led to two main families of approaches. One would remain mainstream with experimental psychology and use statistical methods involving tests of significance and the null hypothesis. The other family developed out the of the study of individual differences, or differential psychology. It emphasized correlational statistics and led to what we now call psychometrics, the specialty within psychology dealing with measurement issues. The sensory and motor functions were early foci for laboratory investigations in physiology, and formed the basis of Fechner's psychophysics. So early psychology sought to measure sensory and motor processes in both experimental and psychometric approaches.

A major pioneer in psychological measurement was the British psychologist, Francis Galton (1822-1911). He developed the first ideas regarding numerical correlation and regression. His student Karl Pearson (1856-1936) refined his approach, giving us the Pearson product moment statistic, or $r$ in 1894. Galton was also a prolific writer in many areas, including meteorology. He also pioneered survey and questionnaire methods. He created a standardized series of weights for tactile sensory testing, a whistle for acoustic testing, and arranged a number of these individual items into the first test battery. He also developed word association technique, the use of twins for studying inheritance. In short, he was quite the innovator of means to quantify behavior. Joseph Jastrow (1863-1944) studied with Galton and later taught at the University of Wisconsin. In the 1893 Chicago World's Fair, Jastrow organized a booth where all of Galton's equipment was there, and for a small fee, a visitor could be tested and receive a card with all the data. His battery involved what he termed anthropometric data; including cranial measurement, visual and auditory acuity, grip strength and reaction time. All but cranial measurement are still part of the psychologist's tool chest as part of a comprehensive neuropsychological evaluation. The craniometric measurement was a hold over from phrenology and earlier physiognomonic theories of personality, both early and mis-guided attempt to link brain function and bodily appearance to psychology. It also reflects a continuation of the trend to study physiognomy, physical structure and appearance, as a sign of character or intelligence (Gilman, 1982). Galton also coined the term eugenics, which was to later develop in support of racial supremacist ideas and sanction forced sterilization of the mentally disabled; we also owe the phrase nature versus nurture to his fruitful pen.

The term *mental test* was coined by James McKean Cattell (1860-1944). He was the first American student to earn a Ph.D. from Wundt in Leipzig. He came back and spent most of his career at Columbia University. His tests, like Galton's were mostly sensory and motor in nature, preferring precision of measurement to usefulness in context. The mental testing movement quickly expanded to include much more verbal material, which further opened up survey research methodology as well as more academically focused tests of intelligence, aptitude and academic achievement. Yet, if we look at the 10 tests recommended by Cattell to be a basic battery (Reisman, 1991), many are in continued use in neuropsychological tests. The hand dynamometer is part of the Halstead-Reitan neuropsychological test battery (Reitan & Wolfson, 1985). The Luria-Nebraska neuropsychological battery (Golden, Hammeke, & Purisch, 1980) included two-point sensation as an item. If one looks at the concept of rate of movement, the Finger-tapping Test of the Halstead-Reitan battery still embodies the concept though the precise measuring instrument changed. Just noticeable difference in weight and reaction time for sound are not used in modern neuropsychology. Line bi-section tasks are still known in neuropsychology. The time for naming colors is incorporated in several short term memory tests tapping into over-learned material (letters of alphabet, days of week backward, etc.). We no longer measure immediate verbal memory by number of letters remembered, but the Wechsler family of intelligence tests shifted the stimulus item to numbers to tap the same area. Thus, Cattell's battery would lead to many of modern neuropsychological concepts through the concept of biological intelligence which Ward Halstead sought to identify (1947). It often happens in psychology that a person's contribution is absorbed into the mainstream, and becomes just part of the background fabric of contemporary practice with few knowing how significant their contribution was. James McKeen Cattell is less well remembered compared with Alfred Binet, whose name lives on in an existing test, but every time a psychologist, particularly a neuropsychologist gives a battery a little nod of appreciation for his role would be in order.

Cattell was one of the founding figures behind the Psychological Corporation, one of today's leading test publishers. The Psychological Corporation was primarily as a clearinghouse for psychologists who wanted to offer their services, and persons or organizations seeking them. By 1937 it had four divisions, clinical, industrial, marketing and advertising. It was taken over by a publishing firm in 1970 and integrated with a number of similar product lines. Most professional psychologists are familiar with its Wechsler family of tests, which it owns and updates from time to time.

The Binet scale was the first individually administered test. It gave the field a practical application of measuring mental abilities. The test was created to fill the need to identify children who are not capable of benefitting from schooling as then available. Intellectual and developmental disabilities as well as congenital sensory impairments often were segregated into special institutions and schools. The need of the Paris public schools to identify students not capable of gaining skills from further education led to the involvement of Alfred Binet (1857-1911) and his colleagues Victor Henri (1872-1940) and Theophile Simon (1873-1961). They developed a scale, first published in 1905, which became the standard by which intelligence was measured for many years to come. His scale shows the trend to use more verbal measure rather than physical ones. A number of items, both verbal and physical, were put together in a battery. Their innovation was to arrange the administration of the items in terms of age, from simple to more complex in difficulty. Binet, like many in that era, started with sensory evaluation, for example, two-point discrimination. He also conceptualized cognition into ideation and imagery, an early version of the visual-verbal dichotomy in current intelligence testing construction. It was known that children's intellectual capacity increases over age and education, so the concept of intelligence which Binet put forth was a ratio of the mental age, as measured by the test, to the chronological age. William Stern (1871-1938) took this quotient of intelligence (I= MA/CA) and made it into the IQ as a single summary measure (Hilgard, 1987)

Another person of note was Edouard Séguin (1812-1880), a student of Itard, the French physician who pioneered work with sensory and developmental disabilities. Séguin also specialized in educating those with retardation or severe sensory disabilities. He first used a form board, a board with removable blocks in various geometric shapes. This later became standardized and used as a test of performance or non-verbal intelligence. A modified version of this survives as the Tactual Performance Test, part of the Halstead-Reitan neuropsychological battery. Later, Janet (1925) would claim that the work of Itard and Séguin was directly part of the stream of transmission creating psychological healing.

Back in America, the education of persons we now would recognize as retarded was segregated into special schools, often large residential institutions. One such was the Training School for the Feeble-Minded at Vineland, New Jersey. Its early director of research was one of G. Stanley Hall's graduates from Clark, Henry H. Goddard (1866-1957), was one of the first to adopt the Binet-Simon scale and adapt it to American uses. Goddard was also the first psychologist to be professional employed full-time outside of an academic setting (Napoli, 1981). Goddard was a strong believer in hereditary influences. His study of the Kallikak family advanced the thesis that a hereditary taint could be passed on in families, leading to mental subnormality, criminality, poverty and other bad outcomes. This fed into both native racism as well as the eugenics movement, which was an off-shoot of social Darwinism.

The person to really capitalize on the Binet-Simon scale was Lewis Terman (1877-1956). He founded the psychology department and laboratory at Stanford University, and in 1916 published another Stanford revision of the Binet-Simon scale. He had a norm sample of 2,100 children (Reisman, 1991). He also developed a classification system to describe the range of scores from defective to superior adult. The Stanford-Binet is still a current test, now in its fifth edition.

Though he is most widely known as a pioneer in the study of primates and comparative psychology, Robert Yerkes (1876-1956) had a part-time appointment at Boston Psychopathic Hospital and there worked on an intelligence test. He and his colleagues developed a point scale on the Binet model; arranging items testing a similar function together, and ordering them in terms of difficulty (Reisman, 1991). This became a model to develop the first group administered measure of intelligence. He and J. D. Dodson developed the Yerkes-Dodson law relating arousal and performance in the now familiar inverted U-shaped curve demonstrating the disadvantageous effects of too little or too much arousal.

World War I (1914-1918 in Europe, American entered only in 1917) had a huge impact on the mental testing movement in psychology. As part of the response to the war, in 1917, an Emergency Committee was formed within APA to aid the government war effort, chaired by Yerkes. They were quickly put to work to devise a screening tool to identify military recruits who suffered from mental and emotional problems that would prevent their successful training as a soldier. The Army Alpha (verbal) and Beta (non-verbal) tests were devised. These were the first group administered tests of intelligence. In addition, they devised a structured interview as a screen for mental illness. These activities were generally accepted as useful, though criticisms of the tests were made even early after the war. In any event, it marked the real entry of psychology into the arena of professional services. We were first of all testers.

## Clinical psychology

Lightner Witmer is recognized for founding the first psychological *clinic* in 1986 at the University of Pennsylvania, and coining the phrase *clinical psychology*. What he did, however, was what we would now recognize as educational or school psychology. His first case was a referral from an elementary school principle concerning a young child who was having problems learning to spell (Napoli, 1981). From there he developed ties with a number of school personnel and began assessing and recommending plans of specialized educational treatment. He began publishing a journal, *Psychological Clinic*, in 1906. In the end, his academic duties won out and he became less involved in clinical practice. This begins the delicate balance among professional roles as educator and trainer of the next generation of psychologists, practitioner, and even administrator.

This new area for psychologists not only became known as clinical psychology, but Witmer attempted to popularize another concept, *psychological orthogenics*. This he conceived of as a pedagogical discipline, a type of training and guidance that included vocational, correctional, educational, hygienic, industrial and social components (Reisman, 1991). This was a grand vision and was a realm outside the scope of medical practice. This new clinical psychology was in actuality more an embodiment of the archetype of the teacher, than the physician, though the use of the term clinical suggests a movement toward the medical roots of healing, while the orthogenetic component represents the pedagogical roots of the rhetor and teacher.

Psychology came from two roots, physiology and philosophy, especially education and pedagogy. Here we see a clear boundary between the domain of medicine and that of psychology get a bit blurry by the appropriation of the concept of the clinic. Experimental science was done in laboratories. Physicians attempted to cure the sick in clinics and hospitals. If knowledge is curative, then schools are the locus of therapeutic philosophy. Reisman (1991) notes that one of the reasons why Witmer's call for a clinical psychology was not met with a vigorous response was that psychologists wanted to make experimentation the basis of the new discipline. They carved out their first niche as a discipline distinguished by experimental methods and a laboratory locus of operations.

While the label we give to the locus of work is important (e.g. laboratory vs clinic) the goal was also different. The psychologists sought to do basic research in human functions; the physicians had the burden of healing, of being able to aid the other. The laboratory was the first entry point into hospitals, clinics and other medical settings. Like all laboratories in a hospital, they served to enlighten the physicians, who were the main consumers of their activities. This is why assessment was the early professional role adopted by psychologists. It was a good bridge between science, measurement, and experiment, and the world of human suffering and its amelioration. It would take some time before the value of psychological practice was more directly felt for the client. In the period between the First and Second World wars, professional psychology made this transition. In particular, the role of psychometric instruments to assess a variety of things moved from he academic research laboratories to schools, businesses, and government agencies as well.

The less appreciated dynamic is between the laboratory and the class room. Witmer's work was focused more on cognitive and behavioral issues than psychopathology, diagnosis and treatment. The applications of psychometric theory to the measurement of human differences and the prediction of academic or vocational suitability would generate a market for structured testing. Both in industry and education psychometric instruments would find a use. So the measurement of difference created a niche role for psychologists.

While many early psychologists also had medical degrees, several who did not worked closely with physicians. Among the earliest was Shepard Ivory Franz (1847-1933). He was the first psychologist at McLean Hospital, and had taught physiology at two medical schools. In many ways, he was the first neuropsychologist and health psychologist. He did research on tactile sensation and cortical localization. He pioneered ablation experiments in neuropsychology. An animal would have a particular area of the brain surgically removed and then the impact on behavior was observed. This new animal model allowed more rapid assessment of localization of function. Through these experiments he was able to establish that other brain areas take over certain functions that were damaged by the extirpation of one area. This became the basis of neuro-rehabilitation. Training individuals to by-pass areas of damage and establish increased function through recruitment of other brain areas. He then went on to pioneer rehabilitation of aphasics, persons with primary language disorder due to brain damage from stroke, for example (Reisman, 1991). The leading neuropsychologist in the generation between the two World Wars (1920s, 1930s) was Karl Lashley (1890-1958) who collaborated with Franz for post-doctoral research. Lashley was trained in genetics and biology, but was very influenced by the integrative theories of psychiatrist, Adolf Meyers (1866-1950) as well as John B. Watson, the early behaviorist.

By the outbreak of World War I in Europe, in 1914, professional psychology in America had grown significantly. Reisman (1991) notes the growth in the number of psychology clinics at major mental or urban general hospitals as well as attached to university departments of psychology. The latter were clearly part of an emerging structure for the training of professional psychologists. He goes on to also identify early sites of formal internship training programs. These are the basic elements in forming a full fledged professional identity. Ideally, you have to have sites where students can be exposed to a wide range of clinical situations under proper supervision, supplementing their academic preparation. This link between practice and instructional model marks the emergence of fully professional training programs which wouldn't manifest until several decades later. Psychology, however, was now a profession, as well as a laboratory science. We took on the care of human beings and an obligation to work for their betterment. It took, however, until 1951 before the profession had sufficiently matured to adopt a code of ethics. That came at a time discussed in a later chapter.

## The child guidance movement

In the decades around the beginning of the twentieth century, a broad movement of social progressivism and reform was underway in the United States. Labor unions and organizing was gaining recognition and some legitimacy. Upton Sinclair's (1906) novel about the appalling work and sanitary conditions in the meat industry around the Chicago stockyards set in motion reforms in work place safety and food purity. The first separate court for minors was instituted in 1899 in Illinois. The Juvenile Psychopathic Institute was founded in Chicago in 1909. It was lead by psychiatrist and neurologist William Healy (1969-1963) and was the first comprehensive program of assessment of juvenile delinquents with advice to the court regarding sentencing was instituted.

There was a strong assumption of optimism, that given some other type of response than imprisonment, these troubled youngsters could be rescued from repeating their errors. Beneficial learning could correct their dispositions to act in anti-social ways. This optimism, though later tempered by the problem of recidivism, nonetheless, started a number of facilities which needed staff to help the courts decide how to deal with the problem of juvenile crime. These ideas were consistent with Witmer's early views on the role of psychology in clinical contexts. The first clinical psychologist was hired to work with the children; Grace Fernald (1879-1950) with a doctorate in psychology began her work under a physician's supervision. Napoli (1981) calls our attention to this fact and notes how much of the rest of psychology's time as a profession has been caught up in second class status vis a vis medical professionals.

The origins of professional social work also occur in Chicago during this period through the work of Jane Addams (1860-1935). She established a settlement house which provided important services to immigrants. Hull House, the institution she founded, provided various classes and an expanding variety of other services, including cultural activities such as arts and gymnasia. Both adults and children took advantage of the many resources that were found at the center. She was influenced by, and in turn influenced the Chicago school of sociology, led by George Herbert Mead (1863-1931), then at the University of Chicago. His idea of the self as constructed through social means, a tradition known as symbolic interactionism, is one of the major concepts incorporated into the current social psychology of the person. The school pioneered field work in urban sociology. These were golden years for the social sciences at the University of Chicago with John Dewey in psychology, education and philosophy, and Mead and his colleagues in sociology.

Other streams fed into the formation of modern social work. Social services of all sorts were generally seen to be the domain of charitable organizations, usually with religious foundations. There were many voluntary aid societies prior to late nineteenth century Chicago. During the Civil War most nursing personnel were volunteers. The Sanitary Commission coordinated the volunteers, including Walt Whitman, the great American poet, who served the needs of the troops, particularly the ill or wounded. Nursing began with the work of the British woman, Florence Nightingale (1820-1910), who attended the wounded in the Crimean war (1854-56) began nursing as a profession aimed at the physical care of others. While nursing cared for the ill in hospitals, social workers used the settlement house as a locus of operations. As noted above, the goals were organized around the task of adapting to and coping with life in a new and unfamiliar country. Finding jobs, housing, ensuring sufficient food, and the other necessities of life were all part of the program aimed at successful adaptation to a new culture. Language acquisition, and passing on knowledge of local customs were likewise part of the social and cultural adaptation process.

## Professional contexts

The late nineteenth and early twentieth centuries were periods of time when the modern social welfare emerged. Institutions for the confinement, segregation and at least theoretically for treating the mentally ill and developmentally disabled had evolved from few to many and the quality of their care inconsistent. While Foucault's (1973/1965), claim of an age of confinement may be exaggerated, clearly many institutions warehoused their patients with little additional aid. These institutions existed in periods of optimism and pessimism about the ability of human suffering to be changed or cured by active treatment.

Most hospitals in America at this point in time were operated by religious organizations, Protestant, Catholic or Jewish. The hospital or the settlement house and later other charitable organizations with a variety of approaches and programs were the early embodiment of altruism, the belief in helping others without thought of gain, but out of kindness. From these beginnings emerged a number of professions who still donate many hours of volunteer time in service, even though they have become health care or helping service professionals. The ethos of charity, however, is often one-sided and can become paternalistic. In the 1970s, the disability rights movement would add another perspective.

From this beginning the basic team for mental health services has been comprised of various combinations of professionals from psychiatry, social work, psychology, and others. Team conferences, team input was considered important in getting a comprehensive picture of the client. In many ways, this inter-disciplinary model was a recognition of what we would now see as the bio-psycho-social model of human experience.

It can be said with some confidence that the work with juvenile justice was the founding context of activity for forensic psychologists. The expansion of the role of professional psychology into the role of expert witness before a court of law, or at least provision of reports to the judiciary for evaluation of sentencing began with work with children. The field of clinical psychology, likewise, got its start in contexts which dealt with children and adolescents. The developmental focus tells us that psychology first sought to make itself useful toward human ends began by turning to the young, the most vulnerable, most dependent and in greatest need. Applying what we could learn to adults came after, but very quickly. Psychology as an applied discipline, a new born profession, began as a child with children.

The step needed for a profession to loom is a degree of autonomy. Thus far, all applied activities were at the invitation of teachers, principals, judges and physicians. One critical requirement for this to occur was establishing that non-medical, i.e., psychological means, as an effective mode of action. A psychiatrist, Morton Prince (1854-1929) provided just this rationale. He was the first to explicitly identify learning as a mode of resolving neuroses. Reisman (1991) noted that all of the varieties of psychotherapy are but different forms of education. So re-learning bad habits, neurotic repressions, and other forms of pathology could be meliorated by psycho-social interaction.

The next requirement for a profession to emerge was a method. The dominant means of doing that was generally seen as a medical tool, hypnosis. As we saw, the first really psycho-social technique for healing emerged out of exorcism and faith healing in the Western cultural context became labeled hypnosis. The induction of trances, or altered states of consciousness was the main method. Freud broke with this to found the discipline of psychoanalysis. The other method was therapeutic discourse, advice giving or counseling in a generic sense.

The two lead streams of professional activity, hypnosis and phrenological counseling, merge into the psychodynamic and behavioral streams of transmission. Freud's publication in 1900 of his independent work came with his work *The interpretation of dreams,* marks the opening dialog about techniques that don't use trances or altered states. It was a phase-shift moment in intellectual history and in the history of healing by psychological means. In 1913, John B. Watson (1878-1958) set out the first behavioral position which was based on reflex conditioning models of learning, which were then current. The humanistic-existential roots emerge next, in the 1920s and 1930s, first in Germany with the Gestalt psychologists of perception, and then in America, with the social Gestalt theorists, Lewin and Heider. They brought a European dialectical tradition, emphasizing holism and integration. The social systems stream emerges at the boundary between other disciplines such as social work and teaching (pedagogy). Each of those streams feeding into the current flow of professional psychology will be separately addressed in their own chapters.

## Applied psychology for business and law

We have touched upon the origins of clinical psychology as one major branch of applied psychology. Some of the other ways and contexts in which psychological knowledge and skills can be used came about during these same formative years. Organizational/industrial psychology, forensic psychology and counseling psychology all share the common goal of putting psychology to work on practical problem solving.

Frederick Taylor (1856-1915) is a founding figure in industrial psychology. He was trained as a machinist and became a foreman. From this he evolved the concept of time and motion studies for efficient completion of a work activity. He started a call for rational management with efficiency as the desired outcome. This was the first attempt to apply science to business, his 1911 book *Principles of scientific management*, started that project. It was also, arguably, the first of an on-going genre, the latest management craze. The pace at which a hot new approach to management has been published has quickened since Taylor's era. Management by objectives, total quality management (TQM), and other pitches for the latest wisdom on how to scientifically organize a business stem from Taylor's pioneering effort. In some ways like Wundt, he was an elementarist and not particularly sensitive to the human issues on the work place. The mechanized efficiency he promoted got the ire of workers and was labeled as *Taylorism*.

The first psychologist to seriously become involved with commerce was Walter Dill Scott (1869-1955), of Northwestern University, who was invited to give a talk to a group of Chicago advertising executives about the new discipline of psychology. This began a long consulting career. In 1909 he became not only a professor of psychology, but in the school of business a professor of advertising (Napoli, 1981). He was influential in bringing psychometric testing for vocational selection and placement to the military, corporations, and universities (McCarthy, 2014). His advocacy for the use of psychology grew from his conviction that " . . . the study of own's own mind and that of others is one of the most pleasing and profitable studies for all persons" (Scott, 1906, p. 9).

Hugo Munsterberg (1863-1916), published *Psychology and industrial efficiency* in 1913. This was the standard bearing call for psychology involved in business. One of his own businesses was forensic consultation. His book, *On the witness stand* (1909a) is a pioneering piece in psychologist as expert witness. In that same year he published *Psychology and the teacher*. Thus, he spans all of the other bases of professional psychology besides the clinical. He covers psychology in education, in the courts and in business. He set out what would later become the areas of concern of personnel selection, vocational guidance, and job placement (Hilgard, 1987). He is also one of the pioneers in attempting to understand the motives of criminals.

Walter van Dyke Bingham (1880–1952) found employment at the Carnegie Institute of Technology and founded the Division of Applied Psychology where he hired L. L. Thurstone while completing his Ph.D. This was the first independent training program in applied psychology (Reisman, 1991). While there he started a bureau of salesmanship research, persuading Walter Dill Scott to take a leave of absence from Northwestern. But he also made vocational counseling and assessment a major focus, which feeds into the stream of modern counseling psychology. The two key concepts assessed and measured in this area are interests and aptitudes.

Scott was later influential in helping the Army develop an entire personnel system, according to Hilgard (1987). After the war he set up the Scott corporation, which is the first psychological consultation entity. One of his psychologists, Beardsley Ruml persuaded the U.S. Civil Service Commission to hire a consultant to ensure adoption of a sound psychometric basis for the civil service examinations.

## Counseling and education

Counseling psychology, along with clinical psychology, are the twin specialties leading to licensed practice as a health care provider. All fifty US states recognize degrees in Clinical and Counseling psychology as eligible for licensing as providers. The historic difference between the two was the location of their early activities. Clinical psychology were more frequently found in hospitals, sites controlled by physicians. Counseling psychologists began providing services in college counseling centers, social service agencies dealing with the disabled and even in primary and secondary schools. These are sites not controlled by physicians but psychologists themselves, social workers or educators. The irony, of course, is that Witmer's original view of clinical psychology is now being performed mostly by psychologists training in school or counseling psychology.

This difference in both the locus of practice and the population one encounters would shape the look and feel of counseling psychology. It saw itself as dealing with essentially normal individuals who were undergoing a developmental process and needed guidance of that process. Coping with life-transitions, particularly the transitions from childhood through adolescence and into adulthood, were major goals of counseling. Psychotherapy was done with people who were seriously abnormal, aimed at major and lasting personality change as opposed to better adjustment. Over the author's own lived experience these dichotomies have become less pronounced and even have disappeared. Counseling psychologists are now found in hospitals and clinical psychologists in schools. The major difference that persists is the greater likelihood of counseling psychologists receiving training in vocational and occupational theory.

One of the earliest applications of counseling with adults was through vocational counseling. Oberman (1965) notes the close association of early vocational counseling as a service provided by charitable organizations working with persons with disability. A psychology of occupation and vocation emerged with the work of Frank Parsons (1854-1908). He conceptualized vocational choice as a function of self awareness of abilities or aptitudes, and interests, coupled with knowledge of the requirements of various jobs available in the market, and a process of moving to a match between job and applicant. This formula stands today as a basic framework for vocational guidance. As with many developments in psychology, war played a part. The National Vocational Guidance Association was started in 1913. The University of Minnesota became a leading center, attracting such seminal figures in counseling psychology as Donald G. Paterson (1892-1961) and two of his students, John G. Darley and C. Gilbert Wren, the fifth and sixth presidents of Division 17, Counseling Psychology.

In the wake of World War I, the Veterans' Bureau, the bureaucratic predecessor to the Veterans Administration and now Department of Veterans Affairs, instituted a vocational counseling and guidance program for disabled veterans from that conflict. This was expanded in the 1920s and 1930s to include non-veteran disabled adults who might benefit from some type of rehabilitation to help them gain employment as a source of independence. Thus, another source of the development of counseling psychology was the growth of vocational rehabilitation. By the end of World War II, rehabilitation psychology emerged as a specialty within psychology, ultimately becoming Rehabilitation Psychology, Division 22 of APA (Larson & Sachs, 2000).

There were a number of disease specific self-help organizations and charities that formed in the early part of the twentieth century. Tuberculosis was a major public health problem and resulted in several charitable organizations aimed at research promotion and service. In 1904 the National Tuberculosis Association was formed and through the next several decades psychologists and vocational counselors became involved in working directly with persons with disabilities aimed at increasing the functional capacities of the individuals (1965).

## The drive to mid century

As noted above, psychologists helped the government classify and screen the large number of men entering military services when the U. S. entered the war. After the war, however, those tests were released for civilian use, and a boom occurred in the testing business. Increasingly industry and commerce were interested in using these or other measures to screen prospective employees and try and match them to the jobs for which they were best suited. Though psychologists were involved in other sorts of professional activities, such as counseling and a very limited degree of psychotherapy, the expanding role in assessment paved the way for the entry of psychologists into hospitals, businesses, schools and the like.

In the science of psychology the era of the grand systems of psychology faded as the diversification of interests made the possibility of a single comprehensive system seem unattainable. The first decades of the twentieth century saw the sort of experimental psychology started by Wundt and brought to America by Edward Titchener (1867-1927) termed structuralism. But American psychology was much more influenced by William James and his pragmatic thrust. In psychology this became known as functionalism, and included men like Dewey and James Angell at the University of Chicago. Behaviorism became the dominant force in the 1920s after Watson launched his call for a more objective psychology. In Germany, the Gestalt psychology became influential in America in the decade preceding World War II, in large measure because of the flight of several key figures as Hitler's anti-Semitic policies made life for Jews in academia impossible. Freud had little impact on American psychology, despite the invitation by G. Stanley Hall to come to Clark University and present his ideas. American psychiatry, however, came to adopt Freudian theory and abandon the more holistic approach advocated by Adolf Meyer (1866-1950) under his rubric *psychobiology*. Now a bio-psycho-social approach (Engel 1977) is bringing back a sort of holism that Meyer envisioned. These are the great systems of psychology, structuralism, functionalism, behaviorism, Gestalt and psychoanalysis.

Intelligence tests went beyond the Binet scale for individual tests or the Army alpha and beta for group administered tests. L. L. Thurstone (1887-1955) criticized the basic concept of IQ as a ratio of mental to chronological age and moved psychology to adopt the use of percentile ranks with respect to persons of similar age. Lewis Terman not only adapted the Binet Scale to emerging American testing practices, but was among the first to study the gifted as a special population.

Personality assessment was dominated by psychoanalytic thought. A whole batch of tests emerged in the 1920s and 1930s which were termed projective (Reisman, 1991). The method of free association which Freud pioneered and emphasized was expanded by others. The projective hypothesis is, given an ambiguous stimulus a person will project onto it the meanings of their unconscious processes. The censoring ego gives socially acceptable answers to objective questions, but the ambiguity can only be shaped by unconscious drives, complexes and so on. One of Freud's early followers, Carl Jung, developed a word association test based on this general principle, though words are less ambiguous than ink blots. Herman Rorschach (1884-1922) developed the ink blot test which now bears his name. It was derived from a parlor game of the period in Germany using ink blots. Henry Murray and a colleague, Christina Morgan, brought out the Thematic Apperception Test (TAT) in 1935. Murray chose works of art that had some content that was more recognizable. He added the element of asking the person to make up a story about what's happening in the picture, and tell the examiner an outcome among other probes. He is also among the first to champion the study of life narratives in psychology. In addition to those relatively ambiguous stimulus situations, a number of other projective methods arose. Drawings of all sorts as well as handwriting were means by which people could project their inner motives. Handwriting analysis is mostly used in the U.S. for document authentication rather than personality assessment, but there is a European tradition for that. Drawings of a house, a tree, and a person form one additional cluster. Kinetic family drawings ask a child to draw their family.

The tide was going against comprehensive systems. Scientific psychology became dominated by learning theory as the central concern and behaviorism as it main theory. Professional psychology grew slowly and mostly in the area of testing and assessment.

## The gathering storm

During the 1930s psychology was growing as an academic discipline. Its principal focus was on laboratory investigations of learning using the white rat. Learning theory, though not the only game in town, still got the most attention. But this decade saw an influx of psychologists to the United States from Germany and Austria as Nazi ideology gained political power, dissent quashed, and Jewish intellectuals threatened with imprisonment in concentration camps. Several Gestalt psychologists, Kurt Koffka came intermittently from 1924 onward, settling permanently later. Wolfgang Köhler came in 1935, and Kurt Lewin in 1933.

World War II was to fundamentally change the face of psychology. The story of how we came to get into the business of psychotherapy comes during and after the war, and will be covered in a later chapter. The roles of psychologists during the war was largely personnel selection and training activities, but increasingly presence in hospitals began occurring.

This chapter focused on the role of standardized psychological tests as the main vehicle by which clinical and counseling psychology made their first appearance as an assessment service. The earliest attempts at a profession of psychology were most successful where measurement of various ability met with a practical social concern. Relatively few psychologists were involved in psychotherapy which was then seen as a medical activity. Counseling, however, was a more open domain. But interventions of all sorts played less of a role in the first half of the twentieth century than in the second half. We now turn to several of the more prominent theories of intervention and examine their historical and theoretical underpinnings.

# 10

# Psychodynamic Approaches

WHILE IT IS FAIR to say that there were earlier forms of therapeutic dialog, most textbooks on therapy credit Freud and his development of psychoanalysis as the beginning of the modern era of psychotherapy technique. This chapter traces the development of that tradition of psychotherapy. The earlier forms of treatment included the moral treatment movement such as Tuke's approach as predecessor of the social milieu approach to treatment. Hypnosis was an early method of treatment based on a psychology of altered consciousness, trance induction. In addition, there were traditions in counseling with a variety of emerging social service agencies (e.g. child guidance, vocational rehabilitation, etc.).

What the psychodynamic approach took on as its specialty was the verbal interchange. What it added was a theory of the unconscious. Henri Ellenberger (1905-1993) takes what he calls dynamic psychiatry as the subject of his history of therapy. He defines that branch of psychiatry by its use of one or another version of a theory of unconscious processes. The notion that below the surface of ordinary awareness is a deep reservoir of thought was made popular earlier by Karl Robert Eduard von Hartmann (1842-1906). When Sigmund Freud (1856-1939) decided to stop using hypnosis, he had to develop an alternative, one that would not rely on a trance, or an artificially induced altered state of consciousness. Out of this came the therapeutic dialog known as psychoanalysis. His theory of the unconscious contained the key to unlocking it with the technique of free association.

A person in a trance might be able to communicate, for example, automatic writing as a hypnotic phenomenon dates back to the late 1700s, according to Ellenberger (1970). The nature of psychoanalysis as conceived by Freud and as elaborated by Adler, Jung, and many others, was conducted as a normal dialog. Normal with one exception, at least, in orthodox analysis. By having the patient on a couch facing away from the analyst, there was a degree of deviation from the normal social context of conversation. But in most of the derivative forms of psychodynamic psychotherapy and counseling, the interchange is live and face to face seated comfortably facing each other. The instructions may still differ significantly from normal conversation, but the superficial external form was conversational, dialogical.

Freud, as a founding figure has had enormous impact on the field of psychotherapy. Just as it is said that all philosophy is a commentary on and derivative from Plato, so all psychotherapies are compared in many ways with psychoanalysis. In the public mind psychoanalysis stands for all forms of therapy, and though erroneous, the terms are often treated as synonymous but people outside the mental health field. Freudian ideas have so percolated into the popular culture that the cartoon portrayal of psychotherapists is based on the visual image of the analyst with client on a couch. Even therapies that derive from learning theory or broke away from Freud exist in a market place of nostrums for human suffering that has in many ways been defined by psychoanalysis. It is the first systematically worked out talking cure that caught on in a big way in both popular and professional discourse. Even the general public frequently conflates psychoanalysis and psychotherapy.

According to Ellenberger, the common thread from psychoanalysis back to mesmerism and hypnosis via Charcot and Janet, is the fact that they all deal with the person as a structure composed of conscious and unconscious components. What makes them psychodynamic is the fact that our behavior is an amalgam, an interplay between conscious and unconscious forces. Whether the basis of this structure is driven by the sex instinct, as Freud taught, or by other physical or socio-cultural forces, as the many post-Freudians would hold, there was attention to the interplay, or dynamics, between the conscious and unconscious. They generally account for both normal development and the formation of psychopathology as grounded in this interplay between material that is fully available to awareness and well formulated and those things which are less well formulated and may be completely out of awareness. The term psychodynamic is used as opposed to psychoanalytic. Psychoanalysis is but one species in the genus of psychodynamic approaches, which itself, is one family among several families of psychological healing, with itself is one family among the order of healing arts and sciences, which itself, is among the classes of occupations available as social roles for people in our and other cultures.

This common thread is shared to a high degree with humanistic-existential psychology, which derived in part from it, though coupled with other influences. Both psychoanalysis and existential and phenomenological approaches are grounded in the Kantian tradition as Rychlak noted (1977). Some cognitive theorists, likewise, might be considered psychodynamic, in the sense that internal and primarily subjective experiences are the result of interplay of conscious and unconscious forces. Erikson's developmental schema has broadened the ideas of the dynamics of personality to a point where it seems to assumptive to any coherent explanation of human behavior and experience. Each of the psychodynamic theorists differs from each other and from Freud in some way. The devil is in the details.

The very concept, dynamic, goes back to Leibniz in his works on mechanism and can be traced as it filtered into philosophy, physiology, and psychiatry. Ellenberger (1970) claims the link to psychiatry was made by the French physician Jean-Étienne Esquirol (1774-1840). The interplay and balance in the brain of neural inhibition and excitation shows how the metaphor of dynamics is literally instantiated in the root basis of consciousness and non-conscious processing. The importance of the balance between excitation and inhibition was pointed out by the British neurologist, Hughlings Jackson. He was one of the early neurologists to emphasis holistic neural processing in contrast to the strong position of the localizationists after Broca's and Wernicke's landmark successes.

One final note on historical context. Freud develops his theory of psychoanalysis at a time known as *fin de siecle*, French for end of an era. The First World War would profoundly change the social fabric not only of Europe where the greatest number of battles were fough, but globally. It brought about the end of the old monarchial dynasties and introduced new weapons of mass warfare. The decades following saw even more social and economic change, but those details come later.

## Janet and psychological analysis

Pierre Janet (1859-1947) was a link between the old mesmerists and magnetizers and the modern world of interpersonal therapy. His views have been eclipsed by the later development of psychoanalysis, which obscures the importance he held among his contemporaries. As noted above, his principal technique was hypnosis, but it was not his sole technique. His magnum opus, *Les Médications Psychologique* (1916), translated into English as *Psychological healing* (Janet, 1926/1916) also catalogued the role of education, guidance, and training in bringing about healing and amelioration of human problems. He cited Itard and Séguin as forerunners of the pedagogical style of treatment. The archetype of the teacher as purveyor of therapeutic wisdom is reinforced from the early work with developmental disabilities. He was beginning to conceive of the focus of his work in terms of consciousness as well as unconsciousness. His description of educational treatments for such things as stammering and other neuro-motor disturbances is remarkably recognizable in terms of the current variety of physical therapies, massage, and above all, cognitive-behavioral approaches. Even trance work was seen as more dynamic in nature, that is, dealing with underlying forces that bring the individual to feel, think or act in a certain way.

His major contributions were two, the importance of traumatic memories and the concept of dissociation, or *desaggregation* in the French. This arose out of a theory of consciousness including conscious and unconscious mechanisms of personality. The existence of multiple personalities in one biological individual was an extreme example of dissociation. A more common example in that era was the hysteric, someone, usually female, who experienced neurologically impossible paralysis or anesthesia (loss of sensation) in some bodily area. The modern categories of histrionic personality disorder and conversion disorder are the diagnostic remnants of hysteria. These were the two categories of abnormal mental states who were most studied. Janet, who was the successor to Charcot, and Freud who succeeded both of them in terms of popularity also focused on this group of patients. The American psychologist Ernest Hilgard (1904-2001) revived the concept of dissociation as the basis for hypnosis (1977).

Both of these ideas are now part of the foundational understanding of the nature of post-traumatic stress disorder (PTSD). The psychological impact of the traumatic event creates a recurring experience of the trauma. In some people this may be repressed by the ego as a means of coping with the unendurable, for others it becomes an intrusive and repeated reliving of the troubling events. The very means by which most people can continue to go forward in life is the splitting of awareness such that the traumatic memories can be isolated enough to allow daily life to resume. The degree to which this is successful, of course, varies with the severity of the trauma and other factors.

## Freud and psychoanalysis

Sigmund Freud (1856-1939) is probably among the most influential minds in Western history. While it is true that his basic idea of unconscious forces which influence human behavior can be traced back through other authors, what he did was develop a method of tapping into that pool of unconscious motivation that did not involve a trance or altered state of consciousness. The tool was free association, that is, the patient is instructed to say whatever comes to mind and not hold back anything. In contrast to his earlier training in hypnosis which used a trance, Freud employed a more conventional form of conversation and the normal waking consciousness. But the instruction to not censor one's comments is harder given the nature of the ego.

Although Freud conducted psychoanalysis through purely verbal means, from the outset, there were significant differences from normal conversation. He set the precedent for having the patient lying down on a couch and facing away from the analyst. The rationale is to de-emphasize the physical and social interactive aspects of the process and allow the client to focus on the internal flow of experience. The instruction for free association is to report whatever comes to mind in an uncensored manner; a dictum to report the contents of awareness without hindrance from concerns with logicality, social propriety or anything else than the stream of ongoing, freely reported, associations in the stream of thought. The aim was to capture the unconscious forces as they emerge through the censoring ego, when the ordinary safeguards of our defense mechanisms are loosened by some circumstance. This dialog coming from the id is what is termed primary process. The ego and superego create secondary processes to filter the content of id to standards and social expectations. The loosening of usual mental set was a goal that was shared with hypnosis, and may be the only vestige of his earlier interest which remained after he formulated his mature technique. The trance is just one, albeit somewhat dramatic way of loosening the boundary between the unconscious and the conscious.

Contrast this use of introspection, or looking within at the contents and processes or mind, with the methodology of Wundt and Titchener. The goal of introspection was not in any way personal, indeed, if anything personal intruded into the introspective report it was considered an error. They had their experimental subjects report a stream of atomistic sensations as they occurred in a highly particular way and were highly trained to report in a certain manner. This was part of their quest for the elements of mind before they were combined to make meaningful wholes; just as atoms can exist in some pure state before combining with each other into recognizable molecules. One can say that persons undergoing analysis likewise learn to report their awareness in a certain manner and under certain, albeit very different rules. The leakage of unconscious material revealed the various unresolved conflicts in the psyche which would allow repressed thoughts and feelings to come back into mind and be absorbed by the reality based ego bit by bit. Freud had his patients report the fragmentary images, thoughts and give voice to the impulses that come to the surface of awareness from deeper realms of the person, and the aim was to relink the conscious and unconscious in the individual that would eliminate troubling neurotic symptoms. Both the experimental and the clinical took the individual experiencing person as the root object of study though they treated in very different ways.

Freud focused his medical practice in neurology, and like many of his day began seeing patients suffering from hysteria. This led him into what would become psychiatry, the medical specialty dealing with mental illness. At this point in time neurology and psychiatry were not seen as separate disciplines (Moore, 1992). He considered his system, however, a system of psychology. However, in the United States, the psychiatric establishment took control of the psychoanalytic movement and restricted training to physicians. In Europe, the requirement of a medical degree for psychoanalytic training was not as hard or fast as it was in the United States. American Psychologists finally succeeded in a law suit to open up training to non-medical mental health professionals.

Freud developed his ideas in an intellectual climate. Sometimes he gave credit for his ideas. For example, in his work, *The ego and the id* (1927), he acknowledge the contribution of Groddeck (1961/1923) to his idea of the id. His notion of repression and the defense mechanisms are clearly influenced by Janet's concept of dissociation. According to Ellenberger (1970), when Freud read his first paper in Paris, he miffed Janet for failing to acknowledge his contribution regarding traumatic memories. Ellenberger traces the many roots of Freud's ideas, including their broad base in ideas that arise out of German idealism and romanticism, which provided the basic framework of an individual struggling to balance feelings with reason and assert the will. His whole ideal for what psychoanalysis would result in was grounded in a theory of progress from both Darwinian biology (Hanna,1970) and the long tradition of Herder, Fichte, Schopenhauer, Goethe and Hegel.

## Psychodynamics; forces and structures

Freud had two basic models of the person at different stages of his career. His earlier model is often called a hydraulic model, as it was based on thermodynamics. By the mid nineteenth century physics had studied diffusion of temperature and pressure so the metaphor of something under pressure seeking release was an obvious source for theory. The basic force concept was libido, the psycho-sexual energy. It manifests as sexual desire, and also serves as the chief motivating force for human activity. As the amount of this energy builds up it seeks discharge, or what he termed cathexis, onto objects of this desire. At its fullest developmental stage libido motivates the person to approach and seek a relationship and ultimate discharge of the sexual aspect of the motivating force through intercourse. Cathexis is a modification of the Aristotelian concept of catharsis or outflow of emotional and psychological energy. We can see the influence of Brentano, discussed two chapters later, in that all consciousness is consciousness of some object, so investing psychological energy in things in the outer world is inherent in human nature.

Freud's theory is deeply rooted in his theory of psychological development. The basic psycho-sexual nature of libido is channeled through a variety of erogenous zones from infancy onward into adulthood. These are areas of the body that give pleasure. The first zone of pleasure is the mouth, from the very suckling on the mother's breast that provides both sustenance and nurturance. The infant cathects its libido onto the mother. Over time as the child matures toilet training begins and the erogenous zone shifts to the anus. The releasing or withholding of bodily waste becomes the next source of pleasure. Next the child enters the phallic stage of development and the erogenous zone shifts to the penis. The male bias here is quite evident and psycho-analytic theory has struggled over time to find a more gender balanced explanation of development. But within his framework, the phallic stage represents a major period of time, since the young boy becomes aware at an unconscious level that his father is competition for the mother. The anxiety about castration leads to a shift in identification with and cathexis of libido to the mother to identification with the father and a normal male identity. Unresolved problems at this stage are the source of classical neurotic problems, all anxiety based. Freud termed this the Oedipal period from the Greek myth concerning a king of Thebes who killed his own father and married his mother, the very scenario Freud saw as undergirding the emerging awareness of the nature of desire in the three to five year old child. After resolving this dilemma libido quiets down as the child moves into what was termed the latency phase of development where the sexual nature of the instinctual urges is not available in awareness (or so the theory of child sexuality would hold). Finally, with puberty, the hormonal flush brings sexual desire to the surface in what shortly will be come the adult sexual identity and pattern of intimate relationships. Although Freud saw people as inherently bisexual, in the end, he believed that heterosexual union was the goal of development;

adult homosexual identity was a fixation of the normal course of development, albeit a relatively minor one in terms of psychic dysfunction. In psychoanalytic thought there were no further stages of psycho-sexual development after entering adulthood and later writers such as Erikson would extend these ideas.

But, of course, not all instinctual energy gets directed toward a receptive object, so the individual experiences blocking of cathexis. In addition society has deemed certain objects to be unacceptable, and this message gets communicated to the child who then represses the awareness of the link to unacceptable objects. This creates a pressure that continues to motivate the individual. If the energy is not discharged in one manner it seeks discharge elsewhere. This is the source of much of our behavior, we find substitute outlets for the energy when there is no ready object reciprocating our desire. Symptoms of neurosis are but one example of how this pool of energy gets channeled in different ways. He later noted that slips of the tongue and dreams reveal much about the unconscious manifestations of libido seeking discharge.

The major blocking force of libido is repression. This is completely unconscious at this stage. Later, when there is a functioning ego, the person can consciously suppress unwanted desires, but at this early stage nearly all psychic activity occurs below awareness. Other defense mechanism then arise in the course of psychological development. Projection, sublimation, acting out, reaction formation, compartmentalization, and dissociation are all different modes of handling psychic material and the accompanying anxiety about the unacceptable sexual or aggressive content of the desires fueled by libido.

Libido also became the focal point of dissent from some of his followers. Both Jung and Adler would break with him and hold other motivating forces to be as important or even more so. Like steam under pressure, libido, or psycho-sexual energy seeks discharge into lower pressure space. This internal force stemming from the id, or core biological basis of personality, and represents instinctual drives, needs, and wants.

Freud's second metaphor is structural, the nature of the person is a three-fold division of the psychic structure of the person between id, ego and superego. But this is basically a static metaphor, a model of the major regions of personality, normal as well as pathological. The two models are, of course, closely related and the shift in degree of emphasis between these metaphors over time in his writings did not deny the underlying unity they were reaching to explain. The structural metaphor for self arises out of the nature of repression. In terms of the developing child's consciousness, Freud taught that the sole governing principle is the pleasure principle. Libido seeks gratification because it is pleasurable. But reality in the form of parents and then the broader outside world thwarts immediate gratification. Out of the conflict between "I want" and "Here's what you're given" the ego emerges. The id is the instinctual source of desire, the superego is the internalized representation of the outside world with its limitations and rules. The ego emerges as the child gains some degree of conscious mastery over impulses to satisfy the outside constraints while finding some way to safely cathect the desirous libido. The ego is the engine of compromise.

Later in his career he added an opposing force to libido. Eros was the tendency of the libido to sustain and enhance life, in contrast with thanatos, or the instinct toward death. Freud by this time was dealing with his own mortality as well as the reaction among both professionals and the public to his emphasis on the sexual nature of our primary motives. But the roots of Freud's Eros/Thanatos polarity were also historical and cultural.

World War I had a profound impact on Freud and all who lived through that conflict. Mechanized warfare with new weapons (tanks, airplanes, poison gas), pointless slaughter on stagnant front lines, and ultimately the fall of major European dynasties. Thanatos was clearly manifested in the horrendous carnage that the war brought on as the old order collapsed and new social forces were unleashed. In the era following the end of the war so many of the social values and stabilizing restraints were cast off and a period of experimentation flourished. The youth threw off old restraints and saw in Freud a champion of a new freedom. His open discussion of sexuality which alarmed the conservative forces, was seen as a fresh breath of air by others. In America, however, Puritanism reasserted itself in passage of a Constitutional amendment prohibiting alcohol. Americans went to speakeasies for bootleg liquor which facilitated the growth or organized crime. It was in these environments that the jazz age in music began. Music, dancing, and illegal liquor fueled young people's rebellion against the old order of society. Short hair cuts for women, short skirts and exposed limbs heralded a new era of openness to sexuality and pleasure. These developments were found elsewhere. For example, the youth of the Weimar Republic in Germany played out a new life of freedom, including sexual freedom, in the cabaret society immortalized by Kurt Weil's music and the musical and movie *Cabaret*. Freud's focus on libido was part of a new understanding of the person as a sexual being. For better or for worse, this aspect of Freud's theory had an impact. Soon political forces unleashed in World War I would lead to the rise of authoritarian regimes. Communism triumphed in Russia, Fascism came to Italy and Spain, and Nazism to Germany. Freud had to flee Austria in 1938 even as he was ailing from cancer.

Having discussed his theory personality, what about therapy? Given that the cause of neurosis is the repression of instinctual urges, the way out is to bring the unconscious to light and allow the healing force of rationality replace the turbulent forces of nature. The claim of reason over emotion has a long history in Western thought so Freud was not new in this. His means, however, are the key to why psychoanalysis flourished. In free association clues to the narrative of repression are given and with skill the talking cure can be evinced by a series of conversations about one's life, development, and current problems. Catharsis may occur but the curative factor is the carefully placed interpretation of the psychodynamics that results in the insight allowing reason to govern affect. Over time Freud and his colleagues came to conclude that the most powerful interpretations were focused on the unconscious transference of feelings by the patient toward persons in their developmental past onto the person of the analyst. Therapy is the unpacking of the psychic contents of the unconscious so as to remove the repression, acknowledge and understand the emotional dynamics and thereby gain mastery over one's psyche.

Psychoanalysis has had as one of its primary features as a discipline the requirement of personal analysis. One salient reason for this is that not only do patients transfer feelings from an earlier object onto the therapist, but the therapist, too, has sentiments about the patient. These are termed counter transference and could be disruptive of the therapeutic process if they were not acknowledged and dealt with. In this sense the principles of personality development apply to all and require that the analyst has a high degree of self awareness. This may only be possible through the personal experience of therapy.

Generally, in training in the mental health field, there is no requirement of personal psychotherapy as a pre-requisite for practice. It may be considered desirable to gain the experience from the other side of the couch, so to speak, but it is not commonly seen as essential. Psychoanalysis requires all analysts in training to undergo their own analysis at the hands of an already credentialed member of the society. Part of the rationale for this is that the dynamic interplay of feelings in an intensive psychotherapeutic relationship require the person be fully aware of their own issues, and the best way of assuring that is going through the clarifying process of therapy. It is humbling, as well, to come to see your own neuroses laid bare. But it certainly has value for personal growth as well as from a training standpoint. Hypnosis is likewise a skill one cannot learn without personal experience of the hypnotic state or session. Mindfulness and other meditative practices also cannot be properly taught to others without personal experience and engagement in the process. So experiential learning requires that involvement. Psychoanalysis is not alone in this regard. The benefit of personal therapy can be understood from another view point as well; through Bandura's theory of observational learning. By seeing how therapy is done from an inside standpoint, one has a model of how things are done. One learns through one's own experience.

This practice of required analysis leads to an interesting embodiment of the stream of transmission of the knowledge and skill of psychotherapy. One can trace not only intellectual influences, but a chain of analysis. For example, Donald Winnicott, a figure we'll discuss later, was analyzed by Melanie Klein, who was analyzed by both Sandor Ferenczi and Karl Abraham, who were analyzed by Freud. So you can trace back not only the didactic but experiential currents. What influence that additional component has depends on the person of both the analyst and the analysand, but the influence is undoubtedly both personal and professional, both in terms of the capacity for self observation and reflection and the skill of enacting it live in therapy.

## Jung

Carl Gustav Jung (1875-1961) was the son of a Protestant minister who was a chaplain at the famed Burghőlzli mental hospital, so early in his life he got exposure to the problems of mental illness. He took his medical training at University of Basel, graduating in 1900. He came into contact with Freud's ideas and sent him a copy of his early studies on word association, recognizing the significance for Freud's free association technique. Jung came with Freud to America, for the lectures at Clark University, he was one of the inner circle of favored pupils. He was also the first of Freud's disciples to break with the master. Since Jung was considered the brightest and best, the heir apparent to the master, his departure from the flock was a hard blow to Freud.

Jung was one of several Swiss psychiatrists to have profound influence on the field of mental illness and psychotherapy. The earliest of prominence was Eugen Bleuler (1857-1939). He gave us three very important terms, ambivalence, schizophrenia and autism. The identification of the modern syndrome of autism came later by another's hand, but the term was first used to describe symptoms of schizophrenia. Bleuler hired Carl Jung at the Burhőlzli hospital. The two founders of existential therapy Ludwig Binswanger, and Medard Boss were also Swiss psychiatrists who were influenced by Bleuler. Hermann Rorschach also trained and practiced at the Burghölzli. Their stories will be told later.

To Jung, the process of individuation was the basis of personhood. We start in that very ambiguous mix of early awareness in dependency with the other, to a more differentiated person, changing over time. The process of interaction with the environment resulted in development of basic ego processes which were embodied in personality types as stable formations in an evolving organism. Borrowing from the dialectical theme in German philosophy, he held that the individuation process took place through reconciliation of opposites. The world and the psyche are structured with numerous oppositions or seeming dichotomies.

He laid out a type theory of personality. This would be distinguished from the trait theories favored by many American psychologists beginning with Gordon Allport. Each trait is independent (hopefully) from all the others. In Jung's type theory there are several dimensions of personality anchored by two polar types. He evolved a theory of 3 dimensions; introvert-extrovert, sensation-intuition, thinking-feeling. The first dimension involves the focal point of psychological energy; where one draws energy from or put energy into. The introvert draws from and invests in the inner world of ideas and feelings, whereas the extrovert invests in and draws energy from the outer world of people and objects. The next two dimensions are functions. The information gathering function is anchored by the polar types of sensing and intuition. The decision making function is anchored by the polar types of thinking and feeling.

Each of these can be conceptualized and measured, psychometrically, as continua, the individual locating him or her self somewhere on those dimensions. The

Myers-Briggs Type Indicator (MBTI; Myers, 1962) is the most widely known test embodying Jung's type theory of personality. The internet is flooded with many briefer versions with little validation. The test authors added a fourth dimension, whether the perceiving or judging function was dominant, yielding a four-letter type, one for each of the dimensions (e.g. INTJ, ESFP, etc.).

Another important innovation of Jung's was the concept of the collective unconscious. He agreed with Freud that our individual experience from birth onward gets encoded in our unconscious mind based on our personal life trajectory. But he felt that there was also a collective legacy from the past. He thought it might be literally part of the genetic inheritance. But our cultural heritage is also passed along through the folk lore, custom, myth, fairy tales and other stories that we have been sharing across the millennia. For Jung, the whole symbolic world contains the full field of meanings which shape personality. Myth, language, custom, all embody these sets of meanings. Our personality emerges as we individuate from the parental other. We draw from this pool for good or ill, but it must be dealt with in therapy. For Jung, the impact of Darwin's version of evolution was to give a biological basis for transmission of new collective symbols from culture to shape the landscape of unconscious psychological processes. In his personality theory, all unconscious motives, drives, forces and objects are a mixture of the residue of individual events in life history and collective or social legacy of the species and one's culture. Of course, the global world makes possible access to symbols deriving from cultures other than one's own, so we partake of a universal pool of archetypal images.

In this sense he is also clearly Kantian in his philosophical stance. The types, symbols, complexes, archetypes and other formative structures of the person are a psychological category of understanding, they reveal the a priori bases of experience. Kant was concerned about describing a philosophical system which accounted for conscious experience; Janet, Freud, Jung, Adler, and others are in a long stream of thinkers who have been influenced by the Kantian synthesis of empiricism and rationalism and sought to account for the unconscious forces in human experience. We embody that experience in signs and symbols which we communicate with each other. The very structural basis of the semiotic process operates in conscious and unconscious modes.

The elements of the collective unconscious coalesce into archetypes which are collections of psychic energy in the land of the unconscious. They are associations of symbols, images, and even social roles. Some key archetypes are about the psyche itself; the self, or view from the I perspective, the persona, or public self shown to others, and shadow, the unacceptable self we often hide from our self, but which must be dealt with for true integration to occur. Other archetypes come from the social world such as mother, child, wise old man, trickster. Gender roles were viewed in the context of the animus for woman and anima for man, psychic model of the opposite sex. The whole variety of human mythic tradition and folk lore contain elaborated themes of various archetypes. James Hillman (1926-2011) was an American Jungian analyst who taken the archetype as the label for his interpretation of the Jungian core. His archetypal psychology makes the self relative to the cultural matrix and populates the psychic world with a variety of psychic forms from our shared human experience, a truly pluralistic view of entities in the psyche or soul as he termed it.

Jung is best known as the student of Freud who took seriously human spirituality as a dimension of psychological life. While Freud saw religion as essentially an infantile adaptation that should be dispensed with in adulthood, Jung took it to represent the very basis of connection with the ground of being, the very basis of individual reality. Jung's impact on the psychology of spirituality and religion cannot be underestimated. He clearly embraced mysticism and the esoteric path as a means of personal self-awareness, understanding and growth through integration. He, and William James, are considered the two founding figures in the psychology of religion and spirituality.

Several of his students expanded the work in the arena of spirituality and religion by exploring mythology and cultural symbols. Marie-Louise von Franz (1915-1998) went on to write about the significance of fairy tales, and the psychological inter-pretation of alchemy. In fairy tales there is the willing suspension of the adult ego of the teller to engage the as-if nature of childhood. So doing allows a bridge in the experiential field of the child and adult alike to once again connect with the liminal and primal nature of psychic reality. Jung saw the process of therapy as analogous to the process of transmutation in alchemy. She also wrote on divination and Jung's principle of synchronicity which complements causation (von Franz, 1980). Sortilege, or casting lots is a random process which underlies the sacralization of randomness in many forms of divination.

Károly Kerényi (1897-1973), often known as Carl or Karl, was a Hungarian born classicist and mythologer. He wrote a series of studies of Greek and other myths from a archetypal standpoint. Of particular interest to psychologists is that of Asclepius (1959) and Hermes (1976b). Hermes was a psychopomp; he led souls of dead into the underworld. In the metaphor of therapy as a descent into the unconscious to alchemi-cally transform the base metal of ordinary self-defeating patterns into the gold of the fully individuated and integrated self, the therapist is a psychopomp. The death of the old self then also implies a role as embodying the archetype of midwife to the new. Of course, my own theory of the evolution of the role of the healer by psychological means sets forth the four archetypal roles through which the transmission of knowl-edge, craft, and art has taken place from earliest times until now.

But perhaps no mythologer has been as closely associated with Jungian thought than Joseph Campbell (1904-1987). His 4 volume masterpiece, *The Masks of God* (1959-1968) stands as a foundational reference. But his most widely used contribu-tion was his discovery of the *monomyth* of the hero's journey (1949). He found basic structural similarities in a wide range of myths from a wide range of cultures that make up the several stages of the journey of a hero. This becomes the mythic backdrop for personal growth and development from a Jungian standpoint. From J. R. R. Tolkien to George Lucas we are immersed in stories about the struggle to find one's true self through rising to the challenges placed before us.

One addition to the techniques of therapy is the active imagination. This is the means of envisioning the various alternate possibilities that unfold in the course of therapy as barriers to growth are overcome and new paths become visible. The whole Western bias has been turned away from imagination as opposed to fact as sources of true knowledge While the will-o-wisp of imagination creates many dreams, cold factual reality dominates the sort of thinking that was rewarded in a competitive commercially oriented society. But Giambatisto Vic (1668–1744) had paved the way by noting that truth can be created by doing as well as reasoning. The focus on imagination also echoes the philosophy of Hans Vaihinger (1852-1933) whose work on the "as if" dimension of thought is the basis for envisioning therapeutic change. So the dream like states of inner psychological work can directly contact the unconscious and do work.

# Adler

Alfred Adler (1870-1937) was like Freud in some important ways. Both were sons of Jewish merchants in Vienna, though fourteen years separated them. The zeitgeist they grew up in was very similar. But early in his career, Adler began seeing clients from a wider range of social status. This shaped his ideas of psychodynamics. Freud held that underneath all of the surface motives we see as guiding our actions, the sex drive, libido, dominates. Alder broke with Freud about the primacy of the sexual nature of primary motivation, he was among the first to emphasize broader social forces as well. But that developed later, he was one of the early people to write back favorably to Freud, and was invited to join the circle of close associates that met at the master's house on a frequent basis.

Yet, despite his early affiliation with Freud, his ideas were always somewhat different from Freud's and it was destined that he would strike out on his own at some point. Freud's biographer, Ernest Jones, notes that Adler was perceived as a rather contentious person who later mellowed as he became successful in his own right and not in the shadow of his elder colleague (Ellenberger, 1970). His broader social exposure led to an early interest in social medicine; he was progressive in his values. Social position, one's relationship to others both at a group and interpersonal level were strong influences on the growth of the psyche. We are not only the internal balance of instinctual drives, including sexuality, but we are the product of the relationships and categories brought by our membership to particular groups of people as well.

His first office in general medical practice was in a working-class neighborhood adjacent to an amusement park and circus. His concept of organ inferiority and compensation was possibly influenced by the fact that some circus performers and workers were clients, including people with very atypical bodily structures or abilities

(Ellenberger, 1970). The goal of the compensatory motive is, of course, an ideal. So he points to the dialectic between ideal and actual as a source of dynamism and energy exchange. Perfection is always out there ahead of us, forever unattainable, but its lure goads us on as we strive for improvement. It sets the highest standard of accomplishment. When Adler and nine other analysts left the Freudian circle and formed their own group, it soon became known as Individual Psychology, which reflects their focus not on the resolution of older conflicts, but on the dynamic balance of striving as a fundamental fact of life.

In this idea, he was following the lead of Nietzsche and Schopenhauer, in particular, and the broader tradition of German idealism and romanticism. Will is an underlying theme in the striving to compensate and live up to our own expectations. This is part of the post-Kantian core of philosophy which serves as the basis of the human sciences, and the independent stream of phenomenology and act psychology. Adler drew from this tradition the focus on the conative or motivation striving by the individual through an exercise of will; this is what it means to be a person. The person is active, not just reactive. In orthodox Freudian psychoanalytic thinking, the active capacity of the individual, while acknowledged, is not as central as the instinctual forces which operate in a more deterministic fashion, and are, in any event, out of the range of our effective conscious control. We are driven by things we only poorly understand and control. Adler, by contrast, focuses on the dynamic aspect of the person in action.

This led him to abandon the sort of static structural metaphors and focus on the style of life, or simply, *life style*, of the individual. He coined this phrase and certainly was its main proponent. The phrase has now taken on a much broader field of meaning, yet we owe Adler a debt for first seeing this concept of personal unity. Life style is now, more than in Adler's era, a commodity which is marketed and packaged for consumption. He did mean to focus therapeutic attention to the choices we make and the patterns we form in relationships. He was less concerned with early developmental data, but used that data in concert with a much wider search for knowledge about the individual's current state of being and acting in the world.

## The successors

Freud set in motion a whole movement. He gathered together an informal circle of students who met in his home in 1902. Later, in 1908, the Vienna Psychoanalytic Society was formed. Though Jung and Adler broke with him, many stuck with him rather than splitting. Anna Freud, Sandor Ferenczi, Karl Abraham, Ernest Jones, his official biographer, and others carried on the tradition of orthodox psychoanalysis. They passed the craft and knowledge on to others through training analysis and teaching. His daughter, Anna, likewise continued the tradition of orthodox analysis. But the group known as the Neo-Freudians (Horney and Sullivan in particular) each deviated from the mainstream in some noticeable ways. We shall turn to some of these successors now and trace some of the further theoretical developments in psychoanalytic and psychodynamic thought.

## Anna Freud (1895-1982)

Freud's daughter became a major figure in psychoanalysis in her own right. She is recognized as a pioneer in child psychoanalysis. She also is a pioneer in a stream within psychodynamic theory termed ego psychology. She remained loyal to her father's basic ideas, even though ego psychology is generally viewed as an off-shoot rather than part of the orthodox stream. She was loyal to Freud in a critical way, moving with him from Vienna to London as Nazi forces closed their grips on European Jewry. He was ill by that time with the jaw cancer that would take his life, and she nursed him through his period of illness and final decline. She carried on her work, especially with children at the Hampstead Child Therapy Clinic in Britain after the war.

## Karen Horney (1885-1952)

She was a German psychoanalyst who was among the first disciples of Freud to begin to question his gender assumptions. She is also known for her clear extension of the forces of the individual to the social. Interpersonal and social influences temper the instinctive and libidinous. Her theory of neurosis was innovative but developed Freud's ideas on the psychopathology of every day life. She blurred the categorical boundaries between normalcy and neurosis and saw them more as a continuum. Neurosis was just an ineffective way of coping with ordinary stress and problems. She saw particular patterns of distortions in neurotic thinking, all based on exaggerations or extensions of normal coping responses. For example, everyone needs affection, but the neurotic can't live without it, idealizes or otherwise holds unrealistic positions. The coping strategies of compliance, aggression or withdrawal were available to try and manage life better. She moved to the United States in 1930 and continued her work there. Her differences with mainstream psychoanalysis were significant enough that she set up her own training organization, the Association for the Advancement of Psychoanalysis.

## Harry Stack Sullivan (1892-1949

Sullivan is known for his interpersonal theory of psychiatry. He was, above all, a practitioner as opposed to a scholar; his major work, *An interpersonal theory of psychiatry* (1953) is a compilation of his lectures redacted by his students. Writing was a secondary mode among his gifts. As a therapist and teacher he was in his medium. One of his unique contributions was the describing differentiations of early mental life into proto-taxic, para-taxic and syntaxic modes of experience. Freud had only given us the idea of primary process, but Sullivan gave a more nuanced understanding of the development of early thought. Mental life develops and grows and simply looking at the dichotomy of conscious/un-conscious is too simplistic. By focusing on a stage theory of evolution of the quality of mental life, Sullivan elaborated on the Freudian dynamic concept of primary or primitive processes, those based in instinct, and secondary processes, or elaborative, reflective and cognitive ones. Normal development leads to syntaxic experience, that which is mediated by language and the culturally mediated world of visual symbols.

He also commented on the quality of same-sex friendship during the latency period (ages five to eleven, more or less), using the term chumship to denote friendship between peers. Sullivan's homosexuality was known about at the time, but like most gay men in that era, especially professionals, he had to remain closeted and very discrete. He had a long-term partner, Jimmy Sullivan, who was significantly younger and adopted his name (Vande Kemp, 2004). He set up a special unit at Shepherd-Pratt hospital in Baltimore focused on treating young male schizophrenic patients. He staffed it with homosexual ward attendants as part of his thought that there was a link between schizophrenia and homosexuality (Wake, 2006). Among the streams of therapy one often sees reference to the interpersonal theory, so the approach of Sullivan retains a presence. The William Alanson White Institute continues this stream.

## Melanie Klein and object relations theory

Melanie Klein (1882-1969) was an important figure in the development of the analytic tradition. She was Viennese, like Freud, but worked most closely with his disciples Sándor Ferenczi (1873-1933) and Karl Abraham (1877-1925). Her life was marked by periods of difficulty and suffering. She experienced serious depression at one point in her life. She moved from Berlin to London and remained there until her death. She was a critical figure in object relations theory. Most of her work clinically was with children. Klein and Anna Freud were at odds about whether or not children could be analyzed with the same techniques as for adults. Klein affirmed the practice, Anna, thought the child's ego not yet stable enough for full instinctual interpretation. Anna advocated a more educational approach (Mitchell & Black, 1995). This resulted in a split within the British Psychoanalytic Association between those who supported Anna and those who supported Melanie, or those who tried to harmonize between the two differing opinions.

Both Sigmund and Anna Freud (who actually dealt with children), felt that the oedipal phase was crucial and the mind then accessible. Klein felt the minds of younger children, even infants were accessible. Later, she went on to work with adult psychotic patients, which Freud saw as unsuited for psychoanalysis. And as authors Mitchell & Black (1999) note, Klein's view of the mind is very different from that of ego psychology, considered below. She saw the flux and flexibility of the child persisting in the adult. The mind of the adult was very different from those two diverging psychoanalytic perspectives.

Klein emphasized the aggressive drive more than Freud did, particularly the oral-aggressive or oral-sadist period of development. Wolman (1981) describes her position by pointing out that the infant swallows or spits out the milk as object. But when the infant begins to chew, to bite, then it can take in solid food and digest it. Thus, the process of taking in objects moves from taking them in whole, to de-constructing them. This idea was later to be picked up by Perls (1969) and made part of Gestalt therapy, in the humanistic stream.

Klein became the foundation of all subsequent object relations theory within the psychodynamic stream. One of her colleagues, W. Ronald Fairbairn (1889-1964), emphasized that the ego is present and whole at birth, but becomes split into good object and bad object over time arising out of defense against frustration. The good and bad breast was the giving and withholding source of both nurturance and the experience of limits, of lack of gratification.

Donald Winnicott (1896-1971) is the most widely read of object relations theorists centered in Britain. He fundamentally reformulated the nature of the metaphysics of the situation. He recognized the psychological implication of the basic biological fact that the isolated organism did not exist, particularly at that state of life. The nursing couple exists; after all, being totally dependent, someone must care for the infant, so the relational unit of care-giver and recipient is the unit of focus. His phrase *good enough* mother emphasizes his understanding of the failures inherent in parenting. His concept of the *holding environment* as the model for therapy emphasizes this supportive, nurturing approach. The concept of *transitional object* follows the developmental path as internalized self becomes stabilized. Already we see a very different sort of therapy from the austere position of distance that Freud practiced. As object relations developed the process took place within a warmer relationship.

Otto Kernberg (b. 1928) blends ego theory with object relations theory by focusing on the development of the sense of self, the ego, as it arises out of the process of differentiation of internal representations of the primal object. There is an original undifferentiated self/object whole, which becomes differentiated, or split, into the all-or-nothing dichotomy of good object and bad object, which finally becomes integrated in subsequent development into a normal sense of self with a stable boundary between self and others. Heinz Kohut (1913-1981) continued his work and focused on the development of the narcissistic personality disorder. He saw the grandiose self, is the all powerful self, and the internalized parent then become a source of deflation to the grandiose self. Again, in normal development these narcissistic wounds are bridged by the developing ego with fixation resulting in personality disorder.

## Ego and self psychology

One of the effects of Nazi persecution of the Jews was a flood of immigration to the United States and Britain by those who could manage to get out by whatever means. Many of the intelligentsia were able to leave, including Freud himself and other German and Austrian psycho-analysts. Gestalt psychology, also came to America at this time. So both psychiatry and psychology in Britain and America benefitted from anti-Semitism in Nazi Germany and Austria.

Among the psycho-analysts to come to the U.S. was Heinz Hartmann (1894-1970). He settled in New York City and practiced there. He is generally seen as the leader in a broad movement termed ego psychology. As Ellenberger (1970) noted, his critical role in moving beyond Sigmund Freud, Anna Freud and including work by the analyst Franz Alexander, all of which put the ego foremost in focus of interest.

Erik Erikson (1902-1994) has given us a primary structure of development in terms of psycho-social competencies. His life-stage theory has almost become axiomatic in the human sciences. Despite the wide acceptance of his views, he needs to be placed within the psychodynamic context. His theory of developmental stages is an extension of the ego psychology developed in the years just prior to and following World War II. The central concern in his theory was identity and its development. His own life history is an example of that struggle. He was known by his step father's name, Erik Homberger. He was blond and Nordic looking, yet he was Jewish. He changed his name to Erikson when he became a naturalized U.S. citizen. Like so many of his era, he fled Nazi persecution and wound up living in New York City.

The core of his theory is the notion of developmental tasks. At each stage in the process of organismic development, the person has a particular set of tasks which must be accomplished. The successful mastering of these tasks allows the person to move on to later stages fully prepared for those developments. Those who have not completed the tasks get stuck in a sense, they experience a less than complete developmental trajectory. Neurosis or some other form of psycho-pathology may result depending on the seriousness of the incomplete developmental tasks and the compensatory mechanisms brought to bear on the situation.

## The social critique of psychoanalysis

### Marxism and Freudian thought

Psychoanalysis was one of the great ideologies of the twentieth century; Marxism is another great ideology, though it began before Freud. Marxism and socialism set down deeper roots in Europe than in America. The autocratic communist regime in Russia under Lenin and Stalin complicated the hopeful language of socialism's ideal of a classless society. After World War II a variety of democratic socialist parties shaped much of Western European politics.

It was inevitable that some psychologists explored their intersection. The Soviet Union was the first Marxist state and psychoanalysis was never prominent there. Stalinist authoritarian politics saw Freud as decadent Western capitalist rubbish, advancing instead a type of biologically rooted reflexology, from a Pavlovian basis. But in Western Europe, particularly in France after World War II, a variety of thinkers saw more points of dialog. French thought today accords more recognition to both Freud and Marx as influential in their stream.

Jacques Lacan (1901-1981) is one of the most original French thinkers in the twentieth century, up there with Sartre and Foucault. He was strongly influenced by the structuralist tradition in French thought. This was a theory of anthropology and sociology. Ferdinand de Saussure (1857-1913) was one of the founders of linguistics and one of the co-founders of semiotics. The anthropologist Claude Levi-Straus (b. 1908) laid out the most systematic case for the use of structure to explain social dynamics. Saussure created a structural theory of language, which Lev-Strauss applied to anthropology. One of the major ways in which Lacan has parted company with Freud has been on the belief in the substantive nature of the ego. To Freud, the ego, when it does develop, becomes a stable object and subject. For Lacan, only the unconscious is real, and the ego is its creature and never a really stable existent, but an on-going process. The child comes to a sense of self through the mirroring experience, seeing self through others' eyes. Desires are expressed as symbols and the analysis of our relationship with symbols constitutes the basic data of the interpretive project of psychoanalysis. Two key unconscious mechanisms, displacement and condensation, are basically linguistic in nature, parallel to the processes of metaphor and metonymy. Lacan's work is considered post-structuralist, as is Foucault's and the other major figure in French literary theory and criticism, including Jacques Derrida (b. 1930).

## Feminism

The women's movement of the nineteen seventies is considered the second wave of feminism, or the quest for gender equality. The first wave was the movement for women's suffrage in the latter part of the nineteenth century. Before that Mary Wollstoncraft's (1792) work *A vindication of the rights of women* was a beacon lit for the movement that followed. The second wave emerged out of the cultural ferment of the nineteen sixties. The consciousness-raising group was a key methodology in transforming the understanding of the origins of suffering from a personal failure to a result of social oppression. Within psychoanalysis there was plenty to critique. As noted earlier, Freud's male centered theory of developmental stages left women out. The Electra complex was later added as even Freud recognized the need for separate paths of libido. The overall patriarchal assumptions were more thoroughly critiques by Juliet Mitchell's (1974) book on *Feminism and psychoanalysis.* She pioneered the attempt to reformulate Freudian thought in light of a different conceptualization of gender and gender roles that was more balanced. Others have expanded a reformulation of psychodynamic theory in light of a critical look at the social construction of gender. This has also been applied as queer theorists critiqued psychoanalytic approaches to sexual orientation.

## Inter-subjectivity and relational analytic thought

Sandor Ferenczi's reputation has been enhanced in recent years, especially after his case book got translated and published. He advocated a more active involvement of the therapist than was considered orthodox. He was known as a consummate clinician who took on the most difficult cases other analysts would not work with. The typical analytic mirror on which the patient projects his or her transference now looked back not just with an empathetic reflection of what was heard but with a personal presence. Ferenczi thought that sharing some of the reactions of the therapist would aid in the analytic process. In this sense he anticipated the developments in humanistic psychology of the 1960s and 1960s.

In the post World War II period, another stream began growing which feeds into modern psychoanalysis as well as humanistic psychology and some cognitive approaches, social constructivism. This is the idea that there are no fixed objective social objects; each object is also a subject and that subjectivity cannot be avoided. Indeed, the skilled therapist can use that subjectivity rather than avoid it. What follows from this is the conviction that our social world is constructed by the actions of people. All the many meanings are meanings that are experienced by someone and expressed in the matrix of communication that constitutes culture. Indeed, all culture is the made human environment, is constructed as a human artifact. Thus, all social categories are fixed by a web of meanings created by the human discourse, one with another.

Inter-subjectivity, then is the approach to the analytic situation that recognizes the dialectical nature of a relationship between two active participants. The relationship is the focus of analytic treatment; all is referenced to the nature and quality of the relationship. This distinguishes it from the more intra-psychic approach where the focus is on the internal world of the client alone. Any reference to the intra-psychic world of the analyst or the dialectical back and forth between the two is minimal and incidental to the task of understanding and reorganizing the subjectivity of one of the participants, the client. In relational psychoanalysis there is an explicit acknowledgment of shared world creating the analytic field. One of the leading proponents of this view is Stephen A. Mitchell (1993)

# 11

# Behavioral and Cognitive-Behavioral Approaches

COGNITIVE-BEHAVIORAL APPROACHES ARE AMONG the most widespread in contemporary psychology and human services. Yet it is only in the last roughly 30 years that the hyphenated version of this position arose. Prior to that period it was simply called behaviorism. We will begin there and work forward. Behaviorism was at its heart an approach to the nature of psychology as a science, particularly its methodology, but more importantly its whole paradigm. Somewhat later it became applied to clinical problems. With the rise of behaviorism in the 1920s and 1930s, interest in human cognitive processes other than learning itself declined. By the 1970s, that interest returned for several reasons discussed below. Now, the cognitive focus in psychology appears dominant, much to the chagrin of some behaviorists. But the hyphenated cognitive-behavioral blend is a significant force in contemporary psychology.

## The reflex and S-R psychology

The model for behaviorism is the reflex arc, the stimulus-response (S-R) metaphor. The current rubric is S-O-R-C; the acronym stands for stimulus, organismic processes, response, and consequences. Over time the simple input-output model has become more detailed and qualified. The model and metaphor arises clearly out of neuro-physiology. As noted earlier, in the nineteenth century physiology had established that the nervous system was the major controlling mechanism of the organism, the body/mind. The basics of the reflex arc had begun to take shape with the discovery of the separate neural tracts for sensation or motor control. By the end of the nineteenth century, the view of the different centers of the nervous system and their influence on producing behavior had become more complex as the roles of the lobes and hemispheres were becoming more clear. But the interesting questions had now shifted to how learning took place, how responses were modified by changes in neural connections. Could new links be added through learning? How could a known but crudely understood idea of a fixed reflex account for more complex and learned responses?

Ivan Pavlov (1849-1936) was a Russian physiologist who offered the first model of learning via a reflex theory, one that was well demonstrated by experimental procedures. He termed it the conditioned response. The presence of the response was *conditional* upon the occurrence of the stimulus. One brings about the other. The emphasis on the term conditional is in the original work and was lost, probably via translation through German, and the term became conditioned, which has largely stuck despite efforts to emphasis the significance of the original term (Fishman & Franks, 1992). The model of determinism is mechanistic; it is like a billiard ball transmitting force to another one, there was a causal link. Pavlov's paradigm was consistent with associationism; a broader approach to learning that emphasized how the pairing or association of two things together closely in time, facilitated links and learning. Pavlov's subject was neural, but not involving the central nervous system or the skeletal muscles; rather, he focused on visceral connections as part of the autonomic nervous systems. He chose the glandular secretion involved in salivation. He demonstrated experimentally that the natural stimuli that brought about salivation could be linked to new stimuli by close association in time.

Vladimir Bekhterev (1857-1927), another Russian, applied these same ideas and the basic paradigm to neuro-motor conditioning of the skeletal muscle system. Together they demonstrated conditional learning with clear cut evidence in both autonomic and peripheral nervous system. All that remained was demonstrating conditioning in the central nervous system. That came later as instrumental conditioning of brain waves developed.

## John B. Watson and behaviorism

John B. Watson (1878-1958) was the first American psychologist to champion a behaviorist position with his classic article (1913), *Psychology as a behaviorist views it*. Six years later, he expanded on this early call and wrote a general textbook in psychology where he applied behaviorism widely across psychology, using the same title as his seminal article. Like Freud's 1900 book on dream interpretation, and Dewey's critique of the reflex arc concept, this piece is a true classic in psychological history. Though Watson was a student of the functionalist psychologist James Rowland Angell at the University of Chicago, he grew increasingly apart from both the structuralist approach to experimentation and his teacher's functional school. His disagreement with functionalism centered around its definition of psychology as the science of consciousness; his work in animal learning made him rankle at having to attribute consciousness to animals (Hilgard, 1978). He was a student of the noted physiologist Jacques Loeb (1859-1924) in his neurology class. This helped move him toward the work of Pavlov and his colleagues. Watson saw in their work a much sounder basis for psychology than the introspective judgments made by trained observers on limited sensory phenomena.

His behavioral position was a complete rejection of subjectivism, whether it was in method, as in the introspective method used by the early experimentalists, or in term of the objects of study, the phenomena of mind. While he acknowledged subjective states and variables, he asserted that the functional relationship between the objectively measurable stimulus and response was the only sure basis for psychology advancing as a science. The response to his call was generally, but not completely favorable. Many psychologists saw the emphasis on objective behaviors as an advance in methodology, away from the problems of subjective experiential data. Behaviorism is consistent with materialistic reductionism as a psychology, though it doesn't require such an extreme position on the mind-body question. So many psychologists would describe themselves as methodological behaviorists, but avoid being labeled philosophical or radical behaviorists, which clearly endorsed material reductionism. Watson was both a methodological behaviorist and a philosophical behaviorist, adopting a materialist ontology and a reductionist approach to the nature of psychology.

The metaphor behind the behavioral rejection of introspection is that of the black box. It was claimed that what went on inside the black box may not be knowable though science, though hope was present that neurology could plug the explanatory gap. But whether it was knowable or just difficult to objectively measure, the more important things were the observables, the input and the output. The throughput was left aside. Even in that era, however, the importance of these organism variables as Woodworth noted could not be denied.

Perhaps one his most important contributions, along with his student Rosemary Rayner, was the demonstration that an emotional reaction could be conditioned in a human child. Little Albert was the subject of the experimental induction of a conditioned fear response. Most introductory texts tell the story of how pairing a loud noise with the presentation of a white furry rabbit resulted in that fearful response. The fear response also was triggered by other similar white furry objects, one of the first demonstrations of stimulus generalization. He did not decondition little Albert and his identity and fate have been the subject of subsequent research (Beck, Levinson & Irons, 2009; Beck, Levinson & Irons 2010; Powell, 2010; Reece, 2010; Powell, Digdon, Harris & Smithson, 2014 ). Later, with his student Mary Cover Jones, he conducted the first extinction experiment with an existing conditioned fear response. This was the first significant application of conditioning to human emotions and paved the way for applications to therapy.

Unfortunately, Watson ran afoul of the times. He fell in love with Ms. Rayner and got a divorce from his first wife in order to marry her. At that time in America, professors were supposed to be not only scientific and scholarly models, but paragons of social respectability. Divorce was just not done by someone in his position, so he was forced to resign. For a period of time he continued to write in professional psychological journals and then expanded as well into the popular press. Eventually he made his living through work in the advertising industry, rising to leadership in the J. Walter Thompson agency. Over time he became less involved in organized psychology. The great *what if* question is how much more he might have been able to contribute to psychology had he not been caught up in the social conservatism prevailing in academia at that time.

Another early attempt to apply conditioning models of learning to human problems came with the Mowrers, O. Hobart and his wife, Willie. They used a conditioning paradigm to tackle bed-wetting, enuresis, using a buzzer connected to a pad which would detect moisture. The child would be wakened after voiding the bladder, but was able to be trained to sense a full bladder and wake without losing control. So soon, there were a variety of approaches to human problems that sought to train or condition according to practices derived from experimental studies of learning.

## Behaviorism between the wars

Edwin B. Holt (1873-1946) was a student of William James, a teacher of James J. Gibson, and a colleague of Edward C. Tolman. He has been described as a progenitor of ecological psychology due to his influence on Gibson (Heft, 2001). Heft called his type of behaviorism philosophical behaviorism, since his writings were clearly behavioral in their conceptual structures; but also, as a student of James, his method of exposition was more philosophical than experimental. He took up James' call for a radical empiricism coupled with a critical realism in order to found a psychology based on an objective perception of meaningful real objects as part of the cognitive processes which constitute human behavior. Holt was part of an interdisciplinary movement called the New Realism, including philosophers and psychologists who sought to advance this epistemological and psychological viewpoint. They hold that we do, indeed, perceive objects which exist independently of our perceptions of them. This is the epistemic warrant of our ordinary knowledge of the external world and thus avoids solipsism. Critical realism is also consistent with the assertion that consciousness is the integration of the subjective and objective perspective.

Edward Thorndike (1874-1949) is considered the major exponent of connectionism. This is an extension of the earlier associationist tradition that came from British empiricism and was continued in the Scottish common sense tradition in the first half of the nineteenth century. His major work was with animal learning, where he emphasized the importance of trial and error learning. But in terms of professional psychology, he is most relevant with his ideas on education as well as his quantitative work on intelligence testing. His broad statements of laws of learning, though derived from animal experimentation, can be seen as applicable to humans. The *law of effect* emphasizes the importance of the consequences of behavior for the probability of learning; the *law of exercise* is a classic statement of the importance of practice, the use-it-or-loose-it adage. His research on this concept paved the way for Skinner's operant conditioning paradigm. Thorndike's law of effect shows his primacy for the operant mode of learning which was much expanded by Skinner somewhat later (Fishman & Franks, 1992)

Clark Hull (1884-1952) sought to establish a sound grounding for quantitative measurement in psychology. He earlier studied engineering, though he wound up in psychology. He did use his skills in this area through constructing experimental apparatus, and he even built an early calculator (the original is in the collection of the Smithsonian Institution). He used this device in teaching statistics to his students as well as in research. Habit was a central concept in his theory of learning. This term goes back into antiquity, but certainly began to be used as a more specialized concept with Locke. Learning for Hull was an increase in habit strength. This was based in drive reduction model of motivation for acting. We can also see that his underlying approach to the biology of learning had gone beyond simple stimulus-response reflexive loops, He avoided instinct as a concept, which was the main biological grounding model in psychoanalysis and in McDougall's hormic psychology. He did not favor instinct as a concept, but drive as a concept could be experimentally manipulated. Since food was a primary motivator, Hull measured drive as simply the time elapsed since last food administered to the laboratory animals who were the subjects of most psychological experiments in learning at this time.

Hull's philosophy of science had a huge impact on American psychology. He was favorably impressed with a philosophy of science known as logical positivism. The work came out of the Vienna Circle, a group of philosophers in that city in the 1920s and 30s. It included such figures as Rudolf Carnap (1891-1970), Herbert Feigl (1902-1988) and others, and was centered around the teachings of Mortiz Schlick (1882-1936). The Vienna Circle took Comte's positivism and updated it, particularly in light of another influence another Viennese philosopher, Ludwig Wittgenstein (1881-1951), a seminal figure in analytic philosophy. This new approach to the philosophy of science was termed logical positivism. It was a thorough-going materialistic reductionism. Though Wittgenstein later modified his views, his early views which were adopted by the logical positivists held that all scientific statements must be about observable objects. Mentalistic concepts were considered literally nonsense, that is, unable to be put to an empirical test. Percy Bridgman (1927) advanced science by elaborating on the canons of clear specification of methodological procedures and operations that would be carried out in making observations. All concepts used in psychological theory must be grounded in the operations undertaken to detect and measure their influence. Karl Popper (1902-1994), another philosopher of science close to the Vienna Circle, advanced the falsifiability hypothesis. This hypothesis is somewhat different from the lay understanding that science proves theories. The logical structure, Popper noted, was that you could never conclusively prove any theory, but you could conclusively disprove it by providing evidence contradictory to the prediction of theory. No amount of empirical evidence can rule out the possibility of later disconfirmation, but a present contradiction requires revision or abandonment of the theory. These views about science leave it as an open-ended quest for further confirmation, modification, or outright rejection of a theoretical framework. Thomas Kuhn (1922-1996) later moved the philosophy of science in a slightly different direction with his work on the role of paradigms in scientific revolutions (1962)

Hull took logical positivism and applied it to psychology. He termed his approach the hypothetico-deductive method. One starts with theories, which he agreed were built around concepts which could be operationally defined. From this theory predictions, or hypotheses, could be deduced. Then the relevant observations or experimental procedure conducted and the results measured. If the data confirmed the theory, well and good; if not, then the theory was abandoned or revised accordingly. This was how psychology was to advance. His program of research on conditioning was along these lines.

He had interests that were more applied. Early in his career he worked on aptitude testing and published a major work in this area. He also did the first experimental research in hypnosis, though he was not involved in any clinical work. His own efforts were focused in teaching, research, and writing, but not in the provision of services.

## B. F. Skinner and the consequences of behavior

B. F. Skinner (1904-1990) was impressed with Pavlov's work and sought to continue the work on the conditioning model of learning. However, he took it into new directions, some of which might be seen as extensions of the earlier model, but one clear difference was his focus on the consequences of behavior rather than the stimuli. The whole focus of the neural model of behavior based in the reflex was concerned in the relationship between stimulus and response. Especially important in classical conditioning is the close proximity in time between the unconditioned and the conditioned stimulus. Too much separation and the link is not made between the two presentations of the stimulus. Skinner was more concerned with what happened after the individual emitted a behavior rather than the pairing of the S-R connection. Reinforcement, therefore became his central concept. In reinforcement theory, it doesn't matter so much how a behavior comes about, whether it is conditioned or not, what matters is whether the behavior is rewarded or not. This takes up Thorndike's law of effect and makes it specific.

Skinner is known for his demonstration of a lawful order in the impact of consequences through the schedules of reinforcement. His favored laboratory animal was the pigeon, and the lab apparatus he designed (the Skinner box) was able to delivery food pellets, the reinforcement, in a precisely controlled manner so as to observe the effects of variation. Thus, the concept of schedules of reinforcement arose as a major explanatory framework. Schedules based on frequency of the behavior itself or on the passage of time, and the reinforcement could be given out on a variable or fixed basis. He set out the basic paradigm of bringing about a desired behavior by means of systematic application of reinforcement to shape successively closer approximations of the desired target. One of his major statements came in 1953 with *Science and human behavior*.

Skinner has often been thought of as advancing a mechanistic theory of the person, which is in good measure accurate. However, he was not so simplistic as to think that nothing of significance happened in between stimulus and response, within the individual. While he did exclude all private events if they were truly private, but he held (1953) that " . . . events which are, for the moment at least, accessibly only to the individual himself often occur as links in chains of otherwise public events and they must then be considered" (p. 229). This is an acknowledgment of the validity of Woodworth's organismic variables in between stimulus and response. Thus, the topic of self control and social control or reinforcement was opened up.

He was a rigorous philosophical behaviorist and a determinist. Mind, while self-evident, was epiphenomenal, that is, mind has no causal impact on behavior if scientifically understood. Our experience of choice accompanies brain events which are the real causative factor, the experiential concomitant is simply a byproduct of brain events. He proposed a theory of verbal behavior in 1953 with a book of that title. This led to a series of public disagreements and rejoinders between Skinner and the noted Harvard linguist, Noam Chomsky, who advanced a theory of linguistics that was more nativist, based in inherent structures. So the Lockean (Skinner) and the Kantian (Chomsky) locked horns again and again over the nature of language and higher cognitive levels. Skinner even wound up writing a utopian novel, *Walden II*, expressing his hope that systematic application of his principles of behavioral engineering would result in a better society.

## Conditioning approaches to treatment

As with Hull, Skinner was a researcher and academic, not a clinician. His influence in that area came through others. Those psychologists in the years in between the two world wars who were clinicians were mostly involved in the psychometric evaluation of patients, and psychotherapy was the province of physicians. Cyril Franks, one of the early behavioral therapists in the 1950s noted that psychiatry was dominated by psychoanalysis, and in Britain, clinical psychologists were under medical supervision as clinicians and trained as scientists. We will see in a later chapter how his experience closely parallels developments in the U.S. But Franks saw the behavioral approach as advocated by Hans Eysenck (1916-1997) at Maudsley Hospital, part of the University of London Institute of Psychiatry, as the key to establishing a truly scientifically based approach to behavior change (Fishman & Franks, 1992).

Perhaps the earliest venture into therapy was the first behavioral reformulation of psychodynamic theory. Dollard and Miller (1950) set out to translate many of the basic ideas then current in therapy into the language of science and perhaps back again. At that point in time the psychodynamic approaches to therapy were dominant, so they found behavioral bridging concepts for the psychoanalytic ones. But psychodynamic therapists saw no need to translate their work into behavioral terms and the movement in behaviorism was to stand on its own feet and devise treatment approaches that directly grew out of behavioral research.

There are several streams feeding into the current arena; one following each of the two models of conditional learning, the respondent or Pavlovian tradition, and the operant or Thorndike-Skinner tradition. More importantly, in the 1970s psychology underwent a further paradigm shift known as the cognition revolution or cognitive turn in psychology. From that time forward cognitive-behavioral approaches to human problems rose in popularity driven by research.

An early application of Pavlovian conditioning principles to clinical issues was the development of the treatment of bed-wetting (enuresis) by the husband and wife psychologists, O. Hobart and Willie Mowrer (1938). Joseph Wolpe (1915-1997), a South-African physician, wrote about behavior therapy (1969), which he saw as a continuation of the Pavlovian classical, or respondent conditioning model. Wolpe, though trained as a psychiatrist felt the prevailing psychoanalytic technique inadequate. He used a concept of reciprocal inhibition was important in explaining how classical conditioning might be useful. Anxiety and relaxation are reciprocal states, one can't be in both simultaneously, one is either relaxed or anxious. If there were a way of producing relaxation, then one could use those relaxed states to break the associative chain between the anxiety provoking stimulus and the anxious response.

Wolpe found in the work of Edmund Jacobson the means to generate deeply relaxed states. The next phase is the construction of a hierarchy of situations that elicit fear or phobic response. One uses Jacobson's techniques to induce a relaxed state while the person imaginally experiences the lowest scene in the fear hierarchy. If the patient reports anxiety, they are asked to let go of the image and relax again. Repeated exposures eventually extinguish the connection to a fearful response and the person can tolerate the image. Then one moves up the hierarchy until at the top when the person should be able to handle real life (in vivo) confrontation with the previously feared stimulus without undue distress. This is the meaning of the phrase systematic desensitization which is what he called his approach to treatment. The initial findings were positive and launched this approach as a popular alternative to years of psychoanalysis. Other applications of Pavlovian conditioning models would follow.

Wolpe also developed the Subjective Units of Distress or SUDS scale. This is the simplest form of quantification other than behavior counting. It was the application of 1-10 scale to the problem of subjective distress or discomfort. It was a rough estimate of magnitude that could be easily administered during normal therapeutic conversation and didn't require even the complicating use of pencil and paper instruments.

Edmund Jacobson (1888-1983) is an interesting figure in his own right. He was born in Chicago of Jewish parents. He went off to Harvard for graduate school and studied under such luminaries as William James, Hugo Munsterberg and Josiah Royce (Jacobson, 1977). He took up experimental research on the startle reflex on which he based in doctoral dissertation. It was in that context that he started training people to relax their muscles. After getting his Ph.D. in psychology he went to Cornell university where E. B. Titchener was the premier experimental psychologist of his era and studied under him for a year. He then returned to Chicago and pursued a medical education at Rush Medical School, getting his M.D. His interest in physiology continued as he worked to develop surface electromyographic (sEMG) sensors capable of measuring very small amounts of voltage in conjunction with scientists at Bell Labs. He also collaborated with A. J. Carlson, a University of Chicago physiologist in further research. He eventually set up his own practice in the Chicago Loop specializing in his relaxation training procedure. The irony is that this technique, such a main stay in behavioral treatment, originated in introspectionist research into the phenomenology of tension and relaxation (Kroker, 2003). His training was based on expanding psycho-physical awareness of subtle sensations from the peripheral muscles.

Another application of the Pavlovian model of behavior therapy was aversion therapy. The technique employed noxious stimuli to punish unwanted behaviors and extinguish them more quickly than simple non-reinforcement. These were often applied to sexual problems such as fetishes and socially undesirable behaviors. Homosexuality was once approached in this manner with unfavorable results and is now generally abandoned for that, though aversion therapy still is applied in other contexts. Finally, a more recent application of respondent conditioning has been the work of Edna Foa (b 1937) who developed Prolonged Exposure Therapy (PET) for Post-traumatic stress disorder (PTSD), obsessive-compulsive disorder (OCD) and other anxiety related conditions.

The other stream of applications of behaviorism come from those influenced more by the operant conditioning models, particularly Skinner's. This branch has come to be known as Applied Behavior Analysis (ABA). Among the first to apply his ideas on reinforcement were Ayllon and Azrin (1964, 1965) who worked with chronic mental patients in a large state hospital. This led to the development of token economies, a large institution-wide approach to enforcing contingencies on the behavior of institutionalized persons. A variety of tokens are given for observed positive behaviors targeted by the team, and exchanged for a variety of primary reinforcers on a graded schedule of points. (Ayllon & Azrin, 1968).

One of the characteristics of the ABA approach is the single-subject design in research and treatment. Skinner's (1953) own views were succinct, "Proving the validity of a functional relationship by an actual demonstration of the effect of one variable on another is the heart of experimental science. The practice enables us to dispense with many troublesome statistical techniques in testing the importance of variables" (p. 227). Thus charts showing stimulus control by application or cessation of reinforcement, or step-wise change with multiple baselines of types of reinforcers became part of the scientific and therapeutic demonstration. Currently ABA has now evolved as a separation stream of professional education with a ladder from certification through doctoral training. The field has been extensively applied in the treatment of autism spectrum disorders.

## Purposive and cognitive behaviorism

Watson started the ball rolling toward the banishment of mentalistic constructs and language from psychology. But it was only a few decades before an experimental psychologist found a way to begin to bring the mind back into psychology, though he might well have been more comfortable with the modern term, cognition, for the variety of processes that go on in the mind. Edward Chase Tolman (1886-1959) is the figure most commonly associated with behaviorism's first turn toward inclusion of cognitive factors. He promoted the mention of purposiveness back into the psychological explanation of behavior. By this, he meant behavior is goal directed and we cannot loose site of that fact. His experimental paradigm involved maze learning in rats. The maze was multi-armed with some arms dead ends and others leading from start to goal box where food could be found sometimes. He established the concept of latent learning of a cognitive map of the maze by allowing the rats to wander the maze several times without food being in the goal box. These were viewed as explorations during which the rat had some degree of latent memory of the various arms of the maze. In the experiment one group was provided food in the goal box every trial, others were allowed to roam freely until the third or the eighth trial at which time food was put in the goal box. The first group showed a steep decline in time to goal box, the other two had little or no learning in the unrewarded trials, but as soon as there was a reason to get to the goal box quickly they showed rapid decline in time. To Tolman this converging tendency toward quick trials to goal indicated the presence of a cognitive representation of the maze that allowed rapid progress toward a goal (Tolman, 1948). He was influenced by not only Watson, but McDougall's earlier hormic psychology based on drive and motivation, Woodworth's dynamic psychology and the Gestalt school as well (Hilgard, 1979). His vision was behavioral in methodology but much broader in its consideration of mentalistic concepts. This was a direct link in the emergence of cognitive behaviorism, the story of which follows later.

## Social learning theory

A third stream emerged in behaviorism along side the respondent and operant conditioning models. One of the first people to articulate a social learning theory was Julian Rotter (1954, 1966; Rotter, Chance and Phares, 1972). He pioneered the concept of expectancy. What he meant by that was the expectancy of reinforcement. People come to understand the contingencies in their environment, and their environment is presented in specific situations. They do so through their own personal experiences with similar situations in the past, as well as observations of the others' fate, as Bandura would demonstrate. He set out an initial theory of generalized expectancies, ones that were not rooted in specific situations but applied across many classes of situations. The primary dimension he termed locus of control with poles of internal and external. General expectancies tend to focus on whether the individual does or does not have control over the contingencies between behavior and consequences.

This has been a productive concept, and has been generalized by Seligman (1992) in his learned helplessness theory of depression. To Rotter's original internal/external dimension, he added two additional dimensions, the generalized expectancies can also be global versus specific with regard to the types of situations for which they apply, and permanent or fixed versus changeable. Those expectancies which are fixed, internal and global tend to be highly associated with depression as a type of learned helplessness. The opposite of helplessness is efficacy, which has been developed by Bandura (1997).

Albert Bandura (b. 1925) added another significant theoretical perspective in his pioneering work on observational learning. The sort of latent learning that was explored by Tolman was also described in the context of human learning experiments undertaken by Bandura. His classic studies on aggressive behavior and the effect of different modeling was recognized as a precise demonstration of what we all know by common sense. We all learn by observing others and the consequences of their behaviors. When models were shown a film with an adult acting aggressively toward plastic bobo dolls (inflated dolls weighted at the bottom so as to return to upright if punched). The children exposed to the film were more aggressive toward the bobo doll than those who had not seen the film. Furthermore, the ones exposed showed novel types of aggressive behavior whereas none of the control group did so. Although a gun was not used in the modeling film, children in the exposure group picked up and used the gun aggressively while others did not. This countered the drainage hypothesis that said watching others enact violence drains the same emotion form the viewer. This goes back to Aristotle's theory of catharsis in drama, and also psychodynamic theory. The social context of the experiment is important to keep in mind. There was growing concern about the role of explicit violence in TV and the movies and the effects on children. Bandura's experiments have been repeatedly cited as evidence for the importance of environmental input in the facilitation of aggressive behavior, whether through live models or through media. Thus, advocates of less violent movie and television programming have found in his basic paradigmatic program an ally against the easy portrayal of violence.

Bandura's emphasis on the role of vicarious learning through modeling in learning is the theoretical underpinning of any sort of behavioral rehearsal and role playing. Enacting and watching others enact social situations allows both experiential and observational learning. Bandura's current contribution builds on the attribution theory of Rotter and Seligman as well as his own work. Self efficacy promotes the importance of attributing to oneself the power to change one's circumstances (Bandura, 1997).

## Cognitivism

Cognitive behaviorism has evolved to become among the most popular streams in therapeutic theory and practice. But the whole of psychology went through a cognitive revolution during the 1970s and 1980s, affecting all areas of investigation and practice. The behavioral tradition had cast out mentalistic constructs, and adopted a logical positivist philosophy of science. Even within a behavioral framework, Tolman's purpose and cognitively based concepts showed the need for broadening the focus of study. Cognition could not be ignored, however, and new approaches other than the old introspection soon made research on cognitive processes begin to stand out.

One thing that is clear, is that the cognitive revolution affected virtually all areas of psychology, and a variety of streams fed into this revolution from divergent starting points. For example, the development of computers and the field of artificial intelligence (AI) played a role through its study of computer modeling of human cognitive processes. Several streams outside psychology also contributed significantly to the cognitive revolution. Among them in particular is the advent of systems theory, information theory, and cybernetics. These topics will be taken up in a later chapter. The work of Jean Piaget got translated into English and made his views on child development more widely known. His philosophical tradition was in the European Kantian tradition rather than the Lockean empiricist tradition. All cognitive approaches to therapy have integrated a narrative structure as well, but the dominance of the narrative turn influenced psychoanalysis and humanistic-existential streams deeply as well. Cognitive theories now are found in developmental, social and other domains of scientific inquiry, and neuro-cognitive studies in particular are experiencing a surge of interest. So from identifying unhelpful thought patterns and changing them to understanding cognitive schemas in basic memory processing, cognitive science is thriving in psychology.

Cognition constitutes a broadly accepted focus in psychology crossing most, if not all, boundaries. Human cognition was first seen as an organismic variable intervening between stimulus and response. This is the $O$ inserted between the S and the R from Woodworth's (1918) psychology. It also became coupled with the subjective $I$ of the personalistic views of psychology, the experiencing subject. Add to this Tolman's work on purposive behaviorism, and a more holistic behaviorism was emerging. Internal self-directed control mechanisms took our inner world as objects that could be observed and changed through the deliberate and systematic application of behavioral principles. Beliefs, attitudes, purposes and dispositions to act are all parts of a cognitive system or structure. We see here the behavioral acknowledgment of a broader synthesis. All of the streams of intervention theory and technique have their own version of the importance of cognitive factors in human behavior.

Jerome Bruner (b. 1915) is one of the most important figures in refocusing attention on the details of cognitive processes. He posited two fundamental processes, one sequential the other holistic. Narrative was an example of the sequential type of thought and getting the big picture was an example of what he termed paradigmatic thought. There were three modes of representation, however, enactment, iconic and symbolic, roughly corresponding to behavioral, visual and linguistic modes. Cognitive structures are built up in hierarchically organized patterns. Categories are the elements which combine in schemas or structures which comprise the cognitive structure of behavior. Bruner is also known for his analysis of narrative structure. In his major statement, *Acts of meaning* (1990) he held that each individual constructs their own world, cognitively speaking. This is a statement of the constructivist position, which is held by both some cognitive-behaviorists as well as many of the other streams of therapeutic thought, especially humanistic-existential.

Another important cognitive researcher was Jean Piaget (1896-1980), the Swiss developmental psychologist whose work only became translated and better known in American during the 1970s. His concept of schemas has been largely adopted as a concept to explain a wide range of cognitive structures from simple to complex. Piaget viewed his work as genetic epistemology and is firmly rooted in the European philosophical tradition that descended from Kant. Both Bruner and Piaget have advanced a structuralist way of looking at ways of thought and behavior, an example of what in Pepper's (1942) terms was a formist epistemology.

## Cognitive therapies

Cognitive therapies begin with the work of Albert Ellis (1913-2007). Like many psychiatrists of his era, he was trained in the psychoanalytic tradition but from his dissatisfaction with that approach he developed Rational-Emotive Therapy (RET). He pioneered the focus on irrational beliefs as a source of human difficulties. He explicitly cited as an influence the doctrine of the Stoic Epictetus who claimed that it is not events themselves which trouble people but our beliefs about them. He had an easy to remember formula, ABC, activating events trigger beliefs which result in consequences. When the beliefs are irrational in nature, the consequences are neurotic symptoms. One theme in the classic set of irrational beliefs is that the world has to fit the individual's needs and wants. He emphasizes human problems arise from the psychological imperatives involving using language such as *have to*, *must*, and *should*, in contrast to language revealing a more realistic view of the world such as *want*, *would* and *like*, and other formulations. This world view acknowledges, as did the Stoics, that there are many aspects of the world over which the individual has little control; though the one thing under individual control are the beliefs and attitudes about events. Ellis' technique was very much a teaching and persuading one, sharing the dialectical type of questioning back and forth of the Socratic method. His interpersonal style was much more characteristic of mid twentieth century New York; tough, aggressive, outspoken and blunt. The style was not congenial to everyone. In a classic film comparing Ellis, Rogers and Perls interviewing one client (Gloria), the client decided she didn't care for Ellis, liked Rogers, but would prefer to work further with Perls.

Aaron Beck (b. 1921) is an American psychiatrist whose early formulation of a cognitive approach focused on depression, our ancient and familiar friend melancholia. While Janet and Freud built their approaches on fairly exotic clinical syndromes, Beck took up the garden variety of everyday suffering, the deep sadness that lingers. Depression is among the most common complaints and a high frequency diagnosis, so the applicability of his ideas to clinical need was important. Like Ellis, his original orientation was psychoanalytic. He found the imbalance between focus on affect and focus on belief troubling and began exploring the cognitive schemas that underlie the thinking of people with depression. Schema is close to a consensus term for a basic unit of human thought as it guides action or behavior. It can be described as a series of statements of beliefs that are explicitly adopted by the client, or implied in the logical nature of description of their behavior using ordinary language. Since beliefs are linked to each other in a web of meaning, schemas are the cognitive equivalent of complexes in psychodynamic thought. They are coherent sub-units within the broader individual set of beliefs, which we might term the client's world view. Schemas are also put together to form rules, and much of behavior is rule-governed rather than triggered by specific stimuli.

## Cognitive behavioral approaches

Among the first clear articulations of a cognitive behaviorism is Michael Mahoney's (1946-2006) book titled *Cognition and behavior modification* (1974). He sets out a variety of mediational strategies for dealing with the organismic variables intervening between stimulus and response. He first discusses the covert conditioning models. This follows Skinner's reasoning that thoughts, though private, are simply covert speech with a subtle muscle component, but part of the chain of behavior. But the way was paved nearly a decade earlier by Homme (1965) who introduced the term *coverants* as the covert operants of the mind. This laid out a theory of thoughts as covert behaviors and made possible the application of not only operant conditioning models but of information processing models, and models emphasizing such cognitive factors as attentional and relational processes. He envisioned a broader use of both cognitive and behavioral principles.

Another early approach was that of Donald Meichenbaum (b. 1940). His views are most aptly summarized as cognitive behavior modification (Patterson & Watkins, 1996), but he gives his own account of his career development (Meichenbaum, 2003).

The basis for his system was constructing a set of self-instructions for changing one's thinking. He came upon his idea when attempting to teach healthy self talk to schizophrenic in-patients. He elaborated these ideas in the concept of stress inoculation training. The stream of thought becomes self talk or internal dialog in behavioral terms. Self observation or monitoring is key to self change. In other words, self-awareness and reflection are important psychological skills. The client is then instructed to give self instructions, initiate a belief or series of beliefs which are incompatible with the maladaptive ones and begin to state the alternative that is the goal of change. These are made stable habits through practice as a discipline. He has now turned more toward narrative therapy as his work with PTSD has expanded.

Meichenbaum and others in the behavioral stream have developed fairly extensive programs using structured psycho-educational group methods. His method is quite explicitly training, coaching and educational in nature. Homework assignments and monitoring are part of the social or interpersonal aspect of behavior change. Drawing from Bandura's social learning theory (1977) which involves rehearsal and modeling as major psycho-social mediating constructs, the therapist creates a structured series of interactions based around a self-instructional model, training the client to use the power to deliberate change, alter, or initiate new ideas, or at least, more positive ones, has a cumulative effect on the whole person if sustained over time. So it links into long-term motivational bases of behavior through Thorndike's law of exercise, the aphorism that practice makes perfect may sound trite and over-worn, yet it pithily conveys an essential truth. In this sense, Meichenbaum's approach draws on a long stream of behavioral metaphors, and links to the teacher as archetype of professional practice.

## Third wave behaviorism

A development that has been almost as dramatic and swift as the cognitive revolution has been the mindfulness revolution. Part of developments that were influential in the formation of transpersonal psychology, to be discussed later, was the arrival of meditation teachers from Eastern cultures and their students. Mindfulness is now taught as a secular psychological skill, though its origin is in Buddhist meditation practice.

Jon Kabat-Zinn (b. 1944) was trained as a molecular biologist, and also became a dedicated practitioner of Zen under such teachers as Phillip Kapleau, Seung Sahn, a Korean Zen master, and Thich Nhát Hanh, the Vietnamese Zen master. He began teaching some meditation techniques to chronic pain patients at the University of Massachusetts Medical School. Over time he formalized his approach (Kabat-Zinn; 1991, 1994) as Mindfulness-based Stress Reduction (MBSR).

Marsha Linehan (1989; 1993a, 1993b) began to integrate mindfulness into behavioral work with clients. The client focus was borderline personality disorders and her initial concern was with self-injurious or suicidal behaviors. Her Dialectical

Behavior Therapy (DBT) is the result of her application of behavioral learning theory augmented by other traditions, Buddhist mindfulness particularly.

Steven C. Hayes imported Pepper's world hypothesis theory and contextualism, specifically. His approach, called acceptance and commitment therapy, seeks to recast the behavioral account of verbal behavior by constructing a rigorous behavioral theory of rule governed behavior. He has likewise become a teacher of mindfulness as a behavioral skill. He has also been influenced by the social psychology of Theodore Sarbin, who has pioneered the theoretical foundations of this narrative movement in psychology (Hayes, Hayes, Reese & Sarbin, 1993). Hayes' main goal is both philosophical and scientific formulation within the Skinnerian tradition and takes seriously his epistemic obligations as a psychologist.

The research on all manner of applications of mindfulness has exploded in the last five years or so and a variety of monographs and edited volumes now chronicle the growing research and theoretical base.

# 12

# Humanistic-Existential Approaches

PSYCHOANALYSIS WAS THE FIRST force in psychology, behaviorism was the second force and humanistic-existential approaches became the third force in psychology. It arose out of a desire to promote a holistic view of the person. While both psychodynamic and behavioral approaches had significant mechanistic aspects, humanistic psychology saw itself as the bastion of individual personhood and choice. Choice may not be entirely free, in the sense of being unconstrained or uninfluenced by determining factors outside the scope of control of the individual but the belief that one can choose to do some things differently is essential in any behavior change process. The lawfulness of the behavioral account of things is quite appealing, but the experience of choice and consciousness is as real a part of human experience as anything else and requires some explanation. The importance of choice came clearly from the philosophical movement known as existentialism, and is echoed in most of the contributors to humanistic psychology.

As noted earlier, the methodological dichotomy between empirical and rational approaches merged into the distinction between the natural science tradition and the human science tradition. The former seeks to adopt objective observation and measurement, the latter seeks to articulate the quality and significance of the experience of the subject of research, the person. These divergent views on the best approach to understand the human condition played out culturally with psychology in the U. S. and Britain following the empiricist and natural science tradition, while the rest of continental Europe developed a focus on the subjective pole of experience. This, again, is Rychlak's tension between the Lockean and the Kantian tradition. Indeed the philosopher who most influenced Freud and the psychodynamic theorists also influenced the founders of this stream as well, Franz Brentano. Both Husserl, the founder of phenomenology and von Ehrenfels, the founder of Gestalt psychology were students of Brentano as was Freud. Also, like some of the founders of cognitive therapy approaches in the behavioral tradition were first trained as psychoanalysts, many of the figures in the development of this stream were also psychoanalysts who thought there was a better path and struck out to find it, albeit in different ways than the behaviorists or analysts.

## Brentano

A leading figure in the development of humanistic existential and phenomenological psychology is Franz Brentano (1838-1917), an Austrian philosopher and psychologist. He was a devout Catholic and became a priest, yet he broke with the Vatican around the doctrine of Papal infallibility. He left the priesthood and moved to University of Vienna to continue his teaching. He was not an experimental psychologist or concerned with applied problems. Yet he started most of the major streams within this broad domain. His work was a transmission of ideas that ultimately infused both theory, empirical science and clinical applications. His major theoretical contribution was in the formulation of act psychology based on a concept of intentionality. He used intentionality to mean that all consciousness is consciousness of some object. Experience is structured as subject in relation to and experiencing of objects. Intentionality is inherently a relational or dialectical concept. Subject and object were inherently related through the experiencing person. We now think of intentionality in the narrower sense of purposiveness, as human agency, as free will, to frame it in the older philosophical terms. But Brentano's emphasis on the act heralded a process orientation. Indeed, Hilgard (1987) contrasts Brentano and Wundt by noting they differed in terms of emphasizing mental acts versus mental contents.

This does reveal an important distinction. Brentano went beyond a structuralist position, which sought to identify elements as static things which could later be understood in terms of their connections between each other. Brentano held one should focus on the process, the activity of the person in order to understand the nature of experience. He emphasizes the importance of the molar elements of behavior that Dewey later pointed out. He keeps alive an active person-centered position that we exist in relationship to the objects in our environment. Our awareness is at heart an awareness of something, and that something informs and guides our response. In contrast to the mechanistic world view, Brentano asserts an individual embedded in context. This arises out of the broad human science perspective outlined above. He then gives a name to the active influence of the person, it is an act. We perform, we do things, we choose. The very embedded quality of subject and object in one person creates a field of meaning which results in its own emergent source of action, choice.

## Phenomenology and the human sciences

The humanistic approach to therapy draws on ideas that arise out of the human sciences (Polkinghorne, 1988; Giorgi 1970). In a previous chapter it was noted that the stream begins with Herder, who emphasized the importance of culture and language in history. History is rigorous because there are canons, standards of evidence. Primary sources can often be augmented by secondary ones. The narrative is invariably a story interpreting the facts and putting them into context. But conclusions of history are about particular people, places and times so it is inherently contextualized by those particularities. Hermeneutics, broadly speaking, is the discipline of interpretation of text. The dialectic of text and context becomes the hermeneutic circle. The tradition of German idealism, from Kant down through Hegel and Schopenhauer gave strength to a focus on the human experience, including the will to choose. The developments in linguistics, comparative religions, and the science of culture (early anthropology) laid the foundation for hermeneutics and pointed to its importance in understanding the human condition.

Edmund Husserl (1859-1938) developed a psychological method, the phenomenological method, as a way of encoding first hand experience in a manner that made it open to and available for study and interpretation. The only way to understand the objects of consciousness was by bracketing off all of our prior assumptions and beliefs, creating a sort of methodological doubt. The goal is openness to experience the other in terms of the other, not one's own. It is a form of radical listening to the other. The phenomenological method seeks to discover the qualities of lived experience; what it is like to be such and such a person in a particular context with goals and initiatives. Husserl was a student of Franz Brentano (1838-1917) and Carl Stumpf (1848-1936), both of whom were influential in the development of Gestalt psychology, another humanistic stream of thought.

Phenomenology was further developed by Martin Heidegger (1889-1976). He is a major figure in existentialism, hermeneutics, critical theory and post-modernism. Yet he remains a controversial figure because of his close associations with the Nazi regime in Germany. He even sacked his old friend Husserl from the university where they taught when it came time to enforce the anti-Jewish race laws. But his ideas were profoundly influential in European thought. He coined the term *dasein* which has been translated as being, or the phrase, *being-in-the-world*, which emphasizes the relational and dialectical quality of phenomenology. This is a further elaboration of Brentano's concept of intentionality. The root fact of consciousness, our phenomenal world, is that the I as subject always is in relationship perceptually to the object of perception. So being apart from specifying the object of being, i.e., the world, makes no sense for a science of the subjective lived experience. From Husserl the transmission of phenomenology influences French existential thinking, discussed below.

Different approaches to the clinical interview illustrate the contrasting views of human and natural science. To the extent that the interview is oriented to uncovering certain behavioral facts, including the objectifying internal thought as cognitions or beliefs, it takes a natural science approach. To the extent that the interview seeks to aid the individual in unfolding the flavor, quality or characteristics of their lived experience, it is based in phenomenological inquiry. The clinical interview has many of the hallmarks of the phenomenological method, in that it is based on subjective self report of the client of their experience. The interview takes place in the overarching goal of meliorating the person's experience, making it better in some way.

## Gestalt psychology and holism

Most of the texts in the history of psychology identify Gestalt psychology as the last of the classical *systems* of psychology to emerge. As research in many areas magnified, the scope of explanatory power was focused more narrowly with less expectation of covering all phenomena. Even behaviorism began to diverge into more focused and less broad or encompassing approaches. The notion that one particular path is fitting to all problems collapsed as research deepened our understanding of the complexity of human experience and behavior. Perhaps systems theory, subject for the next chapter, is a new system or paradigm for psychology remains to be seen. The great era of systems had passed by the Second World War. Brentano's psychology was empirical but not experimental. It took the Gestalt school of psychology to make it both experimental and clinical.

There is one intermediate link between Brentano and the classic triumvirate of Gestalt psychology, Max Wertheimer (1880-1943), Wolfgang Kohler (1887-1967), and Kurt Koffka.(1886-1941). That link was Christian von Ehrenfels (1859-1932), one of Brentano's students. He coined the term *gestalt* for the perceptual whole. This group of three Gestalt psychologists are often pictured in psychology textbooks in terms only of their perceptual psychology. There was more to their research than that. Kohler extended Gestalt ideas into learning theory with his demonstration of insight learning in chimpanzee behavior. The later Gestalt psychologists, Kurt Lewin (1890-1947), Fritz Heider (1896-1988), and the American trained psychologist Solomon Asch (1907-1996) extended Gestalt principles into social psychology. Heider's work was influential in subsequent attribution theory, and Asch's work in social pressure and conformity influenced subsequent work in that area as well.

Lewin used two organizing ideas or theories across his career. His first formulation, topological psychology (1936), introduced the concept of *life space* as a metaphor for psychological and social space. While the body had a physical boundary in the skin, the psychological boundary was larger and connected the individual to the world. He even used graphics to portray the subdivisions within the life space of an individual so as to better convey the dynamics between components of the self. He then moved to field theory by 1942 (Lewin, 1951), seeing the concept of fields in physics as an apt model illustrating the interconnectedness in psychological and social life. His original metaphor maps out psychological space and he then reformulates it within physical field theory to accommodate the social or systemic nature of bodies in a social space. What he pointed to was the integration of individual in environment, what we now we see as ecological psychology. His formulation of this relationship was put in the form of a heuristic equation, $B=f(P, E)$, behavior is a function of the person in an environment. This interconnection between person and environment is based on the primary structure of experience into figure and ground (or background).

The perceptual field is constituted by the individual embedded in a context. The figure/ground distinction is the experience of awareness of an active organism in its environment in search of adaptive survival and possibly even to advantage. We take the object of our focal awareness as figure, and all other incoming stimuli become part of the background awareness. This continues Brentano's concept of intentionality as the basis for the fundamental relational quality of subject/object, figure/ground, self/other. We experience our world in terms of a life space, this brings in the topological metaphor which he emphasized. The very nature of a physical field is its capacity to hold disparate and separated elements together in a whole. We experience the connectedness of the elements in our life as our life space. The boundary between individual and environment is both physical and social. So we include others in our life space.

Lewin made methodological contributions as well. Experiential learning, group dynamics, and participatory action research (PAR, or just action research, AR) are a cluster of concepts and methods he used to address social problems and issues. This is a radical restructuring of the process of research away from the focus on the researcher. It empowers the stakeholders in a project to gain information that is ultimately fed back to them. They help define the questions asked and the methods used. They are the primary consumers of the research. The researcher has the skills in specific methods of inquiry and data analysis. The purpose is improvement of function in the host group, community, or organization.

His model of action research was a process, an on-going feedback process, think, act, reflect and analyze then rethink and act again. He saw research as an on-going process of learning and an open process of reformulation and rethinking. The scientist is the thinker, the actor and the evaluator, and he then teaches the participant to do likewise. He passes on the transmission of knowledge skill and value as a process.

He coined the term *group dynamics* and was a pioneer in the study of groups. He began to understand that people learn about themselves and their interpersonal styles through the experiential learning process of being in a group. Although he still used laboratory space, he also went outside of laboratories to other settings to engage in consultation and research. The classic study of leadership types (Lippitt, 1940, Lewin, Lippitt &White, 1930) was conducted with the background of the rise of Fascism, Nazism and the impending Second World War. He found support for the superiority of democratic leadership styles as opposed to autocratic, or a hands off approach. Lewin found experiential learning and education was a powerful tool in personal and social change.

At the time of his death he was involved with a group that would form the National Training Laboratory (NTL) which became one of the leading exponents of training in group processes and leadership. From this came the T-group (the *t* for training).

It was an experiential learning exercise in group behavior. In the late 1940s it located in Bethel, Maine, and conducted summer workshops for therapists, academics, business people, student personnel specialists, and others who were interested in learning more about behavior in groups (Bennis, Schein, Steele & Berlow, 1968; Bradford, Gibb &Benne, 1964).

The idea of the T-group began to emerge when he was involved with Commission on Community Interrelations of the American Jewish Congress. He worked with a number of community groups in the New York area and found that the experience of small group interaction was beneficial in changing attitudes of the participants. From this came his concept of PAR, or AR, which combined research activity with experiential learning and group work. Action research was a field approach to research, not a laboratory one. It focused on solving social problems rather than gaining basic knowledge in a hypothetico-deductive method.

Lewin's social concerns came from his own experience of being a minority; a Jew in Germany as anti-Semitism grew and found expression in the Nazi Party's racist policies. Though he was a wounded veteran of World War I, he knew this meant nothing to the new Chancellor, Adolph Hitler. He had made a trip to America in 1930, and used his contacts to emigrate with his wife and daughter in 1933. Earlier, in Berlin, he was involved in socialist activities, including adult education groups for the working class. During World War II he conducted active research for the war effort; finding ways to make less desirable meats more popular to housewives constrained by rationing among other projects. Again, all of these activities had a profound commitment to social psychology in an active mode, involved with social and personal change.

Fritz Heider, like Lewin, was primarily concerned with social psychology. His *Psychology of interpersonal relations* (1958) is his major work. In this he outlines some important ideas about cognitive processes. His concept of naive psychology refers to the set of beliefs that each individual has about how human beings work. This is also known as folk psychology, the layman's understanding of what motivates people. His most widely known contributions were balance theory and the beginning of attribution theory. All of those ideas arise out of his interest in social perception.

## Existentialism

One of the consequences of the rise of secular world views was the birth of existentialism, a philosophy that starts with a focus on the human condition. It shares that focus with humanism but that approach has been critiqued as too positive, while existentialism is critiqued as too negative, even nihilistic. A better approach is to see existentialism as a balanced perspective. The basis of it is recognition of the existential givens; those things which just are part of being. Clearly awareness of one's own eventual death is at the core of existential anxiety according to Kierkegaard. While it is also true that existentialism has alienation as one of its core concepts. Much of the literature sparked by existentialism is about the absurdity of life. But it also has a clear necessity of choice and creating significance. If the world lacks inherent meaning and purpose as secular mechanistic world view would hold, then all the more reason to seize the opportunity to create and make meaning.

To understand existentialism, one must place it in the context of the growing willingness over the nineteenth and twentieth centuries to abandon the religious viewpoint with its emphasis on the hereafter and focus on the present with all its many uncertainties. Søren Kierkegaard (1813-1855) is considered the father of existentialism, and one of his main contributions was anxiety, or *angst* in German. Despite his criticism of the Danish state church and the commercialism of society even in that age, he saw the need for a leap *to* faith in God as a way to take responsibility for one's existence and life authentically. Indeed to live with authenticity is one of the positive things one can do in the face of anxiety, uncertainty, or even despair. The Russian author Fyodor Dostoevsky (1821-1881) echoed these sentiments in his novels.

A core principle of existentialism is the thrownness of life. We did not ask to come into the world, nor did we ask for the circumstance of our parentage and upbringing. We have more control over our circumstances as we develop, but there still are inherent limits to what we can accomplish. We are embodied and given both the joys of sense and movement, but the pain of illness and limits of age. This aspect of existential was presaged in the philosophy of the Stoics, who like the existentialists, saw the smallness of human will in the face of Fate, destiny or other concepts of impersonal force of nature. But nonetheless, there is a zone of control where choices can be made and actions taken. We can control our own inner life as well by adopting attitudes toward one's mental and emotional processes. We assert our existence as people by creating meaning, we add some value. It was an extension of humanism despite the uncertainties, relativities and depravities of the world.

But perhaps no one exemplified the new awareness of both the loss of faith in the certainties of religion and a stable society than the German philosopher Friedrich Nietzsche (1844-1900). To him we owe the phrase, the death of God, and he has been closely linked with nihilism, a deeply skeptical view of the world. Another idea relevant to psychology is his dichotomy of Apollonian and Dionysian tendencies in the human psyche named after two of the ancient Greek deities, Apollo and Dionysus. The former represents out tendencies toward being well ordered and rational, the latter reflects out chaotic and irrational aspects.

Between these early figures and the existentialist thinkers, psychologists and psychiatrists to come later a whole new world emerged. World War I brought new implements of war, the machine gun, the tank, poisonous gas, mass bombardment of civilian areas, futile charges from one trench to another only to be mowed down and fall amidst the barbed wire of no-man's land. The old dynasties that ruled Germany, Austria-Hungary, and Russia collapsed. The Bolshevik Revolution (1917) in Russia brought the first communist government into being. In the nineteen twenties, social norms were rapidly loosened and challenged by the younger generation. Hemlines in women's dresses went up and hair styles got shorter. America banned alcohol with Prohibition, creating a new and violent criminal underworld. Then came the Great Depression and economic collapse world wide. This led to the rise of Fascism and Nazism, the Second World War, and the Holocaust. After the war the nuclear era began with the growing threat across the nineteen fifties of the complete annihilation of life on the planet. If anything could create existential dread and anxiety it was those cumulative experiences of humanity.

But intellectual ferment created new ideas that challenged old and important areas of thought resulting in even more dislocation and unhinging from previous anchors. In physics, Einstein's relativity theory was soon followed by quantum mechanics which presented very different understandings of the world than were found in Newton's work. In psychology, Freud became quite popular among the intelligentsia, and the irrational, unconscious, and above all, sexual instincts were elevated as models for human motives. The first major revolution in attitudes toward sex as well as openness to varieties of sexuality were also part of the nineteen twenties and thirties.

A variety of writers reflected these new times and the anxiety that came with the new developments. These anxieties brought about the work of existential philosophers in France. Maurice Merleau-Ponty (1908-1961) was important in shaping the thought of Jean-Paul Sartre (1905-1980) and Simone deBeauvoir (1908-1986). Around these figures much of French intellectual life revolved in the post World War II era. Sartre is one of the most important existential thinkers and deBeauvoir is one of the early feminist authors and progenitors of critical theory.

In psychotherapy the voice of this new movement came from three figures. Ludwig Binswanger (1881-1966) and Medard Boss (1903-1990), both Swiss psychiatrists, formulated a type of fusion of psychodynamic therapy and existential philosophy. Daseinsanalysis oriented the therapy process around the modes by which the client situated themselves in the world. *Being-in-the-world* was a phrase that emphasized the dialectical relatedness of subject and object, self and non-self. The *thrownness* or seeming randomness of external environmental forces create a fertile field for choice in the face of circumstances and that paradoxical existential sense of freedom.

Victor Frankl (1905-1995) was another Viennese Jewish psychiatrist (Freud and Adler were the other two). He and his family were arrested, sent to Nazi death camps, and only he survived. What greater challenge to the meaningfulness of life could be experienced than living in the midst of an industrially efficient organized to systematically exterminate a whole people. Racism elevated to genocide. Torture, deprivation, betrayal by all who might support or aid, a bare struggle to stay alive day by day when the smoke of cremation reminded one of the disappeared; all were part of Frankl's experience, and yet he came out of it convinced of the worth of the individual choice to make life anew again, even in the midst and despite those horrors. He called his approach to therapy logotherapy, and it found fertile ground in anxious times.

Rollo May (1909-1994) was among the early psychologists to bring an existential approach to describing the human condition while working at the therapeutic level to change it. May (1969) talked about the human motivational system through the old Greek idea of *daimones*, literally, little gods. Each motive force jostled for dominance in a dynamically balanced system (at least in health), but when one comes to dominate the whole there is great potential for dysfunctional behavior. Following one's daimons, one's inner purposes or paths, can create meaning in life. His earlier edited volume on existential psychology (1960) highlighted the new interest in American psychology with philosophies from Europe. Though he later resisted the close association of transpersonal psychology with humanistic-existential psychology, May penned his last book on the importance of myth, a major theme in transpersonal psychology.

Irvin Yalom (b. 1931), an American psychiatrist, is perhaps the leading contemporary existential therapist. His works straddle both existentialism (Yalom, 1980, 1998) as well as in group method (Yalom & Leszcz, 1995). He has also branched out into writing fiction as well.

## Humanistic psychology

One of the forerunners of humanistic psychology, indeed, one of its founders, is Gordon Allport (1897-1967). He is one of a pair of brothers, the other being Floyd Allport (1890-1979) who became prominent psychologists. Gordon's focus was on personality theory. Trait theory was his choice as an alternative to either psychodynamic or behavioral approaches. He was first to recognize the value of personal data in psychology (Allport, 1942), the basis of psychobiography and autoethnography. He also conducted one of the first studies on prejudice (Allport, 1958).

Abraham Maslow (1908-1970) was also a founding figure. He, too, focused on personality. But his best known idea is the motivational hierarchy that characterizes all behavior (Maslow, 1951). The most basic ones, of course, are most clearly related to biological survival, higher ones then deal with security and belonging. At the pinnacle are the motives or need for self actualization. Each person has an inward motive force to be fully their self and realize their potentialities. We don't always achieve all we set out to do, as existentialism teaches us, but we seek that sense of fulfillment in life. In contrast to psychoanalysis whose data is the lives of neurotic individuals, and early behaviorism which focused mainly on lab animals, Maslow went out and investigated normal individuals, even those who were eminent or accomplished as well. This was at the other end of the functional spectrum from clinical samples. One thing he found was the frequency of *peak experiences* among people who were self actualizing. These brief moments of high sense of competency, purpose, and direction were intrinsically rewarding. Mihály Csíkszentmihály (b. 1934) went on to expand on this idea with his work on flow, as a state of mind during effortless performance, and likewise an ecstatic experience.

## Carl Rogers and person centered therapy

Carl Rogers (1902-1987) has a primary importance for professional psychology. He was the first person to articulate a major system of therapy and counseling (Rogers, 1942) whose training was solely in psychology. As noted in previous chapters, most of the originators of major therapeutic systems in that era where first trained in medicine as neurologists or psychiatrists. Access to patients required a medical degree. The psychological models of practice were educational in nature or consultative to business, courts and other sources of practice referrals (e.g. Witmer, Munsterberg, Dill, etc.). Carl Rogers articulated a theory of personal change and growth that straddled both normal and abnormal contexts, it provided a clinical method that has now become absorbed as a foundation of all basic practice.

His doctorate was an Ed.D., now a distinct minority among the licensed psychologists in the United States. Most licensed psychologists are Ph.D., with Psy.D.s as a close alternative, and the Ed.D. as a distant third place among the three academic degrees that are recognized for licensing as a professional psychologist. The different degrees represent historical shifts in the understanding of applied psychology. We'll go into detail later on the emergence of the Psy.D., but in the present context it is noted that Rogers' degree was granted from the Teachers' College of Columbia University, highlighting the fact that counseling psychology started not in the hospital or a medical clinic but in a variety of counseling centers. His first major work was influenced from his work at a child guidance clinic in Rochester, New York. He then was asked to move to the University of Chicago where he set up the counseling center. McCarthy (2014) goes on to highlight the importance of the college counseling centers in the development of professional psychology.

He is best known today for his position that effective therapy begins with professional relationship skills, especially the process of active listening and empathetic perspective. These skills and attitudes are now foundational across a number of professions. They are taught as basic clinical interviewing skills in any counseling, social work, psychiatric or other helping profession which seeks to claim the facility of interpersonal communication as a significant component. Many basic texts in helping services reference his contribution to the basic communication and relationship skills, though it's not necessarily taught as a Rogerian approach to therapy. In assessment and basic interviewing the work of Ivey and colleagues extended Rogers' work and has become a standard (Ivey,1984; Ivey, Gluckstein & Ivey1993, 1997; Ivey & Ivey, 1999).

Rogers was also one of the first people to conduct empirical research on the therapy process. He began the tradition of recording sessions for later analysis, something now fully integrated into both thetraining of professionals and research on the process of psychotherapy. Since few involved random controlled trials (RCT) this fact if often overlooked in today's environment emphasizing evidence based practice. Furthermore, he stimulated a stream of research; Truax (1967) and Carkhuff (2000) provided further support for his approach. How he labeled his approach changed as his research program unfolded. He initially termed it non-directive therapy, but he came to describe it as client-centered therapy in a later work (Rogers, 1951).

The person was an active agent and creator of meaning. Each person has the capacity for self development and unfolding, an idea compatible with another figure in humanistic psychology, Abraham Maslow. Frustrations and blockages of the natural course of development of a whole and creative person is part of the unfoldment of life and creates symptoms. Rogers' theory of development emphasized that to the extent the parents or others in the child's environment made their love or appreciation conditional on certain qualities or actions, the basis for low self esteem and symptoms was laid. The only thing that is needed, ultimately, is to remove the blockages to self-healing, because each person possesses a capacity for self-regulation as a living being, self-development as an individual biological organism, and growth as an active experiencing person who makes choices and attempts to control his or her life in the most skillful and adaptive manner.

Roger's basic view of counseling and therapy was summarized in the phrase *therapist provided conditions*. His research found that if the therapist provided three conditions, there was a strong likelihood of a favorable outcome. The therapist must convey an empathetic understanding of the client, must be non-judgmental (he termed this unconditional positive regard), and should be seen by the client as genuine (as opposed to contrived, artificial or distant). The goal of the therapist was to establish a trusting relationship aimed at helping with a client through offering the condition of being understood, of really hearing the client, their needs and their context. There were several specific clinical skills which evolved out of his own practice and theorizing, but active listening and empathic understanding scout the path.

Active listening encompasses the basis skills of just plain listening without necessarily adding guidance or intervention. Indeed, Rogers' approach eschewed the typical expectation that the therapist would provide suggestions for how to solve the problem. The therapist was not the expert, the client was the one most attuned to the needs, goals, and directions that therapy should take. It then seeks to deepen the therapist's understanding of the client's perspective by either asking questions or reflecting the content or affect of the client's immediate past communication in an attempt to generate an on-going stream of disclosures of important information about the nature of the client's perception of their own problem. The therapist provides a non-judgmental and acceptive environment which validates the client's belief that they can be understood and responded to on their own terms. The therapist focuses the change process by highlighting the client's stuck points through mirroring their own ambivalence while supporting their desire for growth. The person heals him or her self, the therapist just acts as a catalyst. This optimistic view of human possibilities characterized not only Rogers' view but humanistic psychology as a tradition.

## Gestalt therapy and psychodrama

Fritz Perls (1893-1970) is acknowledge as one of the seminal and key figures in Gestalt therapy. He was an assistant to the German physician, Kurt Goldstein, whose theory of personality is termed organismic or holistic and was also influenced by the Gestalt school of psychologists, though an academic psychologist (Henle, 1978) claims Gestalt psychology and Gestalt therapy have little in common. Perls was analyzed by Karen Horney and Wilhelm Reich. His wife Laura Perls, a therapist also, was analyzed by Frieda Fromm-Reichman. So Perls' pedigree in psychodynamic thought and technique is strong. Neurosis was the central focus of much psychotherapy prior to the nineteen eighties when the DSM multi-axial formulation swept away concern that diagnostic term. Be that as it may, Perls saw how his clients embodied their neurosis. His psychoanalysis with Wilhelm Reich was a key factor in teaching him the importance of embodiment.

He studied under Kurt Goldstein in Berlin but later he and his wife Laura, moved their family to South Africa as Germany became increasingly tense for Jews with the rise of Hitler and the Nazis. There he was influenced by the South African philosopher and statesman Jan Smuts who pioneered the concept of holism. In 1946 he moved to New York. There he collaborated with Paul Goodman and Ralph Hefferline to publish the first book on Gestalt Therapy (Perls, Hefferline & Goodman, 1951). He and Laura founded a training group which would become the Gestalt Institute. By the nineteen sixties the Esalen Institute in Big Sur, California, became a major center for humanistic approaches to therapy and Perls conducted many workshops there, eventually moving to Los Angeles, California, and began working with James (Jim) Simkin.

Perls the man was one of the most charismatic therapeutic figures of his time. His style is often described as confrontational, though he could be supportive. He certainly was active and directive in contrast to Rogers. He, Carl Rogers, and Albert Ellis participated in a film titled *Gloria* in which each of them interviewed the woman of that name, who then commented on her experience with each of them. This has become a classic in the field and most students in clinical or counseling psychology are exposed to it at some point in their training.

Gestalt therapy is an active form of treatment, requiring the patient to engage in an on-going series of sessions where the client is expected to not just talk about things, but experience them, live and in real time. The guidance of the therapist is important in terms of facilitating a process of development of awareness in the moment which leads to experiences which are validated by insight and enhanced awareness of the person as an active chooser of life paths. The specific use of dramatic re-enactment comes from the influence of Jacob Moreno, considered below.

The emphasis on present-centeredness in therapy came from his philosophical mentor in Berlin, Salomon Friedlander as well as the work of Otto Rank. In Gestalt therapy the *now* is the time to learn. The focus is on immediate experience rather than past experience, the goal is tracking the unfoldment of experience as guided by the therapist and the capacity to dialog in the immediate moment about what one is experiencing. He lays out his early ideas in *Ego, hunger and aggression* (Perls, 1969), where he uses a Kleinian approach based on oral sadism, that is, biting and chewing up the ingested whole in order to decompose it and make it one's own. His genius is to see the embodiment of this metaphor from the psychoanalytic tradition in terms of facilitation within the immediate moment rather than accomplished through build up of reflective elaborations of past experience is a detached analytic process.

The organism contacts the world at its boundary. This is literally the skin of the body, but as Lewin noted, psychological space and boundary extends beyond our physical boundary and include objects in our environment that we invest with psychic energy via cathexis, to use the psychoanalytic metaphor, or who are significant providers of social or primary reinforcement, to use a behavioral metaphor. Our psychological boundary, the line between self and the world, or the figure/ground relationship starts at the physical bodily space and moves outward. The process of experience is contact at the boundary. It begins with basic sensory awareness, including awareness of the inner environment as well as the outer environment.

Perls' theory of pathology was based on a holistic understanding of organismic contact and its problems. The pathology that arises when there is a defective or insufficient boundary between self and others is termed confluence. Today, we would see clinical description as reflected in the Axis II condition of borderline personality disorder. Introjection is another concept Perls embraces. It occurs when we take in psychological material without digesting it, without chewing it up. We swallow the other whole and that introjected object remains unprocessed, something other and foreign. Becoming whole comes through chewing it up and breaking it down in terms of one's own self. This failure of development of normal aggression takes the form of unfinished business. Therapy requires deconstruction of meanings of our experiences can be seen in the various rules, roles, expectancies, and residual of our parental upbringing. They comprise all the bad messages we learned. Projection is the opposite, we give away what is ours, it is self imposed organismic limitation. Chiefly, we give away our power to act, control or just be naturally in the moment. Psychoanalytic theory would recognize introjection as object relations problems and projection is now a generic type of defense mechanism. Finally, retroflexion is the squeezing of self, the self's power used to defeat the self. When we turn things in on our self we are retroflecting. But he used it in such obvious situations as the tense musculature of neurotic clients and the inhibition of the normal relaxed flow of breath. All of these defense mechanisms enabled the individual to cope, but not fully experience the moment and be alive.

Perls felt we lived too much in our head, with our conceptualizations and rationalizations. Like Wilhelm Reich discussed below, he was focused on the bodily experience and flow of energy. So, even though Lewin showed how psychological space goes beyond the body, the body is a very good place to begin examining psychological space We use, misuse or neglect various aspects of our body as part of our characteristic stuckness.

Jacob Moreno (1889-1974) gave Perls a powerful technique in dramatic enactment, role playing. Moreno was an Italian-born psychiatrist whose genius was in making role play take on a therapeutic meaning. He founded the discipline of psychodrama, or deliberate use of role play and enactment as a therapeutic vehicle (Marineau, 1989). This was done in a group and required an open space for movement and action. One person became the protagonist and sketched out a basic need, a situation, a scenario that they wanted to change in their life. Since most such problems involve others, the rest of the group are assigned roles to play as needed to script the scene. Props may be used as well, chairs, etc. The facilitator helps the protagonist and the others get comfortable with their parts, having the protagonist brief each person playing a role in their drama about what words to use, what kinds of stance they should take. When a brief period of such structuring is ended, the protagonist and the players enter their roles and begin the drama. The facilitator may then act as a double for the protagonist, suggesting lines or emotions that the protagonist is oblivious to or needs to try out as an alternative to their neurotic stuck points. In groups that have worked together and have developed a trusting climate, other group members might also act as doubles. At some point the natural action either gets resolved, or at remains unresolved, but the role-playing ends. The facilitator then de-briefs the participants and the rest of the group about what they experienced during the drama. Depending on time available the group moves on to another protagonist or concludes.

Because of the capacity of people to get lost in their roles, it can charge the atmosphere with strong emotions. The facilitator must be comfortable with this type of situation. As we saw earlier, with Freud, the style of therapy is partly related to the personality characteristics of the therapist. Indeed, as we shall see later, when talking about Carl Rogers, this is a central feature of humanistic-existential psychology. Not every therapist feels comfortable working in this very active manner, staying more comfortable, and probably more effective with more restrained discussion of the client's problems. But if the therapist feels comfortable with this type of interaction it can be a rewarding and stimulating way of helping people grow.

## Somatics: Reich and the body

The field of alternative healing approaches is a booming industry. Many techniques are described as mind-body integrative techniques. Body work refers to a variety of approaches to access psychological and emotional matters through the body, or soma (as opposed to psychosomatic medicine which accesses bodily processes through psychological ones). Wilhelm Reich (1897-1957), was a psychiatrist and psychoanalyst whose thought and practice have influenced many later practitioners of body work. Unlike other forms of psychodynamic treatment, Reich was willing to explore catharsis more deeply. Freud always felt it important to practice with minimal physicality, as the patient lay quietly on the couch. But Reich used touch, patterned breathing exercises physical positioning and movement to promote awareness and expression of strong emotions expressing repressed psychological material.

Body work, as it is now practiced involves influences from other practitioners than Reich. The pioneers in massage therapy as a discipline as well as the founders of other types of mind-body training also feed into this stream. But Reich remains the pre-eminent font of the conceptual linkage for this whole spectrum of approaches. He is to psychologists interested in somatic techniques and body workers what Jung is to psychologists interested in the spiritual dimension.

Among the dissenters from Freud, the most common reason is their rejection of his libido theory of psychological energy as the sole or even primary motive in human experience. Reich, however, thought Freud got it right; he just didn't carry it far enough. In his book *The Function of the Orgasm* (Reich, 1973/1942), he noted that the pulsating energetic experience of arousal and climax was a primum bonum, an intrinsic good. When we deny ourselves that experience through either cultural or personal suppression or repression we create problems. We literally embody our history of neurosis in the tensing of muscles as we truncate the full process of release in orgasm. Of course, this spills over into other bodily functions. We soon hold, move and live in our bodies in a certain way that is constricted. The pattern of tension and constriction of organismic flow becomes habituated and locked into place as a chronic state. This pattern of disruption of normal flow of energy is known as our body armor and one can read the defensive structure of the person by the malfunctions and deformations which are literally embodied. Character analysis, for Reich involved reading the unconscious conflicts writ corporeally.

Reich tied his ideas about personal character and our somatic life to our social life. He was concerned about the rising tide of fascism in Europe and wrote a manifesto linking fascism to a repression of the sexual as well as the social (1971/1946). He, too, like many German and Austrian psychologists, psychiatrists and others fled the Nazi regime. But his stay in the United States turned sour when after the war, he became more involved in his theory of life-force energy. Orgone is the name he gave to the broader concept which was not just libido, but a basic physical energy in the universe. Reich's orgone theory, however, bears resemblance to the vital energy theories which originated in both India (*prana*), China (*chi* or *qi*), or Japan (*ki*) and even in the Western esoteric tradition (*pneuma*). This concept is also close to the Odic force hypothesized by the German chemist Carl von Reichenbach. He devised orgone accumulators to supposedly funnel these energies and also used them in cloud seeding activities as well as therapeutic ones. The Food and Drug Administration (FDA) finally prosecuted and convicted him of fraud, claiming these were quack medical devices purveyed through the mail. He experienced a major period of psychological decline, even psychosis and died in prison.

His work was carried on by others, notably Alexander Lowen (1910-2008) on the East coast and Charles Kelley's (1922-2005) Radix Institute, on the West coast. Lowen's (1976) Bioenergetics®, derived from Reich, is probably the more well known of the two neo-Reichian systems. In the mid-1970s another movement came along, primal scream therapy (Janov, 1970), though he was less intellectually honest, not acknowledging his clear borrowing of Reich's ideas.

Thomas Hanna (1970, 1988) developed a system of psycho-physical awareness exercises aimed at helping people understand chronic tension and functional difficulties in their bodies. The means are largely psychological, but with some touch, though not as much as massage therapy. Among the other body oriented systems are the Alexander technique, pioneered by an Australian actor and orator F. Matthias Alexander (Alexander,1974/1910). An Israeli, Moshe Feldenkrais, has designed another set of mind-body exercises involving postural and movement activities as part of the learning process (Feldenkrais, 1972). All of these techniques are closer to psychological practice in that their primary mechanism is enhanced awareness of sensations arising in the body that are indicative of functional or structural issues and are corrected by the individual using that awareness to be in and use their body differently. What training psychologists receive in facilitating embodied awareness comes almost exclusively from Jacobson's progressive relaxation training as filtered through CBT. These approaches could add to that base as Criswell (1995) has suggested.

Reich used the phrase character armor to describe the chronic muscular tension that inhibits a full organismic process to move to completion. Ida Rolf developed a system of deep tissue massage that quite literally unlock this body armor by loosening the myo-fascial tissue which lock tension in the muscles and prevents more fluid function (Rolf, 1989). She represents the stream of practice that leads more directly to the use of physical touch as part of the bodily access to and therapeutic change in the psyche. Like all the other approaches noted above, they stem from core ideas developed by Reich.

## Critical theory

Another important stream within the broad river of humanistic and existential thought is critical theory. This is both an approach to understanding texts, including literature, but also a critique of social structures. It draws from the phenomenological tradition and existentialism. It was most clearly articulated in Europe in the half century after World War II, and has only become a presence in American thought and psychology in the last couple of decades of the twentieth century. Simone deBeauvoir, noted above, began to link humanistic values with a political understanding of the social structure of relationships between the sexes. Her work *The second sex* (1949) was a groundbreaking work.

Much of the work known as critical theory came fom the Institute for Social Research at Goethe University in Frankfurt Germany. It led the way in social critique even before the Nazi era. under the leadership of such luminaries as Max Horkheimer (1895-1973). Horkheimer saw value in the Marxist critique of the class structure in society and tried to articulate a philosophy in which human liberation was possible. He had to leave Germany with the rise of Nazi political power, settling in the U.S. His critique of objective and subjective reason emphasized the was social norms and situations shape thinking. With his colleague Theordor Adorno (1903-1969) he challenged the logical positivist world view that prevailed in the philosophy of science in the twentieth century. His work was influential for two other very important figures in critical theory, Herbert Marcuse (1898-1979) and Jürgen Habermas (b. 1929). Habermas integrates much of the sociology of human communication into his epistemological theory.

The French thinker Michel Foucault (1926-1984) is also important. His whole research focus was on how discourse is used as a means of social control. We have cited him previously in regard to his history of mental illness in early modern Europe (Foucault, 1973). He went on to add another book on the clinic, one on prisons as places of penitence, and a three-volume work on human sexuality. In the latter he argued that the very concept of sexuality as a thing was part of the medicalization of desire. What had been the province of the Church to discipline became the object of the physician and especially the psychiatrist's attentions. His synthesis of theory (1970) and his method (1969/1982) are foundational for understanding the significance of discourse.

## Transpersonal psychology

The term *transpersonal* refers to things beyond the individual. Psychology has since its inception focused on the individual person. It has also studied groups, couples, families, communities and other social entities. But the term is usually taken to mean an interest in phenomena of a spiritual nature and the altered states of consciousness that often are the sources of spiritual experience. The field of transpersonal psychology came into being in the nineteen seventies from two major cultural phenomena; the youth counter culture and experimentation with drugs, and the expansion of interest in meditative practices from Eastern spiritual systems.

Spiritual philosophies and practices were tossed out of Western scientific thought from the seventeenth century onward and in psychology with the growth of behaviorism.It would also be an oversimplification that spirituality was completely excluded. William James, one of the founders of psychology, made a profound contribution to the scientific study of religion. Later, Gordon Allport became interested in the psychology of religion, giving us the dimension of intrinsic and extrinsic motivations for religiosity. But part of the broader struggle of science as a human intellectual and practical enterprise has always been to assert the methods and viewpoints of science over, and usually against, the methods and viewpoints of religion. Science has matured and now achieved success as a major epistemic system or world view. What roles should science and religion or spirituality play with regard to each other?

When the Beatles appeared with the spiritual guru, Maharishi Mahesh Yogi, there was an immediate burst of interest in meditative practices. As noted in a previous chapter, the Indian sub-continent was the home of two religious traditions, Hinduism and Buddhism, that developed extensive traditions of meditation. Americans got their fist significant exposure to teachers of those paths with the 1893 Parliament of World Religions, held in conjunction with the Columbian Expostion in Chicago. Following the Second World War a number of American servicemen were exposed to and took up training in Eastern martial arts which have meditative aspects as well as the more obvious emphasis on physical culture. Zen, likewise, became popular in the West in the decades following that war (Harrington & Dunne, 2015). Following the Beatles involvement, a variety of teachers of yoga and meditation came to the West. The Tibetan diaspora in northern India after the Chinese Communist conquest provided an introduction to Tantric Buddhism. Several Western students, some of whom were exposed via their Peace Corps assignments brought vipassana, or insight meditation back to America (Goldstein, 1976).

Other forms of Western mystical tradition likewise flourish in the nineteen seventies onward. Idries Shah popularized Sufi teachings, the Islamic form of mysticism, with the translation of the tales of the mystical mullah, Nasrudin (Shah, 1972). Gray (1975) brought the Western magical tradition into the realm of transpersonal psychology by highlighting how it is used as a means of psycho-spiritual growth and development. Jung's influence can be seen here as well. Mishlove (1975) provides one of the most comprehensive chronicles of the whole range of ideas and practices that I term the Western esoteric tradition.

Psychology and religion have two organizational homes. The first is Division 36, The Society for the Psychology of Religion. It represents the more purely scholarly goal of advancing a scientific understanding of this area, and members are more likely to be interested in or involved with mainstream Judeo-Christian religions. There is generally less emphasis on practice. The second home is either the independent Association of Transpersonal Psychology (ATP) or within Divison 32, the Society for Humanistic Psychology. That community of scholars and practitioners are often more interested in or involved with Eastern or alternative faith traditions, and more importantly, also are more involved in the use of spirituality in therapy. They also tend to be more open to examining various meditative states of consciousness. It grew up in the 1960s and 1970s when the counter-culture had become exposed to and involved with altered states of consciousness. Whether induced by drugs or by meditation or even by exercise, dancing or, ultimately, through just living, the concern of many here was their state of consciousness. The new psychology of consciousness emerged from and with transpersonal psychology.

Besides spirituality, another early influence on the development of transpersonal psychology were altered states of consciousness that were drug induced, particularly the newly developed psychedelic drugs, the most dramatic impact of which came from lysergic acid diethalymide (LSD). There was a growing body of research on what was then called psychedelic drugs (now the preferred term is entheogens, emphasizing their spiritual potential). Originally confined to medically controlled laboratories, soon however, the drug escaped into the underground market and the psychedelic movement began and formal research ceased as legal sanctions tightened.

The association of drugs with the shamanic path was chronicled by Carlos Castaneda in his controversial 1968 book, *Teachings of Don Juan: A Yaqui way of knowledge*. Though many scholars have questioned the veracity of the story, being the field work basis of a dissertation in anthropology, its appeal as a work of descriptive literature in the spiritual quest keeps it a popular read whether you take it as fact or fiction. The study of shamanistic paths has continued and expanded beyond Castaneda's popularization as was mentioned at the beginning of our story.

Both the growth in interest in meditation as well as understanding the altered states from drugs, transpersonal psychology grew along with a revived psychology of consciousness. Tart (1969, 1975a, 1975b), Ornstein (1972, 1973), were early pioneers in articulating this view, and laying down the research paradigms. The advancement of the technology of physiological recording and measurement gave a new and exciting tool for examining states of consciousness. The multi-channel EEG allowed subtle differentiations in brain waves and Tart's (1969) book contains examples of studies using these new tools. The whole field of sleep research gave insights into our understanding of the altered states of consciousness that are normal for all human beings, sleep and dreams (Farthing, 1992).

The leading contemporary thinker in transpersonal psychology is Ken Wilber. He has accumulated a significant body of writings (1977, 1980, 1996, 2000; Wilber, Engler & Brown, 1986). He talks of centaur consciousness as a type of embodied consciousness as part of evolution of spiritual development. His major statement (2000) summarizes his previous ideas about consciousness existing on four dimensions, an inner, an outer consciousness, and an individual one and a collective one. From those beginnings, transpersonal psychology has evolved (Rowan, 1993) and continues to push for an intersection between both psychology, consciousness, and spirituality.

# *13*

# Social Systems Approaches

## Cultural context

THE APPROACHES THAT HAVE become popular for dealing with couples and families, as well as organizations, have been strongly influenced by a major development in the philosophy of science that came after World War II, the emergence of General Systems Theory (GST). Indeed, thinking in terms of systems has now become a ubiquitous feature of all the sciences. Several factors related to the Second World War contributed to the development of systems thinking. One was the development of the digital computer, and the other was operations research and planning.

First of all, when the U.S. entered the war in 1941, it had already been going on for several years, and we had to fight a two front war; in Europe against Germany and Italy, and in Asia against the Empire of Japan. This required a vast mobilization of manpower, materiel and the transportation logistics to get troops trained, equipped and sent to the theaters of operation. To accomplish this required a degree of coordination and organization that had not been achieved before, and it generated a level of thinking about the whole that would enable the coordination of the parts. In addition, it in part paved the way for the development of the second major factor, the digital computer.

That part of the story begins with cryptanalysis, the technology for breaking codes used for military or diplomatic communications. In World War II the American naval victory at Midway in June, 1942, was made possible in large part by the deciphering of the Japanese naval code, which allowed the U. S. Navy to position its carriers to intercept the Japanese invasion force aimed at Midway Island. In the European theater, the German code system was particularly complex. British cryptanalysis working out of an estate in a London suburb known as Bletchley Park developed an early digital computer to check out the hugely large possible meanings of coded messages. This was before integrated circuit technology, so the machines were operated with vacuum tubes and were large and bulky, with little computing power compared with today's technology. The British mathematician, Allan Turing (1912-1954) was a key figure in this important project. They finally broke the Enigma code, the German's best system and enabled many important Allied victories through the advance knowledge of military deployments and strategic intentions.

## Systems, computers, and the Internet

Information is a key concept in systems thinking and the prominence of that concept was influenced by computer programming. Living systems sustain themselves through homeostatic mechanisms involving information exchange to control bodily functions. As noted previously, the cognitive revolution in psychology owed a good deal of its development to the quest to model human cognitive abilities through computer simulation. From the end of World War II to the nineteen eighties was the era of the mainframe computer. Integrated circuits were first incorporated into transistors, which made possible small hand held radios. But then the shrinking size of processors due to integrated circuit technology made possible the development of the personal computer. Apple developed early models, then IBM and other manufacturers joined the market. This was a second revolution and it allowed individuals to own and use personal computers for a variety of functions, including word processing and spreadsheets, which had immediate business applications. By the nineteen nineties the internet arose linking the world's computers through phone lines initially, then through wireless technology. Our current era has now exploded in terms of the number and types of digital technologies and cellular telephones soon were competing with personal computers for access to markets for goods, services, and above all, information. Thus our modern world was born.

The many functions of computers were made possible by the science of cybernetics, which deals with the general theory and technology of control. The term *cybernetic* was coined by mathematician Norbert Weiner (1894-1964), derived from the Greek word for a steersman (*kubernetes*). The concept of the feedback loop is the key to understanding cybernetics. It is in the feeding back of information about the output of a system, that the system can correct or change it's next output to come closer to the target value or to operate within a range of values (homeostasis). The simple thermostat in a building is a concrete example of an information feedback and control mechanism. Weiner worked on the problem of accuracy in gunnery during the war, so one can see how the concept he evolved came from problem of delivering a weapon across a large distance on target, what the current generation of American smart bombs do fairly well, and which also led to putting humans on the moon in 1969. So, soon the concept of feedback loop was being applied in psychology. Two other important figures in the development of both cybernetics and systems theory are the psychiatrist W. Ross Ashby (1903-1970) and physicist Heinz von Foerster

(1911-2002). Their contributions gave additional precision to and expansion of the concepts implicated in systemic regulation.

A key book applying cybernetics to psychology was Miller, Galanter & Pribram's (1960) *Plans: The structure of behavior*. In this book they talk about the TOTE unit (an acronym for Test, Operate, Test, Exit), which they identified as the basic behavioral and cognitive unit of adaptive control. This book brought both the feedback loop and the concept of information and control in general as an organismic adaptive process that required attention. Control, in classical behavioral theory, is external, but with the definition of a system as a set of internal cybernetic processes which govern and coordinate activity of all the elements requires a theory of internal systemic control systems. An important theory of human control systems has been offered by Powers (1973) who offers a nine-level hierarchical organization of human control systems. Hierarchy is inherent in all cybernetics. The very nature of a system is the control of the whole over parts, a central coordinating purpose and a mechanism for its activity.

Inherent in cybernetics is the requirement for a theory of information. The purpose of communication is to transmit information. The function of our senses is to give us information about the world. Our modern concept of information is informed by a mathematical theory. In 1948 Claude Shannon (1916-2001) published a mathematical theory of information later expanded (1949) with Warren Weaver (1894-1978). Shannon coined the term bit for the unit of information (it was a contraction of *binary digit*). Using a two-valued unit of information made it easier to embody it in electrical circuitry which could be in two states, on or off. A switch could be open or closed, and later magnetized media for storage of information could be encoded north or south polarity. The amount of information in a given message is a logarithmic function in base two. One easier way to grasp the meaning is to use a game similar to 20 questions to illustrate the point. Consider a 4x4 matrix with a target in one of the 16 cells. The challenge is to reduce the uncertainty of the location of the target by half with each question. First one asks is the target above or below the midline. The first answer gives one bit of information, and eliminates consideration of the upper or lower half of the matrix. The next question halves the remaining cells by asking if the target is in the right or left half, yielding a second bit of information and further reducing the uncertainty of location by half. Two more questions repeated the procedure results in identifying the target cells with four bits of information. Thus, the physics of electromagnetic energy and the concept of information are united in the mathematical binary means of encoding.

The language of computers has come to identify a whole body of research in cognitive psychology known as the information processing model. It examines human cognition as the means by which sensory input is processed, informed by memory, and ultimately used to make decisions about acting in the world. One of the visual tools of computer programming is the flow diagram. This graphically portrays the movement of information through various stages of processing and is now widely used to portray relationships among a set of processes and elements linked through arrows showing directionality of influence. Neural network theory evolved parallel to computer network theory, but the success in quantifying models of neural relationships that map into cognitive phenomena has not been so swift. The soft tissue turns out to be remarkable hard to decipher.

## General systems theory (GST)

The cultural forces noted above were important in making a general theory of systems possible. Among the founders of the movement was Ludwig von Bertallanfy (1901-1972), an Austrian-born theoretical biologist. His 1968 book remains a widely used text. The Society for General Systems Theory was founded in 1956, and is now known as the International Society for Systems Science (ISSS – www.isss.org). It's first president was the noted economist, Kenneth Boulding (1910-1993). General systems theory became applied to social systems (Buckley, 1968; Luhmann, 1995); as well as the problems of psychiatry and mental illness (Gray, Dull & Rizzo, 1969). Besides the cultural factors mentioned in the section above, one additional factor in the growth of systems theory was the expansion of cross-disciplinary studies such as bio-chemistry. Scientists needed a common language to communicate across the boundaries of increasingly narrow and specialized sciences.

The system is the base concept. It represents an organized set of elements. Both parts of the definition require elaboration. Complexity is simply the number of elements in the system. The number of stars in a galaxy are the elements of the galaxy as an astro-physical system. The number of complex proteins bounded by a membrane defines a cell as a living system comprised of chemical elements. A system is distinguished from an aggregation, a mere unorganized collection of things by the second part of the definition, the organization. A sand pile is a disorganized aggregation of very fine rock particles, it has no structure as an independent entity. Information is constituted by a particular pattern of organization, one that is opposite of entropy, or disorder. Information is what is necessary to create and sustain a system. The exchange of information is critical for cybernetic or control systems which make homeostasis in living organisms possible.

Living systems are negentropic, that is, they are able to prevent energy from dissipating, indeed growth is creation of additional energy within the system by transforming the nutrition taken in. All living beings, it seems, ultimately do succumb to entropy and die. Their physico-chemical and dependent psychological processes break down and disintegrate. But for however long, each organism enjoys or suffers through a period of life, the added value of systemic organization allows self-organization, growth and development. The Chilean biologists Humberto Maturana (b. 1928) and Francisco Varella (1946-2001) introduced the term *autopoiesis* to refer to the self-organizing capacity of individual biological organisms as well as the concept of embodied mind as a basis for human science (Maturana and Varella, 1998; Varella, Thompson & Rosch, 1991).

One of the most complete statements of systems theory comes from James Grier Miller (1978). His monumental work (1,051 pages of densely footnoted and referenced text) not only was a masterful synthesis of existing ideas and their empirical support, but he added several key concepts. Miller coined the term *behavioral science* to reflect this inter-disciplinary perspective. Miller was the founding editor of the journal *Systems research and behavioral science* which has long featured integrative thinking regarding the links between the different levels of explanation contributed by each of the life and human sciences. He was extremely important in the development of clinical psychology as a profession through his role in the Veterans' Administration (VA), which will be covered in the next chapter. Within systems theory he is best known for his delineation of the critical sub-systems. There are subsystems that process only matter-energy; the ingestor, distributor, converter, producer, matter-energy storage, extruder, motor, support. There are subsystems which process only information; input transducer, internal transducer, channel and net, decoder, associator, memory, decider, encoder, and output transducer. And, finally, there are subsystems which process both matter-energy and information; boundary and reproducer.

But my vote for Miller's most significant contribution goes to his brief few paragraphs identifying three basic types of codes of communication, alpha, beta, and gamma (1978). That insight is part of a broader discipline known as semiotics, or the general theory of signs and their relationships to the meanings embodied in them. Alpha level codes embody information by the very physical/structural shape of molecules. The match between molecular shapes is how information is transmitted, the basic metaphor is the shape of a key in a lock. The message is binary, like computer code, on or off. The term endo-semiotics (von Uexküll, Geigess, & Herrmann. 1993) is used to refer to the communication that occurs at this cellular level. One example of alpha codes, is the match between the shape of a neuro-transmitter and that of the receptor site. Another example is shape of the histo-compatibility factor (HCF) which is the chemical marker on each individual cell of an organism contains as the basis for the immune response. It identifies the cell as generated by the individual as part of the system, rather than a foreign body (pathogen, allergen, etc.). Alpha codes are also the basis of phyto-semiotics, how plants communicate with their environment, sending signals to deal with insect predation among other things.

Beta codes involve scalable variables which encode information by variations in frequency, intensity or amount. Some concrete examples are how the perception of fever is taken as a sign of illness, or how the perception of increased uterine contractions are a sign of impending delivery of a newborn child. Beta codes form the basis of bio-semiotics, the study of communication between non-human animals. With beta codes there is some ambiguity as the match between physical characteristic of the sign and its meaning is not perfect. A shriek could be one of delight or fright, without a context the sign remains ambiguous. It certainly indicates a surprise, but the kind of surprise is not specified. The grandfather of the lead author of the article by von Uexküll et al., the noted Estonian ethologist Jacob von Uexküll (1864-1944), used the phrase attunement processes to identify the means by which complex animal communication takes place. One example is how flocks of birds are able to coordinate their flight and turns without colliding with each other, such as the murmuration of starlings. He also coined the term *umwelt* to describe how animals experience their world. This influenced the work of Heidegger who used the term in his phenomeno-logical philosophy, and the semiotician Thomas Sebeok (1920-2001).

Gamma codes embodied in symbols, are fully conventional in the match be-tween sign and meaning. Language is the prime metaphor, and the arbitrariness of match between a grapheme, or elementary unit of written language, for example *G* for the phoneme, or elementary unit of linguistic sound, *guh*. There is no physical basis for the match between letter and the sound it represents. We could switch the gamma or symbolic code and say it matches with a *puh* phoneme. There is little ambigu-ity between sign and meaning in alpha codes; it's a binary, yes/no, on/off message. With the symbolic systems of gamma codes there is a wide range of ambiguity as the physical relationship between sign and meaning is entirely by convention and arbitrary. The need for context to interpret the sign is essential. This really implicates the importance of hermeneutics, the discipline of interpretation of texts as necessary for comprehending language and other symbolic systems. Brier (1998) has extended the scope of cybernetics to include the relationships between humans and the digital world with the term cyber-semiotics.

Finally, the world as envisioned by systems theory is similar to that implied by the bio-psycho-social continuum now widespread in psychology to represent the in-tegration of the various relationships between levels of explanation for understanding the human condition. The cosmos is a nested hierarchy of interacting systems, from the sub-atomic level to the galactic or even cosmic level. Each system is composed of subsystems and itself is an element, or subsystem, of higher order systems, known as suprasystems. Individual disciplines or studies may focus on one level and seek to relate it to a lower or a higher level of system function. So the term system can be applied to any relative level of interest or focus.

## Gregory Bateson and friends; the birth of strategic systems therapy

We have seen how in the period following World War II systems theory, information theory, cybernetics, and computer science opened up new doors to understanding hu-man communication. A particular nexus of research developed in northern Califor-nia. Gregory Bateson was a seminal figure who worked closely with a number of very talented people who would become influential in the development of family therapy and a style of individual brief therapy known as strategic therapy. Among the others who worked with him or were influenced by he and his associates are Jay Haley, Don Jackson, Jeurgen Reusch, Paul Watzlawick and Virginia Satir. Jackson founded the Mental Research Institute (MRI) in Palo Alto, California, which continues to be a site focusing on strategic family therapy.

Gregory Bateson (1904-1980) was born in Britain and acquired his academic training in anthropology there. He did field work in New Guinea and Bali prior to the Second World War. From 1936 to 1950 he was married to the equally famous anthropologist Margaret Mead. During that war he served with the Office of Strategic Services (OSS), an early intelligence agency in the U.S., as did many other anthropologists and psychologists. This brought him to America where he lived since 1940. He collaborated with the psychiatrist Juergen Reusch (1951/1968) on a monograph entitled *Communication: The social matrix of psychiatry*. Reusch went on to author two other monographs on disturbed and therapeutic communication respectively (1957/1962, 1961/1973) and collaborated on a volume on non-verbal communication (Reusch & Kees, 1974).

Bateson is most well known in the area of mental health for putting for the concept of the double bind, as a style of pathological communication. A double bind is where an individual receives contradictory messages from the same source and is therefore caught in a bind as to how to respond appropriately. He along with Jay Haley and Don Jackson interviewed a number patients and their families at the Palo Alto VA hospital who had the diagnosis of schizophrenia. Out of those interviews the idea of the double bind emerged as an etiological hypothesis. While schizophrenia is now seen to have stronger biological bases the double bind has found its way into the literature on all sorts of pathogenic communication styles.

Don DeAvila (Don) Jackson (1920-1968) went on to become a leading figure in the development of family therapy. He and others worked through the Mental Research Institute (MRI) in Palo Alto California, adjacent to the Stanford campus. It became the nexus for a number of creative minds and the work there ultimately fostered the development of family therapy and a style of brief individual therapy known as strategic therapy. This institute would be the focus of much creative work applying findings in linguistics and other fields to therapy.

One aspect of linguistics, pragmatics, deals with the use of language to not only communicate knowledge, but to motivate people to do certain things. Paul Watzlawick (1921-2007) articulated a theory of human communication based on pragmatics (Watzlawick, Beavin & Jackson, 1967; Watzlawick, Weakland & Fisch, 1974). This area also overlaps with the philosophical approach known as speech act theory. First laid out by the British philosopher, John L. Austin (1911-1960), whose (1965) book titled *How to do things with words*, describes pragmatics as an approach. John Searle (b. 1932) now continues work on this philosophical matter (Searle, 1969). The social uses and functions of language link directly into how individuals, couples, families, groups and organizations function.

Jay Haley (1923-2007) articulated an early position advancing the notion that therapists act strategically (1973) to aid the client in understanding and changing their communicational styles. One of Haley's teachers in the skill of psychotherapy was the noted physician, Milton Erickson, who was probably the most skilled hypnotist seen in several generations. Haley edited some of his work (Erickson, 1967), though a later student, Ernest Rossi, was responsible for the editing of Erickson's later teaching and therapeutic style (Erickson & Rossi, 1981).

The study of several talented masters of psychotherapy such as Erickson, Virginia Satir, and Fritz Perls, led Richard Bandler (b. 1950) and John Grinder (b. 1940) to collaborate on the development of what they called neuro-linguistic programming (NLP). Their approach draws heavily on the whole line of research on human communication covered in this section (Bandler, 1985; Bandler & Bateson 1975a, 1975b; Bandler & Grinder 1979; Dilts, Grinder, Bandler, Bandler, & DeLozier, J., 1980; Grinder & Bandler, 1981). Their work is grounded in a detailed attention to the subtleties of linguistic and para-linguistic elements of communication and stands as a mine of valuable hints to the clinician as to how to frame their interventions.

## Family therapy

The basic assumption of family therapy is, given that people spend most of their lives within families, seeing an individual client in isolation is artificial. Focus on the individual is a special case not the natural ground for intervention. Family therapy adopts the systems perspective which sees the larger communities of organisms as a legitimate focus, and in that sense can be revolutionary. Prior to this movement, the whole history of counseling and psychotherapy from Freud onward emphasizes individual psychotherapy. Systems therapy is inherently interpersonal, what is being treated is the relationship between two or more people. Couples therapy is the most common form of dyadic relational treatment, since humans tend to pair bond. Once children are born one has a family, the basic unit of our social system and the means of passing on our love to future generations. This expands outward to include groups, organizations, communities, and even cultures as well. The central idea, however, is the network of human relationships is foundational to individual experience and behavior.

The symptom bearer and the system is a metaphor for the definition of critical roles in the family as client. It is a figure / ground relationship. The one, the symptom bearer, stands out and is usually the occasion for the referral to a mental health or social service agency, but the sage professional sees not just the individual, but the individual in context, including the family that often brings the identified patient in for treatment. Though one member of the family is thrust forward for scrutiny and aid from beyond the family, it is the family who is having the problem and is the basis of the dysfunction. This is a fundamental reconceptualization of the arena of intervention beyond the individual to the group, but to a naturally occurring group. We saw in the last chapter how many important themes in group therapy and experiential education are based in the work of Kurt Lewin. We now see how those same general extension of the therapeutic realm lead to consideration of families, which are groups arising *in situ, in vivo*, and in real time. These are nature's experiments in group formation with biological creation, adoption and other means of blending generations.

An important figure in developing a family therapy was Virginia Satir, whose (1967) book on conjoint family therapy was a major statement of the new specialty of family therapy, which will be elaborated on later. As noted above, she was part of a broader community of scholars and practitioners that flourished in the San Francisco Bay area in the latter half of the twentieth century.

Another key figure in the development of family therapy was the Argentinian born psychiatrist, Salvador Minuchin (b. 1921). His work at the Child Guidance Clinic in Boston added much to the emerging ideas and practices from the Bay area group headed by Bateson. He emphasized the importance of the structural relationships among the members of the family. Many possible solutions exist from poor to non-existent boundaries which result in members being enmeshed with each other, through rigid and inflexible boundaries, especially as between the parents and children which leaves the family incapable of flexibly responding to outside forces requiring change on internal relationships. His approach, structural family therapy, seeks nature to clarify and to change the relationships within the family to allow for more successful functioning.

Nathan Ackerman (1908-1971), another psychiatrist, was located at the Menninger Clinic in Topeka, Kansas. His original training was in psychoanalysis, but he began moving into a more interpersonal mode of treatment, having been influenced by Harry Stack Sullivan's interpersonal theory of psychiatry. He became a founder of the first journal of family therapy, *Family Process*, along with Don Jackson, a colleague of Gregory Bateson. The journal continues to this day. He identified the healthy family as having a homeo-dynamic balance, which includes the concept of homeostasis, along with the principle of growth and change.

Murray Bowen (1913-1919) was an American psychiatrist who was also a pioneer in family therapy. He trained at the Menninger Clinic in Topeka, Kansas. But his interest in families eventually led him to embark on a five-year research project under the sponsorship of the National Institute of Mental Health (NIMH). He studied the families of individuals with schizophrenia in a long term residential ward; both the patient and the family was in residence. He also pioneered the use of closed-circuit television in observing and changing pathological communication patterns among the family members. His concept of multi-generational transmission processes, helped to cement an understanding of how communication patterns, both adaptive and maladaptive, are passed on across the generations in the family.

In the twentieth century up to the last quarter of that century, it was mostly ministers and social workers who focused efforts on families (Philpot, 1997). Like many developments in the area of therapy, this one was also initiated mainly by psychiatrists who had been trained in the psychoanalytic tradition, but found its theory and techniques limiting when applied to situations other than individual outpatient therapy with neurotics. This movement has given us such concepts as first and second order change, enmeshment, multigenerational transmission, and triangulation. It has also resulted in the founding of a separate profession, Marriage and Family Therapy (MFT), whose practitioners are now licensed in most states. The American Association of Marriage Counselors was formed in 1942 which is now the American Association of Marriage and Family Therapy (AAFMT). Bowen served as president of the American Family Therapy Association from 1977-1981. By 1984 the growth of family therapy within psychology was sufficient to attain division status within the organization, as Division 43 (Philpot, 1997).

## Group counseling and therapy

As people develop they move beyond the primary group, the family, into society and become members of other groups. Psychology has been involved in both the scientific study of group behavior and dynamics, recall the work of Kurt Lewin, but also the use of groups for therapeutic purposes. The beginnings of group therapy can be traced to Boston in the early decades of the twentieth century. The Emmanuel movement sponsored a clinic at the Emmanuel Church. The Rev. Elwood Worcestor (1862-1940) was rector at that church and advanced a social gospel perspective by seeking to do a healing ministry. He had studied with Gustav Fechner, and indeed popularized some of his spiritual writings in America. He was eager to combine psychology with religion. In the clinic located in the church, Dr. Joseph Pratt (1872-1956) worked with patients living with tuberculosis. It was an endemic infectious disease with few effective treatments prior to the advent of antibiotics. He asked the rector for space to hold a group for his patients. This group, probably what we would now call a psycho-educational group was a success and additional groups dealing with problems like alcoholism likewise flourished there as well. Indeed, the groups there had a significant influence on the formation of the 12-step recovery programs (McCarthy, 1984). Lay therapists trained at the church began meeting with ordinary people who were not mentally ill, but unhappy. The medical establishment, however, was critical of the involvement of lay therapists even if supervised by physicians; the supervision was not close enough for them. Caplan (2001) notes that this was the cause by which the medical profession took jurisdiction over the talking cure. They wanted to remove or control the practice of therapy from lay people without medical training. Clinical psychologists would have to struggle to enter the realm of psychotherapy over many decades in the twentieth century. The Emmanuel movement was part of a larger movement for medical psychotherapy in the Boston area, in which William James, Josiah Royce, Hugo Munsterberg, and Boris Sidis were also involved. A member of an earlier parish where Worcester was rector was S. Weir Mitchell, the founder of the rest cure for neurasthenia.

Psychoanalysts were also involved in the development of group work, despite their focus on long-term individual therapy. Trirgant Burrow (1875-1950), an American psychoanalyst started group psychoanalysis. Paul Schilder (1886-1940) likewise used psychoanalytic techniques in his group work. In addition to his work with groups, he also gave us the concept of body image, pioneering what would later be called body work. Alfred Adler also began working with groups, couples and families. His student Rudolf Dreikurs (1897-1972) extended Adler's focus on the social bases of individual behavior, as well as founding what is now the Adler School of Professional Psychology.

Samuel Slavson (1890-1981) is another key figure in the development of group therapy. He originally trained as an engineer but then moved into social service work. He started self support groups for Jewish youth. He is credited with starting the first groups with children and adolescent, writing an early textbook on the subject. He was one of the founding members of the American Group Psychotherapy Association (AGPA). Despite being a lay therapist, he continued to contribute research and textbook writing into the post-World War II era, combining psychoanalytic theory with sociological perspectives. During World War II, the sheer number of casualties made group therapy very appealing, and Karl Menninger one of the leading psychiatrists of his era said that group therapy was one of the gifts of military psychiatry to its civilian sibling (Scheidlinger, 1995).

Perhaps one of the most significant developments was the work of Kurt Lewin and his students. They developed the T-group, or training group and went on to influence psychology, management, and student personnel through the workshops on interpersonal communication at the National Training Laboratory (NTL) in Bethel, Maine. This morphed into the encounter group movement which arose within humanistic psychology. Such people as Carl Rogers and Will Schutz (1973) developed this form of group work for normal individuals who seek growth and enhanced functioning. The movement ultimately became somewhat controversial as an off-shoot of the counter-cultural zeitgeist of the nineteen sixties and seventies, but empirical evidence supported its potential usefulness (Lieberman, Yalom & Miles, 1973). Also associated with the human potential movement was psychodrama, which was founded earlier by Jacob Moreno (1889-1974). He also gave us the technique of sociometry for graphically representing relationships among groups of individuals. Fritz Perls borrowed extensively from Moreno's fusion of drama and therapy and his hot-seat-empty-chair technique owes much to that source.

Finally, the circle has come around once again to the psych-educational group where group work began. As noted above, this was the first format for working therapeutically in groups. It now has become the basis for much of the work in cognitive-behavioral approaches, especially those that are aimed at training specific skills such as assertiveness, stress management, and interpersonal communication.

# Community psychology

Community psychology grew out of the activism of the 1960s. Psychologists were not content to deal with just individuals. Couples, families or organizations, entire communities could be the object of focus of study and consultation with the participants, change can be a goal. An early pioneer was Kurt Lewin, especially after he fled Germany to the United States and became involved in practical consultations and study the group dynamics of prejudice and intra-group social conflict. From this most productive period of his life came such approaches as action research, which is data gathering in context of action and intervention. The key aspect of participatory action research (PAR) is the collaboration with the stakeholders in the investigation to formulate the questions asked and the means whereby data is gathered and used to find patterns and understand functions. This is the sort of psycho-social research which empowers people and links understanding to advocacy. He gave us the whole concept of group dynamics, and pioneered attempts to deal with social problems by getting out of the classroom and getting into communities, to go into the field.

A variety of forces were moving psychology to understanding the broader social factors which shape behavior, and to intervene at these additional levels. In particular, the struggle for social justice by minorities became one of the central factors in the development of community psychology. It was in the 1960s that increasingly psychologists moved out of college, universities, clinics and hospitals, and began working in a variety of projects based in a primarily urban environment. As noted above, Lewin's action research was an early model of applied social psychology, of using psychological knowledge, especially scientific investigation, to understand and change social systems.

Another major development was the Community Mental Health Act of 1963. This single piece of legislation changed the face of mental health treatment. It created the current model where the focus of treatment is not in large centralized institutions (PL 88–164), but in the patient's community. It sounds nice, despite the reality that many of those suffering with several and chronic mental illnesses such as schizophrenia or bipolar disorder may not have strong ties with a particular geographic community. After a history of multiple hospitalizations and no steady work history, they become dependent disabled. More later to pick up this thread. Like many Americans in the post-World War II era, a high degree of mobility is available across a wide range of social class. The coordination of care between in-patient and out-patient treatment has always been a problem for the mental health field for a long time. By way of contrast to the current situation there is a film of hospital life from 1927-1936. It shows life in the state mental hospital in that period. It includes a visit from *extra-mural social service* as part of the continuity of care. It also shows the dedication of the cemetery; implicitly documenting the fact that some patients lived out their lives in the facility (Larson, 2005).

The shift toward more emphasis on treatment using communities is as old as the hospices for the mentally ill at the Shrine of St.Dymphna in Gheel, Belgium in the middle ages, and Tuke's York Retreat in England and its progeny in America beginning in the early 1800s. It is interesting that both the tradition in Gheel and the institution of the York Retreat are still operational and providing services. There are examples of enduring foci of the therapeutic community. There was something in the iteration of this idea that was fresh in the 1960s (Almond, 1974). The use of therapeutic communities in the United States has been primarily for residential or half-way house care for drug abusers in recovery, or felons returning to society. The classic example of this is the Synanon community in California, founded by Charles E. (Chuck) Dederick. In the United Kingdom, there has been greater use of it in the care of the mentally ill. R. D. Laing's (1927-1989) radical psychiatry (1960, 1970) there was a basic principle that if you created a safe and accepting place for people to fall apart, they will be able to piece themselves back together is a much better way than the prevailing use of psychotropic medications to prevent psychotic symptoms from coming together. The key to his method was the openness and radical acceptance of disorder. Underlying this is an assumption of self-healing capacity in each individual which can be enhanced and brought forth in a therapeutic community. Maxwell Jones (1907 -1990) was one of the pioneers of this movement. His work was largely in Great Britain. He took his ideas on using the milieu of the community for treatment to Dingleton Hospital in Scotland.

Community psychology encompasses the study of naturally occurring communities, their problems and the dynamics of how the people who live in them are affected by the larger scale social structures as well as intentional communities, i.e., the therapeutic community movement. Both of these streams share a similar model of self-help and healing by involvement in the social struggle to change the structures of society to accommodate human needs. Social justice and personal understanding are part of the concerns which find expression in a modern community psychology.

# 14

## Maturation of Professional Psychology

### Historical background

WE HAVE NOW SEEN the evolution of four major archetypes of professional psychology and four streams of theory and practice of psychotherapy. Over the course of the twentieth century psychology became increasingly involved in therapy, but particularly after World War II. Prior to that time our involvement in work with mental illness, psychiatry and medicine had been research and evaluation. Shepherd Ivory Franz (1916) made it quite clear that the boundary between the role of the psychologist and the psychiatrist was quite firm. He summed our entire professional role in one word, investigation. We were scientists not clinicians. The involvement of psychology in developing testing was our point of entry into the realm of practice. It was our first practical application; measuring and describing patterns in personal attributes. During and after World War II our role expanded into direct treatment as well as research and assessment. That story begins with the Veterans' Administration (VA). But first we nee to provide context by describing the broad historical forces at work in the third quarter of the twentieth century, this macro layer of forces then was fully global.

The twentieth century can be understood by looking at the impact of four major events and movements; first, the two World Wars taken collectively, the Great Depression, the Cold War, and the civil rights movements. The First World War brought the end to the old European dynastic monarchies and saw the emergence of various republican governments as well as the totalitarian regime of Lenin's early Soviet Union. There was also a period of cultural ferment and loosening of old restriction before the onset of the Great Depression, where basic personal and societal survival became an open question. That was a global economic collapse.

By 1945 the Allied powers had defeated the Axis, Germany, Italy and Japan ending the second world war. The Second World War (WWII) drew to a close with the advent of the nuclear age. The atomic bomb had devastated Hiroshima and Nagasaki bringing about the surrender of Japan, the last Axis power surviving by then. But from the ashes of that conflict another one arose almost immediately, the Cold War. The tensions between socialist and capitalist countries dominated the forty years from the close of World War II to the fall of the Berlin wall in 1989 and the subsequent dismantling of the Soviet Union. The communist countries rapidly expanded. Chinese communists under Mao Tse Tung took over mainland China, communist party governments were installed in the European territories under Soviet occupation. These countries became the Warsaw pact against which the North Atlantic Treaty Organization (NATO) was its Western counterpart. The closest crisis to nuclear annihilation was the Cuban missile crisis in 1962; but somehow the doctrine of mutually assured destruction (MAD) kept us from going totally mad.

All throughout those decades of conflict the threat of nuclear annihilation hung over the world's collective head. For the first time in human history we had the power to not only kill, but to probably end life as we know it on earth. What would survive after the nuclear winter predicted as a consequence of such a large detonation of nuclear weapons is anybody's guess, though little of civilization as we know it would survive. This sense of anxiety was different in magnitude from the anxiety felt by earlier existentialists and was different from the neurotic anxiety of Freudian world view.

The U.S. economy boomed in the post World War II era. This was the time period when a returning men and women of the armed forces, thanks to the GI Bill, could get a college education and get a Federally underwritten mortgage for a house. They married and the resulting post-war baby boom shaped American demographics to this day. Tract homes in the suburbs were rapidly built, and the roads that connected them with urban centers. The automobile became the center around which urban America was built. Commercial airlines replaced railroads and steam ships for long distance passenger transportation.

This is the era of the rise of the American middle class. In the nineteen thirties, the Roosevelt administration got the National Labor Relations Act passed by Congress, which put a seal of approval on labor unions. Many men of working class backgrounds got well paying jobs in the expanding industrial heartland of America and were able to enter the middle class by buying a home and sending their children to college. Prosperity and high employment fueled an economic expansion and material wealth and an abundance of consumer goods characterized the new society. Abroad, the ambitious Marshall Plan spread the bases of industrial regrowth and prosperity to Japan and a Europe which had lost much of industrial infrastructure.

But there were some negative consequences in American culture. Rampant anti-communism fueled a witch hunt in academia, government and the film industry for those suspected of disloyalty and sympathizing with communist thought. The McCarthy era, named after Senator Joseph McCarthy, ushered in a period of fear and suspicion. The expectation of conformity to corporate America was also criticized in the caricature of the button down mind that went along with the grey flannel suit of the large American multi-national corporations. This would set the stage for the youth revolution of the nineteen sixties.

No better image of corporate America could be put forth than IBM, Modern developments in computer science, programming, and digital technology has resulted in fundamental changes in modern society; all of which can be termed an information revolution. known as Big Blue in reference to its corporate logo. It was the largest purveyor of the large mainframe computers to help organize the flow of data.

The civil rights movement shaped the domestic situation in America beginning in the post-war years. Overt racial segregation and discrimination through Jim Crow laws were endemic to the South. The great migration of African-Americans out of the rural south to the Midwest or other areas for unionized manufacturing jobs set the stage for the civil rights movement. As the economy expanded after the Depression with war-time production, jobs were created in the industrial heartland of the country, the northeast and Midwest. African-Americans began a decade of migration to find better opportunities and hopefully less hostility.

The initial civil rights movement started with working through the legal system. The landmark decision of *Brown vs. Board of Education of Topeka* (347 U.S. 483) said separate education was not equal education and mandated desegregation of schools. Southern states resisted, protesters were beaten but only continued. Lunch counter discrimination, discrimination on public transportation (Rosa Parks case); these are the flames of discontent made manifest in a sustained movement for social change. Rev. Martin Luther King (1929-1968) and his Southern Christian Leadership Conference (SCLC) became the most visible, articulate and ultimately powerful figure in the civil rights movement. Anger often boiled over into violence in urban areas. This brought about calls for law and order, code words for stronger police reaction.

The country was torn by the assassination of President John F. Kennedy (1917-1963), and his successor, Lyndon Johnson (1908-1973) both deepened American involvement in the war in Vietnam, but also signed the Civil Right Act of 1964 (PL 88-352), a major validation of the civil rights movement. America viewed the situation in southeast Asia as a potential for expansion of communism. The worry that the governments would fall like dominos prompted increasing involvement of the military; first in training and aid, then direct combat involvement. By the mid nineteen sixties, the war in Vietnam was in full swing. The year 1968, however, was pivotal. It began with the Tet offensive in February and the significant and rapid penetration of South Vietnamese and U.S. embassy security shocked the TV audience at home. A hopeful sign was the Prague spring when reform minded forces in Czechoslovakia under Alexander Dubcek eased cultural restrictions. The Sorbonne erupted in student protest against the Vietnam war. The shocks were worse to come; Martin Luther King was assassinated in March, with cities erupting in violence. The progressive hope invested in Robert F. (Bobby) Kennedy was snuffed out by his assassination in June while campaigning for the presidency. The Warsaw pact invaded Czechoslovakia and replaced the more democratic Dubcek government with party functionary loyal to Moscow. At the Democratic National Convention in Chicago riots erupted as large number of student radicals and others protested; being met with clubs by police. The election was tense and Nixon won. The war would continue and the counterintelligence program, COINTELPRO, and other surveillance programs would thrive until the Watergate scandal brought Nixon's downfall.

The other feature to note was the youth counter-culture of the nineteen sixties. The post-war baby boom had come of college age and coming from middle class backgrounds entered universities in great numbers. This leavening effect of exposure to knowledge, skills, and opinions coincided with generally loosening the bonds toward experimentation. As we noted in talking about the origins of transpersonal psychology, one of them was the wide spread experimentation with drugs such as marijuana, LSD, and other psychoactive drugs by youth in colleges. Rock and roll emerged from jazz. Soon a full scale cultural shift was taking place; male long hair came back into fashion, sexual experimentation was prevalent. This coincides with the rise of feminism and the movement toward sexual orientation and gender identity equality; a thread to return to later.

## The Veterans Administration and the expansion of professional psychology

Professional psychology would not be where it is today in numbers or the diversity of its scope of services without the Second World War, and the key role of the Veterans Administration in its aftermath (Moore, 1992). The press of need resulted in a number of military psychologists starting to practice psychotherapy in field hospitals or rear echelon facilities. The resistance of men and women trained in psychology to just do testing and leave therapy to physicians had eroded during the 1930s. Now, the war need threw out all practical objection to entering the arena of healing.

As the Second World War wound down, President Truman saw the need to expand the veterans facilities to accommodate the needs of thousands of wounded and disabled veterans. The anticipated numbers were enormous, both in terms of the physically disabled and the emotionally damaged. There was a high psychiatric casualty rate because of the intensity of the combat. A key appointment was General Omar Bradley to head up the new Veterans Administration (VA). That organization was a consolidation of the National Home for Disabled Volunteer Soldiers and Sailors, founded after the U.S. Civil War, the veterans' pension and benefit program, including vocational counseling, and the operation of the national cemeteries for military veterans. Bradley was known as the soldier's general for his concern for the welfare of his troops, and this would translate into confidence among the returning veterans that they would be well cared for.

One of his deputies was James G. Miller, who we encountered as a major figure in general systems theory. He was the first Chief Psychologist in the VA. Miller had both a Ph.D. in psychology and an M.D., both from Harvard. He was able to facilitate the meeting of interest between the VA and the APA to put together a proposal for training more clinical and counseling psychologists. The need was great enough that many had jobs upon completion. This connection resulted in the first major training model for clinical psychology which emerged from a conference held in Boulder, Colorado, in 1949 (Raimy, 1950). This became the scientist-practitioner model, emphasizing the Ph.D. and a solid base of training in research as a major activity.

The number of jobs and training slots were huge. Most psychologists who took their training from the late 1940s onward received some, if not most, of their clinical training in VA Hospitals and Medical Centers. This benefitted counseling psychology as well. The growth of college counseling centers had begun earlier, prior to the war, but now the need, especially for career and vocational counseling was significant with the number of returning veterans with educational benefits enrolling in college (often the first of their family to do so). Part of the expansion in many college and university counseling centers was funded by VA contracts (McCarthy, 2014). Counseling psychologists were also located in offices of the Veterans Benefit program, providing vocational rehabilitation and guidance for disabled veterans as well. Many also were located in hospitals as well, so increasingly professional psychology in both clinical and counseling emphases were moving significantly into applied practice. Even in 1977, when I was hired as a psychologist after doing my internship with the VA, it was the largest employer of psychologists.

The most important aspect of the growth of college counseling centers in the post-war period is that they were largely under the control of other psychologists or college administrators rather than physicians. Clinical psychology always had to be supervised ultimately by physicians when it came to patient care activities in any setting controlled by physicians such as hospitals, clinics, etc. No matter how collegial the personal relationships were, there was the inevitability of the pecking order with physicians on top. College counseling centers did not have that close relationships with physicians. In many instances the college health center was separate from the counseling center. Keep in mind that Carl Rogers, who we discussed earlier with respect to humanistic psychology, first worked in a Child Guidance center in Rochester, New York, before moving to Chicago to found the counseling center at the University of Chicago. And, of course, his 1942 book, as noted above, was the first psychotherapeutic theory written by someone not trained in medicine. The growing adoption of Carl Rogers' theories and techniques also made them a bastion of humanistic psychology but also the basis of generic helping professionals' training in relationship and communicational competency.

The sheer number of professional psychologists who were turned out into the market in the 1950s and 1960s allowed the profession to build toward licensed

independent practice as a health care provider and inclusion in a variety of reimbursement structures for payment of professional services. The emergence of the third-party
payer is another story. State mental hospitals likewise employed psychologist and state
vocational rehabilitation programs needed counselors. Social work expanded its role
in mental health direct therapy, as well as masters level counselors which have now
coalesced in their professional organization, the American Counseling Association
(ACA).

## Neuropsychology, rehabilitation and clinical health psychology

The previous four chapters have covered the development of specific broad theories
of therapy. This chapter began with the growth of clinical and counseling psychology.
But one of the developments that characterizes the current era is the growth of interventions in the area of biological psychology. This domain includes interests that are
tied to specific divisions with APA. Neuropsychology (Division #40), rehabilitation
psychology (Division #22), and health psychology (Division #38). Each sponsors a
professional journal, conferences and presentations at the annual convention. Beyond
the realm of therapy for medical disorders, many psychologists are involved in sport,
exercise and performance psychology (Division #47). The recent trend toward positive psychology reprises the earlier human potential movement in the humanistic-
existential tradition. Another aspect of psychology for the well and functional is the
emphasis on work place wellness, with programs in stress management and habit
control for corporate or social service agencies. Developments in genetics as well as
growing awareness of our internal biome and its relationship to behavior are opening
up even more opportunities for engagement by psychologists in the realm of biological psychology. We turn now to looking at these developments.

Many of the earliest pioneers in psychology as an independent discipline started
out in physiology; for example, Gustav Fechner and Wilhelm Wundt. William James
was trained in medicine, though he never practiced it. So the biological roots of psychology are substantial. That being said, psychology saw itself as an experimental discipline so our presence in hospitals was not as prominent as our expanding number of
laboratories in academic departments.

Shepherd Ivory Franz (1874-1930) was one of the first psychologists to work
in a hospital setting. His role was largely that of researcher, and as a testament to his
value he received an honorary doctor of medicine degree from George Washington
University, where he taught physiology for a number of years. As early as 1911 there
was a conference jointly sponsored by the American Psychological Association and
the Southern Society for Philosophy and Psychology titled "the relations of psychology and medical education." Franz and J. B. Watson were psychologists who presented
papers there along with such key figures from psychiatry as Adolf Meyer and Morton
Prince (Thompson, 1991)

Adolf Meyer (1866-1950) deserves particular attention. Trained in psychiatry he advocated an integrated approach. He supported the importance of obtaining a detail history from the patient and considering biological, psychological and social factors in formulating the case. He serves as an early pioneer for what is now termed the bio-psycho-social approach (Engel, 1977). He focused interest on dysfunctional behavior rather than brain pathology.

One of Franz's students was Karl Lashley (1890-1958). Indeed the two authored two articles on the effects of ablation of the cerebral cortex in rats on habit formation and retention (Franz & Lashley, 1917; Lashley & Franz, 1917). Lashley went on to do significant additional work in the area of brain-behavior relationships. Though he sought to find the *engram* or locus of a memory in the brain, his work gave support for distributed storage.

Ward Halstead (1908-1968) was part of the generation of psychologists that created the standardized instruments used to diagnose brain damage and describe its effects of cognitive functions. His major interest was biological intelligence, or the neurological structures of cognition. He developed a variety of neuropsychological assessment tools which were later standardized and put into a comprehensive battery by Ralph Reitan (1922-2014). The Halstead-Reitan battery has been one of the major tools in clinical psychology for several decades, though the field has moved away from comprehensive batteries to a more prescriptive approach. The Russian neuropsychologist Alexander Luria (1902-1977) was known for his use of techniques from behavioral neurology. These became standardized through the Luria-Nebraska Neuropsychological Battery (Golden, Hammeke, & Purisch, 1980). The field has now moved on beyond large comprehensive batteries to a host of smaller for focused instruments for prescriptive use for evaluating specific functions.

Larson & Sachs (2000) told the story of the development of rehabilitation psychology. The role played by psychologists working with the VA was significant here. Also, early studies on the impact of disability. Involvement by psychologists with people living with disability comes from three sources; private charities, state or county government affiliated social service agencies, and Federal VA sponsored programs for disabled veterans. Two students of Kurt Lewin, Tamara Dembo (1902-1993) and Beatrice Wright (b. 1917) were early leaders in the field. Their monograph on adjustment to misfortune (Dembo, Leviton & Wright, 1956) and Wright's (1983) work on the psycho-social aspects of disability helped take the field out of strictly vocational considerations to the broader goal of restoration of functional capacity.

Stone, Cohen & Adler (1979) edited an early book laying out the shape of psychological service to people with a variety of medical conditions. Clinical health psychology is a fast-growing area of psychology as the research and public awareness of the impact of psychological factors, especially stress, on the body can generate, aggravate, and sustain troublesome conditions. Being ill is no picnic and the psycho-social consequences of chronic illness on the individual and family are now areas of concern as well.

One area of research and practice where psychologists have been heavily involved is biofeedback, and the emerging specialization of neurofeedback, or EEG biofeedback (Schwartz & Andrasik,2003) The technology for measuring and recording physiological signals of very low amplitude allowed the detection of muscle activity in the range of microvolts, millionth of a volt (Crisswell, 2011). Physiological data can be fed back to the person so they can learn to control their bodily processes to various degrees. Computer technology has advanced so that the data can be presented in even more sophisticated ways, including incorporation of video game technology. Clinical protocols have been established for evidence-based practice across a wide range of conditions (Moss &Shaffer, 2016). Increasingly, mind-body integration uses both sophisticated digital technology, ancient contemplative practices from Eastern cultures, and other forms of relaxation training originating in the West (Moss, McGrady, Davies, & Wichramasekera, 2003). The Association for Applied Psychophysiology and Biofeedback is a base for professional communication of research and practice in this area.

Primary care psychology has now emerged as a significant area of practice (Frank, McDaniel, Bray, & Herdling, 2003). As psychologists have moved further into the mainstream we are now defining ourselves not just as a mental health profession, but as a health care profession. Part of this is assuming responsibility along with psysicians, nurses, and others for the total care of the patient. This is now mandated by the Affordable Care Act, discussed below.

## Civil rights movement and the roots of multi-culturalism

As noted above, the situation of African-Americans was fraught with overt discrimination by statute as well as custom. The struggle for equality began to change in earnest after World War II. The manpower needs were such as to force the country to induct large numbers of minorities into the armed forces. Desegregation of the military did not occur until 1948 under the Truman administration.

The Association of Black Psychologists (ABPsi) was founded in 1968 to begin to organize psychologists of color. Guthrie (1998) chronicles the relative invisibility of African-American psychologists in the history of our field. Mexican-Americans, or Chicanos also awoke to begin organizing for their interests. Cesar Chavez (1927-1993) worked to organize migrant farm workers in California and sparked additional movements among Latinos. Second wave feminism critiqued the patriarchal system of male dominance in all matters. The Christopher Street reaction to police oppression of gay and transgender youth likewise added sexual orientation and gender issues to the mix of social change. From the nineteen sixties onward various factors of human diversity became objects of attention from psychologists. The number of divisions within APA representing these minority interests expanded; including Division 35, Society for the Psychology of Women, Division 44, Society for the Psychological Study of Lesbian, Gay, Bisexual, and Transgender Issues, Divison 45, Society for the Psychological Study of Culture, Ethnicity, and Race. This has ultimately prompted the association to make multicultural competency a major focus. To serve an increasingly diverse population, psychologists must be sensitive to and knowledgeable about the power relationships between majority and minorities groups within the whole.

## Professional and economic developments

One of the marks of a profession is regulation of its practice. Licensing of occupations is based on the premise that some occupations could endanger the health and safety of the public if practiced by people with little or no training. Indeed in the preamble to various licensing laws passed across many jurisdictions, there is a finding that the practice of the profession has such an impact and therefore the law is needed. Prior to government intervention, many professions have sought to self regulate by promulgating codes of ethics and instituting proceedings against practitioners who violate the code. As a profession becomes more numerous, then there are increasing calls for outside regulation, usually by governmental bodies. In the United States, the individual states are responsible for occupational licensing and regulation. As the Federal government has played an increasing role in health care, then its influence over the nature and direction of occupational regulation has increased. Sinclair, Simon & Pettifor (1995) recounted the history of the development of both a code of ethics and various approaches to credentialing and regulation of psychology.

There were little or no regulations concerning the practice of medicine and competing schools of medicine with varying commitments to science. The Carnegie Foundation sponsored a study by Abraham Flexner on the state of medical education. The report which came to be known as the Flexner Report of 1910 suggested adopting the emerging biomedical sciences as foundations, reducing the numbers of medical schools, centering training there and partnering with states to license the practice. It had the desired effect and the number of schools with little or no science closed. Of the many schools of medicine two major theoretical approaches were present, allopathic and osteopathic. There were several decades before Allopathic medical schools granting the Doctor of Medicine (M.D.) degree and the Osteopathic physicians (from schools granting a Doctor of Osteopathic Medicine, D.O.) were both recognized by state licensing agencies as containing equivalent curricula in science. The osteopaths have additional course work and supervised practice in manual medicine. Chiropractic, which also existed before the Flexner Report continues, but with limited medical license. They cannot prescribe nor perform surgery. They have a particular theory of spinal subluxation as an etiological factor in disease and their particular use of manual medicine for spinal adjustments. But these developments in medicine didn't effect psychology, which at this time kept its role in applied practice largely to psychometric assessment and research. Following World War II the professions of counseling and clinical psychology greatly expanded the number of psychologists in private practice, at least part-time.

In keeping with the fact that the growth of professional psychology came largely following World War II, the American Psychological Association set up a committee to draft ethical standards in 1947, finally completing the task and approving the first formal code in 1953. There have been major revisions in 1959, 1963, 1977, 1981, 1989 and 1992. As with all forms of private regulation the internal disciplinary proceedings can only result in termination of membership in the association, as the state controls the ability to practice by granting, suspending, or revoking a license.

The history of credentialing and licensing is complex in itself. There have been several stages or levels. At the lowest level is registration. Here the role of the state is to maintain a list of people who have completed a given course of preparation in an occupation. Above that level is certification, where the state not only maintains the list, but certifies that the people have actually received the requisite training. At the highest level of regulation is licensure where the practice of the profession and the use of a specific tile are restricted only to those that the state finds qualified to practice. In addition to the educational requirements, there is often an examination, review of transcripts of training, and sometimes an interview or oral examination as well. Each state has specific mental health laws regarding involuntary hospitalization as well as laws governing the confidentiality of health related information and the procedures that must be followed for the release of medical information from the provider to others. Most states also now have mandatory reporting laws for child abuse and neglect or elder abuse and neglect.

By the time America celebrated its bicentennial as a nation in 1976, professional psychology had achieved some form of legal recognition, such as certification, registration or licensing, in many states, and had become seen as a mental health profession along side psychiatry, social work and psychiatric nursing. The next quarter century saw the solidification of these gains for the profession, but also the emergence of a new threat to the independence of the profession in managed care.

Private specialty and advanced practice credentialing began immediately after WWII with the founding of the American Board of Professional Psychology (ABPP) in 1947. They initially credentialed candidates with 5 years practice in counseling, clinical, school and industrial/organizational. Later, numerous additional specialty boards have been added in such fields as neuropsychology, forensic psychology, group, family, clinical health, rehabilitation among others. The organization has now spun off separate credentialing boards in the above areas dealing with the specific of their field.

## The Psy.D. and the professional practitioner model

While the scientist-practitioner model was the first model of clinical training, it had limitations. Most of the actual jobs created for clinical and counseling psychologists required virtually full-time provision of service with little time left over for research. Indeed two studies (Kelly & Goldberg, 1959; Levy, 1962) showed that the modal number of publications since graduation of clinical psychologists was zero. There was a significant discrepancy between the goals of the training model and the outcome. In many instances little more than rudimentary coverage of practice skills was covered in course work; most programs assumed those skills would largely be acquired on practicum or internship training from supervisors on site. This led to calls for a fully professional training model. Medicine had that with the M.D. it was primarily focused on training clinicians, not researchers. If one wanted to do more research, one could get a Ph.D. in microbiology, or some other discipline relevant to one's interests.

Finally by 1976 the calls for an alternative model had begun to bear fruit and a variety of programs began to offer the Doctor of Psychology degree (Psy.D.) which was more clinical in its emphasis. That year the second major conference on training professional psychologists was held, this time in Vail, Colorado, and it endorsed the Psy.D. as an alternative to the Ph.D. (Korman, 1976). Clinical training had now arrived. The National Council of Schools and Programs in Professional Psychology (NCSPP) emerged as the group representing the interests of these training programs. Heretofore, all training had been done at major state or private research universities, now free-standing graduate schools became part of the mix. There were some who were structured as for-profit institutions. The Illinois School of Professional Psychology was founded in 1976. It is now known as Argosy University and remains a for-profit institution,. Other free-standing graduate schools were not-for-profit, such as the Chicago School of Professional Psychology, founded in 1979. In addition there were several program located in traditional universities.

One in particular deserves mentions. The University of Illinois at Champaign-Urbana offered the first Psy.D. in clinical psychology (1968-1980). As one of its key figures noted (Peterson, 1997), the reason it did not survive as a program is that it wasn't truly independent of the rest of the academic department of psychology. It did not control its curriculum and other vital functions. In the end, neither the students in that program nor the faculty were satisfied and the program was discontinued in 1980. A counter example is Wright State University's School of Professional Psychology. The founding Dean, Dr. Ron Fox, learned from the experience of University of Illinois and worked with the state legislature to create a separate college, like the schools of medicine and nursing. It was not housed in an academic department of psychology, affiliated with a College of Arts and Sciences, but a separate college with its own Dean. It had control of admissions, curriculum, faculty hiring and advancement. Within a few years of its start it even opened the Frederick A. White Ambulatory Care Center in Dayton, Ohio, as a training site for its students. This degree of independence allowed it to sustain its vision of clinical training. I was fortunate to have been in the first group of adjunct faculty hired and taught history and systems to its charter class on up to the fall of 1986; which is how this text evolved.

## Managed care and economics

The rise in the cost of health care created concerns for balancing the needs of this sector of the economy with the other sectors. In the nineteen eighties and nineties, the rate of health care inflation exceeded the general rate of inflation. If left unchecked, the inflation of health care costs would consume the budget available for other important priorities. There are several reasons for this rapid rise, many of which are good in the long run, though costly, others however are due to careless accounting or just plain demographics.

The first good reason for inflation with the rapid developments in basic medical science with the computer. Nearly all laboratory techniques were automated and expansion of physical and chemical analysis refined results. Radiographic studies were enhanced by computers with Computer-Assisted Axial Tomography (CAT) scans, and now supplemented by Magnetic Resonance Imaging (MRI) technology. Functional MRI (fMRI) studies now are at the cutting edge of neuroscience. All this costs money, especially for early developers and adopters. It starts with Federal grants to academic teaching hospitals and bio-medical engineering programs jointly working with basic science.

The practice of medicine expanded beyond the scope of what one person could competently know, so residency training in a post-graduate medical specialty became the norm. Those post-graduate programs cost money but staffed higher level academic medical schools and hospitals and their outpatient clinics. In the end, they even designated a specialty in Family Practice medicine to begin to make the old General Practitioner or GP return from the simpler days of earlier decades. The need for primary care practice has become central as well for additional reasons. Allied practitioners, first nurse specialists with usually a masters degree in nursing and physicians' assistants (PA) came bachelors programs in medicine. Many returning military medics and corpsmen from the Vietnam war found a place in that entry point. These physician extenders as they were termed then, were given latitude to perform a number of medical tasks with some independence of practice.

The addition of Medicare and Medicaid in the 1965 amendments to the Social Security Act (PL 89-97). Title XVIII became Medicare, a completely Federal program, and Title XIX became Medicaid, as a state-Federal partnership. For Medicare, health insurance became a component of the Social Security system allowing retirees under Social Security Retirement Insurance (SSRI) and those on Social Security Disability Insurance (SSDI) benefits to receive coverage for medical care. This expanded health care to the elderly. Along with general improvements in quantity of food available and more regular medical care, more people were living into old age. Thus the population of the elderly rose as in part a testament to improvements in general health. But as one ages, more systems begin to wear out and chronic conditions occur that need regular medication to manage, so the demographics of a growing aging population at the same time meant an unavoidable increase in health care costs. Indeed most health care expense come at the end of life, despite changing cultural values on end of life, or hospice, care. Medicaid was given over to the states to administer, hence there are 50 plus different programs with varying coverage. The target population are termed the medically indigent, that is they are unable to pay for health care. There is a means test for entry into the program so some elderly poor can't qualify. Most of the expense of nursing homes is funded by Medicaid in the United States. The statutes generally require the estate of the dependent elder in the nursing home to be liquidated to pay for care before state benefits are eligible. Some exceptions for a non-disabled spouse living in the home are possible, but this essentially bankrupts lower and middle income families of any inheritance from their family.

All these forces came together to bring in managed care. That was the phrase that covers a variety of means to control the runaway health care inflation at the end of the twentieth century. The health insurance system did not really expand until after WWII as a growing economy allowed large corporations to lead the way and offer health care insurance as a benefit of employment. America favored the free market of insurance, so any attempts to provide government solutions were resisted. The American Medical Association protested Medicare as socialized medicine. They soon, however, saw the benefits to their practice and went along. The cumbersome systems of indemnifying an insured upon his or her submitting the claim was replaced by the routine assignment of benefits, which allowed the practitioner to directly bill the insurance company for services.

The first line of defense was utilization review. This meant an immediate shift of clinical nurses to insurance company employees hired to review claims. At first this done retrospectively, but that became unmanageable, so prospective utilization review is now in place. Staff at provider offices verify coverage and benefits before services are provided. The forces for Medicare reforms resulted in a large study undertaken by Yale School of Public Health which proposed changes to Medicare to better manage care. The study put new structures on Part A, for hospital care, and Part B, for outpatient services. On the in-patient side diagnostic related groups (DRG) had a consensus for the number of days needed to treat the 467 groups. If hospitals discharged the patient sooner, they got the full amount, and likewise if the stay went over the limit (exceptions for complicated cases could request a waiver). For out-patient, units of service could be adjusted for relative-value units (RVU) reflecting such things as local office costs.

As the Federal government went, the private market followed and various other options for managed care emerged. The Health Maintenance Organization (HMO) radically restructured care by providing all the care needed for a pool of subscribers, in exchange for a fixed amount per capita (hence the term capitation fee) per year from the employer and employee combined. It had limits, however, one had to go to a participating physician or hospital regardless of closer options. Participation in HMOs was low given consumer reluctance to give up choice of care giver. The

Preferred Provider Organization (PPO) became the dominant force in the insurance market. The structure returns to the fee for service model where the base is the Usual, Customary, and Reasonable (UCR) fee for the service. The cost is contained by offering the provider access to a large population of subscribers in exchange for a reduced fee in lieu of the UCR. Plans are administered so customers can go to a provider in the PPO network and get maximal amount of payment of the UCR as discounted, or out of network and get a reduced percentage of the UCR as reimbursement.

All practitioners in the delivery of health care services are now, as of December 2016, awaiting the fate of the Affordable Care Act (ACA; PL 111-148). This promised to change the health care landscape by a number of reforms. The primary aim was to provide a means for more Americans to get health care insurance, even mandating coverage with a penalty, which did not sit well with many consumers. It did provide a shield against discrimination due to a previous condition and kept young people on their parents' insurance to age 25, which were population. The act also mandated more integrative primary care through the concept of patient-centered medical care home; an institutional locus of care. Electronic health care records (EHR) are now mandated to make both ease of sharing for continuity of care, as well as privacy concerns brought forward. The network of health care insurance pools was most vulnerable to state by state decisions. Republicans repeatedly repealed the act only to be unable to sustain an Obama veto. But as the political wind has shifted with the election of 2016, the repeal is promised to get through and uncertainty will dominate the health care funding situation for some time to come.

## Conclusion

We have brought the story of psychological healing up to the current situation. Professional psychologists are now filling a wide range of services. Among the most important for our future will be the higher level competencies such as supervision, research and evaluation, consultation, and management and administration. As noted earlier, the front line staff for most mental health and social services are at the masters level. The added value of a doctoral degree will be in those areas where we work very closely with other health care professions.

One of the key ideas laid out here is that all health care professions share a similar background. It is not just the health service psychologist (HSP) who stands on the shoulders of the shaman, the physician, the teacher and the scientist. We all do. The archetypal roles and their accompanying values and assumptions are common to many diverse occupations. These are the streams of transmission that led us from the past to the present and project forward into the future.

Especially the key skill in human communication is shared not only among health care providers, but among a wide range of service occupations. The very heart of what we know to be human is the capacity to use words to make meaning and share meanings, and yes, of course, to change meanings. The existential ground of humanity is our capacity to create significance as we adapt to and shape our environment across time and culture. The most important of the practical skills is rhetoric, the discipline of persuasive speech. It is the oldest subject that was taught by professional teachers. It is a foundational skill for a wide range of functions, including the therapeutic one.

The global nature of our world will not change, barring some form of catastrophe. We are composed of individuals who have a unique personal history, but who are also members of groups of other humans and share with them many things in common. Above all, there is our common humanity shared by all. Beyond that there is the shared life on this planet we share with all other living beings. One of the most profound statements of this shared legacy comes from the work of Kluckhohn and Murray (1948; a collaboration between an anthropologist and a psychiatrist: "Every man is in certain respects a. like all other men, b. like some other men, c. like no other man" (p. 2). An ecological awareness will be vitally important in coming years to ensure that this common legacy of millennia of development is secured and protected against harm.

While there are many reasons why we want to be able to use our self awareness to identify our own values, presuppositions, and beliefs, one of the most important ones for our purposes is to be able to bracket them off and enter into the world of the other. The prime tool for accomplishing the goal of aiding the other is the establishment of a personal trusting relationship through skilled communication between client and counselor. This idea originated in implicit and explicit forms before Carl Rogers focused us on the empathetic nature of human communication, but it is his formulation of the critical importance of the personal connection between therapist and client built that subsequent theories build. Pike and others gave us the emic/etic distinction which applies to our awareness and sensitivity toward differences based on group membership. The competency of individual and cultural differences requires us to do the same not only with regard to the individual client but to their particular cultural matrix.

More than many other professions, we have this fiduciary duty to act ethically on behalf of the interests of the other. Knowing how we all came to be who we are, where we are, and when we are is of vital significance for the task of improving the lives of those we serve. This is why the knowledge of history, geography, and cultures is just as important as the knowledge of individual beliefs, feelings, and motives. They are all interwoven the our common archetypal matrix.

One clear lesson of the history of psychological healing is that our theories will continue to evolve. We have seen that hypnosis, a well established technique by now, went through several phases where other explanations were given, tried and found wanting. We saw that neurasthenia so easily morphs into stress related conditions and the treatments evolved for that are just as current today, even though we have greatly refined our understanding of nervous energy. We should be humble with regard to our current theories. In the future they may seem as misdirected and even quaint as the theory of four humors does today. Time and again, we have come upon good techniques or identified patterns, but have explained them in terms of the intellectual tools then available. As science progresses, those explanatory tools evolve as well.

The essence of good news is that healing by psychological means is a craft based on a science requiring certain skills and critical attitudes that can be taught. Some may have particular gifts in some areas with some people, but education and training can make a person more likely to be successful in the quest to help another in distress. The aim of this book has been to provide a thorough grounding in the historical and philosophical foundations of practice of the craft of psychological healing, a witcraft for healing. Our awareness of our roots gives us an appreciation of those whose lives and work provided us with today's tools. Our job is to take those tools, improve on them, and pass them on to the next generation of professional psychologists. We are but one link in a long stream of transmission and we must pass it forward.

# References

Ackerknecht, E. H. (1943). Psychopathology, primitive medicine, and primitive culture. *Bulletin of the History of Medicine, 14,* 30-69.

Alexander, F. M. (1974) *The resurrection of the body.* New York: Delta. (Original work 1910-1942).

Alexander, F. G. & Selesnick S. T. (1966). *The history of psychiatry: An evaluation of psychiatric thought and practice from prehistoric times to the present.* New York: Harper & Row.

Algeo, M (2014). *Pedestrianism: When watching people walk was America's favorite spectator sport.* Chicago: Chicago Review.

Allport, G. W. (1942). *The use of personal documents in psychological science.* New York: Social Science Research Council.

Allport, G. W. (1958). *The nature of prejudice.* Garden City, NY: Anchor. (Original work 1954).

Almond, R. (1974). *The healing community: Dynamics of the therapeutic milieu.* New York: Aronson.

Altman, I. & Rogoff, B. (1987). World views in Psychology: Trait, interactional, organismic and transactional perspectives. In D. Stokols and I. Altman (Eds.) *Handbook of environmental psychology.* New York: John Wiley & Sons.

American Psychological Association (2003). Ethical principles of psychologist and code of conduct. *American Psychologist, 35*(12), pp. 1060-1073.

American Psychological Association Committee on Training in Clinical Psychology. (1947). Recommended graduate training program in clinical psychology. *American Psychologist, 2* 539-558.

Andreassi, J. L. (2007). *Psychophysiology: Human behavior & physiological response* (5th ed.) New York: Psychology Press.

Attneave, F. (1959). *Applications of information theory to psychology.* New York: Holt, Rinehart and Winston.

Austin, J. L. (1965). *How to do things with words.* New York: Oxford University.

Ayllon, T. & Azrin, N. H. (1964). Reinforcement and instructions with mental patients. *Journal of the Experimental Analysis of Behavior, 7*(4), 327-331.

Ayllon, T. & Azrin, N. H. (1965). The measurement and reinforcement of behavior of psychotics. *Journal of the Experimental Analysis of Behavior, 8*(6), 357-383.

Ayllon, T. & Azrin, N. H. (1968). *The token economy: A motivational system for therapy and rehabilitation.* New York: Appleton-Century-Crofts.

Bachofen, J. J. (1967). *Myth, religion and mother right* Princeton, NJ: Princeton University. (Original work published 1861).

Bandler, R. (1985). *Using your brain – for a change: Neuro-linguistic programming.* Moab, UT: Real People.

Bandler, R. & Bateson, G. (1975a). *The structure of magic. vol 1.* Palo Alto, CA: Science and Behavior.

Bandler, R. & Bateson, G. (1975b). *The structure of magic. vol. 2.* Palo Alto, CA: Science and Behavior.

Bandler, R. & Grinder, J. (1979). *Frogs into princes: Neuro linguistic programming.* Moab, UT: Real People.

Bandura, A. L. (1977) *Social learning theory.* Englewood Cliffs, NJ: Prentice-Hall.

Bandura, A. L. (1997). *Self efficacy: The exercise of control.* San Francisco: W. H. Freeman.

Barker, R. G. (1968). *Ecological psychology: Concepts and methods for studying the environment of human behavior.* Stanford, CA: Stanford University.

Barker, R. G., & Associates. (1978). *Habitats, environments and human behavior: Studies in ecological psychology and eco-behavioral science from the Midwest Psychological Field Station, 1947-1972.* San Francisco, CA: Jossey-Bass.

Bartlett, J. (1968). *Bartlett's familiar quotations* (14th ed.), Boston: Little Brown & Co.

Bateson, G. (1982). *Steps to an ecology of mind.* New York: Ballantine.

Beck, H. P., Levinson, S. & Irons, G. (2009). Finding Little Albert: A journey to John B. Watson's infant laboratory. *American Psychologist, 64*(7), 605-614.

Bell, L. V. (1980). *Treating the mentally ill: From colonial times to the present.* New York: Praeger.

Benjamin, L T. DeLeon, P. H., Friedheim, D. K. & Vandenbos, G. R. (2012). Psychology as a profession. In D. K. Friedheim (Ed). *Handbook of psychology, Volume 1, History of psychology.* New York: John Wiley & Sons. pp. 27-45.

Bennis, W. G., Schein, E. H., Steele, F. I., Berlow, D. E. (1968). *Interpersonal dynamics: Essays and readings on human interaction* (rev. Ed.). Homewood, IL: Dorsey.

Benson, H. (1976). *The relaxation response.* New York: Harper & Row.

Bentley, J. H. (1993). *Old world encounters: Cross-cultural contacts and exchanges in pre-modern times.* New York: Oxford University.

Bernheim, H. (1965). Hypnosis and suggestion in psychotherapy. New Hyde Park, NY: University Books (Originally published, 1884).

Berry, J. W. (2003). Conceptual approaches to acculturation. In K. M., Chun, P.B., Organista, & Marin, G (Ed.), *Acculturation: Advances in theory, measurement, and applied research.* APA: Washington DC. (pp. 17-37).

Berry, J. W. (1997). Lead article: Immigration, acculturation, and adaptation. *Applied Psychology: An International Review, 46,* 5-34.

Berry, J. W., Uichol K., & Boski, P. (1988). Psychological acculturation of immigrants. In Y. Y. Kim & W. B. Gudykunst (Eds.). *Cross Cultural Adaptation: Current Approaches* Newbury Park, California: Sage (pp. 62-89).

Billig, M. (1996). *Arguing and thinking: A rhetorical approach to social psychology* (2nd ed.). Cambridge: Cambridge University.

Boring, E. G. (1950). *A history of experimental psychology.* New York: Appleton-Century-Crofts. (Original published, 1929).

Boyer, C. B. & Merzback, U. C. (1991). *A history of mathematics* (2nd ed.). New York: John Wiley & Sons.

Bradford, L. P., Gibb, J. R. & Benne, K D. (1964). *T-group theory and laboratory method: Innovation in re-education.* New York: John Wiley & Sons, Inc.

Brier, S. (1998). The cybersemiotic explanation of the emergence of cognition: The explanation of cognition signification and communication in a non-Cartesian cognitive biology. *Evolution and Cognition, 4*(1), 90-105.

Bromberg, W. (1937). *The mind of man: The story of man's conquest of mental illness.* New York: Harper & Brothers.

Brown, D. (2003). *The DaVinci code.* New York: Doubleday.

Bruner, J. (1990). Acts of meaning. Cambridge, MA: Harvard University Press.

Buber, M. (1958). *I and thou.* New York: Charles Scribe's Sons.

Buckley, W. (Ed.) (1968). *Modern systems research for the behavioral scientist: A source book.* Chicago, IL: Aline.

Campbell, J. (1949). *The hero with a thousand faced.* Princeton, NJ: Princeton University Press.

Campbell, J. (1955). *The masks of god: Primitive religions.* New York: Viking.

Campbell, J. (1962). *The masks of god: Oriental mythology.* New York: Viking.

Campbell, J. (1964). *The masks of god: Occidental mythology.* New York: Viking.

Campbell, J. (1968). *The masks of god: Creative mythology.* New York: Viking.

Caplan, E. (2001). *Mind games: American culture and the birth of psychotherapy.* Berkeley, CA: University of California.

Carkhuff, R. R. (2000) The art of helping in the 21st century (8th ed.). New York: HAD.

Castaneda, C. (1968). *The teachings of Don Juan: A Yaqui way of knowledge.* New York: Ballantine.

Clements, F. E. (1932). Primitive concepts of disease. *University of California Publications in American Archaeology and Ethnology, 32*(2).

Crisswell, E. (Ed.)(2011). *Cram's introduction to surface electromyography* (2nd ed.). Boston, MA: Jones & Bartlett.

Crook, J. H. (1997). The indigenous psychiatry of Ladakh, Part I: practice theory approaches to trance possession in the Himalayas. Anthropology & Medicine, 4(3), 289©307.

Cushman, P. (1995). *Constructing the self, constructing America: A cultural history of psychotherapy.* Boston, MA: DaCapo.

DeLeuze, J. P. F. (1879). *Practical instruction in animal magnetism.* (Rev. Ed., Trans. Thomas C. Hartshorn, 1843.). New York: Fowler and Wells (Original work 1819)

Dembo, T., Leviton, G. L. & Wright, B. A. (1956/1975). Adjustment to misfortune: A problem of social-psychological rehabilitation, *Artificial limbs, 31,* 15-70 reprinted in *Rehabilitation Psychology,* (1975), 22, 1-100. (Original work 1956).

Dewey, J. (1896). The reflect arc concept in psychology. *Psychological Review, 3,* 357-370.

Dewsbury, D. A. (Ed.) (1996) *Unification through Division: Histories of the Divisions of the American Psychological Association,* vol 1. Washington, DC: American Psychological Assoc.

Dewsbury, D. A. (Ed.) (1997) *Unification through Division: Histories of the Divisions of the American Psychological Association,* vol 2. Washington, DC: American Psychological Assoc.

Dewsbury, D. A. (Ed.) (1998) *Unification through Division: Histories of the Divisions of the American Psychological Association,* vol 3. Washington, DC: American Psychological Assoc.

Dewsbury, D. A. (Ed.) (1999) *Unification through Division: Histories of the Divisions of the American Psychological Association,* vol 4. Washington, DC: American Psychological Assoc.

Dewsbury, D. A. (Ed.) (2000) *Unification through Division: Histories of the Divisions of the American Psychological Association*, vol 5. Washington, DC: American Psychological Assoc.

Dilts, R., Grinder, J., Bandler, R., Bandler, L. C., & DeLozier, J. (1980). *Neuro-Linguistic Programming: Volume I: The study of the structure of subjective Experience*.

Dollard, J. & Miller, N. E. (1950). *Personality and psychotherapy: An analysis in terms of learning, thinking, and culture*. New York, NY: McGraw-Hill.

Eliade, M. (1961). *The sacred and the profane: The nature of religion* (Trans. Willard R. Trask). New York: Harper.

Ellenberger, H. F. (1970). *The discovery of the unconscious: The history and evolution of dynamic psychiatry*. New York: Basic.

Ellis, A. (1962). *Reason and emotion in psychotherapy*. New York: Lyle, Stuart.

Engel, G. L. (1977). The need for a new medical model: A challenge for biomedicine. *Science, 196*(4286), 8 April, pp. 129-136.

Entralgo, P. L. (1970). *Therapy of the word in classical antiquity*. (Trans. L. J. Rather & J. M. Sharp) New Haven, CT: Yale University.

Erickson, M. H. (1967). *Advanced techniques of hypnosis and therapy: Selected papers of Milton H. Erikson, M.D.* (J. Haley, Ed.). New York: Grune & Stratton.

Erickson, M. H. & Rossi, E. L. (1981). Experiencing hypnosis: Therapeutic approaches to altered states. New York, NY: Irvington.

Farthing, G. W. (1992). *The psychology of consciousness*. Englewood Cliffs, NJ: Prentice-Hall.

Feldenkrais, M. (1972). *Awareness through movement: health exercises for personal growth*. New York: Harper & Row.

Fields, R. (1986). *How the swans came to the lake*. Boston: Shambala.

Fischer, R. (1971). A cartography of the ecstatic and meditative states. *Science, 174*, 897-904.

Fishman, D. B. & Franks, C. M. (1992). Evolution and differentiation within behavior therapy: A theoretical and epistemological review. In. D. Freedheim (Ed.). *History of psychotherapy: A century of change*. Washington, DC: American Psychological Association. pp 159-196.

Fouad, N. A., Crus, C. L., Hatcher, R. L., Kaslow, N. J., Hutchings, P. S., Madsen, M. B., Collins, F. L. & Crossman, R. E. (2009). Competency benchmarks: A model for understanding and measuring competence in professional psychology across training levels. *Training and education in professional psychology, 3*, 4(Suppl.), S5-S26

Forster, M. (2001). Johan Gottfried von Herder. In E. N. Zalta (Ed.). Stanford Encyclopedia of Philosophy (Winter 2001 edition), downloaded March 20, 2005 from URL http://plato.stanford.edu/archives/win2001/entries/herder/.

Foucault, M. (1970). The order of things: An archaeology of the human sciences. New York: Vintage

Foucault, M. (1973). *Madness and civilization: A history of insanity in the age of reason*. (Trans. R. Howard) New York: Vintage Books (Original work 1961).

Frank, J. D. & Frank J. B. (1991). *Persuasion and healing: A comparative study of psychotherapy* (3rd ed.). Baltimore, MD: Johns Hopkins University.

Frank, R. G., McDaniel, S.,Bray, J. H., & Heldring, M. (Eds.)(2003). *Primary care psychology*. Washington, DC: American Psychological Association.

Franz, S. I. (1916). The functions of a psychologist in a hospital for the insane. *American Journal of Insanity, 72*, 457-464.

Franz, S. I. & Lashley, K. S. (1917). The retention of habits by the rat after destruction of the frontal portion of the cerebrum. *Psychobiology, 1*, 3-18.

Frazer J. G. (1950). *The golden bough: A study of magic and religion*. New York: Macmillan. (Original work 1922).

Freud, S. (1927). *The ego and the id* (Trans. Joan Riviere) London: Hogarth. (Original work 1923).

Freudenberger, H. J. (1975). The staff burn-out syndrome in alternative institutions. *Psychotherapy, 12*, 73-82.

Fuller, B. A. G. & McMurrin, S. M. (1960) *A history of philosophy* (3rd ed.). New York: Holt, Rinehart & Winston.

Gallo, F. P. (2005). *Energy psychology: Explorations at the interface of energy, cognition, behavior, and health* (2nd ed.). New York: CRC.

Gardner, H. (1983). *Frames of mind: The theory of multiple intelligences*. New York: Basic.

Gellhorn, E. & Kiely, W. F. (1972). Mystical states of consciousness: Neurophysiological and clinical aspects. *Journal of Nervous and Mental Disorders, 154*(6), 399-405.

Gergen, K. J. (1973). Social psychology as history. *Journal of Personality and Social Psychology, 26*(2), 309-320.

Gilman, S. L. (1982). *Seeing the insane*. New York: John Wiley & Sons.

Gimbutis, M. (2007). *The gods and goddess of old Europe, 7000 to 3000 BC: Myths, legends and cult images*. Berkeley, CA: University of California Press. (Original work 1974).

Giorgi, A. (1970). *Psychology as a human science: A phenomenologically based approach*. New York: Harper & Row.

Godwin, J. (1981). *Mystery religions of the ancient world*. San Francisco, CA: Harper & Row.

Goffman, E. (1959). *The presentation of self in everyday life*. New York: Doubleday Anchor.

Golden, C., Hammeke, T. A., & Purisch. A. D. (1980). *The Luria-Nebraska neuropsychological battery: Forms I and II: Manual*. Los Angeles: Western Psychological Services.

Goldstein, J. (1976). *The experience of insight: A simple and direct guide to Buddhist meditation*. Boulder, CO: Shambala.

Gould, S. J. (1986). Evolution and the triumph of homology, why history matters. *American Scientist, 74*, 60-69.

Grant, M. (1982). *From Alexander to Cleopatra: The Hellenistic world*. New York: Charles Scribe's Sons.

Gray, W., Duhl, F. J., & Rizzo, N. D. (Eds.). (1969). *General systems theory and psychiatry*. Boston: Little, Brown.

Gray, W. G. (1975). Patterns of Western magic: A psychological appreciation. In C. Tart (Ed.). *Transpersonal Psychologies*. New York: Harper & Row. pp 433-472.

Green, H. (1986). *Fit for America: Health, fitness, sport and American society*. New York, NY: Pantheon.

Grinder, J. & Bandler, R. (1981). *Trace-formations: Neuro-linguistic programming and structure of hypnosis*. Moab, UT: Real People.

Groddeck, G. (1961). The book of the it. New York: Mentor Books, (Originally publish 1923).

Guthrie, R. V. (1998). *Even the rat was white (2nd ed.)*. Boston, MA: Allyn & Bacon.

Hadot, P. (2002). *What is ancient philosophy?* (Translated by Michael Chase). Cambridge, MA: Harvard University.

Haley, J. (1963). *Strategies of psychotherapy*. New York: Grune & Stratton.

Halstead, W. (1947). *Brain and intelligence*. Chicago: University of Chicago.

Hanna, T. (1970). *Bodies in revolt*. New York: Dell.

Hanna, T. (1988). *Somatics: Reawakening the mind's control of movement, flexibility and health.* Cambridge, MA: Perseus.

Harner, M. (1990). *The way of the shaman.* San Francisco, CA: Harper.

Harrington, A., & Dunne, J. D. (2015). When mindfulness is therapy: Ethical qualms, historical perspectives. *American Psychologist, 70(7),* 621.

Harvey, G. (2006). *Animism: Respecting the living world.* New York: Columbia University

Hayes, S. C., Strosahl, K. D. & Wilson, K. G. (1999). *Acceptance and commitment therapy: An experiential approach to behavior change.* New York: Guilford

Hayes, S. C., Hayes, L. J., Reese, H. W. & Sarbin, T. R. (Eds.) (1993). *Varieties of scientific contextualism.* Reno, NV: Context.

Headland, T. N., Pike, K. L. & Harris, M. (1990). *Emics and etics: The insider/outsider debate.* Newbury Park, CA: Sage.

Heft, H. (2001). *Ecological psychology in context.* Hillsdale, NJ: Lawrence Erlbaum & Assoc.

Heidelberger, M. (2004). *Nature from within: Gustav Theodor Fechner and his psychophysical world view.* Pittsburgh, PA: University of Pittsburgh.

Heider, F. (1958). *The psychology of interpersonal relations.* Hillsdale, NJ: Lawrence Erlbaum.

Henle, M. (1978). Gestalt psychology and Gestalt therapy. *Journal of the History of Behavioral Sciences, 14(1),* 23-32.

Hilgard, E. R. (1977). *Divided consciousness: Multiple controls in human thought and action.* New York: John Wiley & Sons.

Hilgard, E. R. (1987). *Psychology in America: A historical survey.* San Diego: Harcourt Brace Jovanovich.

Hippocrates (n.d./2003). Aphorisms. Sec. 1, 1. (Trans. F. Adams) retrieved from http://classics.mit.edu/index.html January 16, 2004.

Hofstader, R. (1944). *Social Darwinism in American thought.* Boston: Beacon.

Homme, L. E. (1965). Perspectives in psychology: XXIV. Control of coverants, the operants of the mind. *Psychological Reports, 15,* 501-511.

*Howells, J. G. (Ed.). (1975). World history of psychiatry. New York: Brunner/Mazel.*

*Howells, J. G. & Osborn M. L. (1984). A reference companion to the history of abnormal psychology (2 vol.) Westport, CT: Greenwood Press.*

*I Ching or book of changes.* (Trans. R. Wilhelm) (1952). Princeton, NJ: Princeton University.

Ivey, A. E. (1994). *Intentional interviewing and counseling: Facilitating client development in a multicultural society* (3rd ed.). Pacific Grove, CA: Brooks/Cole.

Ivey, A. E., Gluckstern, N. B., & Ivey, M. B. (1993). *Basic attending skills* (3rd ed.). North Amherst, MA: Microtraining Associates.

Ivey, A. E., Gluckstern, N. B., & Ivey, M. B. (1997). *Basic influencing skills* (3rd ed.). North Amherst, MA: Microtraining Associates.

Ivey, A. E. & Ivey M. B.(1999). *Intentional interviewing & counseling: Facilitating client development in a multicultural society* (4th ed.). Pacific Grove, CA: Brooks/Cole.

Jacobson, E. (1977). The origins and development of progressive relaxation. *Journal of Behavior Therapy and Experimental Psychiatry, 8,* 119-123.

James, W. (1958). *The varieties of religious experience* New York: Mentor. (Original work published 1902).

Janet, P. (1925). *Psychological healing: A historical and clinical study.* (2 vol., Trans. E. & C. Paul). London: George Allen & Unwin, Ltd. (Original work published 1919).

Janov, A. (1970). *The primal scream: Primal therapy: The cure for neurosis.* New York: Delta.

Josselson, R. & Lieblich, A. (Eds.). (1993). *The narrative study of lives, Vol. 1.* Newbury Parl, CA: Sage.

Judith, A. (1996). *Eastern body, Western mind: Psychology and the chakra system as a path to the self.* Berkeley, CA: Celestial Arts.

Kabat-Zinn, J. (1991). *Full catastrophe living: Using the wisdom of your body and mind to face stress, pain, and illness.* New York: Delta.

Kabat-Zinn, J. (1994). *Wherever you go there you are.* New York: Hyperion Books.

Kelly, E. L. & Goldberg, L. R. (1959). Correlates of later performance and specialization in psychology: A follow-up study of the trainees assessed in the VA Selection Research Project. *Psychological Monographs, 3*(12, Whole No. 482).

Kerényi, C. (1959). *Asklepios: Archetypal image of the physician's existence.* New York: Pantheon.

Kerényi C. (1967a). *Eleusis: Archetypal image of mother and daughter.* Princeton, NJ: Princeton University.

Kerényi, C. (1976b). *Dionsysos: Archetypal image of indestructible life.* Princeton, NJ: Princeton University.

Kerényi, C. (1976b). *Hermes: Guide of souls.* Putnam CN: Spring.

Kipling, R. (1989). *Kim* (edited and with an introduction by Edward Said). New York: Penguin Books (Original work 1901).

Kluckhohn, C. & Murray, H. A. (1948). *Personality in nature, society, and culture.* New York: Alfred A Knopf.

Korman, M. (Ed.). (1976). *Levels and patterns of training in professional training in psychology.* Washington, DC: American Psychological Association.

Kroker, Kenton (2003). The progress of introspection in America: 1896-1938. *Studies in history and philosophy of biological and biomedical sciences. 34*(1), 77.

Kuhn, T. S. (1962). *The structure of scientific revolutions.* Chicago, IL: University of Chicago.

Labov, W. & Fanshel, D. (1977). *Therapeutic discourse: Psychotherapy as conversation.* New York: Academic.

Laing, R. D. (1960). *The divided self.* New York: Pantheon.

Laing, R. D. (1970). *Knots.* New York: Pantheon.

Lakoff, G. & Johnson, M. (1980). *Metaphors we live by.* Chicago, IL: The University of Chicago.

Lao-Tzu (1974). *Tao te ching* (Trans. G. Feng & J. English). New York: Vintage.

Larson, P. C. (2016). The intersection of humanistic psychology and Pagan spirituality: Personal and professional perspectives. Divination and psychological assessment. *Society of Humanistic Psychology,* conference, San Francisco, March 18, 2016.

Larson, P. C. (2015). Stress management: A transpersonal perspective. *Society for Humanistic Psychology conference,* Chicago, IL, March 28, 2015.

Larson, P. C. (2006). Clinical theory as rhetoric. *Proceedings of the International Academy of Linguistics, Behavioral and Social Sciences.* Vol. 8 (CD-ROM)

Larson, P. (2005). Longview State Hospital: The video. Paper presented at the Annual Convention of the American Psychological Association, Washington, DC, August 20, 2005.

Larson, P. (2002). Teaching "history and systems" from a clinical perspective. *History of Psychology, 5*(3), 249-263.

Larson, P. C. & Sachs, P. (2000). Division 22: Rehabilitation Psychology. In D. Dewsbury, (Ed.) *Unification Through Division: Histories of the Divisions of the American Psychological Association,* vol 5. Washington DC: American Psychological Association.

Lashley, K. S. & Franz, S. I. (1917). The effects of cerebral destruction upon habit-formation and retention in the albino rat. *Physiological Psychology, 1,* 71-140.

Leahey, T. H. (2000). *A history of psychology: Main currents in psychological thought* (5th ed). Upper Saddle River, NJ: Prentice-Hall.

Levy, L. H. (1962). The skew in clinical psychology. *American Psychologist, 17,* 244-249.

Lewin, K. (1936). *Principles of topological psychology.* (Translated by F. Heider and G. Heider). New York: McGraw-Hill Book Co.

Lewin, K. (1951). *Field theory in social science.* New York: Harper & Brothers.

Lewin, K., Lippitt, R. & White, R. K. (1939). Patterns of aggressive behavior in experimentally created "social climates." *Journal of Social Psychology, 10,* 271-299.

Lieberman, M., Yalom, I. & Miles, M. (1973). *Encounter groups: First facts.* New York: Basic.

Linehan, M. M. (1989). Dialectical behavior therapy for borderline personality disorder: Theory and method. *Bulletin of the Menninger Clinic. 51,* 261-276.

Linehan, M. M. (1993a). *Cognitive-behavioral treatment of borderline personality disorder.* New York: Guilford.

Linehan, M. M. (1993b). *Skills training manual for treating borderline personality disorder.* New York: Guilford.

Lippitt, R. (1940). An experimental study of the effect of democratic and authoritarian group atmospheres. *University of Iowa Studies in Child Welfare, 16,* 45-195.

Lowen, A. (1967). *The betrayal of the body.* New York: Collier.

Lowen, A. (1975). *Bioenergetics.* New York: Collier.

Luhmann, Niklas (1995). *Social systems* (Trans. J. Bednars). Palo Alto, CA: Stanford University

Lutz, T. (1991). *American nervousness, 1903: An anecdotal history.* Ithaca, NY: Cornell University.

Lyddon, W. J. (1995). Forms and Facets of Constructivist Psychology. In R. Neimeyer and M. Mahoney (Eds.) *Constructivism in Psychotherapy.* Washington, DC: American Psychological Association.

Macdonald, M. (1981). *Mystical Bedlam: Madness, anxiety, and healing in seventeenth-century England.* New York: Cambridge.

Mahoney, M. J. (1974). *Cognition and behavior modification.* Cambridge, MA: Ballinger.

Marcuse, H. (1955). *Eros and civilization: A philosophical inquiry into Freud.* Boston: Beacon.

Marcuse, H. (1964). *One-dimensional man.* Boston: Beacon.

Marineau, Rene F. (1989). *Jacob Levy Moreno, 1889-1974: Father of psychodrama, sociometry, and group psychotherapy.* New York: Routledge.

Maslow, A. H. (1954). *Motivation and personality.* New York: Harper.

Maturana, H. R. & Varela, F. J. (1998). *The tree of knowledge: The biological roots of human understanding.* Boston, MA: Shambala.

May, R. (Ed.) (1960). *Existential psychology.* (2nd ed.). New York: Random House.

May. R. (1969). *Love and will.* New York: W. W. Norton.

Mayor, D. & Micozzi, M. S. (Eds.) (2011). *Energy medicine East and West: A natural history of Qi.* New York: Elsevier.

McCarthy, K. (1984). The Emmanuel movement and Richard Peabody. *Journal of Studies on Alcohol, 45,* 59-74.

McCarthy, T. (2014). Great aspirations: The post-war American college counseling center. *History of Psychology, 17,* 1-18.

McDonald, F. (1985). *Novus ordo seclorum: The intellectual origins of the constitution.* Lawrence, KS: University of Kansas.

Meichenbaum, D. (2003). Cognitive-behavioral therapy: Folk tales and the unexpurgated history. *Cognitive Therapy & Research, 27*(1), 125-129.

Meyer, M. W (Ed.). (1987). *The ancient mysteries, a source book: Sacred texts of the mystery religions of the ancient world.* San Francisco, CA: Harper & Row.

Miller, G. A., Galanter, E. & Pribram, K. H. (1960). *Plans and the structure of behavior.* New York: Holt, Rinehart & Wilson.

Miller, J. G. (1978). *Living Systems.* New York: McGraw-Hill.

Millon, T. (2004). *Masters of the mind: Exploring the story of mental illness from ancient times to the new millennium.* New York: John Wiley & Sons.

Mishlove, J. (1975). *The roots of consciousness: Psychic liberation through history, science and experience.* New York & Berkeley, CA: Random House.

Mitchell, J. (1974). *Feminism and psychoanalysis.* New York: Penguin.

Mitchell, S. A. (1993). *Hope and dread in psychoanalysis.* New York: Basic.

Mitchell, S. A. & Black, M. J. (1995). *Freud and beyond: A history of modern psychoanalytic thought.* New York: Basic.

Moore, D. L. (1992). The Veterans Administration and the training program in psychology. In D. K. Freedheim (Ed.). *History of psychotherapy: A century of change.* Washington, D.C.: American Psychological Association. pp 776-800.

Moss, D., McGrady, A., Davies, T. C., Wichramasekera, I. (Eds.)(2003). *Handbook of mind-body medicine for primary care.* Thousand Oaks, CA: Sage.

Moss, D. & Shaffer, F. (Eds.) (2016). *Foundations of heart rate variability biofeedback: A book of readings.* Wheat Ridge, CO: Association for Applied Psychophysiology & Biofeedback.

Mower, O. H. & Mower, W. M. (1938). Enuresis: A method for its study and treatment. *American Journal of Orthopsychiatry, 8,* 436-347.

Munsterberg, H. (1909a). *On the witness stand.* New York: McClure.

Munsterberg, H. (1909b). *Psychology and the teacher.* New York: Appleton.

Munsterberg, H. (1913). *Psychology and industrial efficiency.* Boston: Houghton-Mifflin.

Myers, I. B. (1962). *The Myers-Briggs Type Indicator.* Princeton, Educational Testing Service.

Nagel, T. (1974). What is it like to be a bat? *Philosophical Review, LXXXIII,* 435-50.

Napoli, D. S. (1981). *Architects of adjustment: The history of the psychological profession in the United States.* Port Washington, NY: Kennikat.

Neugebauer, R. (1979). Medieval and early modern theories of mental illness. *Archives of General Psychiatry, 36,* 477-483.

Nussbaum, M. C. (1994). *The therapy of desire: Theory and practice in Hellenistic ethics.* Princeton, NJ: Princeton University.

Oberman, C. E. (1965). *A history of vocational rehabilitation in America.* Minneapolis, MN: T. S. Denison.

Ornstein, R. E. (1972). *The psychology of consciousness.* San Francisco, CA: W. H. Freeman.

Ornstein, R. E. (Ed.) (1973). *The nature of human consciousness: A book of readings.* San Francisco, CA: W. H. Freeman.

Parsons, F. (1909). *Choosing a vocation.* Boston: Houghton-Mifflin.

Patterson, C. H. & Watkins, C. E. (1996). *Theories of psychotherapy.* (5th ed.). New York: Harper-Collins.

Peirce, C. S.(1955). *Philosophical writings of Peirce* J. Buchler, (Ed.). New York: Dover.

Pepper, S. C. (1942). *World hypotheses: A study in evidence.* Berkeley, CA: University of California.

Perls, F. S. (1969). *Ego, hunger and aggression: The beginning of gestalt therapy.* New York: Vintage.

Perls, F. S., Hefferline, R. & Goodman, P. (1951). *Gestalt therapy; Excitement and growth in the human personality.* New York: Dell.

Peterson, D. R. (1997). *Educating professional psychologists: History and guiding conception.* Washington, D. C.: American Psychological Association.

Peterson, R. L., McHolland, J.D., Bent, R. J., Davis-Russell, E., Edwall, G. E., Polite, K., Singer, L.and Stricker, G. (1991). *The core curriculum in professional psychology.* Washington, DC: American Psychological Association.

Peterson, R. L., Peterson, D. R., Abrams, J. C., and Stricker, G. (1997). The National Council of Schools and Programs of Professional Psychology Educational Model. *Professional Psychology: Research and Practice, 28*(4), 373-386.

Philpot, C. L. (1997). A history of Division 43 (Family psychology): It's all in the family. In D. Dewsbury (Ed.) *Unification through division: Histories of the divisions of the American Psychological Association, volume II.* Washington, DC: American Psychological Association.

Pike, K. L. (1954). *Language in relation to a unified theory of human behavior.* (3 vol). Glendale, California: Summer Institute of Linguistics.

Plucker, J. (2003) *Jean-Marc Gaspard Itard.* Retrieved from http://www.indiana.edu/~intell/itard.shtml 3/8/04 7:26p

Pohl, W. (1991). The concept of ethnicity in Early Medieval studies. *Archaeologia Polona, 29,* 31-49.

Polkinghorne, D. (1988). *Methodology for the human sciences: Systems of inquiry.* Albany, NY: State University of New York.

Pollak, R. H. & Brenner, M. J. (Eds.) (1969). *The experimental psychology of Alfred Binet.* New York: Springer Publishing.

Powell, R. A. (2010). Little Albert still missing. *American Psychologist, 65*(4), 297-303.

Powell, R. A., Digdon, N., Harris, B., & Smithson, C. (2014). Correcting the record on Watson, Rayner and Little Albert: Albert Barger as psychology's "lost boy." *American Psychologist, 69*(6), 606-611.

Powers, W. T. (1973). *Behavior: The Control of Perception.* Chicago: Aldine.

Pryzwansky, W. B. & Wendt, R. N. (1987). *Psychology as a profession: Foundations of practice.* New York: Pergamon.

Raimy, V. R. (1950). *Training in clinical psychology.* New York: Prentice-Hall.

Reece, H. W. (2010). Regarding Little Albert. *American Psychologist, 65*(4), 297-303.

Reich, W. (1971). *The mass psychology of fascism.* (V. R. Carfagno, Trans.). New York: Farrar, Straus, & Giroux. (Original work 1946)

Reich, W. (1973). *The function of the orgasm.* (V. R. Carfagno, Trans.). New York: Farrar, Straus, & Giroux. (Original work 1942).

Reisman J. M. (1991). *A history of clinical psychology* (2nd ed.). New York: Irvington.

Reitan, R. M. & Wolfson, D. (1985). The Halstead-Reitan Neuropsychological Test Battery: Theory and clinical interpretation. Tucson, AZ: Neuropsychology.

Reusch, J. (1972). *Disturbed communication* New York: W. W. Norton. (Original work 1957).

Reusch, J. (1973). *Therapeutic communication* New York: W. W. Norton. (Original work 1961).

Reusch, J. & Bateson, G. (1968) *Communication: The social matrix of psychiatry* New. York: W. W. Norton. (Original work 1951).

Reusch, J. & Kees, W. (1974). *Non-verbal communication: Notes on the visual perception of human relations*. Berkeley, CA: University of California.

Robinson, D N. (1981). *An intellectual history of psychology* (Rev. Ed.). New York: Macmillan.

Roccatagliata, G. (1986). *A history of ancient psychiatry*. New York: Greenwood.

Rodseth, L. & Novak, S. A. (2000). The social modes of men: Toward an ecological model of human male relationships. *Human Nature, 11,* 335-366.

Rogers, C. R. (1942). *Counseling and psychotherapy: Newer concepts in practice*. New York: Houghton-Mifflin.

Rogers, C. R. (1951). *Client-centered therapy: Its current practice, implications and theory*. Boston: Houghton-Mifflin.

Rolf, I. P. (1989). *Rolfing: Reestablishing the natural alignment and structural integration of the human body for vitality and well-being*. Rochester, VT: Healing Arts.

Rosen, G. (1968). *Madness in society: Chapters in the historical sociology of mental illness*. Chicago: The University of Chicago.

Rotter, J. B. (1954). *Social learning and clinical psychology*. Englewood Cliffs: Prentice-Hall.

Rotter, J. B. (1966). Generalized expectancies for internal versus external locus of control of reinforcement. *Psychological Monographs: General and Applied, 80*(1), 1-28.

Rotter, J. B., Chance, J., & Phares, E. J. (Eds.). (1972). *Applications of a social learning theory of personality*. New York: Rinehart & Winston.

Rowan, J. (1993). *The transpersonal: Psychotherapy and counseling*. London: Routledge.

Rubin, N. J., Bebeau, M., Leigh, I. W., Lichtenberg, J. W., Nelson, P. D., Portnoy, S., Smith, I. L. & Kaslow, N. J. (2007). The competency movement within psychology: A historical perspective. *Professional Psychology: Research and Practice, 38*(5), 452-462

Rudolfa, E., Bent, R., Eisman, E., Nelson, P., Rehm, L. & Ritchie, P. (2008). A cube model of competency development: Implications for psychology educators and regulators. *Professional Psychology: Research and Practice, 36*(4), 347-354.

Rumbaut, R. D. (1972). The first psychiatric hospital in the Western world. *American Journal of Psychiatry, 128*(10), 125-129.

Rychlak, J. F. (1977). *The psychology of rigorous humanism*. New York: John Wiley & Sons.

Sabar, A. (2014). *The outsider: The life and times of Roger Barker*. Seattle, WA: Amazon Digital Services.

Said, E. (1979). *Orientalism*. New York: Vintage .

Sarbin, T. R. (1986). The narrative as root metaphor for psychology. In T. R. Sarbin (Ed.). *Narrative psychology: The storied nature of human conduct*. Westport, CT: Praeger. pp 3-21.

Satir, V. (1967). *Conjoint family therapy: A guide to theory and technique*. Palo Alto, CA: Science and Behavior.

Scheidlinger, S. (1995). The small healing group – A historical overview. *Psychotherapy, 32,* 657-668.

Schön, D. A. (1983). *The reflective practitioner: How professionals think in action*. New York: Basic.

Schön, D. A. (1987). *Educating the reflective practitioner*. San Francisco: Jossey-Bass Publishers.

Schutz, W. C. (1973). *Elements of encounter: A bodymind approach*. Big Sur, CA: Joy.

Schwartz, M. S. & Andrasik, F. (Eds.)(2003). *Biofeedback: A practitioner's guide* (3rd ed.). New York: Guilford.

Scott, W. D. (1906). *The psychology of public speaking*. Philadelphia, PA: Pearson Brothers.

Schwartz, G. E. . (1984). Psychobiology of health: A new synthesis. In B. L.Hammonds, & C. J. Scheirer (Eds.) *Psychology and Health*, (pp 149-193). Washington DC: American Psychological Association.

Searle, J. R. (1969). *Speech acts: An essay in the philosophy of language*. Cambridge, UK: Cambridge University.

Seligman, Martin E. P. (1992). *Helplessness : on depression, development, and death*. New York : W. H. Freeman

Sellars, J. (2009). *The art of living: The Stoics and the nature and function of philosophy* (2nd ed.). London: Bristol Classics.

Shah, I. (1972). *The exploits of the incomparable mullah Nasrudin*. New York: E. P. Dutton

Shannon, C. E. (1948). A mathematical theory of communication. *Bell Systems Technical Journal*, 27, 379-423.

Shannon, C. E. & Weaver, W. (1949). *The mathematical theory of communication*. Urbana, IL: University of Illinois.

Shapiro, D. H. & Astin, J. (1998). *Control therapy: An integrated approach to psychotherapy, health and healing*. New York: John Wiley & Sons.

Silverman, J. (1967). Shamans and acute schizophrenia. *American Anthropologist*, 69(1), 21-31.

Skinner, B. F. (1953). *Science and human behavior*. New York: Macmillan.

Skrbina, D. (2007). *Panpsychism in the West*. Boston, MA: MIT.

Snellgrove, D. (1987). *Indo-Tibetan Buddhism: Indian Buddhists and their Tibetan successors* (2 vols). Boston: Shambala.

Sokol, M. (2001). Practical phrenology as psychological counseling in the nineteenth century United States. In C.D. Green, M. Shore, & T Teo (Eds.). The transformation of psychology: Influences of 19th century philosophy, technology and natural science. Washington, DC: American Psychological Association. (pp. 21-44).

Stone, G. C., Cohen, F., Adler, N. E. (Eds.)(1979). *Health psychology: A handbook*. San Francisco, CA: Jossey-Bass.

Sullivan, H. S. (1953). *The interpersonal theory of psychiatry*. New York: W. W. Norton.

Tart, C. T. (1975). *States of consciousness*. New York: E. P. Dutton.

Tart, C. T. (Ed.) (1969). *Altered states of consciousness: A book of readings*. New York: John Wiley & Sons.

Tart, C. T. (Ed.) (1975b) *Transpersonal psychologies*. New York: Harper & Row.

Taves, A (1999). *Fits, trances and visions: Experiencing religion and explaining experiences from Wesley to James*. Princeton, NJ: Princeton University.

Taylor, A.. M.. (1977). *Societal transformations from paleolithic to contemporary times*. (pp. 323-399). Great Britain: Gordon and Breach Science.

Tedlock, B. (2001). Divination as a way of knowing: Embodiment, visualization, narrative and interpretation. *Folklore*, 112, 189-197.

Thompson, R. J. (1991). Psychology and the health care system: Characteristics and transactions. In J. J. Sweet, R. H. Rozensky & S. M. Tovian (Eds.). *Handbook of Clinical Psychology in Medical Settings*. New York: Plenum Press. pp. 11-25.

Tick, E. (2001). *The practice of dream healing: Bringing ancient Greek mysteries into modern medicine*. Wheaton, IL: Theosophical Publishing House.

Tolman, E. C. (1948). Cognitive maps in rats and men. *Psychological review*, 55, 189-208.

Truax, C. B. (1967). *Toward effective counseling and psychotherapy: Training and practice*. New York: Walter de Gruyter.

Turner, V. (1995). *The ritual process: Structure and anti-structure*. New York: Aline de Gruyter. (Original work, 1969).

Underhill, E. (1961). *Mysticism*. New York: E. P. Dutton. (Original work 1911).

van Bertalanffy, L. (1968). *General system theory: Foundations, development, applications*. New York: George Braziller.

van Gennep, A. (1960). *The rites of passage* Chicago, IL: University of Chicago. (Original work 1909).

Vande Kemp, H. (2004). Harry Stack Sullivan (1892-1949): Hero, ghost, and muse. *The Psychotherapy Patient*, 13(½), 7-61.

Vandenbos, G. R., Cummings, N. A. & DeLeon, P. H. (1992). A century of psychotherapy: Economic and environmental influences. In D. K. Freedheim (Ed.). *History of psychotherapy: A century of change*. Washington, D.C.: American Psychological Association. pp 65-102.

Varela, F. J., Thompson, E. & Rosch, E. (1991). *The embodied mind: Cognitive science and the human experience*. Cambridge, MA: MIT.

von Franz, M. (1980). *On divination and synchronicity*. New York: Inner City.

von Uexküll, T., Geigess, W & Herrmann, J. M. (1993). Endosemiosis. *Semiotica*, 96(½), 5-51.

Wake, N. (2006). "The full story by no means all told:" Harry Stack Sullivan and Shepherd-Pratt 1922-1930. *History of Psychology*, 9(4), 325-358.

Walter, M. N., & Fridman, E. J. N. (Eds.) (2004). *Shamanism: An encyclopedia of world beliefs, practices, and cultures* (2 vols.). Santa Barbara, CA: ABC-CLIO.

Watzlawick, P., Beavin, J. H., & Jackson, D. D. (1967). *Pragmatics of human communication: A study of interactional patterns, pathologies, and paradoxes*. New York: W. W. Norton.

Watzlawick, P., Weakland, J. & Risch, R. (1974). *Change: Principles of problem formation and problem resolution*. New York: W. W. Norton.

Whiteley, J. M. (Ed.). (1980). *The history of counseling psychology*. Monterey, CA: Brooks/Cole.

Wilber, K. (1977). *The spectrum consciousness*. Wheaton, IL: Theosophical Publishing House.

Wilber, K. (1980). *The Atman project: A transpersonal view of human development*. Wheaton, IL: The Theosophical Publishing House.

Wilber, K. (1996). *A brief history of everything*. Boston, MA: Shambala

Wilbur, K. (2000). *Sex, ecology, spirituality: The spirit of evolution*. (Rev. Ed.). Boston: Shambala.

Wilber, K., Engler, J., & Brown, D. P. (Eds.). (1986). *Transformations of consciousness: Conventional and contemplative perspectives on development*. Boston: New Science Library.

Wolman, B. (1981). *Contemporary theories and systems in psychology*. New York: Springer.

Wolpe, J. (1969). *The practice of behavior therapy*. New York: Pergamon Press.

Woodworth, R. S. (1918). *Dynamic Psychology*. New York: Columbia University.

Worthington, V. (1982). *A history of yoga*. London: Routledge & Kegan Paul.

Wright, B. A. (1983). *Physical disability: A psycho-social approach* (2nd ed.) New York: Harper-Collins.

Yalom, I. (1980). *Existential psychotherapy*. New York: Basic.

Yalom, I. (1998). *The Yalom reader: Selections from a master therapist and storyteller*. New York: Basic.

# References

Yalom, I. D. & Leszcz, M. (2005). *The theory and practice of group psychotherapy* (5th ed.). New York, NY: Basic Books.

Zilboorg, G. (1941). *A history of medical psychology.* New York: W. W. Norton.

# Index

gratification, forms of denial of ordinary, 39
the great awakening, 108
Great Depression, 198, 223
Great Schism, in 1054, 79
great teachers, in China, 74
Greatrakes, Valentine, 91
Greco-Roman world, transmission of the classic
    books of, 93
Greece
    pantheon of deities prior to writing, 41
    philosophy, technology and arts of, 43
Greek magic, 52
Greek medicine, 48
Greek philosophy and medical skill, as a
    foundation, 44
Greek view, of mind and matter, 103
Greek world, 47–48
Gregory the Great, 79
Grimm brothers, 121
Grinder, John, 217
Groddeck, 159
group, concept of people as, 120–121
group counseling and therapy, 219–220
group differences, nature of, 16
group dynamics, 195, 221
group psychoanalysis, 220
group therapy space, 11
guilds, 87–88
Gutenberg, Bible first book printed by, 96

Habermas, Jürgen, 207
habit strength, learning as an increase in, 179
habits, 20
Haiti, slave rebellion in, 99
Haley, Jay, 216, 217
Hall, G. Stanley, 136–137, 152
Halstead, Ward, 142, 229
Halstead-Reitan battery, 142, 229
Hammurabi, code of laws, 45
Hampstead Child Therapy Clinic, 169
hand dynamometer, 142
handwriting analysis, 153
Hanh, Thich Nhát, 189
Hanna, Thomas, 206
Hanukkah, holiday of, 46
harmony
    among constituent elements of the human
      body, 69
    to the natural order of things, 74
Harner, Michael, studied under shamans, 36
Hartmann, Heinz, 172
Harvey, William, 115
Hayes, Steven C., 190
Hayes. Steven, 19

healing, 4–6
    as a social event, 39
    through music, 46
    by touch, 91
    by word, 51–52
healing professions, origins of, ix–x
healing rituals, Napier performing, 95
health and illness, in an animistic world view, 33
health care
    moving toward a more integrative model of
      service delivery, 8–9
    rise in the cost of, 234
health care professions
    education required, 2
    sharing a similar background, 236
health care provider, role of the professional
    psychologist as, ix
Health Maintenance Organization (HMO),
    restructured care, 235
health psychologists, as consultants to individuals
    and groups, 125
health psychology (Division #38), 228
health service psychologists (HSP), ix, 10, 236
health service psychology, 9–12
Healy, William, 146
heart, as the basis of circulation, 115
Hebrew Bible, 44
hedonism, 60
Hefferline, Ralph, 202
Hegel, George Wilhelm Friedrich, 103, 119
Heidegger, Martin, 193, 215
Heider, Fritz, 194, 196
the Hejira, 82
heliocentric theory, 113
helio-centric view, of the universe, 87
Hellenic period (ca 800 bce - 330 BCE), 47
Hellenistic era, 48, 59
Hellenistic philosophy, 61
the helper, social role of, xii–xiii
helping relationship, asymmetrical nature of, 1
Henri, Victor, 143
hepatomancy, 38
Heraclitus, on process of change, 53
herbal remedies, integral to TCM, 74
Herbart, Johann Friedrich, 130
Hercules (Heracles), 24
Herder, Gottfried Wilhelm, 120, 193
hereditary taint, passed on in families, 143–144
heresy, defining in Christianity, 95–96
hermeneutic circle, 121, 193
hermeneutics
    described, 193
    discipline of, 120
    importance of, 215

# Index

male and female deities, 41

male erectile dysfunction, 124

Malthus, Thomas, 116

managed care, 232, 235

mania and melancholia, polar images of, 88

Manichaeism, 61

mantic function, 38

mantra, 71

*manual of psychological medicine*, 107

Mao Tse Tung, 224

Marathon, battle of, 48

Marcus Aurelius, as an example of Stoic philosophy, 60

Marcuse, Herbert, 106, 207

Marie Antoinette, 126

market place, as a central element of classical liberal thought, 106

Marriage and Family Therapy (MFT), 219

Marshall Plan, effects of, 224

martial art, form of, 75

martyrs, 83

Marx, Karl, 106, 116, 119

*The Masks of God* (Campbell), 166

Maslow, Abraham, 199, 201

mass death, major impact of, 92

mass extinctions, of life forms, 29

mass media, development of, 101

massage therapy, as a discipline, 205

masters level practitioners, granted independence of practice, 3

masturbation, considered self pollution, 123–124

material cause, as the matter out of which it is made, 58

material substrate, 138–139

materialism, early versions of, 112

materialistic reductionism, 179

mathematics, 112, 113

matter, 104, 112

Maturana, Humberto, 213

May, Rollo, 199

maze learning, by rats, 184

McCarthy, Joseph, 224

McDougall, William, 138, 184

Mead, George Herbert, 147

Mead, Margaret, 216

meaning

as the currency of psychological healing, 5

as extremely context dependent, 8

interpretation of, 121

measure is man, of all things, 55

measurement of difference, created a niche role for psychologists, 145

Mecca, pilgrimage to, 83

mechanism, 19

mechanistic world hypothesis, 113

Medicaid, 234, 235

medical conditions, where stigma is present, 3

medical model, xii

medical necessity, 12

medically indigent, 235

Medicare, 234

medication, physician's sole right to prescribe, 48

medicine

close identification of healing with, 5

emphasizing physical means of healing, 48

traditionally allowing only doctoral level practitioners, 3

Medieval Christianity, sponsored pilgrimages to places holding the relics of saints, 91

Medieval scholastic philosophy, 87

medieval society, 92–93

Medina, 82

meditation

basis of, 68

benefits of, 76

Hinduism and Buddhism developed extensive traditions of, 208

practiced in both Western and Eastern religions, 66

teachers from Eastern cultures, 189

techniques of, 23, 38

meditational strategies, 188

*Meditations* (Marcus Aurelius), 60

meditative practices, 38, 208

Meichenbaum, Donald, 188–189

melancholia, figure for, 88–89

melancholic temperament, 51

memory

compaction of, 21

importance of, 16

pure process of, 132

Menninger, Karl, 220

mental abilities, measuring, 143

mental age, ratio to chronological age, 143

mental disorders, becoming the province of neurology, 122

mental health

coordination of care, 221

history of, xii

mental health laws, of each state, 232

mental health services, team for, 148

mental health specialists, 11

mental illness

as emotional problems, 118

graphic history of, 88

having a cyclical course with periods of lucidity, 90

medical specialty dealing with, 159

reflective self awareness, 17
reflective self-examination, 103
reflex arc, 134, 175
reflex arc physiologists, 135
reflex conditioning models of learning, 149
refrigeration, for food safety, 115
registration, at the lowest level, 232
regulation of practice, by a profession, 231
rehabilitation psychology
    development of, 229
    Division 22 of APA, 151, 228
Reich, Wilhelm, 202, 204–206
reimbursement for services, mode of, 12
reincarnation, 67
reinforcement theory, 180
Reitan, Ralph, 299
relational psychoanalysis, 174
"the relations of psychology and medical
    education," conference on in 1911, 228
relationship
    as the focus of analytic treatment, 174
    between self and other, 17
relationship competency, 15, 16
relative-value units (RVU), for out-patient
    services, 235
relativity
    Einstein's theory of, 198
    theories of, 113
*The relaxation response* (Benson), 67
relaxation training procedure, 183
relaxed states, 182
religion, defined, 27
religion and spirituality, psychology of, 166
religions, era of formal organized, 40
religious experience, study of, 134
religious leaders, role in healing, 32
religious syncretism, 40, 59
religious tolerance, in areas controlled by the
    Moors, 93
religious wars, in Europe, 97
the Renaissance, 93–95
Renouvier, Charles, 134
repressed memories, recovering via hypnosis, 128
repression, 161, 162
*Republic* (Plato), 56
repulsion, 28
research, as an on-going process of learning, 195
residency training, in a post-graduate medical
    specialty, 234
resilience, of clients, 5
respondent or Pavlovian tradition, of conditional
    learning, 182
rest cure, 124
resurrection, doctrine of, 114–115

retardation, 143
retroflexion, 203
Reusch, Jeurgen, 216
revolutionary France, optimistic ideology of, 107
rhetoric, 13
    bases of persuasion as reason, emotion, and
        character, 55
    domains of, 54
    as the most important of the practical skills,
        237
rhetors
    of ancient Greece, 52
    described, 13
    as the first professional teachers, 54
*Rig Veda*, 65
"ring around the rosey," as a cultural remnant, 92
rites of passage, 15
ritual series of actions, 39
Robert-Fleury, Pinel painted by, 107
St. Roche, patron saint of plague, 92
Rock and roll, emerged from jazz, 226
Rogers, Carl, 200–201, 202, 220
    on conditions for successful therapy, 14–15
    founded the counseling center at the
        University of Chicago, 227
    on the personal connection between therapist
        and client, 237
Rogoff, used Pepper's schema of classification, 19
role archetype theory, Larson's, 24–26
role play, 204
roles. *See also specific roles*
    capacity of people to get lost in, 204
    forming the structure of social interactions,
        9–10
Rolf, Ida, 206
Roman empire, geographic extent of, 80
Roman power, effects of the fall of, 81
Romantic movement, as a reaction to the
    elevation of reason, 117
romanticism, 117–119
Rome
    dispersed Jews throughout the empire, 46
    first sacked in 410 CE by Alaric, 81
Roosevelt, Theodore, 124
root metaphors, Pepper's world views organized
    around, 19
Rorschach, Hermann, 153, 164
Rorschach test, 38
Rosa Parks case, 225
Rosetta stone, 120
Rossi, Ernest, 217
Rotter, Julian, 184
Rousseau, 124
royal touch, exercised by a sovereign, 91

Taoism, author of, 73
Taoists, as mystics, 74
Tarot card reading, 38
Tasman, Abel, charted parts of Australia, 99
taxonomies, variety of, 113
Taylor, Frederick, 149–150
*Taylorism*, 150
teacher
    archetype of, 51, 54–55
    first professional in Classical Greece, 25–26
    as purveyor of therapeutic wisdom, 157
    seen as a progenitor of psychotherapy, 54
    transmitting the collective wisdom of the profession, 21
teacher to teacher, tracing one's lineage from, 23
*Teaching of Don Juan: A Yaqui way of knowledge* (Castaneda), 209
technological developments, compounding and creating a momentum of change, 30
technology, as magic, 34–35
temperament, as the bedrock of our personal planet, 20
temperance movement, in America, 108
temple complexes, spirituality focused around, 40
temples
    centers of learning and of healing, 49
    as communities, 40
    priesthoods serviced, 31
temporal boundaries, 15
Ten Commandments, 45
Terman, Lewis, 137, 144, 152
*terpnos logos*, in Greek, 52
Tertullian, 79
Tet offensive, in Vietnam, 225
Teutonic knights, in northern Europe, 85
text books, previous relating the history of the science of psychology, xii
texts, canons of interpretation of, 120
T-group (training group), 195–196, 220
Thales of Miletus, 52–53
thanatos, 162
Theban Sacred Band, defeated by Phillip of Macedon, 57
theistic forms of spirituality, 27
Thematic Apperception Test (TAT), 153
Theodosius
    closed the pagan temples, 62
    made Christianity the official state religion, 79
theories
    disproving, 179–180
    nature of, 87
    of psychological healing will continue to evolve, 237
theory of signs (semiotics), 121–122

*Theory of the earth* (Hutton), 113
therapeutic community movement, 222
therapeutic conversation, 10, 18
therapeutic discourse, 149
therapeutic impact, basis of, 61
therapeutic interview, 21
therapeutic relationship, 7, 15
therapeutic touch, 35, 48
therapist
    active involvement of, 174
    aiding the client with communicational styles, 217
    conditions provided, 201
    creating structured interactions, 189
    curbing self-interest, 6
    expecting compensation for services rendered, 6
    having sentiments about the patient, 163
    providing a non-judgmental and acceptive environment, 201
    sharing reactions of, 174
    working backward from the present layers, 20–21
therapy
    earliest venture into, 181–182
    empirical research on the process of, 200
    requiring deconstruction of meanings, 203
*Therapy of the word in classical antiquity* (Entralgo), 51
Theravada, 70, 71
Theravada Buddhism, 70
thermal energy, 112
thermostat, 211
things, having spirits, 32
thinking-feeling, 164
third party payment, forms of, 12
third wave behavioral approaches, 71
Thirty Years War (1618-1648), 97
Thomas, Apostle, 65
Thoreau, having translations of Hindu scriptures, 63
Thorndike, Edward, 178
Thorndike's law of exercise, 189
thought field therapy, 75
thought reform camp (*sophronisterion*), for people with bad ideas, 56
threshold, limen as, 15
thrownness of life, 197, 198
Thurstone, L. L., 150, 152
Tibet, as the roof of the world, 72
Tibetan Buddhism
    known now as the Vajrayana path, 70
    path of, 72
    transmission of authority, 23

Made in the USA
Las Vegas, NV
19 August 2022

53437808R00166